TOMORROW THE WORLD

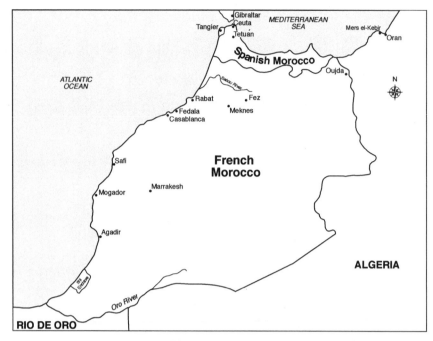

Morocco, 1940–42

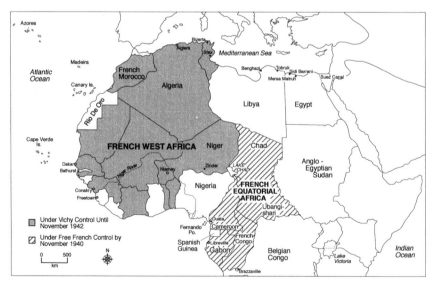

Northwest Africa, June 1940–November 1942

TOMORROW THE WORLD

Hitler, Northwest Africa, and the Path toward America

Norman J. W. Goda

Texas A&M University Press
College Station

Maps courtesy Cartographic Service Unit,
Department of Geography, Texas A&M University

The paper used in this book meets the minimum requirements
of the American National Standard for Permanence
of Paper for Printed Library Materials, Z39.48-1984.
Binding materials have been chosen for durability.

Library of Congress Cataloging-in-Publication Data

Goda, Norman J. W., 1961–
    Tomorrow the World : Hitler, Northwest Africa, and the path
toward America / Norman J.W. Goda. — 1st ed.
        p.   cm. — (Texas A&M University military history series ;
57)
    Includes bibliographical references and index.
    ISBN 0-89096-807-1
    1. World War, 1939–1945—Germany. 2. Hitler, Adolf. 1889–
1945. 3. Germany—Foreign relations—1933–1945. 4. Strategy.
I. Title. II. Series.
D757.G56   1998
940.54′013—dc21   97-43802
                                                             CIP

To my parents

Contents

❧

List of Maps	IX
Preface	XI
Introduction	XIII
CHAPTER 1. The Window on the Atlantic	3
CHAPTER 2. The Demand for Casablanca	16
CHAPTER 3. The Specter of de Gaulle	33
CHAPTER 4. The Riddle of the Rock	52
CHAPTER 5. September Shifts	71
CHAPTER 6. October Illusions	94
CHAPTER 7. Winter Collapse I: Iberia	113
CHAPTER 8. Winter Collapse II: France	136
CHAPTER 9. Passing the Torch	165
Conclusion	194
Notes	203
Bibliography	272
Index	295

Maps

&

Morocco, 1940–42   *frontispiece*

Northwest Africa,
   June 1940–November 1942   *frontispiece*

Preface
⌘

This study began innocently enough. As a graduate student at the University of North Carolina, I wished to write my first seminar paper on why Hitler's Germany did not capture the British naval base at Gibraltar during the Second World War. The desirability of such an operation seemed logical, and both Germany and Franco's Spain had seemingly vital interests in doing so. In reading through the published discussions between the German and Spanish leaders in the fall of 1940, however, I discovered that they barely discussed the issue of Gibraltar. Instead, they bickered over a seemingly unrelated issue—the German desire for a naval base in the Canary Islands. In pursuing the issue for the next several years, I began to conclude that German aims in the southwest had perhaps less to do with Gibraltar or the Mediterranean as such, and perhaps much more to do with a whole network of bases off the Northwest African coast—bases intended for a future war against the United States. Germany's pursuit of this aim and the reasons behind it form the subject of this book.

For an author to say that he owes "a great debt to many people" for the completion of a book is a cliché, but I truly am neither rich enough, smart enough, nor patient enough to have done this on my own. The generous financial support of the University of North Carolina, The *Deutscher Akademischer Austauschdienst,* and the Fulbright Commission made my research in Germany, Spain, and the United States possible. The staff of Dr. Marie Keipert at the *Politisches Archiv des auswärtigen Amtes* in Bonn, especially Herr Claus Wiedey, provided valuable help, as did the staff under Dr. Manfred Kehrig at the *Bundesarchiv/Militärarchiv* in Freiburg. Dr. Gerhard Schrieber of the *Militärgeschichtliches Forschungsamt* provided insights over coffee during my stay in Germany. In Madrid, Doña María Josefa Lozano, Ignacio Ruíz, Concepción Contel Barrea, and Pilar Casado all helped me to navigate Spain's confusing rules of archival access while providing help in the *Archivo General del Ministerio de Asuntos Exteriores,* the *Archivo de la Presidencia del Gobierno,* and the *Archivo General de la Administración* in Alcalá de Henares. Timothy Mulligan and Harry Rilley of the National Archives in Washington, D.C. were patient with me and extremely helpful back when I did not know a roll of microfilm from a home movie.

The demanding undergraduate seminars led by Francis L. Loewenheim at Rice University challenged me to expand my intellectual horizons and kindled my interest in pursuing German international history as a profession. His death last year was a great and irreplaceable loss for that institution. Michael P. Fitzsimmons convinced me in my senior year at Rice that my interest in the Second World War would be served best by studying with Gerhard L. Weinberg in Chapel Hill, and I have never regretted that decision. Professor Weinberg was, and still is, a model adviser. His rare combination of unparalleled scholarship, commitment to undergraduate teaching, and practically unlimited time for graduate students is one that all scholars would do well to emulate. The manuscript's thesis in one form or another has been read in whole or in part by Frederick Behrends, Rodler Morris, Samuel Williamson, Konrad Jarausch, John Headley, Gillian Cell, George Kent, Arthur Funk, Charles Burdick, Donald Detwiler, Russel Van Wyk, David Grier, Scott Lackey, Daniel Rogers, and Steven Miner, and all have made helpful comments. My new colleagues at Ohio University have also provided me with valuable suggestions and support since I moved here in the fall of 1996.

Nothing, however, is possible without family. My wife, Joy, has been a constant source of happy inspiration despite my moods and professional anxieties. Coming home to her each evening is the highlight of my day. My two little boys, Grant and Lucas, remind me every evening that the time we spend together reading about dinosaurs, making paper airplanes, and kicking soccer balls is far more meaningful than anything I could have done in the pages that follow, despite my rather silly disposition to think otherwise sometimes. My parents, Herbert and Lilyan, and my sisters, Saralee and Esther, have supported everything I have tried in life and have provided me each time with the very best chance to succeed. All of these people share in whatever is good about this work. Whatever is flawed is my responsibility alone.

Athens, Ohio
1997

Introduction

❧

We work in stages. . . . Have no fear,
we will not proceed in anarchy
or without a plan.
— Adolf Hitler

In the early morning hours of 7 November 1942, the United States battle-ship *New York*, the light cruiser *Philadelphia*, and a collection of destroyers and transport vessels disengaged from a large American convoy bearing eastward across the Atlantic Ocean. The detachment set a course for the old fishing town of Safi, 140 miles south of Casablanca on the Atlantic coast of French Morocco. By 11:30 P.M., the American vessels had moved to within 8 miles of the Moroccan coast. An hour before first light on 8 November the destroyer-transport *Bernadou* approached the narrow shoreline within the port of Safi. At 4:45 A.M. the specially-trained Company K of the Forty-seventh Infantry Division disembarked from the ship. Moments later amid enemy fire, Company K landed on the beach, becoming the first regular American troops to fight in the Euro-Mediterranean theater of war. Thus began the American occupation of French Morocco, which along with Anglo-American landings in Algeria, comprised Operation *Torch*—the Allied invasion of French North Africa.[1]

In his message to the French chief of state, Marshal Henri Philippe Pétain, on 8 November, President Franklin Delano Roosevelt justified the Anglo-American undertaking:

> *Today, with greedy eyes . . . Germany and Italy are proposing to*
> *invade and occupy French North Africa in order that they may*

execute their schemes of domination and conquest over the whole
of that continent. . . . Such a conquest of Africa . . . would be the
prelude to further attempts by Germany and Italy to threaten the
conquest of large portions of the American Hemisphere. . . . An
invasion and occupation of French North and West Africa would
constitute for the United States and all of the American Republics
the gravest kind of menace to their security—just as it would sound
the death knell of the French Empire.[2]

Pétain was furious and unconvinced. He acidly retorted to the president: "You invoke pretexts which nothing justifies. You attribute to your enemies intentions which have not ever been manifested in acts. . . . We are attacked; we shall defend ourselves; this is the order I am giving."[3]

Like Marshal Pétain, historians of the Second World War have traditionally argued that the president overstated his case—that Adolf Hitler's Germany had no more than an ephemeral interest in Northwest Africa and no global designs against the United States. This study will examine this very issue and will argue otherwise. From the capitulation of France in 1940 to the Allied North African landings of 1942, the parameters of this book, Hitler's Germany tried consistently to develop German bases in French Northwest Africa and the outlying Spanish and Portuguese islands. The bases were to be employed in a future struggle with the United States. Allied success in 1942 owed little to a lack of interest on the part of Berlin. It owed much more to a very interested yet failed German policy.

The issue of German aims in Northwest Africa during the Second World War directed at a transatlantic struggle with the United States fits into the larger historiographical debate on the nature of German war aims. Did Adolf Hitler *have* policies and aims or did he act solely out of opportunism? If Hitler, his National Socialist movement, and his military *did* have specific geopolitical aims, then what was their nature? Were they directed at a mere revision of the Versailles treaty? Did Hitler's Germany strive ultimately for Lebensraum in the East while creating a militarily unassailable position on the European continent? Or was the final objective nothing less than actual *world* hegemony for the Third Reich?[4] If indeed Germany seriously entertained the idea of using the Northwest African coast as a base of operations against the United States even *before* the entry of the United States into the conflict in December 1941, then it would seem that the aims of the Third Reich were truly *global* in scope. German strategic considerations and political policy toward Northwest Africa thus provide important keys for understanding the nature of the German and European side of the Second World War.

There will always be those who are understandably relunctant to ascribe rational calculation to political movements such as Nazism that seemed to glorify the irrational. Sir Alan Bullock's argument that Hitler was "an opportunist entirely without principle" will long have a following, as will the neorevisionist approach to the Third Reich, which views the Nazi dictatorship as a fundamentally weak and aimless government that adopted belligerent policies in order to hold popular support.[5] Most historians of German foreign policy and strategy, however, have ascribed to Hitler the aim of continental dominance at least. The late Andreas Hillgruber, the preeminent German historian on Hitler's strategy, formed a paradigm for future discussion in the 1960s in which Hitler's policies comprised a coherent *Stufenplan*— a step-by-step program for European conquest whereby Germany would eliminate its continental enemies one by one in a series of lightning campaigns. First, Germany would build a powerful strategic position in central Europe. Next, it would clear its western flank by smashing French military power for all time. Finally, it would crush the Soviet Union, thus garnering the vital German Lebensraum in the East.[6] Indigenous peoples would be moved out; German colonists would move in. Yet Hillgruber and many of those who built on his work have refrained from extending the idea of a German program to worldwide proportions. To be sure, they have taken notice of top-level discussions in the Third Reich on globally oriented issues such as a blue-water navy and bases on the West African coast. Yet to Hillgruber and others, such discussions had very limited importance. These issues, they say, arose temporarily and never affected the immediate progress of the war for *European* conquest. They were also *defensive* rather than *offensive* in nature, focusing on the need to defend German conquests from the increasing power of the United States, for which Hitler and the German government had great respect. Only once before Hitler's declaration of war on the United States on 11 December 1941 did he consider offensive action against the Americans, and this occurred in the overly optimistic early days of the campaign against the USSR.[7] As Günter Moltman argued in 1961, "One cannot say that a military world strategy existed on the German side in the Second World War. . . . To be sure . . . future perspectives in 1940 were expressed in but an ephemeral way and were only occasionally uttered and discussed. Soon the prosecution of the war once more claimed Hitler's full attention. . . ."[8]

There are, however, other ways of considering these issues. As Gerhard

L. Weinberg, the preeminent U.S. scholar of Nazi foreign policy, has shown, Hitler's crude race-based assessment of the world's peoples, combined with his notion that racial struggle was the Hegelian motor that drove history forward, meant that the geographic implications of German aggression were, in principle, unlimited. Moreover, Hitler adjusted his ideas concerning the United States after 1929, thereafter viewing American society with repugnance rather than respect.[9] It is problematic, then, that Hitler thought of the German relationship with the United States in defensive terms. Other research by German historians Jost Dülffer and Jochen Thies on German naval and Luftwaffe contracting indicates that the German leadership viewed global power as more than a pipe dream. Germany's government, as well as its naval and air force contractors, devoted significant monetary and workforce resources to giant battleships and long-distance bombers—hardly defensive weapons—*before* the war in Europe was even launched.[10] A sketch of these issues, by means of introduction, follows.

Hitler tied state policy to his crude social Darwinist beliefs, which he had gained from such dubious sources as Houston Stewart Chamberlain, Richard Wagner, and the *Protocols of the Elders of Zion,* all filtered through even more dubious early Nazi party ideologues, and which he himself enunciated in *Mein Kampf* and his so-called second book.[11] To the National Socialist mind, the natural human condition was one of perpetual struggle among races. A dominant race was one that maintained its natural instinct for struggle and thus the ability to conquer geographic space for its own further proliferation. The Nordic race, to which the Germans belonged, was the highest human type of all and the founder of all true human progress. The great antagonist to the Nordic was the Jew—"the inexorable mortal enemy of all light, a hater of all true culture."[12] Hitler argued that the Jews' method of survival lay in the elimination of the natural instinct for struggle that higher races possessed and employed. Jews had polluted the blood of the superior groups by intermarriage with lower racial types. Worse, they had preached supposedly nonsensical notions of human equality while encouraging intraracial squabbling with political narcotics such as democracy, trade-unionism, and socialism. The result of it all would be the use of the proletariat to impose a classless and raceless bolshevism. An artificial, cesspool-like, global pacifism would prevail, in which the Jew could survive but in which the Germanic institutions of strong government and war would lie buried. To Hitler, this process was complete in the Soviet Union and on its way to completion in any country in which races lived together beneath one flag and one law and in which all people enjoyed the freedom to vote or strike.

France was but one such example. If not halted, this global Jewish conspiracy would plunge the world into utter darkness.[13]

In order to meet this threat, the Nordic race needed to rediscover the instinct for struggle. It would keep its blood pure; it would ignore Jewish-Marxist and pacifist rhetoric; it would replace weak democracy with strong dictatorship; and through war it would attain Lebensraum in which Germans could proliferate further. In the first volume of *Mein Kampf*, completed in 1924, Hitler noted that Germany's Lebensraum lay in the Soviet Union. But again, the geographic implications of perpetual racial struggle, as was the case with Karl Marx's notion of perpetual class struggle, were limitless. The dialectic was a permanent human condition; struggle could end only with final victory or utter destruction. Global peace between races—Hitler's version of the end of history—could not exist until the racial question was solved one way or the other and on a world scale. "Anyone," argued Hitler, "who really desired the victory of the [Jewish] pacifist idea in this world would have to fight . . . for the conquest of the world by the Germans. . . . The pacifist-humane idea is perfectly all right . . . when the highest type of man has previously conquered and subjected the world to an extent that makes him the sole ruler of this earth. . . ."[14]

Hitler's conviction that racial struggle was a worldwide phenomenon became more, not less, concrete with time. In the second volume of *Mein Kampf,* completed in 1925, Hitler concluded that "a state which in this age of racial poisoning dedicates itself to the care of its best racial elements must some day become lord of the earth."[15] In his unpublished "second book" of 1928, he stated unequivocally that "wherever our success ends, it will only be the jump-off point for a new struggle."[16] In the same year in a speech in Oldenburg, Hitler predicted: "Eventually the most valiant *Volk* will rule the earth. We do not know which *Volk* it will be. But we would like not to exclude our *Volk* from this competition."[17] In a speech to supportive students at the University of Erlangen on 13 November 1930, Hitler summarized his argument as follows: "Each *Volk* strives for *Weltherrschaft*. A *Volk* that is too cowardly or which no longer possesses courage or strength enters . . . the route of renunciation and self-surrender, which finds its conclusion in destruction. There are only two roads. The first road leads incessantly forward . . . the second route leads downward."[18]

Even though Hitler spoke in terms of world racial struggle from an early date, his views on the United States evolved—or devolved—more slowly. Through 1928, Hitler viewed the United States as a formidable force on the world stage. It was a social-Darwinian paradise that had siphoned away

Europe's best and most energetic Nordic elements. They had proliferated in America's limitless space while not mixing with lesser Negroid and Asiatic types. Hitler had already predicted in 1924 that "the Germanic inhabitant of the American continent, will remain [master] as long as he does not fall victim to defilement of the blood."[19] By 1928, he saw in America a sleeping giant that one day would strive for world domination.[20] "The American union," he noted in his second book, "is emerging . . . as the sharpest competitor to all European nations fighting as export nations for the world's markets. . . . It is reckless . . . to believe that the contest between Europe and America will always be only of a peaceful economic nature."[21]

Hitler's solution to the growing problem was global struggle at some point in the "distant future."[22] As part of the conquest of Europe, Germany would marshal the best racial elements of the continent. Such a German-led Europe would one day confront the Western Hemisphere, led by the United States.[23] "In the future," predicted Hitler, "only the state which has understood how to raise the value of its *Volkstum* . . . will be able to face up to North America. . . . It is . . . the task of the National Socialist movement to . . . prepare . . . [the] Fatherland for this task."[24]

Yet Hitler's assessment of America changed dramatically in the early 1930s, most likely from the American inability to deal with the worldwide economic depression.[25] He revoked his earlier laudatory statements and concluded that a Jewish-controlled United States had fallen "victim to defilement of the blood" after all. The United States still had its population, space, and industrial potential. According to Hitler, Washington also had a stranglehold on the raw materials of Latin America.[26] The United States would thus remain a competitor that Germany would have to confront—all the more so since it was apparently dominated by Jews. Yet the racial corruption that Hitler saw as evident in America made it, to him, a toothless beast. The United States, argued Hitler before coming to power in June 1931, could never be a nation, thanks to its "ideological, religious, ethnic, and racial rivalries," and it would "never be able to dictate to us our historic path." Events would instead "take the USA by surprise."[27] These views would not change. In 1942, Hitler would comment that he did not "see much future" for the United States—"a decayed country" with a "racial problem and social inequalities." "It goes without saying," he continued, "that we have no affinities with the Japanese. They are too foreign to us. . . . But my feelings against Americanism are feelings of hatred and deep repugnance. I feel myself more akin to any European country, no matter which. Everything about [America is] half Judaised, the other half negrified. How can one expect a state like that to hold together?"[28]

On taking power in 1933, then, the new Nazi government would pay little heed to the United States or its preferences in spite of deteriorating relations, and this attitude continued through the outbreak of war six years later. America's seemingly Jewish pacifist–inspired neutrality legislation, which forbade loans and arms sales to belligerents; its deplorable military unpreparedness; and its weak-minded unwillingness to intervene forcefully in global battlegrounds such as Manchuria, Ethiopia, or Spain, to Hitler's thinking in the 1930s, meant that America was a nonfactor. Hitler viewed the German ambassador's post in Washington as one of the world's least significant assignments; American bondholders who had loaned money to the Weimar government were quickly defrauded out of their principal and interest; financial consideration owed for German sabotage in the United States was not paid; Austrian debts to the United States were repudiated after the German-Austrian *Anschluß*; and trade relations grew ever more sour in the course of the decade. In the meantime, Berlin brushed aside or ignored American official and public concerns regarding Germany's anti-Jewish, anti-Catholic, and antidemocratic policies while Hitler blithely ignored the increasing damage that the pro-Nazi, swastika-bearing "German-American Bund" had done to the American public's perceptions of Germany. This disdain for American opinions prevailed despite reports from the German embassy in Washington on the hardening anti-German mood in the American public and the prediction that America would side with the Western democracies in the event of war. The laughter and outright contempt toward the United States displayed by the Reichstag on hearing Hitler's public ridicule of Roosevelt's peace appeal of 14 April 1939 demonstrated these attitudes for anyone who cared to look.[29]

Despite the alarm that Germany's early victories over Poland, Denmark, Norway, the Low Countries, and France had generated in the United States, Hitler proceeded into the 1940s oblivious to any decisive American military threat to the emerging new order in Europe. This ambivalence persisted despite the United States' efforts to expand its defense capabilities in 1940. Increased congressional appropriations for defense in the second half of that year—which included increased aircraft production, the four-billion-dollar two-ocean navy bill of July, and the first American peacetime conscription law in September—were viewed in Berlin as nothing more than a giant bluff. This idea was confirmed by the German military and air attaché in Washington, General Friedrich von Bötticher, whose racially based assessments of American politics confirmed Hitler's own predilections.[30] Perhaps the Jewish-controlled American government was rearming to meet the German threat, but whatever threat the United States could muster would be in the *distant* future—perhaps five years, perhaps *twenty-five* years away, depending on changing political circumstances in Europe, Asia, and America itself. But in any case, it would be too late to change the verdict then emerging in Europe. German military intelligence from 1940 to 1942 confirmed that any interference the United States could muster in the *immediate* future would be annoying at best and inconvenient at worst. The only true concern in Berlin, as shall be seen in the chapters to come, lay in the fear that the Americans would seize base sites in the East Atlantic in which the Germans were interested—base sites from which they would be difficult to dislodge.

Whatever America's racial characteristics were and whatever its weapons timetable was to look like, Hitler understood early that Germany would need a high-seas fleet to combat the United States.[31] Still a believer in the outdated notion of the *Entscheidungsschlacht,* he wanted the future German navy built around a state-of-the-art "superbattleship," which would combine speed, durability, and power, and which would dwarf the battleships of other countries.[32] Though an amateur in naval affairs, Hitler understood that the time lag between a battleship's contracting and christening meant that the former had to occur as early as possible. The Anglo-German Naval Agreement of 1935, which set Germany's future warship tonnage at 35 percent of that of the Royal Navy, was nothing more than a political soup bone. The German government let the contracts for the construction of the battleships *Bismarck* and *Tirpitz* in the very same year, and each would have a displacement of 42,000 tons—well over the internationally accepted limit of 35,000 tons.[33] This was not all. By December 1937 the German navy, surely at Hitler's instigation, approved a plan for the construction of six H-class battleships (*Bismarck* and *Tirpitz* were G-class) of 56,000 tons each.[34] The ships were to be completed by 1944. This date, moreover, was not coincidental. On 5 November 1937 Hitler had informed his top military aides, at the famous Hoßbach conference, that he planned to solve the German Lebensraum problem in Europe by 1943 to 1945 at the latest.[35] If indeed Europe by that time were to have fallen under the German boot, then the H-class ships could only have been meant for a future global struggle with the United States. Surely ships of this scale were not needed to retrieve Danzig and would not have been ready for use in time for the war that Hitler expected against Great Britain and France. To be sure, the navy in 1944 would not have been very balanced. Yet the fleet such as it would exist in 1944 would *look* impressive and would thus suffice to protect German autarchy in the Eastern Hemisphere while allowing German industry the time to turn the nucleus of the future fleet into something much larger.[36]

This argument's thrust is confirmed by the fact that Hitler's own construction priories contrasted with those of the German navy and its commander in chief, Grand Admiral Erich Raeder. Raeder, who had served as commander in chief since 1928, was surely not averse to naval construction. The Naval Command since the imperial period had nursed a tradition of jealousy of Great Britain's colonial and sea power; Raeder was an heir to this tradition and to the bitterness over the naval limitations imposed by the Versailles treaty.[37] Yet the Naval Command preferred a more balanced and versatile fleet that could engage in commercial raiding. Raeder had often tried to convince Hitler of the need for balance and he became more adamant as war with Britain became likely in the late 1930s. Short on large vessels, he argued for a delay in the construction of two H-class ships and increased production of pocket battleships and submarines. Hitler refused. The navy's final prewar construction program, Plan Z of January 1939, though providing for a balanced fleet by 1948, still called for the completion of the H-class ships by 1944. Due to the priority on battleships, Germany's shipyards could build no new pocket battleships, nor could they expect to reach the target number of 249 submarines until 1948. Hitler would have his way, and in April and May 1939 the Navy awarded contracts for the six H-class ships.[38]

New naval weapons were not Hitler's only concern. While contracts were being let for the new surface fleet, the Messerschmitt aeronautics firm was at work on the Me 264—the so-called Amerika-Bomber—which, with a range of more than 12,000 kilometers, would be able to bomb the East coast of the United States. Luftwaffe commander in chief Hermann Göring had been calling since 1938 for the development of an aircraft that could drop a five ton payload on New York City and return without refueling. Messerschmitt had in fact begun working on the four-engine bomber the year before, and in 1940 received an official government contract to develop six versions of the bomber. Hitler spoke for the first time in November 1940 about terrorizing the United States from the air. He expected the Me 264 to be in production by the fall of 1941. The first test flight actually took place in December 1942, and some seventy test flights in all were made. Ultimately the bomber never went into full developmental production thanks to shortages and other projects that followed the German disaster at Stalingrad.[39] But the high expectations regarding the aircraft would indeed influence German policies in 1940 and 1941.

The thought of global struggle and the idea of transatlantic war at some future date also raised concerns over the future of German interservice co-operation. The army, naval, and air force commands would have to cooperate in a way hitherto unknown. Hitler indeed gave voice to this worry in December 1940 after a dispute on the deployment of air torpedoes had caused a rift between the German navy and Luftwaffe. He emphasized to Chief of Armed Forces High Command Wilhelm Keitel and to Chief of Operations Alfred Jodl the need for a strong central High Command framework in the future because, "A man could one day step into [the Führer's] shoes, who . . . does not have . . . as much military knowledge and ability. Such a man would need a very strong *OKW* [Armed Forces High Command], for otherwise there would exist the great danger that the . . . three armed forces branches would fall apart instead of becoming combined. . . . The armed forces would . . . never be able to perform at their best, a condition which in war, where the existence of the Reich would be at stake, is unthinkable."[40] When Hitler made this statement, he viewed the war in the West as won and expected that the conquest of the Soviet Union would be complete by the end of 1941. The war to which he referred could only have been against the United States. Even if one of the Reich's new vassal states had revolted against the New Order in Europe after Hitler's death, the existence of the Reich would hardly have hinged on this kind of interservice cooperation.

On one hand, the above sketch makes a more-than-circumstantial case for a global view on Hitler's part and for his expectation that one day Germany would struggle with the United States for world dominance. On the other hand, there remain a number of problems. Critics of this thesis often speak of the lack of operational planning for a premeditated war with America, and of course the fact remains that though Hitler would declare war against the United States, he would do so at a time that would appear to belie the timing delineated above. It would seem, then, that he was an unprincipled opportunist after all, or that at the very least, there was no *coherent* German thinking concerning a war with the United States. To suggest otherwise—to attach concrete importance to Hitler's musings and military contracts—would seemingly create formidable methodological problems. Norman Rich, author of a two-volume study entitled *Hitler's War Aims,* indeed discussed the issue of *"morgen die ganze Welt"* in skeptical terms and argued that for this issue, historians are ultimately "dependent on Hitler's own statements about his intentions, on plans prepared by state and party officials, and on speculation, with speculation often the major or sole resource available."[41]

Thus, the methodological challenge lies in the translation of broad statements, musings, and unrealized plans and projects into something beyond mere speculation. To start, one must note that broad statements themselves *do* indeed have a historical importance of their own—if nothing else, they reveal the nature of those who uttered them and of the regimes in which they were uttered. Moreover, in the case of Nazi Germany, the absence of operational plans and their implementation *does not* limit the historian to completely idle speculation. It is true that the German leadership did not blueprint its long-range operational planning with the complete paper trails that historians would like. Thankfully, it is also true that Germany did not attack the United States with long-range bombers from bases in Northwest Africa. But in the search for meaningful intention, one must remember that Hitler retained *tactical* freedom within broader *strategic* conceptions; he indeed commented that there were many issues that he preferred to keep to himself and many that he did not think out in detail until the proper time arrived.[42] Thus, while it is true that Nazi Germany had no operational plans to sail up the Chesapeake Bay (as imperial Germany did) or to bomb New York City, it is also true that there was not yet a battle plan to attack Poland when Hitler demanded Danzig, none to attack France while Germany was at war with Poland, nor any to invade Great Britain or the Soviet Union while German troops marched through France. Germany managed to attack each of those states anyway. Moreover, though a shooting war between Germany and Czechoslovakia was averted in September 1938, few historians would deny that Hitler's statements concerning his determination to destroy Czechoslovakia through war or that *Fall Grün*—the operational planning to invade Czechoslovakia—demonstrate an intent with historical significance beyond mere speculation. The Nazi regime had a broad outline of aggression despite tactical shifting, as Propaganda Chief Joseph Goebbels explained in April 1940:

> *National Socialism . . . has never had a doctrine in the sense that it discusses details. . . . If today someone asks how [we] visualize the new Europe, we must say that we do not know. Certainly we have an idea. But if we clothe it in words, this immediately brings us enemies and increases resistance. Once we have the power, they and we as well will see sure enough what we can*

make of it. . . . If necessary one must try to attain the goal in
stages. The individual segment is more easily understood because
it appears to be attainable and because everyone can see that it
can be attained. . . . Today we are saying "Lebensraum." Every-
one can make of this what they want. At the proper time we shall
surely know what we want.[43]

Yet how may one determine the more *concrete* importance of broad statements and planning? One must still anchor loose intentions within the cement of reality, and here the issue of where Germany intended to *station* its new naval and air weapons is key. Whatever its industrial and techno-logical capabilities, the Reich itself enjoyed no easy access to the ocean, and strategic bases, like battleships or new aircraft designs, demanded a long lead time for development. The most favorable area for German base devel-opment was Northwest Africa—a region defined here as running from French Morocco to Senegal and including the outlying archipelagoes of Spain's Canary Islands and Portugal's Azores, Cape Verde Islands, and Madeira. If the Reich followed a clear, coherent policy aiming at the acquisition of base sites in this region at the expense of those states that enjoyed colonial lord-ship over the sites in question (France, Spain, and Portugal) and at the ex-pense of those states that wished a greater imperium over those same areas (Italy, Spain); and if this policy were followed as a true priority—to the detriment of other, short-term advantages—then would this not make a strong case for the existence of a strategy of true global hegemony?

The idea of bases in the East Atlantic had surfaced before the war in both military and political circles. In the navy it had found willing reception in the *Marineakademie* and in strategic considerations of the late 1930s.[44] In 1937, during the civil war in Spain, Raeder demanded the procurement of bases in western Spain and in the Azores and Cape Verde Islands.[45] In June 1938, Admiralty Staff Officer Helmuth Heye toured the Iberian Penin-sula and Spanish Morocco to examine the possibilities of submarine bases, and in mid-1938 and mid-1939 Göring sent "fishing expeditions" to the Canary Islands to garner photographic and cartographic intelligence for a possible base there.[46] After the outbreak of war, the Germans made success-ful arrangements with the Spanish government for the secret reprovisioning of submarines in western Spain and the Canary Islands. Several such refuel-ing operations had already occurred before the French capitulation.[47]

Yet the German victory over the Allied forces in France in June 1940 for the first time made the issue of bases in Northwest Africa a true possibility.

The French were defeated. Italy had entered the war on Germany's side in order to fulfill territorial aims of its own. Spain was about to do the same and argued that it could make an alliance with Portugal as well. All of the states involved were convinced, moreover, that Great Britain itself was on the edge of surrender and that the United States could do nothing to halt the German march to total victory in Europe. Those who question the notion of German long-term aims should consider that in late 1943—with the Red Army having yet to enter Polish territory and with American and British armies half a year away from invading France—British, Soviet, and American representatives were nevertheless discussing the eventual zonal division of Germany. In the summer of 1940, Germany looked much closer to realizing its aims in the West than the Allies looked to realizing theirs in 1943. The idea that the German government would plan its next steps and move to implement them is not at all implausible. Hitler and the Naval Command indeed discussed the outlines of Germany's territorial and strategic future in the West and were in broad agreement on Germany's future strategic needs. Germany would have a large raw materials empire in central Africa. It would also have to prepare for an eventual war with the United States. Bases in Northwest Africa were thus essential—they were not a luxury—and the notion of *borrowing or sharing* installations was no longer sufficient. Germany needed to *own* the necessary sites in order to develop them especially for the new aircraft and warships that it would deploy following its European victories. The time had come, moreover, to attain these base sites, ideally with the acquiescence of the states that owned or coveted them (France, Spain, Italy, and Portugal), but if necessary without it. What no one understood in June 1940 was that Hitler's uncompromising attempt to gain base sites from these states would waste precious months, cost precious advantages, and ultimately affect the course of the conflict to Germany's detriment. And in the end, Northwest Africa would become a springboard for an American, not a German, global role.

In explaining German policy aimed at acquiring bases in Northwest Africa, this study will thus make a case—with the use of published and unpublished German, French, Spanish, Italian, and Portuguese records—for the importance of this policy within the context of a global strategy on Germany's part. In so doing, this study will seek answers to the following questions: When, why, and to what extent did the issue of Northwest Africa surface in German discussions? Was the issue more offensive or defensive in nature? Did Germany take serious diplomatic steps with the colonial powers that controlled Northwest Africa and the outlying islands to win a per-

TOMORROW THE WORLD

Chapter 1

The Window on the Atlantic
ᏇᏋ

The war in the West is over.
—Adolf Hitler

The first item on the German agenda in late June 1940 was the armistice with France. The swift German victory cleared Germany's western flank so that the Reich could launch an isolated war for Lebensraum in the East. Yet the French collapse also meant something else. The opportunity now arose for German base sites in French Northwest Africa and possibly the outlying islands as well. Though discussions on base sites began even before the armistice treaty was signed, Hitler, as this chapter will reveal, was restrained during the cease-fire process. The first order of business involved the immediate liquidation of the war against the Western democracies. Sticky questions involving overseas possessions were to be reserved for a final peace settlement, which seemed imminent to the German leadership. The armistice convention thus gave Germany no political or strategic advantages in Northwest Africa for either the short or long term. Since the expected peace conference never came, German policies in Northwest Africa would be permanently bound by the hasty and poorly thought out decisions of June 1940.

Even to the younger Hitler, France had always been the eternal "*mortal enemy of our nation.*"[1] Never to be trusted, the French in Hitler's mind wished for European dominance and hoped for the return of the weak and fragmented Germany of 1648. In keeping with this aim, the Jewish-controlled Third Republic had supposedly engaged in the poisoning of white European blood with that of imported negroes from French colonies in Africa.[2] Whatever its methods, the fundamental French aim of a crippled Germany would never alter course—after all, the French population was declining in numbers and in racial quality and would thus act to preserve itself. "I never believe," Hitler wrote in 1925, "that France's intentions toward us could ever change. . . ."[3]

The new French government, soon to be located at Vichy under the leadership of Marshal Henri Philippe Pétain, took its nation's defeat by Germany as proof of Germany's demographic superiority and also as confirmation of a long French societal degeneration under the Third Republic. To France's new leaders, a resurgence was essential and possible but would also demand certain prerequisites. First, France would have to extricate itself from the defeat as inexpensively as possible, which meant the minimization of German armistice and peace terms. Second, France would have to recast its society in a more authoritarian and nationalistic mold—far to the right of the republican past. Finally, France would have to find a place in the new German-led Europe commensurate with its past glory and what Vichy leaders hoped would be its future significance. Toward that end, Vichy was willing to cooperate with the Germans very closely in the areas of economics, racial engineering, and foreign and military policy. In the last area, Vichy would reveal a certain affinity for firing on France's former allies while allowing its former enemies the use of French territory, both in the *Metropole* and in the overseas empire. Yet Vichy would expect significant rewards. France was to keep ownership over those things that had made it great— namely its overseas empire and a good portion of its military might. In this way it could maintain a position in Europe proportional with its presumed importance.[4] Hitler would be willing to move down the road of collaboration to a certain extent in pursuit of German political, military, and economic aims. But France would never be allowed to recover its strength and would never earn his trust. "France remains hostile to us," Hitler would remark over dinner one evening in January 1942, and contained "a blood that will always be foreign. . . . The French are trying to profit from our moment of weakness to get the greatest possible advantage. . . . But with me they will not succeed. . . ."[5]

Hitler learned shortly after 9:30 A.M. on 17 June 1940 that the new Pétain government wanted a cease-fire. Before noon he charged Generals Keitel and Jodl with the drafting of an agreement.[6] Despite his long-term preferences, Hitler aimed to infuse a certain reticence into the terms. The British appeared very close to defeat but had still yet to ask for a cease-fire; draconian armistice terms for France would hardly convince London that peace was in its best interests. Moreover, the French navy was still intact, and the French government still could have fled France for England or North Africa to continue the war should the armistice terms have appeared unacceptable. Hitler therefore insisted that the priority of the armistice lay in ending Allied resistance as soon as possible. Thus, the French army would lay down its arms, and Germany would occupy the northern three-fifths of France to continue the war against Great Britain. Yet the French government would remain sovereign in unoccupied France and in the empire. The French navy would be neutralized rather than taken. Germany, meanwhile, would make no territorial demands either in France or overseas.[7]

Germany's Italian allies were far less reserved in their view of the armistice. Domination of the Mediterranean and free access to the Atlantic and Indian Oceans had been Benito Mussolini's grand strategic aim since the mid-1920s.[8] As the French and the British neared defeat in June 1940, Mussolini pulled Italy into the war to gain whatever territorial booty he could before their seemingly imminent surrender. Italy, in Mussolini's conception, would conduct a war *parallel,* rather than identical, to that of the Germans. *Il Duce* understood that Italy could not withstand a long struggle, but he thought that he had entered the war at a fortuitous time.[9] The Italians, as it turned out, gave a dismal showing on the French Alpine front. Still, on 17 June Mussolini approved an Italian-French armistice drafted by his son-in-law and foreign minister, Count Galeazzo Ciano and his army chief of general staff, Mario Roatta, which embodied all of his aims. The French would demobilize all troops in the *Metropole and* in the empire, while handing over to Italy all armaments, *including* the French navy and air force. Italy would occupy France to the River Rhône as well as Corsica, Tunisia, and Djibouti, with the option to occupy further territories. Italy would also occupy the naval bases of Casablanca, Mers-el-Kebir, and Algiers. Finally, the French would neutralize Beirut.[10]

Hitler had always seen the Mediterranean as the "natural area of Italian expansion."[11] He would not, however, allow the Italians to ruin the chances of a quick peace with the Western democracies. Nor would he allow them to thwart his aims in Northwest Africa. In discussions with Mussolini, Ciano, and Roatta at Munich on 18 June, Hitler and his foreign minister, Joachim von Ribbentrop, pared the Italian list accordingly, mortifying the Italians in the process.[12] They flatly informed their allies that there could be no French "holy war" and that the navy would have to remain in French hands. Hitler and Ribbentrop also stated that they wished a quick settlement with Great Britain in which the latter would accept the German continental conquests. An extended war would mean only the destruction of the British Empire with the United States as the prime beneficiary. Finally, though the Germans accepted Italian claims to Nice, Corsica, French

Somaliland, and Tunisia, they bluntly rejected any Italian aspirations in Morocco.

Ribbentrop's comments on this last point deserve scrutiny due to their significance for Germany's Northwest African policy. He told Ciano that Germany had its own historic claims in Morocco, perhaps mentioning as well that Germany wanted certain ports on the Moroccan Atlantic coast. Ribbentrop then spoke "at great length" about the recently received Spanish claim to that protectorate.[13] It was true that the Franco government in Madrid had changed its status from neutral to "non-belligerent" on 12 June 1940, occupied the international zone of Tangier on the fourteenth, and informed Hitler on the sixteenth through Army Chief of Staff Juan Vigón that Spain wished for a united Morocco under Spanish protection. But there is nothing to suggest that Hitler seriously considered handing French Morocco to the Spaniards outright at this time. Vigón had met with Hitler and Ribbentrop only two days before the Munich discussions, and the Germans told him only that a solution for Morocco would be found that was satisfactory to all sides.[14] Moreover, as will be seen below, the Germans did not begin to take the idea of Spanish entry into the war seriously until mid-July. It is less likely that the Germans were acting as the grand protectors of Madrid's interests at Munich than that they were forwarding their own aims in Morocco under the smoke screen of Spanish claims. In any event, Hitler and Ribbentrop slammed the hatch on an Italian window on the Atlantic and began to open one for Germany. In the meantime, Hitler began to consult with his naval expert about the need for German bases in the Northwest African region.

The German Naval Command was certainly familiar with the idea of bases in the East Atlantic. German submarines were already secretly using Spanish ports for reprovisioning.[15] In May 1940 with the war in the West apparently won, Grand Admiral Raeder ordered studies of which bases the navy would need to protect Europe and a future German empire in Central Africa, presumably to be taken from the losers.[16] The studies that emerged made it very clear that the navy would need a large number of bases, and that the navy expected Germany's future enemy to be the United States. The chief of naval operations, Admiral Kurt Fricke, visualized an empire stretching from Senegal to the former colony of German East Africa, including the French colonies south of Senegal and the Belgian Congo. Although he recommended naval bases off the African coast, he named no island groups specifically and seemed to concern himself more with the Indian Ocean.[17] General Admiral Rolf Carls, commander of *Marinegruppenkommando Ost*, named a dazzling number of bases specifically.[18] In Europe, Germany would control Trondheim, Brest, and possibly the Channel Islands. In the Indian Ocean, it would have Madagascar and possibly the Seychelles. In West Africa, Germany would have Dakar and possibly Bathurst. Finally, to secure the route to the empire in Africa, Germany would give Gibraltar to Spain and take Casablanca for itself. If a German base at Casablanca collided with Italian or Spanish aspirations, Carls said, then perhaps Germany could erect a base in the Spanish Canary Islands instead. Who would Germany's future enemies at sea be? Both naval studies assumed a rapprochement with Great Britain and a future conflict with the United States. Fricke's suggestion of a trade of German Southwest Africa for Kenya reflected the expectation of compromise with the British, as did Carls's comments that all German demands on British territories depended on political feasibility. Carls also noted the expectation that France and Britain would one day make common cause with Germany to defend European interests, and Raeder accordingly was highly skeptical of any German claim on the Channel Islands, Bathurst, or the Seychelles.[19] On the other hand, the idea of conflict with the United States was certainly present. Carls advocated a future fleet ratio between Germany, Italy, Great Britain, and France of 4-2-2-1, with the latter two countries having mainly older defensive units and no submarines. He then spoke of the need *"from the bases to prosecute an offensive war."*[20] If the 4-2-2-1 ratio were to become reality, and if France and Britain were to ally with Germany, then the war that Carls was describing could only have been with the United States. The Naval Command registered general agreement with this aspect of the Carls study, and Raeder himself showed particular enthusiasm with Carls's suggestion for naval bases in Dakar and in the Canary Islands.[21]

Yet the claims of the German navy rested ultimately with Hitler. On 20 June 1940, one day before the opening of cease-fire negotiations with the French at Compiègne, Raeder presented the Führer with a memorandum that synthesized the navy's claims for bases in the postwar world.[22] In connection with the continuing war against Great Britain, Raeder pointed to the importance of Dakar. For the postwar period, the memorandum claimed that a system of new bases must permanently eliminate the *British* threat to Germany and its new overseas possessions. Perhaps the navy had already come to the conclusion that even if peace with the British were possible, true rapprochement was not. To protect Germany itself, the Naval Command recommended permanent installations at Trondheim, in Iceland, and along the Channel Coast. In East Africa, the navy advocated installations in Madagascar and in the French island groups off the coast. In West Africa, the memorandum recommended the development of bases in the "colonial area," which probably referred to Dakar, Point Noire, and Duala. In Northwest Africa, the navy wanted an agreement with Spain and Portugal for the purchase and development of bases either in the Azores *or* in the Canary *and* Cape Verde Islands.

There was an important trend to emerge from the 20 June meeting. As will be seen, Hitler would soon press for German bases in the Canaries, Cape Verdes, and Azores. Yet he demonstrated no interest at all in the navy's suggestions concerning the Indian Ocean. Madagascar, he told Raeder, would become a reservation for Europe's Jews, not a naval base. Hitler's focus on the Atlantic rather than the Indian Ocean meant in essence that he did not share the navy's concern of a postwar British threat to that area and was thus apparently unworried about the possibility of *any* British threat after the war. After all, the future German colonies on the Indian Ocean would have been particularly vulnerable to British pressure had London chosen to pose a threat there. Hitler still believed that he would either reach a settlement with the British or destroy their power completely. Hitler's interest in Atlantic bases and disinterest in bases in the Indian Ocean thus suggests that the future enemy, as far as he was concerned, was not Great Britain, or even Great Britain in alliance with the United States. It was the United States exclusively.

During the evening of 20 June, after his discussion with Raeder, Hitler returned to the prevailing issue of the armistice treaty with France. As before, he still believed that the war in the West was essentially over and that peace would be more easily attained if Germany were to handle territorial questions in a later peace conference rather than during the cease-fire process. Nonetheless, the specter that Hitler feared most at this time—continued French resistance in the colonies—had risen in the form of General Charles de Gaulle. On 18 June, de Gaulle issued his famous radio address from London calling for continued French resistance from Great Britain or from the French Empire. Hitler now had greater cause for concern than before. If the armistice terms were too demanding with regard to France's overseas interests, the French colonies would defect to de Gaulle and German aims in the French Empire would fall into doubt. With his own hand then, Hitler altered the clauses that dealt with the French navy. A solemn pledge was added that Germany would not seek to use the French fleet for its own purposes, nor would it claim the fleet in the peace. Hitler also added to the treaty draft the possibility that the French government could perhaps return to Paris in the near future. Paris would surely have added legitimacy to the Pétain government in the eyes of the colonies and the armed forces there, thus deflating the Gaullist danger. These actions turned out to be symptomatic of the armistice process as a whole as it touched the French Empire. The separate German and Italian armistice treaties with the new French government demonstrated incredible political reticence and even shortsightedness on the part of the Axis toward French Africa.[23]

The German peace delegation under Generals Keitel and Jodl met with a French delegation under General Charles-Léon Huntziger on 21 and 22 June at Compiègne. The resulting German-French armistice treaty focused primarily on the French *Metropole* and dealt with France's empire only to an indirect degree.[24] The military restrictions were hardly unexpected. France was to cease all hostilities in the *Metropole* and in all of its overseas possessions (Article 1), and could be compelled to hand over all weapons used against Germany even if located in the unoccupied area (Article 5).[25] French prisoners of war, be they metropolitan or colonial troops, would remain in captivity until the final peace settlement (Article 20). The French government was obliged to prohibit members of the French armed forces from following de Gaulle's example (Article 10) and was to prohibit the transit of war materials to any third country. France also had to submit to economic restrictions during the armistice period. Merchant shipping (Article 11), civilian air traffic (Article 12), and radio transmissions (Article 14) were all suspended until further arrangement. The Germans could revoke the treaty at any time should the French government not fulfill the conditions. Otherwise the agreement would remain in force until the conclusion of peace (Article 24), and France would bear all costs of occupation in the meantime (Article 18). A German Armistice Commission would supervise the implementation of the treaty with the cooperation of a specially composed French delegation (Article 22).

The armistice treaty was not an easy one for the *Metropole* or the empire. Still, it contained a certain latitude with regard to the latter. First, there was no German demand to occupy French territory outside of the *Metropole*. Second, although the French navy was to disarm, Germany pledged to claim no part of the fleet either before or after the peace. In the meantime, France was allowed to retain the naval units needed to protect their colonial interests. Moreover, although the letter of the fleet provisions in Article 8 of the convention stated that the French warships would disarm in their peacetime stations, Keitel assured Huntziger on 22 June that the Germans would decide on a case-by-case basis whether the disarmament of the ships in the

North African ports after demobilization would be more practical given the British air threat to the French mainland Atlantic harbors.

Hitler had gauged correctly that the key questions for the Pétain government lay in the fleet and in the empire. Before Huntziger's delegation left the government's temporary headquarters in Bordeaux for Compiègne, the marshal had warned them that terms concerning the surrender of any part of the fleet or the occupation of any part of the empire would be unacceptable and would warrant an immediate breaking off of armistice talks.[26] To be sure, Huntziger was apprehensive. The new German Armistice Commission, he pointed out, could conceivably make demands over and above the letter of the treaty. There was also grave concern regarding the still-unknown Italian cease-fire demands. The German cease-fire was contingent on one with Italy (Article 23), and despite Huntziger's invective against Rome's jackal-like behavior and military incompetence, Keitel and Jodl refused to discuss the issue.[27] Finally, the German delegation would give no clue as to what the final peace terms would look like. Yet although many questions remained unanswered, the French government felt it could live with the cease-fire arrangement. French honor, as they had defined it, remained intact.[28] General Maxime Weygand, Pétain's minister of national defense and Huntziger's immediate superior, believed that the German view of Italy corresponded with the French one, and that Berlin would do little to forward Italian demands in North Africa or the Levant.[29]

While the Germans were presenting the French with terms reticent toward Africa, the Italians were softening their terms as well. As late as 20 June, Mussolini and the Italian general staff planned to occupy France east of the River Rhône, Tunisia, French Somaliland, and perhaps Corsica and a part of Algeria as well. Yet on the evening of the twenty-first, the Italian dictator substantially reduced these demands. He would settle for general demobilization and a series of demilitarized zones instead.[30] Expediency led to Mussolini's change of stance. He was very much worried by rumors on 21 June that the French government was planning a flight to Algeria. He asked for Hitler's opinion on a possible suggestion to Franco that Spanish forces occupy French Morocco to cut the lines between Casablanca, Oran, and Algiers.[31] Had the French government in fact moved to North Africa along with the French navy and air force, Italy would have faced certain disaster at sea in the Mediterranean, and the Italian army then in Libya under the command of Marshal Italo Balbo would have faced a two-front war.[32] As it was, the Italians had yet to achieve any breakthrough on the Alpine front. Yet if the French were to remain passive, the war would end and Italy could raise more extensive demands at the peace table.[33] Mussolini's explanation to Hitler, that he wished "to facilitate the acceptance of the Armistice by the French" and that he "wished to avoid difficulties at the present very important moment," certainly rings true.[34] *Il Duce* unceremoniously ignored the impassioned pleas by Roatta and the general staff that abstention in North Africa, particularly in Tunisia, would constitute a major error.[35]

The Italians hosted Huntziger's armistice delegation at Villa Incisa on 23 and 24 June. The Italian delegation, headed by the chief of the *Commando Supremo*, Marshal Pietro Badoglio, seemed more embarrassed than victorious, and Mussolini was eager that the talks conclude as soon as possible.[36] The Italians thus showed unusual flexibility, particularly with regard to Africa. The main issue for the French government was the maintenance of its colonial authority. Huntziger warned Badoglio that if France's colonial subjects were to gain the impression that French sovereignty had been weakened, the resulting unrest could engulf Italy's colonies as well. Badoglio thus allowed a debilitating ambiguity in the treaty of 24 June. All areas belonging to France were to demobilize in theory. But the French were presented with no general deadline for demobilization, and they were allowed to maintain the forces needed to preserve order overseas. The German Armistice Commission together with an analogous Italian Armistice Commission were to determine the strength of these forces. The latter, in determining French military strength, would attach special importance to the conservation of order in North Africa, Syria, and French Somaliland (Article 9). In the meantime, the deadlines that the French received were made unenforceable. France was given ten days in theory to demilitarize 200-kilometer zones in Tunisia, Algeria, French West Africa, and French Equatorial Africa where each bordered Libya. Yet here the Italians would permit the French to maintain the military strength needed to preserve order (Articles 3 and 4). The French had fourteen days to demilitarize the naval bases of Toulon, Mers-el-Kebir, Bizerte, and Ajaccio (Article 6). Yet again the Italian Armistice Commission could make exceptions on a case-by-case basis (Article 7). Badoglio even assured Huntziger that the time limits on demilitarization of the Libyan border zones and the naval bases would receive lenient enforcement. For the remainder, the clauses in the Italian treaty referring to the French fleet, air force, merchant shipping, civilian air transport, and radio transmission mirrored the German treaty. Such was also the case with continued illegal participation in the war of French nationals and war materials.[37] The Marshal's government was relieved with the Italian treaty. Pétain said on 23

June that Italy's exaggerated claims would have brought catastrophe had the Italians demanded their implementation.[38] Mussolini demonstrated severe disappointment with the convention, acidly remarking that it was at least a good document to have in hand.[39]

Berlin was remarkably apathetic toward the elasticity of the Italian-French agreement, even given the belief there in a quick ending to the war. There could hardly have been less coordination between the German and Italian governments during the armistice negotiations, and Germany did not even learn the terms of the Italian treaty until the day after its signing. The Foreign Ministry and the embassy in Rome then allowed the treaty to pass without comment.[40] Hitler, meanwhile, had shown no concern either. Mussolini's announcement of 22 June that the Italians would opt for demilitarized zones rather than occupation in Africa won only Hitler's comment that Germany would go along with Italian preferences, "however you decide."[41] To Hitler, the Mediterranean had always been Italy's natural theater anyway.

Given the strong German and Italian interests in the French African empire, the leniency of the armistice treaties for the region was surprising to say the least. The treaties bound the overseas French forces with rubber bands rather than iron fetters. The German-French treaty allowed certain French naval forces to defend French colonial interests while restricting maritime, air, and radio traffic but otherwise did not deal with the empire in a direct way. Berlin, as Hitler and Ribbentrop had made crystal clear, planned to make its colonial claims known to the French only after the war had ended.[42] The Italian treaty dealt with Northwest Africa but in the weakest possible way. Italian troops would occupy no territory. Though Italy called for French disarmament, there was no firm policy for the delineation of French strength. Given the contemptuous French attitude toward the Italians, Italy's military weakness, and Weygand's belief that Berlin would do little to further Rome's aims in Africa and the Middle East, any Italian policy in Africa would be very difficult to implement.[43] Ciano, meanwhile, harbored doubts as to Pétain's ability to execute the treaty's few requirements regarding the French navy and empire. Here was an even more uncomfortable thought, especially given the Italian foreign minister's private belief that the war had only just begun.[44] At the time, however, Ciano's belief was unique. It was true that the armistice conventions set very narrow parameters for what the Axis powers could demand in French Africa. But in the heady days of June 1940, these parameters did not seem to be a problem. The war seemed nearly over, and the parameters set in the armistice process were to vanish during the peace process. In fact the war was far from over, and the parameters that the Axis powers set for themselves in Africa would be excruciatingly difficult to alter.

Due to miscalculations concerning the length of the war, there were also numerous built-in problems in the armistice machinery itself. In the first place, the treaties dealt almost solely with immediate military questions. They gave scant attention to political and economic issues, and they did not touch military questions that could possibly emerge in the future. The Armistice Commissions themselves were viewed as temporary organizations for the implementation of cease-fire terms. The German commission did not even receive a permanent chief of staff until July 1940.[45] The armistice machinery was ill-equipped to deal with military issues not covered in the treaties or the larger political and economic issues that were bound to arise should the war not end within a matter of weeks. Yet as the war continued, it was these political, economic, and military issues omitted by the treaties that would gain importance. German, Italian, and French demands and counterdemands would appear that flew over and above the terms of the armistice conventions. Hitler had in fact recognized that the German treaty was limited in its scope and had attempted to have it written with greater elasticity. On 17 June he had instructed Lieutenant Colonel Hermann Böhme from Jodl's staff, who would in July become the chief of staff for the German Armistice Commission, to write the articles broadly so that Germany could raise further demands. Such language was impossible with most terms, so Hitler opted for a preamble that was to act as a "general clause." It stated that the treaty's purpose was to provide Germany with all necessary securities for the continuation of the war. Yet the preamble, though read aloud to the French at Compiègne, was never signed as such. The French never viewed it as part of the treaty.[46] Thus, any demands that went over the letter of the actual terms, even if supported by the preamble, would only increase the apprehension between the parties. The French would view the Germans and Italians as adding illegal conditions to the armistice conventions, while the Axis would view French stubbornness and attempts at negotiation as an insidious ploy to escape the war as inexpensively as possible.

The armistice conventions also failed to delineate geographic spheres of authority between German and Italian armistice agencies.[47] According to the treaties, the German and Italian Armistice Commissions were to have joint authority over the resumption of French merchant shipping, air transport, and radio contact. Disarmament itself was a joint responsibility in many cases. Yet when the Armistice Commissions were created on 25 June in Wiesbaden and Turin respectively, there was no delineation of authority spheres. The chairman of the German commission, General Carl-Heinrich von Stülpnagel, received only the vague directive from Hitler that his main task was the implementation of the armistice treaty in coordination with the Italians. Later instructions from the High Command merely harked back to the generalities of the previous week's German-Italian discussions in Munich, employing the vague formula that Germany would be responsible for the *Metropole*, while Italy imposed the cease-fire terms in the Mediterranean.[48] Nothing was said about the French holdings elsewhere.

The closest facsimile to a high-level written agreement on spheres of responsibility came during a meeting in Wiesbaden on 29 June between Generals Stülpnagel and Roatta. The two men discussed the issue of spheres and signed a written protocol. Yet even these so-called Roatta Agreements of the twenty-ninth were vague in the extreme. Germany was to control the strength of the French armed forces in most of the French *Metropole* while Italy would be responsible for this task in the French Mediterranean possessions, namely Syria, Tunisia, Algeria, and Morocco. Italy would also handle disarmament in French Somaliland. For warship disarmament, Germany would supervise the Atlantic, Pacific, and Indian Ocean ports and Italy would supervise the harbors in the Mediterranean, the Red Sea, and the Gulf of Aden. The theory behind the Roatta Agreements evidently lay in the German recognition of the Mediterranean as an Italian sphere of inspection activity, but in such a case there already existed several problems. In the first place, Berlin was careless regarding Morocco. Ribbentrop had already informed Ciano in Munich that Germany had powerful interests there. Moreover, though French Morocco had a long Atlantic coastline with several important ports and a Mediterranean coastline of no more than fifteen kilometers, that protectorate was thrown to the mercy of Italian supervision. Exacerbating this problem all the more was the Italian belief that the areas of supervision were in fact exclusive spheres of interest; an impression that the Germans, as will be seen, never wished to give.[49] The Germans would not find it easy to rid the Italians of this notion. Secondly, the Roatta Agreements mentioned nothing at all about the supervision of the tremendous expanses of French West and Equatorial Africa. When Axis powers turned their gaze toward these areas in September 1940 as a result of the activities of Charles de Gaulle, the lack of an agreement on the supervision of these regions would cause additional friction between Berlin and Rome.[50]

The blurry relationship between Wiesbaden and Turin would become blurrier by the scarce high-level contact between the leaders of the Armi-

stice Commissions. Stülpnagel, a career general staff officer and most recently commander of the German Second Army Corps, had little respect for
the Italians and showed no interest in a meeting with the Italian chairman,
General Pietro Pintor, who himself was no Germanophile. The German High
Command never pushed Stülpnagel on the issue, since the alliance with Italy
was one of a parallel war in any case. Stülpnagel's attitude carried down
into the hierarchy of the German Armistice Commission. The first personal
meeting between the German and Italian chiefs of staff did not come until
February 1941, ironically in order to overhaul the Roatta Agreements.
Though the German and Italian subcommissions concerned with the French
air force maintained close contact, those for the French army and navy questions did not. The only permanent contact between Wiesbaden and Turin
lay in liaison officers, and neither even arrived at his respective post until
late July.[51]

Hostilities with France ended officially at 1:35 A.M. on 25 June. On the
evening of the twenty-fourth while awaiting the historic moment, Hitler
met with a small circle of German officials in his temporary headquarters at
Bruly-le-Peche. Happily considering the present and future, the Führer
confidently remarked, "The war in the West is over. France is defeated and
in the shortest time I will come to an agreement with England."[52] It would
become clear soon, however, that there would be no peace conference in the
immediate future to redistribute territories in Europe and in Africa. Instead
the Germans, French, and Italians would exist in an intermediate stage of
cease-fire. In this stage, many military, political, and economic questions
had been left unresolved, and there was no easy way to settle these questions as they arose. Had Hitler thought that the war would last even throughout the year, he surely would have protected his interests in Africa better. As
it was, his aims in Africa would be bound by the hasty armistice arrangements and nonarrangements for which he himself was responsible.

Chapter 2

The Demand for Casablanca

Mers-el-Kebir can and must help us.
—Paul Baudouin

But the French do indeed remain the French.
—Joseph Goebbels

On 15 July 1940, the new Pétain government received a startling note from Germany. Adolf Hitler had demanded that France provide Germany with positive support in the latter's continuing war against Great Britain. Specifically Hitler wanted bases in French Morocco. The French government was to place at Germany's disposal eight airfields near Casablanca, to be chosen by a special German commission. They were to develop the areas in accordance with Germany's specifications and to make available all facilities necessary for operation, including ground personnel. They were to provide adjacent land for the setup of antiaircraft batteries. They were to allow unrestricted use of North African ports, French cargo ships, and the Tunis-Rabat railroad so that the Germans could outfit the bases properly. They were to allow full access to North Africa's communications network and weather stations. All of the services listed in the note were to operate under German command, and Berlin would hold the French government at Vichy responsible for any acts of sabotage. Finally, the Führer expected that France would communicate its assent immediately.[1]

Few historians have examined the Casablanca demand of 15 July 1940 in detail. Those who have done so have seen the episode as a *Zwischenspiel*—an isolated incident dealing with an issue of ephemeral importance. Perhaps Hitler was attempting to provide the Luftwaffe with the means to combat British supply traffic in the eastern middle Atlantic. Perhaps he was attempting to intimidate Great Britain into surrender by presenting it with a united front from the North Cape to Morocco while protecting the latter from British attack. In any case, Vichy refused Hitler's demand and the Führer dropped the issue, never to raise it again.[2] A close look at the surviving documentation, together with Hitler's views concerning progress of the war in the summer of 1940, suggests that other explanations may be more satisfactory. The Casablanca demand was indeed part of a consistent German policy. Hitler was not hoping to gain access to a single cluster of airfields for immediate and temporary use against the British. Casablanca was to be the first of a whole network of permanent German air and naval bases in the Northwest African region. Their development, moreover, was intended for a future global struggle against the United States. In mid-July 1940, the military and diplomatic constellation seemed suitable for Germany to demand strategic control over Casablanca and thus gain an initial foothold in Northwest Africa.

The Germans had already discussed the question of bases in Northwest Africa before the armistice, although Hitler himself had preferred to wait until the final peace arrangements to make actual territorial demands. German silence on the issue clearly appealed to the Pétain government, which hoped to exit the war as inexpensively and with as much national dignity as possible. Indeed, the fate of the French Empire, convulsed by the defeat, and with German, Italian, Spanish, and Japanese wolves waiting at its various doors, was an especially acute concern in France. General Maxime Weygand, Pétain's minister of national defense, directed the French delegations to the German and Italian Armistice Commissions in accordance with his own hope to preserve the empire intact despite the German victory. From the start, the French did what they could to assert the authority of the new government overseas.[3] For the rest, Weygand was willing to fulfill the cease-fire terms as they were written but unwilling to give the Axis powers anything in the empire that overshot the treaty provisions without substantial compensation.[4]

Yet crucial to the fate of French Africa was London's refusal to wait calmly for the results of this ambiguous French policy, particularly with regard to the French navy. A transfer of French naval vessels to the Axis powers would have eliminated British fleet advantages gained during the German conquest of Norway during the preceding spring and would have meant disaster for the already overextended Royal Navy. Few in London trusted German assurances regarding the French fleet in Article 8 of the Armistice Convention, especially since Berlin could simply revoke the treaty on pretext. Prime Minister Winston Churchill, moreover, placed little faith in the assurances of Admiral Jean-François Darlan, the French naval minister, that the fleet would not fall into Axis hands. Thus on 3 July, the British launched Operation *Catapult*, which aimed at the control, disablement, or destruction of all French warships within reach. At the Algerian port of Mers-el-Kebir, *Catapult* turned particularly grim. French resistance led to a British attack in which one French warship was destroyed, three damaged, and more than eleven hundred French sailors killed.[5] The French government, and Darlan in particular, were predictably outraged, but to Weygand the attack provided the opportunity and indeed the necessity of easing the armistice terms with regard to disarmament in the colonies. On 6 July he penned the following policy outline to the chairmen of the French delegations in Wiesbaden and Turin, General Charles-Léon Huntziger and Admiral Emile-André-Henri Duplat respectively: "If we do not wish to run the danger of losing to both sides we must direct the attention of Germany and Italy to the considerable sacrifices to which we are agreeing."[6]

The relaxation of the armistice terms was easy to a point because Hitler was willing for the time being to have the French keep the British at arm's length from Africa. On the afternoon of 3 July, before the outcome of Mers-el-Kebir was clear in Europe, Hitler ordered General Stülpnagel, the chairman of the German Armistice Commission, to tell the French that the Führer was following their actions with great interest. Hitler added vaguely that the French performance in this test of loyalty to the armistice would add weight to the securities given to the French fleet in the Armistice Convention. On handing the French the note with this message the same evening, Stülpnagel noted further that the German Armistice Commission was prepared to suspend those provisions of the armistice that ran counter to the measures that the French government was taking at that time.[7] The next day, the French began to press for specific measures. Admiral Fritz Michelier, chief of the French subdelegation for naval affairs in Wiesbaden, requested the suspension of the naval disarmament clauses in the armistice treaty, freedom for French war and merchant ships to pass through the Strait of Gibraltar, the release of French naval personnel held prisoner in Rochefort, and the return of the confiscated files of the French Naval Ministry. Michelier's opposite number in Wiesbaden, Commander Paul Wever, was unusually affable. Counter to all custom, he gave Michelier a warm handshake before relaying the requests to Berlin.[8] Within three hours, Hitler himself had approved Michelier's entire list.[9] The Armistice Commission also allowed a partial suspension of French air force and antiaircraft disarmament.[10] The

German concessions of 4 July were far-reaching enough so that the naval and air force subcommissions in Wiesbaden soon complained that they had no work to do.[11] Vichy had hoped for more, namely a full revision of the notion of the armistice. On 7 July, Huntziger made an argument to Stülpnagel, which Vichy would repeat often in the coming months. "Normally," he said, "an armistice is an intermediate stage between war and peace . . . but our Armistice is irregular, for . . . France finds herself almost at war with the same enemy as her victorious adversary. . . . regular procedures are no longer sufficient. . . . For new situations, new measures!"[12]

Yet Berlin had already traveled as far down the road of Franco-German friendship as it wished. No one in Berlin was even remotely ready for a fundamental shift in policy. There were several reasons for this unwillingness. One was the quick reemergence of German suspicions of French reliability as Vichy's outrage over Mers-el-Kebir failed to turn into truly decisive action. Despite much noise about naval and air force alerts in North Africa and general attack orders from Darlan, the French took little retaliatory action against the British.[13] In the days following Mers-el-Kebir, Vichy contented itself with a largely symbolic air strike on Gibraltar and a formal break in diplomatic relations with London. On 8 July, the British carrier *Hermes* attacked the French battleship *Richelieu* at Dakar, inflicting damage to the new battleship's stern. *Richelieu* had left Brest in late June, having never completed its trials or firing practice, and the crew had never fired the main battery. Still, German circles remained unimpressed with the ship's performance. Wever commented that the result of the British raid should have been different and concluded by the tenth that Vichy was not really serious about defending strategic areas after all. By the end of the month, he even suspected secret ties between Vichy and London.[14]

The miscarriage of total cooperation between France and Germany suited senior officials in Berlin in any event. The list of territorial demands to be made on France would have to have shrunk considerably if the French were to have given Germany active help in the war against Great Britain. Such thinking permeated the Naval Command especially. Raeder and his cohort viewed the disarmament concessions that followed Mers-el-Kebir as temporary expedients that were to allow the French to defend themselves but no more.[15] Raeder shuddered at the thought of a fundamental policy shift and was not willing to allow the French to force Berlin's hand. When the French admiralty pressed on 8 July for separate French and German operative naval zones, full operative freedom, and an extension of the approved 20-mile attack zone to one of 100 nautical miles off the West African coast, the

German navy balked.[16] The recognition of France as an ally, cautioned the Naval Command, did not lay in Germany's political interests. "The French goal," they remarked, "is obviously to demand considerable concessions with the conclusion of peace by reason of a joint struggle against England." Raeder followed the same line with Hitler on 11 July when the latter asked about the wisdom of allowing French offensive operations in the Atlantic. Germany, stated the grand admiral, should allow France nothing more than the defense of its West African bases.[17]

Hitler in fact needed little convincing. It was one thing to allow the French to defend their colonies and bases from the British for the time being. Even before the armistice, Hitler wanted a French government that commanded the obedience of France's overseas holdings. Yet Hitler's attitude toward France had long been one of fundamental mistrust, and it would take much more than Mers-el-Kebir to change it. Help from the French in a war that seemed all but won would have been militarily pointless and politically expensive. Immediately after the Mers-el-Kebir raid, he ordered Propaganda Minister Joseph Goebbels to have the German press subdue all Francophilia arising from the British-French engagements. "If we wanted," remarked Goebbels the following day, "we could completely win over the French. But we do not wish to do so."[18] German written polemic against France in fact *increased* after the episode at Mers-el-Kebir.[19] Hitler vented his continued mistrust to Ciano during a long discussion in Berlin on 7 July. The French, he warned, would still destroy Germany and Italy if they were to become able. The Axis, he concluded, would continue to treat France as an absolute enemy.[20]

Thus, despite the suspension of naval and air disarmament in the colonies, Vichy received nothing from Germany that would have allowed it to establish a firm grip on Africa at the expense of German aims there. The German Armistice Commission, for instance, allowed the return of the files of the French Naval Ministry but rejected a request for the return of the files of the French Colonial Ministry on the grounds that the German authorities had not yet finished with them.[21] The French request to set up civilian air transport to Algiers, Oran, Casablanca, and Dakar was handled in a dilatory fashion by the German Armistice Commission, in part because of a German desire to set up Lufthansa service to Dakar.[22] The Germans were also in no hurry to allow the resumption of merchant shipping to and from the French African colonies.[23] The risks of diminished economic contact between France and its overseas possessions were well known in Berlin. German and French observers in Dakar noted that respect for French authority was slipping, and that British influence from Gambia, Sierra Leone, Nigeria, and the Gold Coast was increasing due in large part to the economic decline caused by the stoppage of French air and sea transport.[24] German observers also detected the hope for independence in North Africa.[25] Yet Berlin did nothing about this series of problems at this point, partly due to the possibility of French merchant ships falling to the British as prizes, but also due to Germany's own economic and political interests in the French colonies.[26] Not until General Charles de Gaulle's August 1940 coup in French Equatorial Africa demonstrated the consequences of neglect did Berlin move to settle these issues, and then only at the price of extended German influence in the politics and economy of French Africa.[27] In the meantime, the attack on Mers-el-Kebir and the German concessions on disarmament allowed certain opportunities for Berlin. In his own mind, Hitler had made several magnanimous gestures to Vichy, and there was no time like the present to take advantage of his generosity. The Germans had been talking about bases in Northwest Africa since before the war, and the political constellation seemed right to gain an initial German foothold there, even before the expected peace conference. Berlin would demand bases in Casablanca.

The immediate impetus for the Casablanca demand seems to have been an Italian initiative. During the Mers-el-Kebir crisis, the Italian government had been as forthcoming as that of Germany with the suspension of disarmament clauses. On 4 July, the Italian Armistice Commission approved French requests for the suspension of demilitarization in French North Africa and Syria, with the inclusion of all naval bases therein.[28] Rome's stance was as self-serving as that of Berlin. The Italian navy saw in the French fleet a convenient instrument with which to combat the Royal Navy in the Mediterranean without risking Italian units.[29] Yet the commander in chief of the Italian armed forces, Marshal Pietro Badoglio, felt that Italian concessions could be used to Italy's advantage regardless of the reasons behind them. On 5 July, two days after the Mers-el-Kebir raid, he had the Armistice Commission at Turin broach the idea of an Italian air base in Algeria for joint Franco-Italian operations against British vessels in the area.[30] The French cabinet learned of the request the same evening. The next day Darlan, still fuming over the first British attack on Mers-el-Kebir, and having just learned of a follow-up attack that morning by the British carrier *Ark Royal* on the French battle cruiser *Dunkerque,* wanted to give Rome a positive answer. Pétain agreed and ordered a study on the basing of Italian aircraft in Algeria to help protect the French fleet and for possible attacks on Gibraltar.[31] Even Weygand was ready for a brief time to grant Italy's request.[32] According to

the diary of French foreign minister Paul Baudouin, voices against the opening of Algeria to the Italians won Pétain's favor by the next day.[33] But the
French reserve had still come too late to stop a 7 July note that accepted the
Italian suggestion in principle.[34] In fact, Rome had already begun to pull
back from collaboration with Vichy and by 9 July had stopped discussing
the issue.[35] Italy's reserve likely came at the behest of Mussolini, who feared
that collaboration with Vichy would mean a shrinkage of Italian war booty.
According to Ciano, the Duce was "concerned over the fact that France
[was] trying to slip gradually into the anti-British camp."[36]

Berlin learned of the Italian request for an air base in Algeria on the
same day as Badoglio's request but apparently did not learn of the positive
French answer until 11 July.[37] Nonetheless, Hitler told Ciano on 7 July that
he intended to demand two airfields in French Morocco for the Luftwaffe,
one east and one west of the Spanish Moroccan border. His stated motive
was to intervene if the Royal Navy were to launch any more attacks.[38] The
German Armistice Commission received orders to coordinate a German
demand with that made by Turin and to approach the French delegation on
the issue of air bases.[39] On 10 July, Wiesbaden informed Turin of the forthcoming German demand and asked for an immediate Italian agreement so
that Germany and Italy could face the French with a united front.[40] If the
Germans had indeed drafted a demand at this point, then the text no longer
exists. Yet the demand at this point was likely rather limited. The available
sources suggest that it mentioned but a single base in North Africa and was
in line with the comments that Hitler made to Ciano on the seventh. The
Italians, contrary to their stance a few days later when the Germans presumably widened the sweep of the demand, raised no objection to the news
from Wiesbaden. Rome simply replied that the French had accepted the
Italian request in principle.[41]

In fact, Berlin was already extending the scope of the original demand.
Later on 10 July, Wiesbaden received new orders to draw up a demand for
bases in North Africa for the Luftwaffe *and* for the navy.[42] Later the same
day, Berlin changed its mind again. Wiesbaden was told to draft yet another
version, this time omitting the mention of naval usage. The reason for the
omission is not clear. Perhaps Hitler was concerned that the mention of
naval usage would appear to threaten the assurances given the French navy
in the Armistice Convention, thus forcing the French fleet to the British side.
The omission meant little in any case, since the initial foothold of air bases
would be decisive. Control of the skies would mean control of adjacent
harbors. Wiesbaden drafted a new demand in accordance with the latest

specifications and sent it to Turin on 11 July. The text of the 11 July draft does not survive. But later discussions regarding the demand suggest that it strongly resembled the final draft, described above, which Stülpnagel handed to the French delegation on 15 July. The only difference appears to have been that the 11 July version included a demand for a German base at Oran in addition to those at Casablanca, whereas the 15 July version, thanks to Italy's insistence described below, included Casablanca only.[43] In any case, the demand was no longer the limited request for the prevention of another Mers-el-Kebir, nor did it aim at the mere disruption of British cargo traffic off the Northwest African coast. The demand, by virtue of its sheer scope along with the time and manpower needed for its implementation, aimed at a permanent German position in Northwest Africa. The demand, moreover, was directed at a prospective long-term enemy, and to Hitler this enemy was not Great Britain but rather the United States. A look at Hitler's view of the global situation in mid-1940 lends strong credence to this interpretation.

It is true that the Casablanca demand began with the rather benign assertion that it merely called on France to provide Germany with support in the continuation of the war with Great Britain. Yet this claim aimed at little more than the cloaking of an illegal demand in legalistic garb. It was an allusion to the elastic preamble to the German-French armistice treaty, which declared that the treaty's purpose lay in providing the Reich with all securities needed to continue the war. In fact the demand held no such intent. In the first place, the bases in Casablanca did not fit into Hitler's current conception of the war with Great Britain. He believed at the time of the French collapse that Great Britain, like it or not, would have to bend the knee and recognize German continental supremacy.[44] As June turned to July this belief became stronger in spite of the British attack on Mers-el-Kebir. Churchill's stubbornness, Hitler believed, was the last gasp in a long tradition of English continental interference. Hitler told the Italians on more than one occasion in early July that Great Britain was finished and that Whitehall was dreaming of American or Soviet intervention, which would never materialize. Yet if the Churchill government wanted Great Britain's total destruction, stated Hitler, they could have it.[45] Actually, the Führer preferred negotiation to destruction. If the British Empire were to collapse in 1940, he reasoned, the beneficiary would have been the United States rather than Germany.[46] Berlin thus sent peace feelers to London in late June. Hitler also tried a public "appeal to reason" from the *Reichstag* on 19 July—four days *after* the Casablanca demand—which he truly felt would work wonders in London.[47] Ciano, who heard the appeal, noted that "[the Germans] are hoping . . . that this appeal will not be rejected. . . . I believe [Hitler's] desire for peace is sincere. . . . When the first cold British reactions to the speech arrive, a sense of ill-concealed disappointment spreads among the Germans."[48] If negotiation were to fail, Hitler was willing if necessary to force Great Britain to the peace table, primarily with air power. Here again, he had no doubt of success. He estimated in early July that he could defeat Great Britain within four weeks, primarily through aerial bombardment.[49] On 2 July, he also ordered the armed forces branches to begin the theoretical work for the last resort—Operation *Seelöwe*—the proposed military landing in England that would come once the Luftwaffe had secured air supremacy over England. "[If] London should reject our last offered chance [for peace]" noted Goebbels, "then they shall be crushingly defeated. Apparently the English have no idea at all what stands before them."[50]

None of Hitler's conceptions regarding Great Britain in July 1940 connected with air bases in Casablanca. Hitler was still hopeful regarding his peace overtures when the demand was drafted. He also made it clear that a continuation of the war would mean taking the war to the home islands through bombing or invasion. Such projects would have demanded that the Luftwaffe set up on the English Channel—not hundreds of miles away in Morocco. The time needed to choose airfields in Morocco and make them operational through sea transport and the Tunis-Rabat railway would have far exceeded the time frame that Hitler felt was needed to defeat Great Britain through direct means in any case. The possibility that Hitler wished to station aircraft in Morocco to sink British transports headed around the Cape for the Middle East is problematic. The Luftwaffe was already weakened from its busy spring of campaigning and did not have the aircraft to spare for such a tangential project.[51] Besides, German submarines could already operate in the East Atlantic, thanks to their secret refueling bases in Spain and the Canary Islands.[52] The Casablanca demand, moreover, would have invested too much materially and risked too much politically to have been aimed at a few transport vessels bound for a non-German theater. The notion that Hitler aimed to prevent a British attack on Casablanca is also unlikely. True, Hitler commented to Ciano on 7 July that he wanted to be able to intervene if the British made another raid in North Africa. Yet if the Royal Navy raided Mers-el-Kebir on 3 and 6 July and Dakar on the eighth, then Berlin could not help but notice by 15 July that Great Britain probably had no intention of attacking Casablanca, where the only French warship worth attacking was the unfinished battleship *Jean Bart*. Even if Berlin truly expected another British attack in North Africa, there existed easier and faster ways to station German aircraft in the area than that which Hitler demanded.

Is it possible that Hitler made the Casablanca demand for the contingency that the war with Great Britain could, counter to all of his expectations and statements, become a long one of attrition? If this were the case, bases in Morocco would indeed assume greater importance as the war progressed, particularly for the British. Yet this argument is also difficult to maintain. It is true that in early July Hitler was sensitive to the possibility that Great Britain could attempt the occupation of French Morocco. On 1 July, he commented to Italian ambassador Dino Alfieri that the inability of Franco's Spain to fulfill a wish of Mussolini's—the occupation of French Morocco in order to forestall its defection from the Pétain government—had actually been a boon to the Axis. Such a Spanish action, Hitler had said, would have prompted a British occupation attempt.[53] Likewise on 7 July, he rejected Ciano's idea for a separate peace with France. Such a peace would include a German demand for the return of its colony in the Cameroons. This demand, warned Hitler, would have triggered a British assault on French Morocco.[54] Yet by mid-July the Führer seemed rather unconcerned with the possibility of a British attack in Africa. After all, if Spanish intervention in French Morocco would have provoked a British landing there in early July, then the development of German air bases near Casablanca would certainly have done the same. German bases would also have sent an unmistakable message to London that the entire French Empire was up for grabs. Hitler surely felt when he made the Casablanca demand that Great Britain, staring at German swords and olive branches from across the Channel, would be unable or unwilling to undertake grand projects in Africa. The timing of the Casablanca demand thus confirms more than challenges the notion that Hitler expected a speedy arrangement with London.

It would appear more likely that the Casablanca demand fit into the context of a future war with the United States. To be sure, Berlin did not believe that Washington presented an immediate threat to the unfolding order in Europe. Ribbentrop had made this belief clear to Ciano in their Munich meeting of 18 June, and Hitler had not even mentioned the United States in his long discourse to Ciano on 7 July. It remained far from certain that the supposedly pro-Jewish President Roosevelt would even win reelection in November 1940.[55] Nonetheless, a confrontation with the United States down the road appeared inevitable, and preparations could not begin too soon. In the diplomatic realm, Ribbentrop had already begun to bully the Latin American states away from increased economic contact with the

United States. Germany, he told them, would soon become their most important raw materials market and their prime supplier of finished goods. Poor behavior now, said the foreign minister, could be punished with trade sanctions later.[56]

Armament issues relevant to war with the United States were also moving to the forefront of German thought. On 11 July, while the Casablanca demand was in development, Hitler and Raeder discussed warship production for the period after the British surrender, which both saw on the horizon.[57] To the navy, the identity of Germany's future enemies had become clear. While Hitler might have felt that the British would mend their fences with Germany and become a vassal of the Reich, the navy felt that Great Britain would, in defeat, become the junior partner of the United States. "The fate of the British World Empire after this war is uncertain," predicted the Naval Command. "Yet it can be assumed that Great Britain [will] have to renounce all interference in Europe and recognize German European supremacy. In its weakened state Great Britain will seek the support of the United States, which [will] still have a firm interest in a strong European England. [Thus] will the USA become an enemy of Germany. Both Anglo-Saxon Powers will maintain their great sea power either to defend or to expand further their world Empire, and [will] thus become the first natural enemy for Germany to consider."[58] Accordingly, Raeder called for stepped-up fleet construction to meet the Anglo-Saxon threat. The outbreak of war in 1939 had arrested work on the two H-class battleships already begun and annulled the contracts of the remaining four.[59] The navy called for the immediate completion of the suspended contracts, along with design innovation for future vessels to make them more resistant to enemy bombing. Since such construction would demand years and leave Germany with a weak fleet in the meantime, the Naval Command suggested the construction of an "interim fleet" based on two hundred submarines.

Hitler might have disagreed with Raeder's political projections regarding Great Britain but concurred with the main thrust of the navy's arguments regarding fleet construction.[60] He approved the immediate development of the submarine fleet. As for battleships, he called for the completion of the two H-class ships already begun, while pressing for design improvements for all remaining battleships to be contracted. Fleet development was not the only weapons issue on the German agenda. It was at this time that the Messerschmitt firm received the official contract to develop the Me 264, the so-called Amerika-Bomber, on which it had been working since 1937. The firm was to produce the aircraft in six versions, four of which were to have a range of 11,900 to 16,300 kilometers. Actual production turned out to be far less spectacular than the contracts.[61] But Hitler was optimistic about the prospects of the bomber. He would hint to Mussolini in June 1941 that it would be in production by the end of that year, in other words, when the USSR would supposedly be defeated and Germany would stand as the master of Europe.[62]

Germany could produce naval vessels and aircraft by itself, but it could not produce its own forward base sites. It would have to take these from other countries. Hitler and Raeder discussed this key issue in their 11 July meeting as well. One installation was to be at Norway's great natural harbor of Trondheim, which would serve as a state-of-the-art base and shipyard, capable of producing a new battleship each year. There would also be a large German city there, complete with two indoor swimming complexes, which would be accessible from Germany by a new Autobahn.[63] With regard to the East Atlantic, Hitler approved Raeder's suggestions of 20 June, focusing primarily on the Canary Islands. He mentioned that he wished to trade French Morocco, doubtless minus Casablanca, the demand for which had already been drafted, to Madrid for one of the islands. Raeder was to examine which of the islands, aside from the two main islands of Gran Canaria and Tenerife, would serve most suitably as a German base.

It would be difficult to argue that the Casablanca demand, the plans for naval and aircraft construction, and the projects for bases in Norway and the Canaries were not parts of the same whole. Each of the projects would take considerable time to bring to fruition. An H-class battleship would take at least six years to complete, and no one knew for certain about the Me 264's timetable. The Trondheim Autobahn was placed on a fifteen-year completion schedule. The lesser Canaries had no natural ports and needed extensive dredging and construction to harbor battleships. Even the setup of bases in Casablanca for an initial German foothold in Africa would have demanded weeks or months, especially if dependent on the Tunis-Rabat railroad to make them operational. None of these projects could have fit into German timetables regarding the war with Great Britain. They could only have fit into a timetable regarding a more distant conflict with the United States.

Yet if the Casablanca demand was aimed at a conflict that was far in the future, then the timing of the demand remains a mystery. Why would Berlin pose the demand while the war with Great Britain was still in progress, while the United States was still perceived as a paper tiger, and while the danger still existed that French Africa could defect from Vichy? Actually, the timing of the Casablanca demand made good diplomatic sense. With regard to Vichy, the placement of the demand before the conclusion of peace no doubt seemed quite wise. By making the demand while hostilities with Great Britain were still in progress, Hitler could use the preamble to the armistice treaty as legal justification. By making the demand shortly after the British raid at Mers-el-Kebir, Berlin could point to the air bases as a quid pro quo for the German concessions to the French navy. This Hitler in fact did in the final text of the demand, and Huntziger for one viewed the Casablanca bases primarily as payment for the German favors on French disarmament.[64] If Hitler were to have waited for the conclusion of peace, he would have had a more difficult job to demand the bases either on the grounds of the preamble or on those of the disarmament suspensions. The war with Great Britain would have ended and the French navy, one can safely assume, would not have survived into the postwar period. In addition, Vichy seemed in July 1940 as though it would be quite amenable to the German demand. It had, after all, accepted in principle the Italian request for an air base in Algeria. Vichy had also hinted via Wiesbaden that it might be in favor of French-German-Italian naval collaboration in North Africa.[65] The timing of the demand also made good sense with regard to Germany's relations with Spain. In the third week of June, a few days before the French surrender, General Francisco Franco's government had registered with Berlin a claim to French Morocco and other portions of Northwest Africa that supposedly belonged to the Spanish patrimony.[66] Hitler, as he had made clear to Raeder, was willing to let Spain have most of French Morocco in return for one of the Canary Islands. Surely Madrid would gladly have traded a small island for a united Morocco under its protection. Yet how happy would Franco have been about German military enclaves on the outskirts of Morocco's most important city and primary harbor? During the civil war in Spain, Hitler had become quite familiar with Franco's stubbornness over German participation in Spanish mining concerns.[67] Franco would have been easier to deal with over Morocco if Germany were to have gained its foothold there *before* a peace settlement. The Spaniards would then have had to accept a French Morocco with German strategic enclaves or no French Morocco at all.[68]

Ironically, the initial opposition to the German demand came before it was even presented to the French government, and from Rome rather than from Vichy. Mussolini had earlier rejected the idea of gaining an Italian base in Oran before a peace settlement. Now that the Germans were interested in bases in Northwest Africa, the Duce aimed to dissuade Berlin from present-

ing the demand or, if dissuasion were to fail, to join Berlin so as not to be left
out of the division of some early war spoils. In any case, he could not have
been pleased with the prospect of a German air base in Algeria, which he
considered an Italian interest sphere.[69] At 9:00 P.M. on 11 July, the Italian
chargé d'affaires in Berlin, Guelfo Zamboni, visited State Secretary Ernst
von Weizsäcker and relayed Mussolini's misgivings. The German demand,
he argued, would allow the French to adopt a stance of passive solidarity
with the Axis. Yet if Germany were to persist, then Italy would demand a
base in Oran simultaneously. Either way, Mussolini wanted the matter postponed until Rome and Berlin could coordinate a joint policy.[70] To accom-
modate the Italians, Berlin postponed the presentation of the demand in
Wiesbaden and reworked it. On 12 July, Weizsäcker informed Ambassador
Alfieri that the German High Command would refrain from creating a German air base in Oran. Italy was welcome to have a base there if it liked. Yet
the German High Command valued a base at Casablanca and would pursue
this demand regardless of Italian misgivings. Rome accepted this development and dropped all objections to the German *démarche*. Mussolini never
demanded the base at Oran; apparently he was pleased enough to keep the
Germans out of Algeria.[71] With all diplomatic roads clear, Hitler could finally
have Stülpnagel present the German demand to the French at Wiesbaden.
Huntziger received the note on the evening of 15 July, and the marshal's
cabinet saw it at 10:00 A.M. the next day.

It is possible that Vichy, already taking steps toward true collaboration
with Germany, wished to use the Casablanca demand to become an "associated power" of the Axis.[72] On the other hand, it is clear that neither the
marshal nor his ministers wanted to see the Germans established in French
Africa. Moreover, if the sanctity of the empire was one of the expressed
conditions of honor on which Pétain had made the signing of the armistice
treaty contingent, then Morocco was in a class by itself. Morocco had been
a hotbed of international intrigue and espionage since the turn of the century. Endemic pan-islamic conspiracies—aided by German gun-running,
which was in turn supported and sponsored by Hamburg shipping companies and German consular officials—aimed to spur tribal resistance and revolt against French rule. During the First World War, these efforts had
increased, as the Germans and their Turkish allies poured agents, money,
and guns into the protectorate through the Spanish zone. The French, through
counterespionage and economic favors to the natives, were able to negate
German actions, but the apparition of German intrigue in Morocco through
real and fictitious business fronts never vanished. In fact, the specter grew

by the late 1930s, thanks to additional intrigue by Italian fascists and Spanish nationalists.[73] And although German consular representation in French Morocco was prohibited in the interwar period, Berlin's General Consulate in Tetuán, the capital of the Spanish zone, maintained contact in the late 1930s with pan-Islamic elements in the French zone while sending money and propaganda materials.[74] Hitler's demand for Casablanca, then, was particularly ominous; as Baudouin clearly understood, it dealt not with a temporary German establishment in Northwest Africa for limited military aims but rather a permanent and dominant German presence there. Vice Premier Pierre Laval, already a most eager advocate of Franco-German collaboration who had predicted a Franco-British war days earlier, now spoke pessimistically of universal German domination.[75] According to Baudouin's diary, the cabinet agreed that France could not accept the demand as part of the armistice treaty. Such acceptance would have meant humiliation along with the possible loss of the empire. Huntziger received orders to tell the German Armistice Commission that, since the demand lay outside the scope of the Armistice Convention, the marshal would write to Hitler personally. Baudouin meanwhile received orders to draft a reply for Pétain to send to Hitler.[76]

The reply to which the marshal affixed his signature, dated 17 July 1940, showed that Vichy, although perhaps willing to move toward greater cooperation with the German war effort, did not wish to include French Africa in any bargains. Pétain noted that France had signed the armistice because it had been in keeping with the honor of the nation, and that he was thus "painfully surprised" by the German demands. France, he said, had stood by its signature despite the bloodshed at Mers-el-Kebir. France would continue to do so regardless of the price. The Casablanca demand, however, lay outside the Armistice Convention, outside the scope of French honor, and in fact, completely out of proportion to any suspensions in the Armistice Convention that Germany had granted. "There exists in fact no doubt," continued the marshal, "that these new demands [would deliver] North Africa, its natives, a highly excitable people, its military and air forces, [and] its means of existence and transport to the discretion of . . . the Reich. Can [this] be regarded as an equivalent consideration for the deferment of certain conditions of the Armistice? I think not."[77] Should Germany insist on pursuing these demands, finished Pétain, then the French government would find itself in an entirely new diplomatic position with regard to the conqueror. The two countries would have to enter new negotiations entirely. After the dispatch of the letter, the French government waited with apprehension. Baudouin expressed the concern that German troops might sweep into unoccupied France. Laval meanwhile proposed to Otto Abetz, Ribbentrop's representative in Paris, that France bomb Gibraltar in return for German reticence concerning Casablanca.[78]

The German reaction when Huntziger presented the Germans with Pétain's letter on the evening of the nineteenth was mixed. Stülpnagel was reputed to have made the angry comment to Huntziger that the cease-fire alone had prevented German forces from occupying the remainder of France and French North Africa in June.[79] German diplomats saw Vichy's reply as a ploy to eliminate the Armistice Convention and attain equal negotiating status with Germany.[80] Hitler's own reaction on reading Pétain's letter is not documented. Yet the fact that he allowed the issue to drop for the time being provides a few clues. Clearly he chaffed at the idea of negotiating with the French as equals. He also had little desire to take North Africa by force, thus initiating a new front there. His intent lay in ending the war in the West so that he could start a new one in the East. By mid-August, Hitler had adopted the view that he should put the Casablanca demand on ice, especially if Germany could not make the prospective bases there operational quickly. The British government had given no sign of making peace easily and could have decided to attack the French African empire, particularly if provoked by a German presence there. Stülpnagel warned on 12 August that Berlin should maintain the Casablanca demand only if it would be of immediate help in the war with the British and only if its terms could be implemented quickly. Otherwise it would provoke British attacks in French Africa, which would in turn delay French disarmament there while encouraging the French to press for a new political status vis-à-vis the Axis. Hitler expressed concern on the same day that German bases in Casablanca could trigger a British attack on Dakar. He thus concurred with Stülpnagel for the time being.[81] Marshal Pétain's letter would receive no answer for now. The Casablanca issue, on the surface anyway, appeared to have died a natural death. The issue of bases in Northwest Africa, however, would resurface quickly enough.

The German demand for air bases in Casablanca on 15 July 1940 was a diplomatic gamble. Hitler and his top aides had already begun to look past the conquest of Europe and toward a transatlantic struggle with the United States. Toward that end, they began to discuss and contract the weapons that Germany would need for such a conflict and started to look for Atlantic bases at which to station them. Casablanca, with its forward location and modern harbor, provided an excellent site, and Great Britain's attack at Mers-el-Kebir provided a timely pretext for Germany to demand an early military presence there that could expand following the expected peace. If the French government accepted the demand, so much the better. If they refused, Berlin would simply pursue the issue at another time. Indeed, the French rebuff was only the beginning of Germany's attempt to become situated in Northwest Africa. The episode was hardly one of marginal or isolated importance. It was the first step in a consistent policy that, though unsuccessful, reveals the ultimate aims of Hitler's Germany.

Chapter 3

The Specter of de Gaulle

❧

*Duty consists in holding every point of
the Empire for France against the
Germans and the Italians.*
　　　　—General Charles de Gaulle

*A joining of the colonies with England and
a secession from France means . . .
endangerment of our own possibility of
dominating the African area. . . .*
　　　　—German Naval Command War Diary

Marshal Pétain's rejection of Hitler's demand for German air bases at Casablanca did not change Hitler's mind on the issue. Rather than drop the matter, Hitler changed his focus, this time toward the strategic benefits of Spain's entry into the war. The Strait of Gibraltar would offer a route into Northwest Africa where Germany could impose its will despite the marshal's refusal. Yet the immediate issue in August and September 1940 was the surprising coup by Charles de Gaulle in French Equatorial Africa and the possibility that the fire of revolt could spread to more strategically important areas on the continent. Hitler had always been concerned with the possibility of a continued French "holy war" in the colonies, and de Gaulle's coup led to a lively debate in Berlin over future German policy in French Africa. The answers came from Hitler himself, who remained distrustful of Vichy and who intended a dominant German role in Northwest Africa. France would receive small concessions to deal with the crisis but would receive no more than it absolutely needed to remain in temporary control of the empire. In return for its generosity, Berlin received from Vichy permission to take a more active role in Africa. Germany began to set up a commission in Northwest Africa to monitor French military measures, an economic commission to contend for African goods, and German consulates to monitor political activity. Berlin would also send a team of officers to Northwest Africa to reconnoiter base sites. The planning for extended German influence in Northwest Africa came despite Rome's claim that the area was an Italian sphere of interest. It also came at the same time that Berlin was negotiating with Madrid over the enlargement of Spanish territory in Africa as a price for Franco's participation in the war. Hitler meant to augment German influence in Northwest Africa regardless of his allies' wishes and would use de Gaulle's coup as the convenient lever for doing so.

By mid-summer 1940, de Gaulle had become a forgotten man in Berlin. Despite the rebel general's theatrics, Pétain had formed a government and surrendered, and de Gaulle was considered no more a threat to the new order than the Polish government in exile.[1] The German High Command evaluated de Gaulle's movement in mid-August and found it lacking both in bodies and in resonance. German intelligence numbered de Gaulle's troops at a mere two to three thousand. French war weariness and the great prestige of Pétain and Weygand were cited as reasons for de Gaulle's meager success. His influence in the French Empire was seen as particularly slight.[2]

At the same time, Berlin felt reasonably comfortable, all things considered, with the position of the Vichy government in Africa. The Germans based their assessments more on an evaluation of the colonial leaders than on the opinions of the populations at large. Some suspected the loyalty of Resident-General Charles Noguès in French Morocco, but most trusted Governor-General Pierre Boisson, who commanded the West and Central African colonies. German observers worried only about the Cameroons, where they judged the governor, though not the population, to be pro-British.[3] All in all, Berlin miscalculated both the strength of de Gaulle's voice and the strength of its echo. These miscalculations determined German policy concerning Vichy's economic and military strength in Africa before de Gaulle's coup.

One of the major concerns of the Pétain government with the signing of the armistice lay in the establishment of firm authority in the empire. Economic contact with the colonies had to be reestablished to prevent distress, and the armed forces had to be maintained as much as possible to deter revolt and incursions by would-be interlopers.[4] The Axis had similar interests. A new military front in French Africa was not an agreeable thought and territorial transfers, it was hoped, would come bloodlessly during the peace settlement. Yet because the Axis states *did* have extensive aims in French Africa, and because the French could not be trusted, a firm bond between Vichy and the colonies could not be allowed to develop. It was best to keep the French imperial bond as weak as possible without allowing it to break.

The policy concerning economic contact between the *Metropole* and Africa was formed largely by the German Naval Command. The British had included the *Metropole* in their blockade since 25 June, and Raeder and his associates did not wish to see the British seize French cargo.[5] Thus, while the navy left Mediterranean shipping to Italian discretion, they strictly prohibited traffic to and from West Africa.[6] The detrimental economic and political consequences of this German policy were clearly visible in West Africa both to the French and to the few Germans who visited in the summer of 1940.[7] Yet French protests concerning the deterioration of imperial bonds netted little result.[8] Darlan sent a special mission to Wiesbaden to press the Germans on the subject in late July, and in August he began calling for armed French convoys to run the Strait of Gibraltar as well as for the bombing of Gibraltar.[9] Laval meanwhile worked on a scheme to revive merchant shipping while including the Germans in the division of the cargo.[10] Yet while Italy, perhaps fearing unrest in Africa, allowed French food transports in the Mediterranean, Hitler declared that Germany would treat all merchant vessels in the area of France conquered before the armistice as prizes, a measure hardly calculated to solve the French transport problem.[11] The potential implications of such measures were obvious, especially when de Gaulle called on French colonial officials to reject the economically ruinous armistice and to place themselves on the British side on 30 July.[12] Still, colonial products such as peanuts, sugar, and coffee remained in the congested Atlantic ports of Africa.

In August, Berlin slowly arrived at the conclusion that political problems in the French Empire did not lie in their own interests either. This realization struck the German navy first with reports from Wiesbaden that the colonial situation was becoming precarious.[13] The Naval Command remained unready to allow the French to challenge the British at Gibraltar, especially since Anglo-French confrontations could lead to a reduction of German war booty in Africa. "Incidents by English actions which force the French into active participation against England on the side of Germany," they stated, "do not lie in the German interest."[14] Yet they did recognize that economic decline in the colonies could cause the collapse of Vichy's authority overseas and that such a turn of events would be detrimental to German territorial claims as well.[15] Thus in late July and early August, the navy began to approve voyages for a very small number of French merchants carrying fats and perishable goods from Casablanca and Dakar to the *Metropole*. The merchants had to scuttle themselves rather than fall into British hands and had to land in Bordeaux (occupied zone) instead of Marseille (unoccupied zone).[16] This slow and limited case-by-case solution to the problem of colonial shipping hardly struck the French as satisfactory. Yet the Germans remained unwilling to change their minds, especially since goods arriving at Bordeaux could be in part "purchased" by Germany against the balance of French occupation costs.[17] Darlan's delegation to Wiesbaden argued that such limited economic contact would mean imperial ruin, but in the end the French glumly concluded that the meager arrangement from Berlin was the most they would get.[18]

The lone German voice for increased economic contact was that of General Stülpnagel, chairman of the German Armistice Commission in Wiesbaden. On 22 August, three days after hearing an impassioned plea by Huntziger that predicted the defection of the colonies to Great Britain, Stülpnagel cabled a lengthy report to the German High Command. The possibility of French North and West African defection, he argued, could have large implications for the German war effort. He proposed that Germany abandon the system of case-by-case permission for cargo shipments and turn instead to some system of unified general regulation, while allowing the French a test vessel to attempt a passage through the Strait of Gibraltar to Marseille to see if such passage was indeed possible, as the French had been arguing.[19] Yet for the moment, Stülpnagel had no listeners in Berlin. As late as 27 August, the Naval Command was still determining permission for French shipping on a ship-by-ship basis.[20]

The French government also hoped to maintain its empire by evasion of the colonial disarmament and demobilization clauses in the armistice. At the official close of hostilities in late June, the French army in North Africa numbered about 400,000 men, of which 200,000 to 250,000 men were armed and deployable. The eight to ten divisions in North Africa possessed some heavy artillery and armor but suffered from shortages in material and from the fact that much of their heavy weaponry was outdated. In French West Africa stood 122,000 men under arms, whose material situation was not as good as those in North Africa, and whose numbers were spread out over the wide expanse of territory that made up the West African colonies. The colonies of French Equatorial Africa had a mere 15,500 troops over nearly one million square miles.[21] The French air force in North Africa was relatively well equipped, since so many aircraft had fled France for the other side of the Mediterranean during the final days of hostility. The best postwar count of the airplanes in North Africa after the armistice places 2,648 aircraft of all categories and degrees of battle readiness in North Africa in July 1940, of which anywhere from 630 to 1,150 were capable of action.[22] Still, the actual value of the air forces in North Africa was less than the numbers would suggest. Fuel stocks allowed no more than fifteen days of operations and neither the air force ground organizations nor the supply depots were able to flee France along with the aircraft in the days before the armistice, despite the presence of some 1,500 trained pilots in North and West Africa.[23]

The French government wished to preserve as much as it could of its colonial forces. Huntziger had made this point to Badoglio during the armistice negotiations, and Baudouin and Weygand both agreed that if France were to garner anything positive from Mers-el-Kebir, it would be a postponement or cancellation of French disarmament in the empire. At first this hope seemed vindicated. The demobilization of French North Africa was an Italian responsibility, and the day after Mers-el-Kebir the Italians suspended the general disarmament clauses for the region. On the eve of de Gaulle's coup in Equatorial Africa, this condition remained essentially unaltered, thanks to Italian ineptitude. Italy's control organs for North Africa did not even arrive there until mid-August.[24] When they did arrive they proved indecisive, thanks to lack of intelligence concerning French forces and French threats of another British attack and of native revolt.[25] The German military was irritated.[26] Stülpnagel, though trusting of Noguès, held much of the Vichy administration in North Africa in suspicion. He also gave little weight to French arguments that Britain could launch another raid and that British propaganda leaflets would spur native revolt.[27] Yet the High Command's inquiries with Badoglio in Rome yielded little aside from the comment that Mussolini wished to observe the situation in North Africa for two more weeks before deciding what to do.[28] All the Germans could do was limit North African air strength by prohibiting the transfer of ground crews from the *Metropole* while trying to pin the Italians down on limitations for the French army and air force.[29]

Stülpnagel ran out of patience by late August. It was perhaps understandable to allow the French enough naval units to defend their African bases, but the Italian concession of a full army was another matter. In a lengthy report to the High Command, he complained that the Italians had used Mers-el-Kebir to write off their duties in North Africa completely.[30]

Conditions in North Africa, he said, demanded disarmament with the same tight supervision that the Germans were employing in the *Metropole,* and since the Italians were too timid to make the necessary tough decisions and demands, Germany should do it for them.[31] In brief, Stülpnagel recommended that the High Command junk his own agreement with Roatta, along with the German policy of having Italy handle the disarmament of the Mediterranean area, and that Germany take over inspection functions in North Africa.

Hitler shared similar concerns. He distrusted the French in North Africa and was well aware that the Italians had done little to disarm them. Nevertheless, he had Stülpnagel informed that because the Mediterranean was an Italian "sphere of interest," Italy had to handle the issue. Though Wiesbaden could use moral influence, German demands on Italy would not be allowed.[32] The Führer thus remained unwilling to offend Italian sensibilities and hoped for now that subtle pressure from Wiesbaden could achieve the desired ends in French North Africa. On the other hand, he lacked full confidence in the Italians and had already ordered Admiral Wilhelm Canaris, Germany's military intelligence (Abwehr) chief, to make the surveillance of the connections between France and North Africa his business.[33] For the rest, Hitler was beginning to lean toward an operation against Gibraltar, which would place German troops in Spanish Morocco and thus keep in check the French troops south of that area.[34] Such remained the German policy on the eve of de Gaulle's coup. Berlin would allow France no more than was absolutely necessary to keep the colonies loyal to Vichy for the time being. Germany would also do nothing to hurt Italian sensibilities, however, even if Rome were to move more slowly than Berlin might have liked.

For de Gaulle, the idea of setting up a base of operations in Africa was logical. It would give Free France an area to create an army while providing a basis for a return to Europe when the time came. A Free French foothold in Africa could also help defend French possessions against enemies, while deterring transgressions by allies.[35] As for the chances of success, de Gaulle brought a more thoughtful analysis to the problem than had Berlin. North Africa was out of the question for Free French enterprises. De Gaulle had already made futile attempts before the armistice to place his services at the disposal of Noguès in Morocco, and after Mers-el-Kebir, de Gaulle's stock in North Africa was extremely low.[36] The best prospects lay, in spite of Pierre Boisson's loyalty to Vichy, in French Equatorial Africa and especially in Chad, where Governor Félix Éboué, an African native with a humanist education, found National Socialism repulsive. Éboué had decided in principle to join de Gaulle from the first call of mid-June. A good chance of success in de Gaulle's eyes also existed in the French Cameroons, where according to de Gaulle's appraisal, no one wished a return to German rule.[37]

The coup itself occurred with relative ease. The British flew de Gaulle's "missionaries" to Lagos, from where they traveled to Fort Lamy in Chad. Here Eboué formally proclaimed his loyalty to Free France on 26 August. Thus began the flood of defections in French Equatorial Africa. Cameroon joined de Gaulle on the twenty-seventh, the French Congo along with the Equatorial African capital of Brazzaville joined on the twenty-eighth, and Ubangi-Shari joined on the thirtieth. In Brazzaville, de Gaulle's "alternate self," Colonel Edgard de Larminat, declared himself the new governor-general of French Equatorial Africa.[38] The week's only failure came in the colony of Gabon, where Vichy reacted in time to reverse the coup attempt at the capital at Libreville. Vichy sent air force general Marcel-Louis Têtu to that city with several Glenn Martin bombers and the title of governor-general of French Equatorial Africa. The Gaullists would not take Gabon until 10 November, but de Gaulle had still scored a political victory that would bring consternation in Berlin and in Vichy alike.

News arrived slowly, but by the evening of the twenty-ninth it was clear that something was wrong in central Africa. Late that evening, the French delegations in Wiesbaden and Turin asked permission to send three cruisers and three destroyers to quell the revolt. The French also asked for a general suspension of demobilization in French Africa, permission to send six Senegalese battalions then in unoccupied France to West Africa, and permission to send two groups of transport aircraft to lift supplies to the people of the Chad colony.[39]

The Germans, now that the French Empire now seemed in danger of large-scale defection, now changed their tune concerning Vichy's authority in the colonies. In Wiesbaden the concern was especially serious, for despite Stülpnagel's original skepticism toward French warnings, an entire territory had now defected from Vichy.[40] Moreover, French Equatorial Africa provided a link between the British territories of Nigeria and Egypt via the Sudan, thus giving the British an alternate route to supply their forces in the Middle East. Finally, the possibility existed that the rejection of the Vichy regime in central Africa would spread to more important sections of the continent. In the small hours of 30 August, Böhme told the High Command that Wiesbaden advocated the French request for the release of the warships to the African Atlantic coast.[41] The Naval Command shared Wiesbaden's view. Raeder and his cohort feared the revolt might spread to West Africa, in which case Germany's aims in that area would be ruined, perhaps by United States intervention. "A reconciliation of the colonies with England and a secession from France," warned the Naval Command, "means . . . endangerment of *our own possibility of dominating the African area.* . . . one can also not ignore the danger of a grab by the USA at the French West African colonies."[42] Thus, in spite of the risks that the six warships would not pass Gibraltar without a fight, that they would achieve no positive result even if they reached Gabon, and that they would later need reinforcement from the Mediterranean, the Naval Command advocated the French warship requests. This was not all. The Naval Command, suddenly sympathetic toward the economic woes of the French Empire now that their *own* interests were threatened, advocated a generous reestablishment of merchant shipping. Regular economic contact, they hoped, would alleviate the problems in the colonies, which in everyone's view had contributed to de Gaulle's success. Yet the Italians suddenly had other ideas. Noting that French demobilization had in fact yet to begin in Africa, the Italian Armistice Commission decided that the present crisis would be the best opportunity to get tough with the French. Thus, they told the Germans that they planned to reject the French requests to send land and sea forces from the *Metropole,* arguing that the forces already in Africa would have to suffice. Turin agreed to grant the French request for the transport aircraft, but these would have to come from French stocks in North Africa.[43]

For the time being, Italy's word was law due to Hitler's support. The Führer's initial reaction to de Gaulle's coup remains unknown. The news was cause for concern, but it apparently did not worry Hitler enough at first to force a change in his fundamental policy. Italy's stance harmonized with Hitler's distrust of the French anyway. It pressed French disarmament forward while allowing Vichy to fight dissidence in central Africa with only North African forces, hence weakening possible rebel forces in that more important region. Thus Hitler commented on 31 August that, although he agreed in principle with the French request to send naval forces to Africa, Italy would have to deal with the situation itself because the forces in question lay in the Mediterranean area. He repeated that Germany would put no pressure on Rome to grant the French requests.[44]

Thus the French, who had hoped for a true policy shift by the Axis powers, remained disappointed. On 31 August, Huntziger argued to General Friedrich Mieth, the temporary acting chairman in Wiesbaden, that the Gaullist revolt could easily infect the entire French Empire and that Vichy could find itself obliged to send the requested forces *without* Axis approval.

Later in the day he told Hans-Richard Hemmen, the Foreign Ministry's economic delegate in Wiesbaden, that the root of the entire problem lay in the
interruption of economic contact between the colonies and the *Metropole*.
He maintained that the most important countermeasure to imperial dissolution was the immediate resumption of regular cargo traffic between France
and West Africa. Herein, asserted Huntziger, lay the best method of strengthening the confidence of the native peoples in the French government.
Huntziger also pointed out *for the first time* that de Gaulle's success came in
part from his claim that the colonies would revert to France after the war if
they joined him. The marshal's government was hamstrung, said Huntziger,
for lack of similar guarantees from Germany and Italy. Yet Huntziger was
stonewalled. Mieth told him that military decisions lay with Italy because,
as Mieth *incorrectly* phrased it, the area threatened by de Gaulle lay within
Italy's interest sphere.[45] Hemmen expressed little concern for anything other
than the 65 billion francs in Polish, Belgian, and French gold that the French
had moved to Dakar in June. He urged Huntziger to have the gold placed
out of the British reach in the *Metropole* and helpfully offered German airplanes for the task, a suggestion that Huntziger studiously dodged.[46] Hemmen
concluded from Huntziger's stance that the French were not serious about
quelling the spread of dissidence.[47]

Yet German policy would soon change. The German High Command
began in early September to consider the French arguments more seriously.
Stülpnagel concluded within a few days that Vichy's desire for greater freedom of movement came from a sincere desire to preserve the empire. He
strongly suggested that the German military and political establishments
give the French requests a closer look.[48] This they did. A High Command
report presented to Jodl and Keitel on 2 September agreed that the French
colonies could not live on their own and that, if the *Metropole* did not
support them, they would seek support elsewhere. The report continued
that, because the Italians had rejected the earlier French requests, the danger existed that the fire of revolt could spread to North Africa, in which case
the British would acquire bases in Casablanca and Dakar. Thus, the High
Command report proposed that the Foreign Ministry push the Italians toward greater leniency concerning French requests and that the French be
allowed to stabilize the economic situation in the colonies, at least within
the scope of the possibilities that the condition of war in the Atlantic
offered.[49]

How seriously Hitler took the High Command's assessment of French
sincerity is debatable, but a policy shift on the part of Berlin in early Sep-

tember is certainly discernible. The Germans, certainly with Hitler's approval, began to make small economic and military concessions to Vichy to help quell the spread of revolt in Africa, but with several provisos which reflected Hitler's stamp. First, the concessions would not be enough to allow the French a formidable grip in Africa, just in case Vichy remained untrustworthy. Second, Italian sensibilities, at least on the surface, would not be harmed. Finally, Berlin granted favors to the French only at the price of a German presence in Africa, through which Germany would be able to wrangle a permanent political, economic, and strategic presence. In the end, the German policy shift would bear little fruit. But the evolution of new procedures and their aims show the direction in which Hitler now wished to go.

The German Foreign Ministry, in cooperation with the Naval Command, became more lenient on the issue of merchant shipping in the first week of September. On the fifth, Hemmen told Huntziger that France could establish regular intracolonial routes so long as the French reported movements in advance and the ships prevented themselves from falling into British hands. This step would at least allow colonial products to move within the empire. With regard to transport between the colonies and the *Metropole,* Germany still reserved the right to inspect each individual case. Ships bound for the *Metropole* would still head for Bordeaux rather than Marseille. Yet Hemmen gave the French to understand that Germany would now grant permission not only to individual ships, but rather to groups of ships and series of voyages.[50] Hemmen commented that Berlin would not have made these concessions, which Hemmen thought were quite magnanimous, had it not been for de Gaulle's coup. In reporting to Vichy, Darlan's commission noted that the new arrangements were still unsatisfactory, but that France could at least decongest its colonial ports while provisioning the colonies to a certain degree.[51]

Yet even this largesse did not come for free. In return for these rather meager concessions, the Naval Command and the Foreign Ministry had expected colonial products and inspection rights in the empire.[52] Hemmen also mentioned to the French that Germany expected permanent economic representation on the African west coast.[53] Finally, he made the ominous request for the establishment of German consulates in the more important cities of the French Empire. The French reported to their Colonial Ministry that such consulates would present Vichy with certain disadvantages, but that it would be impolitic to reject the German request with the empire's economic livelihood hanging in the balance. Darlan's mission took comfort in the fact that the Germans could not set up such consulates while still in a state of war with France.[54] On this last point they would be proven wrong.

Military issues concerning the de Gaulle coup were more complicated, for it was here that Berlin needed to take the Italians into account. Yet it was also here that the Germans would begin to erase the notion that Northwest Africa was an Italian sphere of interest while replacing it with the idea that it was their own. On 4 September, General Alfred Jodl of the High Command and State Secretary Ernst von Weizsäcker from the Foreign Ministry sat down to hammer out a new policy concerning the French and Italians in Africa.[55] They quickly decided that Berlin's best alternative lay in a solution wherein "Germany could grant France a certain measure of freedom and demand, under the threat of countermeasures, that she promptly restore order with her own resources." Such an alternative appeared preferable to silent acquiescence of the revolt or intervention with German resources, either one of which could only aggravate the situation while perhaps inducing British intervention. Yet this policy contained problems. In the first place, the Axis powers had never established which of them was responsible for disarmament and supervisory issues in French West and Equatorial Africa. If Berlin were to allow Vichy military concessions in Africa, then it would have to reach agreement with Rome on modes for granting and overseeing French measures there. Neither Jodl nor Weizsäcker thought for a moment that Italy should supervise French measures alone, despite the fact that French forces released for duty in central Africa would certainly have come partly from the French Mediterranean coast or North Africa, where Italian authority was clear. Yet it was also well known that Hitler wished to leave Mediterranean issues to Rome's discretion and that the Italians regarded the areas in question as their special sphere of interest.[56]

The Foreign Ministry deduced while studying the issue of armistice responsibilities that the issue of West and Equatorial Africa had been dangling since the armistice came into force.[57] The Roatta Agreements had given Italy supervisory responsibility over land and air forces in French *North* Africa while dividing the supervision of the French navy in such a way that gave Italy responsibility for the African Mediterranean ports and Germany responsibility over the African Atlantic ports. Subsequent understandings with Italy carried the arrangements pertaining to the French navy to the French merchant marine as well.[58] Yet arrangements of this kind for army and air force questions in West and Equatorial Africa did not exist. The German Armistice Commission, when asked, stated that it had left such issues with the Italians due to Hitler's desire to avoid conflicts of interest with Rome.[59] Yet Weizsäcker winced at the suggestion that all of this meant that French Africa was an Italian *sphere of interest*. General Mieth's earlier comment to Huntziger that the area threatened by de Gaulle was an Italian interest sphere was clearly a faux pas. Weizsäcker raised one eyebrow when learning of the comment and raised the other on learning that Italy had unilaterally rejected Vichy's request to send naval and troop units to West Africa on this assumption.[60] He and Jodl thus decided that Italy had no claim to hegemony in Equatorial Africa and that the Italians should simply be informed of the measures that Germany chose to take there.[61]

The issue of the Axis *supervision* of measures allowed to Vichy also needed resolution, and again, no one in Berlin thought this job would fall to the Italian control agencies in North Africa. Some sort of German control body was needed. Proposals for German inspection missions in Africa had been raised since early August by both the army and the navy, but Hitler had rejected them, apparently to avoid clashes of authority with the Italians.[62] Hitler also rejected a later proposal by Jodl for a German commission on Morocco's Atlantic coast with the comment that although this area was in principle a German responsibility, Germany would dispatch no control agencies to Africa. Shortly after de Gaulle's coup, the Naval Command, concerned for its interests and not shy about proclaiming *German* interest spheres, tried again to carry through its wishes. "It lies in the pressing interest of Germany," argued Germany's admirals, "to gain as soon as possible a running insight into the military, economic, and political conditions in the French colonies which belong to the German interest sphere (Dakar, Casablanca) . . . by dispatching a permanent commission." If such an official commission were not politically feasible, then the navy suggested that Germany send officials under the cover of business interests such as Lufthansa. Total abstention however, would run the risk that developments in Northwest Africa could take Germany by surprise.[63] Weizsäcker, in his meeting with Jodl on 4 September, altered the navy's assertions to make them more acceptable to Rome, by tactfully raising the idea that Germany attain this kind of insight through a mixed German-Italian commission.[64]

Meanwhile, the idea that Germany needed to supplant Italian supervision in Africa gained energy due to more Italian steps. Starting on 1 September, the Italians angered the Germans again by unilaterally reconsidering and approving the French requests of 30 August for the three cruisers, three destroyers, and six Senegalese battalions, while at the *same* time presenting the French delegation in Turin with a note that reimplemented in principle the general land, sea, and air disarmament clauses that had been suspended after Mers-el-Kebir. Details were to follow. Turin justified this demand by noting that the British had made no threat to the French holdings in Africa in the two months since the attack.[65] The impetus for the command doubtless came from Mussolini, who feared allowing the French to wriggle over to the Axis side and who, as Badoglio had said in mid-August, had planned to make a final decision on French disarmament in any case.[66] The unilateral nature of the Italian actions angered Stülpnagel to the point that he now made to the High Command the most far-reaching proposals yet heard concerning Germany's African policy.[67] Stülpnagel was convinced that Germany had to view the de Gaulle movement in Africa in the context of the war as a whole and that Germany should under no circumstances leave the matter to the Italians, regardless of previous agreements. Italian decisions, he said, had been based too much on Italy's Mediterranean aims and not enough on the situation in Africa as a whole, particularly with regard to central Africa and the Atlantic—areas crucial for the German war effort. The Axis, Stülpnagel argued, had to allow Vichy to retain control of its African empire with a more farsighted policy. All recently placed demands for disarmament, he continued, should be shelved until the clarification of the situation in Africa. Until then, Vichy should be allowed to use forces already in North Africa, where the Axis wanted to weaken French power anyway. Germany should also allow the repatriation of African troops presently in the *Metropole*. *Both* Armistice Commissions would hear requests for additional naval units from the Mediterranean coast of France, and French petitions should receive a generous hearing. French air formations in Africa, he said, were strong enough to eliminate the need for reinforcements from France anyway. With regard to Axis supervision of French measures, Stülpnagel proposed *German* control commissions, which would operate in Casablanca, Dakar, Fort Lamy, and elsewhere as the situation in French Africa developed. These military commissions would be disguised as economic commissions so that they could inspect both military measures and merchant traffic. Stülpnagel's proposals were vast. He had changed his stance considerably on the tempo of French disarmament but had intensified his attitude toward Italian authority. Italian demands for disarmament in French Africa would be set aside, Italian decisions on the movement of forces from France and North Africa would be shared with Germany with, one can assume, Germany holding the decisive vote, and Italian control agencies in Africa would become obsolete with the arrival of German agencies. In brief, Germany would assume the control of Africa as its *own* sphere of interest due to the importance of the West African coast. The High Command accepted these proposals. On receiving the report, they suggested that the French be given the means to restore the situation in Africa and that there be German control commissions established in Casablanca and Dakar.[68]

All proposals, whether from the Foreign Ministry or the High Command, had to have Hitler's approval, and while the Führer shared some of the concerns of his subordinates, he disagreed with them on procedure. He remained unready to trust Vichy or to insult Rome. On the other hand, his concern for the spread of Gaullism was growing. On 2 September, the British and the Americans announced the Destroyer-Base Deal that gave the latter eight bases in the western Atlantic. As will be explained in more detail in the chapters to come, it also seemed to Berlin that Washington would attempt to use de Gaulle to gain bases in Africa before Germany could do the same. Hitler wished then, despite Rome's claims, to extend a greater German presence in the French colonies. On 8 September, he thus announced a new policy directive that aimed to square the circle of Italian authority and German concerns.[69] At one stroke, Germany would prevent the spread of Gaullism, weaken Vichy's strength in North Africa, preserve Italian prestige, and extend German influence into French Northwest Africa.

First, Hitler left unmolested the most recent Italian decisions. Vichy, he agreed, could request additional land and air forces for the restoration of Equatorial Africa aside from those already approved, but these forces could come only at the expense of North Africa, an area that would simultaneously undergo its own disarmament.[70] Supplementary naval forces from the *Metropole* were a possibility, but only if the six warships already approved had achieved some success. Hitler took more overt steps to protect German interests in Northwest Africa. To help supervise French disarmament and anti-Gaullist measures, Hitler ordered the setup of a mixed German-Italian control commission in North Africa. The commission would operate as a "roving" commission and would work in conjunction with the Italian control agencies already present in North Africa. Italian supervisory authority in Africa would thus nominally remain. Yet without Rome's knowledge, Germany would take additional steps in Africa. The original draft of Hitler's policy order charged the Luftwaffe Command "with the preparation of German air bases in Dakar and Casablanca." Hitler deleted this command from the final draft, perhaps to prevent the possibility of a leak to the French or the Italians.[71] Nonetheless, the Luftwaffe Command began preparatory work for the occupation of these bases, discussing problems of ground defense and preparing reconnaissance missions to Casablanca and Dakar.[72] At the same time, as will be seen in the following chapters, Hitler was planning on the capture of Gibraltar and the stationing of forces in Spanish Morocco

and the Spanish and Portuguese islands as well. Thus, Germany would mitigate threats to Northwest Africa from within by disarming the French forces
there while allowing those not disarmed to move to central Africa. Germany would meanwhile mitigate similar threats from without with a system
of bases which included Casablanca, Dakar, and the Atlantic islands. And
as Hitler would make very clear, he did not mean for the bases to serve a
simple defensive function. Germany hoped to occupy the bases soon to prevent the British and Americans from doing the same, but would further
develop the bases *after* the war for the prosecution of a truly global struggle.

For now, however, Germany needed Italy's approval for the more immediate aspects of Hitler's policy statement, which was not easily attained,
thanks to the latter's reluctance to see German involvement in North Africa.
The negotiations were conducted from 9 through 11 September between Badoglio and General Enno von Rintelen, the German military attaché in Rome.
Badoglio made little secret of his government's disapproval of the plan for
the mixed control commission.[73] The first issue of contention lay with the
new commission's area of competence. After Hitler's order of 8 September,
Berlin decided that the commission would work from the Headquarters of
the French armed forces commander in chief in Africa and would change
location as did his headquarters.[74] After Rintelen's first discussion with
Badoglio on the subject, the German High Command changed its mind.
The commission would set up in North Africa and supervise only the French
African Atlantic coast and French Equatorial Africa. The change came obviously at the insistence of Badoglio, who aimed to protect the Italian position in North Africa. The Italians would lose nothing, since the Atlantic
coast was already a German area of supervision and since there had never
been a firm decision on Equatorial Africa either way. A "roving" commission, on the other hand, could have infringed on Italian interests in North
Africa.[75] Badoglio's comment of 11 September, that Italy already *had* an
active commission in Morocco, was not accidental.

The other point of contention with the Italians dealt with the chairmanship of the commission. Though Weizsäcker had originally assumed that
the chairman would be German, there was no such mention in Hitler's policy
statement. Rintelen was thus told to say nothing on the issue.[76] Yet Badoglio
insisted, at Mussolini's behest, that the chairman be Italian since, as Badoglio
put it, the entire area lay within the Italian interest sphere. Rintelen communicated this statement to Keitel, who apparently checked with Hitler and
then wired back that the chairman could indeed be Italian, while remaining
mute on Badoglio's justification for the Italian chairmanship.[77] Evidently

Hitler wished to humor Mussolini and did not care enough about the chairmanship to argue about it.[78] The important issue lay in the placement of German military officials in Northwest Africa, and as shall be seen, an Italian chairmanship would amount to little anyway. Meanwhile, the tacit acceptance of Badoglio's claim that the entire area lay in the Italian sphere of interest was quickly recognized in Berlin as a major blunder by the German High Command, which Weizsäcker, with Ribbentrop's approval, was obliged to correct through the embassy in Rome.[79]

The new policy was presented to the French in Turin and Wiesbaden on 10 and 11 September, respectively. Included was the threat that the Axis powers reserved the right to change their stance should the French government fail to restore order in the threatened areas.[80] The French reaction was mixed. On one hand, there was a certain relief that the Germans had not demanded an actual troop presence in Africa.[81] Thus Huntziger, when discussing the German note with Stülpnagel on 12 September, accepted the mixed control commission with nary a protest. On the other hand, the French cared little for the distrustful tone of the note, for as Huntziger mentioned, Vichy was doing all it could to prevent the revolt from spreading.[82]

This was true. The most notable French step in this regard had been a governmental reshuffling of 6 September, which made Huntziger the new minister of war and gave Weygand the new noncabinet post of delegate-general of the French government in Africa, with the functions of solidifying Vichy's authority in Africa, guaranteeing the military security of the area, and making preparations for the return of the dissident colonies. Due to injuries sustained in an airplane crash landing, Weygand would not arrive in Africa until the first week of October. Yet on his arrival, the seventy-four-year-old general would carry out his mission with dispatch, traveling all over French Africa from his headquarters in Algiers, helping to bring the African empire's administration and its armed forces more firmly behind Pétain. Weygand's policy would lie in balancing the African imperium between the belligerent camps. He would be determined to resist all German encroachments in Africa, but at the same time, the thought of joining the Allies without Pétain's approval was repugnant to him. For Weygand's trouble, he would earn the pathological distrust of Hitler himself.[83]

The French also objected to Axis insistence on continued French disarmament. The Italians on 9 September had presented the French with a note defining the specifics for army demobilization in North Africa. The note allowed a force of a mere 30,000 men for the entire region, including police forces, a figure far below the French request of 150,000 men, which, according to Huntziger, was below even the peacetime strength.[84] Huntziger argued to Stülpnagel on 12 September that, given the excitable nature of the natives, the disappointing harvest, and British propaganda, the minimum requirement for North Africa was 120,000 men. "If you want to bring these people into the English orbit," warned Huntziger, "then continue disarming. I guarantee you success." Germany, he continued, could not demand that France keep its empire while denying it the means of doing so. Stülpnagel concurred with Huntziger's analysis that 30,000 troops was too small a contingent, and he pledged to raise the issue in Berlin. Yet a decision on this question would not be reached until after the British-Gaullist raid on Dakar in late September.

In the meantime, Berlin took decisive steps to stake a position in French Africa. The British-Gaullist attack at Dakar in late September would temporarily interrupt German planning in this regard, but the preparations that the Germans actually made in mid-September and early October clearly demonstrate Berlin's intention to use the threat of de Gaulle as a lever for the economic and strategic exploitation of Northwest Africa, in spite of agreements with Rome and ongoing discussions with Madrid. On 12 September, Hemmen began work on the composition of the permanent economic commission for the west coast of Africa, which would have its seat at Dakar. The commission was to include a representative from Lufthansa, and a member of the War Economy and Armaments Office, and would be under the chairmanship of a certain Herr Klaube, the former German consul at Bathurst, who had already worked with a prisoner repatriation committee that had gone to Dakar in July.[85]

Berlin was also quite busy with the composition of their military commission. By early October, Stülpnagel had carried out a mid-September order from the High Command to outline the makeup and duties of the German contingent to the mixed control commission.[86] The German group would be 160 to 180 men and would be under the command of a Luftwaffe officer with its seat in Casablanca. Its official function would lay in the implementation of the armistice in its designated area—French Morocco's Atlantic coast and French West and Equatorial Africa—and in the supervision of the forces released to Vichy to combat the Gaullist movement. It would also evaluate political and economic developments in conjunction with Klaube's commission. Turin and Wiesbaden, in theory anyway, would share equal responsibility for the mixed commission. Yet the mixed nature of the commission did not mean that Berlin planned to share power in its own areas of interest. The German and Italian contingents to the mixed commission each had their own spheres of control, and according to Stülpnagel's delineation, which had High Command approval, the German contingent would have sole authority in most of French Morocco and French West and Equatorial Africa despite Italian chairmanship of the mixed commission. For Morocco, the mixed commission would have a subcommission under German chairmanship. Stülpnagel made no mention of the Italian control bodies already in Morocco, but it is apparent that they were to become obsolete. For Equatorial Africa, the Italian contingent would supervise nothing but the slivers of French territory that bordered Algeria and Libya, with the remainder falling under German supervision. The Germans would have sole authority in French West Africa. Stülpnagel, as he stated, meant to secure German strategic concerns in Africa while excluding Rome from any share in the decision making in areas that were German areas of interest.[87] De Gaulle's attempt to land at Dakar in late September put a permanent hold on the work of this particular commission, but had this plan gone into effect, Stülpnagel would have succeeded in his aims.

During this planning stage, Germany in fact sent preliminary groups from the two commissions to their respective stations to begin work. Berlin decided on 19 September that a part of the economic commission would travel to Dakar via Casablanca as soon as possible, to which Keitel, at the urging of the Foreign Ministry and the Naval Command, added a naval officer in civilian disguise.[88] It was also decided at this time to send a Luftwaffe reconnaissance group to collect intelligence on prospective air bases in Casablanca. Interestingly, Berlin made these decisions during the *very same week* in which a Spanish delegation was in Berlin to discuss Madrid's claims in Morocco as a price for Spanish entry into the war.[89] The preliminary economic commission under Consul-General Schellert arrived in Casablanca on 23 September and proceeded to make observations on the situation in Morocco. In the afternoon they traveled to Rabat, where they met with Noguès, who promised full economic cooperation and listed phosphates, iron ore, and manganese as the products that French Morocco could supply immediately to Germany. The Germans also discussed with Noguès the ramifications of de Gaulle's recent attempt to land at Dakar. Schellert was convinced that while Noguès was no friend of the Germans, he would oppose a British landing in French Morocco to the utmost.[90] Shortly after Schellert's arrival in Casablanca, the Luftwaffe delegation of six officers arrived under Lieutenant Colonel Erdmann, the chief of the Luftwaffe Organizational Department. Unlike the Schellert commission, this one landed unannounced, much to the indignation of French authorities. Though Erdmann told the French that his task lay in the observation of British influence in Casablanca, the actual job of the group, as confirmed by an attached army officer, lay in the accumulation of information for the eventual setup of German air bases.[91] Both the Schellert and Erdmann missions were to continue to Dakar, but the High Command would cut their trips short due to the Anglo-Gaullist attack there.[92]

Yet as shall be seen, Hitler viewed the return of the preliminary commissions as a temporary setback. He had still managed to employ the de Gaulle movement in central Africa to stake a strong claim vis-à-vis his allies and enemies in Northwest Africa. He had shaped new rules and limitations for the French armed forces in the region, which were entirely in tune with German interests, and his efforts to extend a powerful German influence there would only become stronger with time. German negotiations with Spain, and later France, would indeed demonstrate that German efforts in this direction were only beginning.

Chapter 4

The Riddle of the Rock

ೞ

You cannot imagine what Morocco means to the
new Spanish generation and particularly
to the present Spanish leaders. . . .
they are much more interested in
Morocco than in Europe.

—Sir Samuel Hoare

The consequences of the alliance with these
unfathomable people cannot be predicted.
We will have an ally for whom we
[will] have to pay dearly.

—General Franz Halder

In the late summer of 1940, Germany's interest turned toward Gibraltar—the great white Rock from which the Royal Navy has guarded the western Mediterranean since the eighteenth century. Historical studies which have examined Germany's interest in Gibraltar have viewed the Rock's significance in terms of a German peripheral strategy against Great Britain. The argument runs as follows: Unable to force Great Britain to the peace table through blockade, bombardment, or invasion, Hitler seized upon the suggestion that Germany could end the war with an attack on Gibraltar and support for an Italian drive on Suez. As summer turned to autumn, Hitler increasingly hoped that such a strategy could end British resistance so that the German flank would be clear for his ultimate aim—the annihilation of the Soviet Union, which he had decided would begin in the spring of 1941. The attack on Gibraltar was thus part of an interim "Mediterranean strategy," which sought to create the conditions for an isolated war in the East that the defeat of France alone had failed to create.[1]

The argument here will be that Gibraltar was a piece to a different puzzle. To Hitler, the British stood on the brink of defeat, and if a final blow were needed, he meant to deliver it in England, not in Spain. Spain was important for reasons having perhaps less to do with Great Britain and more to do with the United States. Hitler's desire for bases on and off the Northwest African coast has already been documented, as has his first abortive overtures toward this end with Vichy. After Pétain's rejection of the Casablanca demand, Hitler pursued a new diplomatic route to Africa via Spain. The Strait of Gibraltar offered the easiest route to Morocco. Hitler and his navy also coveted a base in the Canary Islands, which Hitler felt could be gained in trade for French Morocco. Finally, Hitler believed that Germany could launch operations from Africa and the Canaries to seize bases in the more forward Portuguese archipelagoes. Hitler considered these possibilities at the time of the French armistice. Spain's participation became more attractive with Vichy's refusal to allow the Germans into Africa, and even urgent once Berlin feared that Great Britain and the United States, seemingly with de Gaulle's help, could conceivably beat the Germans to the areas in question. Berlin's challenge in the second half of 1940, then, would lie in convincing Madrid of this urgency.

To Hitler's mind, Spain—unlike France—was no eternal enemy to Germany, nor was it racially polluted. Spanish blood, according to Hitler, was a potent mix of Gothic, Frankish, and Moorish elements.[2] Hitler felt as early as 1928 that Spain was a potential German ally, thanks to its jealousy of the French Empire in North Africa.[3] As shall be seen, however, the problem between Berlin and Madrid would lie in mutual distrust between Hitler and the Spanish chief of state, General Francisco Franco y Bahamonde. Franco had good reasons for caution with Berlin. German and Italian aid during the Spanish civil war helped to place him in power, but Hitler had used the civil war to wrench iron ore mining concessions from Madrid. As Berlin provided weapons and air support in measured drams, German firms nosed their way into Spanish mineral concerns. Franco was obliged in April 1938 to join the Anti-Comintern Pact and to lift his restrictions on foreign participation in Spanish mining companies in November.[4] In the meantime, the feeling of irritation had become mutual. The slowness of Franco's offensives aggravated Berlin and Rome and gave each a better assessment of Spanish military power than the *Caudillo* probably would have liked. Franco's declarations of neutrality during the Sudeten crisis of September 1938 and three days after the outbreak of war in 1939 seemed the height of ingratitude and won few friends in Berlin.[5] Thus, in the summer of 1940 when military collaboration came up again, each side viewed the other with a strong degree of cynicism. Yet in 1940, Franco was eager to help share in the spoils of Germany's victory. Much of the original scholarly literature on Spain's policy during the war, which thanks to a paucity of Spanish sources had to rely on Spanish postwar polemic, argues that Franco deliberately avoided German pressure to enter the conflict. The *Caudillo*, according to this argument, kept Hitler north of the Pyranees with stalling tactics and sporadic raw material deliveries.[6] More recent writing, which benefits from access to Spanish records, acknowledges that Madrid had more aggressive policies which, despite Spain's weakness, Franco attempted to pursue within the parameters of opportunity.[7]

As Spain degenerated into civil war in 1936, Franco's successful military career had already made him one of the darlings of the Spanish Right. As would be the case with Pétain in France, Franco had come to view himself as a national savior, thanks to the numerous plaudits and honors that he had received from right-wing admirers.[8] As a soldier, however, Franco had little use for abstract political ideas. His sole meeting with José Antonio Primo de Rivera, the founder of the Spanish *Falange,* had left the latter quite unimpressed.[9] In April 1937 after José Antonio's murder, Franco simply united the various elements of the Spanish Right into a more efficient and malleable conglomeration called the *Falange Española Tradicionalista y de las Juntas de Ofensiva Nacional Sindicalista (FET y de las JONS)* under his own command.[10] He was in large part the authoritarian career army officer whom his military aide and cousin Francisco Franco Salgado-Arraujo once described as "Francoist above everything . . . one hundred percent Francoist."[11]

Yet despite his refusal to follow the leadership of the *Falange* or any other right-wing party, he did share with them certain ideas. At home, he defined his mission as the eradication of degenerate republicanism in Spain, which had brought communism, anarchism, and atheism in its wake. Brutal repression of the Spanish Left became the rule. Abroad, Franco hoped to reconstruct Spain's ancient empire, or at least the parts of it that were within reach. Franco focused specifically on French Northwest Africa, specifically French Morocco—the focus of Spain's most recent imperial gains and disappointments. The Spanish emotional claim to the region was centuries old, and most recently it was in Spanish Morocco where Franco had made a glorious career fighting the Rif tribes of Abd-el-Krim in the mid-1920s.[12] It had thus held special meaning to him and to all of the *Africanistas* in the Spanish army. In 1924 when the Spanish dictator Miguel Primo de Rivera had argued for a military withdrawal from the Spanish protectorate, which was small, unprofitable, and increasingly expensive in both manpower and treasure, then–lieutenant colonel Franco passionately countered that "Morocco is Spanish earth because it has been acquired at the highest price and paid for with the dearest coin—Spanish blood."[13] On the eve of his own victory in Spain in 1939, General Franco commented that the possibility of restoring Spain's greatness lay ultimately in Africa.[14] Franco, wrote his brother-in-law and interior minister, Ramón Serrano Suñer, after his death, "was a man of Africa. In Morocco he had brilliantly made his entire career, and in Morocco his destiny seemed to lay."[15]

The delineation of the French and Spanish Moroccan protectorates had long been a sore point with Spanish nationalists. In 1902, French foreign minister Théophile Delcassé had promised Madrid a sizable zone of influence in Morocco, which included northern Morocco down to the Sebu and Mulaya Rivers and a large chunk south of Agadir. Yet after the Entente Cordiale with Great Britain in 1904, the French reduced much of the proposed Spanish zone. The final division of 1912 shrank Spanish Morocco to what King Victor Emmanuel III of Italy called the bone of the Moroccan cutlet—a mountainous coastal strip of 20,000 square kilometers, nearly impossible to conquer and barely worth improving.[16] The Spanish zone would not include the port city of Tangier either, which had been placed under international administration in 1923.[17] In 1925, the French further occupied the rich and populous Beni Zerual and two smaller tribal areas on the Spanish side of the border as part of their contribution to the effort against Abd-el-Krim. A French-Spanish border agreement of 1925 had obliged the French to leave these areas, but as of 1940, the French had still not pulled out.[18]

Franco's government had worked to build Spain's place in Morocco at France's expense even before the war. The most active figure was Colonel Juan Beigbeder y Atienza, an expert on Morocco who had served as the Spanish high commissioner in Tetuán from April 1937 to August 1939.[19] During the Spanish civil war, Beigbeder kept the tribal leaders behind Franco and supplied Franco with 70,000 Moroccan troops by granting the native leaders an autonomy hitherto unseen in either zone, while hinting that such freedoms could blossom into independence. Beigbeder's interests spread into the cultural arena as well, with a new Institute for Moroccan Studies and the rebuilding of mosques and Arabic schools. He also allowed the Moroccan nationalist press in the Spanish zone to blast the neighboring French administration. After the civil war, the caliph, the sultan's representative in the Spanish zone, told Beigbeder that Franco had won the heart not only of

Morocco but of all Islam.[20] None of this sat well with the French, who had enough problems without the addition of nationalist agitation in Morocco. There was even an invasion scare in the Spanish zone in May 1938, and in February 1939 the French asked Foreign Minister Count Jordana to counter the pan-Islamic movement, the center of which, they stated, was in Tetuán.[21]

The Germans helped Spain exacerbate French headaches in Morocco. Relations between the high commissioner and the German consulate in Tetuán, under Herbert Georg Richter, were friendly and cooperative. Beigbeder set up German contacts with the Moroccan nationalist leaders in the French zone, and during the Franco-German war Richter had funneled cash to nationalist groups in French Morocco while promoting German propaganda in both zones.[22] Beigbeder had doubtless expected that Spain would be the beneficiary of this sort of activity, especially in the event of an eventual French defeat, and Richter understood this. When praising Beigbeder to the German Foreign Ministry upon the colonel's promotion to the office of foreign minister in August 1939, Richter commented that "Beigbeder's personal wish is to incorporate Tangier into the Spanish zone and also to advance the frontiers against French Morocco; nonetheless he openly admits that this [would only be] possible in the event of a general conflict."[23] The new Spanish administration in Tetuán was also headed by staunch *Africanistas* friendly to the German consulate. The high commissioner was General Carlos Asensio, a divisional commander during the civil war, and the new general secretary of the administration, Tomás García Figueras, was an expert on Morocco who had written a polemical book on the Spanish protectorate.[24]

Franco had not planned on entering the war when it erupted in September 1939. Spain, he had told Ciano in June, needed five years of peace to recover from the civil war, and on 4 September Madrid proclaimed strict neutrality.[25] Yet the French disasters of May and June 1940 opened new doors that seemingly offered inexpensive passage. "We believed then certainly in a German victory," wrote Serrano Suñer, "and we had to . . . foresee the accommodation of Spain in the European order."[26] Air Minister Juan Yagüe was not joking when he commented to the Germans in May 1940, "The Spanish Air Force rejoices in this victory as if it were our own."[27] All evidence points toward the fact that Franco especially was fully convinced of a German victory.[28] In the first week of June, Beigbeder informed the German ambassador Eberhard von Stohrer that Spain's national aspirations included Gibraltar, French Morocco, and an enlargement of Spanish Guinea, and he stated that he would regret it if the Italians desired to occupy Morocco.[29] The Spanish press began to speak openly about national demands in Africa, and during a speech commemorating the military rebellion on 18 July, Franco himself announced that it was necessary "to make a nation, to forge an empire. To do that our first task must be to strengthen the unity of Spain. There remains a duty and mission, the command of Gibraltar, African expansion, and the permanence of a policy of unity."[30] In the final few days of France's belligerence, action would accompany polemic, and it is key that Madrid did not consult Berlin in any substantial way concerning this action. Spain's preferred course was to act alone without help from or obligation to Germany. On 12 June, the government announced that it was no longer a neutral, but a "non-belligerent."[31] The aim of a united Morocco under Spanish protection now became Franco's overriding aim.

Tangier was the first objective. Despite Tangier's international character, France enjoyed primacy since the chief of the Tangier control commission had always been French. This practice had always piqued the Spaniards in general and Beigbeder in particular.[32] France's problems gave Beigbeder a chance to act. France had proposed in April a joint French-Spanish military occupation to guarantee Tangier's neutrality against possible Italian encroachments. Neither Beigbeder nor the rest of the Spanish government cared to act jointly with a belligerent power in Tangier, especially a rival on the brink of defeat. Beigbeder had the French informed in June that Spain wished to proceed alone with a temporary occupation.[33] Though General Noguès vehemently opposed from Rabat any concession to Spain in Tangier, there were no objections in the French Foreign Ministry.[34] An agreement emerged on the evening of 13 June, on the condition that Spain's occupation remain provisional.[35] The French were not expecting the swift Spanish action that followed, for they had not informed any of their representatives in Morocco on the agreement with Madrid. On the same evening, Beigbeder ordered Asensio to mobilize two troop detachments for entrance into the city at seven o'clock the next morning. At the time of the occupation the chief of the control commission and the *Mendub* (the sultan's representative in Tangier) were to be informed that Spain was temporarily assuming security functions "in the name of the Sultan" and that Spain would respect all international rights. Noguès was to be informed of the occupation at 6:45 A.M with the comment that the occupation had come with the agreement of the French government.[36]

The following morning, the operation proceeded as smoothly as Beigbeder had described it, to the surprise of all but the Spanish authorities there.[37] It was a fine victory for Beigbeder, who for several days was visibly pleased with the proceedings.[38] He even convinced Stohrer and Hitler himself that there had been no contact with France.[39] And though Beigbeder publicly characterized the occupation as temporary, the truth was different. His notes to Berlin and Rome studiously omitted the statement given to all other capitals that the occupation was a provisional measure in the sultan's name. Spanish measures in November and December to replace the international administration with that of Tetuán revealed even more plainly that Tangier was to become part of Spanish Morocco.[40]

Yet would Madrid be as daring with French Morocco? Here Spanish intentions are less clear, but from the available evidence it appears that Madrid seriously considered an invasion in the days preceding the French surrender.[41] On 15 June, the day following the Tangier occupation, Stohrer visited Beigbeder and found the latter fully preoccupied with maps of French Morocco. The ambassador quickly cabled Berlin that Spain was prepared to take action in the French zone soon, though he remained unsure when.[42] On the same day in Tetuán, Asensio told Richter that a Spanish action was forthcoming.[43]

On the sixteenth, Franco's chief of staff Jorge Vigón met Hitler and Ribbentrop in France, delivered a letter from Franco, and made several exploratory remarks.[44] Vigón announced Spain's expectation of a united Morocco under its protection, and that it counted on German material aid should the Americans land there. Vigón offered Hitler no promises of any kind from Franco, and apparently wished only to sound Hitler out on German support in deciding Morocco's postwar fate.[45] Yet Hitler's remarks could not have pleased Madrid. Although the Führer supported a devolution of Gibraltar to Spain and promised to fight an American landing in Morocco, he balked on the issue of Morocco's ultimate protector, stating that Germany and possibly Italy had interests there. Ribbentrop quickly interjected that the interested powers would need to find a solution satisfactory to all sides. Madrid could only have concluded that it would have to make its own rules in Morocco.[46] Richter meanwhile reported considerable troop movement at the French Moroccan frontier during the entire week, and Asensio predicted that there would be a large advance into the French zone. Reliable sources told Richter that the marching order was to have come from Madrid on 16 or 17 June 1940 but that the order had been postponed. Meanwhile, a nervous Asensio hourly awaited orders to invade the French zone.[47]

If Franco had intended to invade the French zone during the final week of the Franco-German war, then why did Spanish troops not march? A political explanation could lie in Baudouin's shrewd request in the small hours of 17 June for Spain to mediate a Franco-German cease-fire.[48] The request stunned the Spaniards, who had expected that the French would ask the Swiss for this favor, and as Madrid's ambassador in France noted, the request was an appeal to the moral stature of Spain and of Franco himself.[49] Could Franco have invaded French territory under such circumstances? It is surely no coincidence that Beigbeder opened a channel to the French government in Bordeaux in search of small territorial concessions in Morocco later the same day. Even if Franco could have forsaken his own honor and marched into the French zone, military considerations apparently convinced him not to do so. Noguès kept his troops moving along the northern frontier of the French zone to bluff the Spaniards into overestimating his strength, and in fact the Spaniards, as García Figueras told Richter on 19 June, estimated that the French forces were still quite strong. Richter agreed that the invasion would not have met with the ease that the Spaniards had originally expected, and he was relieved when the Spaniards called it off because, as he said, "One cannot describe the Spanish military organization here in bad enough terms."[50] The pre-armistice movement of French aircraft to North Africa cooled Spain's ardor even more. On 23 June, Beigbeder admitted that Spain could pursue no operations in the area due to French airpower.[51]

While the Spaniards were weighing mixed signals from Hitler, intelligence reports from Africa, and the French request for mediation, Beigbeder attempted on 17 June to wring whatever concessions he could from the French before the expected European peace settlement. Yet despite his argument that France would be better off losing parts of its empire to Spain rather than Germany, Beigbeder met with no success. Noguès and the French Foreign Ministry had no intention of allowing another Tangier to occur, especially with the peace terms still unclear. Beigbeder's proposal included the Beni Zerual, which according to the 1925 border agreement was to have gone to Spain anyway, and the Beni Snassen area on the Algerian border. The French Foreign Ministry stalled Beigbeder and was willing to "concede" nothing more than the Beni Zerual. Yet Noguès's shrill objections killed even this concession, and when Baudouin finally received a proposal for negotiation in August, it included a truncated version of the Beni Zerual that Noguès himself designed on the basis of security. In short, Spain could expect nothing from France.[52]

Thus the Spaniards, with the road to imperial expansion closed in Morocco and in France, decided to make a long detour via Germany. Madrid was too late to take advantage of Germany's victory over France, yet perhaps there was still time to capitalize on Germany's impending victory over

Great Britain. On 19 June, Beigbeder informed Stohrer that Spain would enter the war against Britain under the following conditions: Spain demanded a united Morocco under its protection, the Oran district of Algeria, an extension of Rio de Oro to the twentieth parallel, and an extension of Spanish Guinea. Spain also demanded the materials for an attack on Gibraltar, German submarine help in defending the Canary Islands, and food.[53]

Why did Madrid make this offer now? The most plausible reason appears to be that it was Madrid's last hope for an empire in French Northwest Africa. With the exception of Gibraltar, all Spanish claims were on French territory. Spain had made no suggestion up to this time that it wanted a war with Great Britain. Aside from angry street demonstrations in Madrid, the Spanish government had not pressed the British on Gibraltar and in fact lacked any prepared plans for an attack on the Rock.[54] Spain's actions of the nineteenth were symptomatic of desperation. Its aspirations, combined with its military weakness and France's stubbornness, had forced the Spaniards further into Germany's court than when Vigón had met Hitler three days earlier. Yet once Madrid's proposal was on the table, it was up to Berlin to act.

It would take Berlin nearly six weeks to act on the Spanish offer of 19 June and array itself for an operation against Gibraltar. Historians have not fully examined the reasons for this delay, but Berlin's wandering path to the Gibraltar operation provides an important key to understanding Hitler's war aims. Gibraltar became important to the Germans not because its capture would lead to victory over Britain, but because the Strait of Gibraltar provided a speedy route into Northwest Africa. Once Gibraltar had fallen, Germany could protect Northwest Africa from either a Gaullist coup or an American strike, while developing the coast for the demands of global warfare. This was a German objective even before the Spanish offer. Before the French refusal of the Casablanca demand in July, it was hoped that Spanish help might not be needed. Yet the refusal of the Casablanca demand, the decision to turn German forces east the following spring, the threat of de Gaulle in Africa, and concern over a preemptive American strike in Africa brought the Germans to focus on Spanish participation and the capture of Gibraltar later in the same month.

Hitler expected peace with the British shortly after the French capitulation. His comments to foreign dignitaries, his plans to reduce the army to peacetime strength, his Munich discussions with the Italians in mid-June, his faith in the peace appeal of 19 July, and even his Casablanca demand clearly demonstrate this expectation.[55] Yet what if London refused to surrender? The prevailing logic in Berlin argued for taking the war to Britain itself. In a famous memorandum of 30 June 1940, General Jodl prioritized attacks on Britain's sea transport, its air defenses, its strategic targets, and perhaps its civilians.[56] Germany could even land troops in England, once the Luftwaffe and navy had softened its defenses. Jodl mentioned the transfer of the war to the British Empire and the possible inclusion of the Spaniards in an attack on Gibraltar as an alternative, but this idea was something of an afterthought. Hitler apparently saw Jodl's memorandum and approved it. On 2 July, the High Command relayed his comment that under certain conditions, the main one being air supremacy, a landing in England could come into question.[57] This thought would form the basis of Operation *Seelöwe,* the preparations for which were ordered on 16 July. But a week after the armistice came into force, Hitler remained confident that a landing would not be necessary.

Spain did not fit into these considerations, and the Germans in fact ignored Madrid's *démarche* of 19 June. A high-priced alliance with a destitute country for the capture of a distant British naval base seemed unnecessary. After three days passed with no answer from Berlin, Ambassador Stohrer had to ask the German foreign ministry what his own country's policy *was!*[58] No answer came from Berlin until the twenty-fifth, a week after the Spanish offer, and here Weizsäcker made the dry comment that Berlin had taken note of the Spanish desires in North Africa, and that if Germany needed Spain's help, it would call.[59] For July and August, the Spaniards were left with few options. Despite their efforts, they learned nothing about German thinking on the issue of peace terms.[60] Thus, they attempted to negotiate with the French for small territorial concessions in Morocco, while repeatedly pressing Germany and Italy for a more strict enforcement of French disarmament in North Africa.[61] Spain's intentions regarding the last point are not entirely clear. One must balance Beigbeder's claim of the time that he feared a revolt in Morocco against the rumor that Spain planned to advance once the French had been sufficiently disarmed.[62] In any event, Spain received no satisfaction. Even Weizsäcker, who chafed at Italy's authority in Africa, claimed ignorance when faced with Madrid's complaints.[63]

Yet despite the official coolness toward Spain's offer, Hitler began to talk increasingly in July 1940 about a role in the war for Spain, primarily in connection with his interests in Morocco. On 1 July, after telling Italian ambassador Dino Alfieri that the war against Britain was won, Hitler stated that a Spanish occupation of French Morocco to stem French dissidence was undesirable, since it would provoke a British landing there. He then

noted in the same breath that Spanish participation in the war *was* desirable
and that Gibraltar "would have to be attacked."[64] A week later in a meeting
with Ciano, Hitler renewed his concerns over Morocco's safety and said
that the German military had already considered the problem of Gibraltar
at length.[65] It was also in this discussion that Hitler began to toy with the
idea of demanding bases in Morocco from the French as a return gesture for
the German concessions of three days before, which followed Mers-el-Kebir.
If Germany could establish itself on the Northwest African coast with French
approval, then perhaps an arrangement with Madrid would become superfluous. Yet Morocco was a postwar consideration. On 11 July, Hitler met
with Raeder at the Obersalzburg. While discussing the war with Britain,
they focused on naval blockade, aerial combat, and a possible landing in
England but did not mention Gibraltar once.[66] The remainder of the discussion dealt with *postwar* questions such as heavy battleship construction and
Hitler's desire to trade French Morocco, doubtless minus German interests,
to Spain for one of the Canary Islands. Two days later, Hitler approved the
army's theoretical work on the landing in England and ordered that the
army begin practical preparations so that Germany could execute the operation by 15 August. Yet at the same time, the Führer stated that he wished
"to bring Spain into the game."[67] The receipt of Vichy's rejection of the
Casablanca demand on 19 or 20 July brought Hitler more firmly to the idea
of Spain's participation. On 24 July, he informed General Wolfram Freiherr
von Richthofen, ex–Condor Legion commander and present commander of
the Seventh Air Corps, that he wished to take Gibraltar, hopefully without
Spanish participation, but if necessary with it. Four days later, Richthofen
was in Biarritz discussing an assault on the Rock with Vigón.[68] Was there a
connection between Berlin's desire to bring Spain into the conflict and the
war with Britain? If Hitler were truly concerned with Gibraltar's importance for the war against Britain, then why did he not mention it to Raeder
on 11 July? Why did his War Directive 16, issued on 16 July 1940—Operation *Seelöwe*—call for a landing on the coast of England and not a push
through Spain?[69] Why had the Germans not even begun serious reconnaissance work near Gibraltar until the end of July?[70] Why had the Foreign
Ministry done nothing up until this point to analyze the Spanish *démarche*
of 19 June? For Hitler, Gibraltar and Morocco were targets intended not so
much for the defeat of Britain, as for the period immediately *after* the British surrender. Britain sat on the edge of defeat and Hitler planned to deliver
a final blow to England itself. Yet Germany would also establish itself in
Northwest Africa, so that when the white flag went up over London, the

swastika would fly over Northwest Africa. Germany would present the world with a fait accompli in the East Atlantic.

By August, the Gibraltar operation became more urgent in Hitler's eyes, thanks to the decision to attack the Soviet Union the following spring. On 21 July, Hitler met with Raeder and General Franz Halder, the army chief of staff. He repeated that Britain's position was hopeless and held forth on *Seelöwe*. The operation would have to run by early September, since the weather in the Channel would deteriorate thereafter. Hitler noted that if the armed forces could not complete their preparations by the beginning of September, Germany would have to consider "other plans."[71] Did these "other plans" refer to the possible transfer of the war to the Mediterranean periphery? Hitler unveiled the "other plans" in a pivotal meeting of 31 July. Here the Führer revealed to his chiefs that Gibraltar and Suez were diversionary interim measures insofar as they concerned Britain. Clearly he felt a decisive strike against Britain could only come against Britain itself. And yet the possibility of *Seelöwe* for 1940 was fading, for as Raeder commented, the navy could not complete its preparations until mid-September and would be more comfortable with a target date in May 1941. Hitler responded that he would make a final decision on *Seelöwe* after eight days of intensified aerial combat and that, for the interim, he would move the execution date to 15 September. If the Luftwaffe were successful, he continued, *Seelöwe* would run in 1940. At this juncture, Raeder left the room and Hitler divulged the "other plans" to which he had already referred on the twenty-first. They concerned the annihilation of the Soviet Union for the following spring.[72] Hitler's logic was that London continued its hopeless struggle because it expected support from the Soviet Union and the United States. The destruction of the Soviet Union would eliminate what Hilter saw as Britain's continental sword, while simultaneously removing the threat to the Japanese flank in the Pacific. Japan then could keep Britain's transatlantic sword, the United States, in check as well. Germany would have to gain its Lebensraum in the East sometime anyway, and now was the optimum time. The operation was to begin in May and would presumably need five months for completion.

Spanish participation in the war became more urgent, thanks to the new course that the war would take, but not because Hitler believed that a diversionary operation against Gibraltar would force the British to the peace table. Spain's participation, as will be seen, was far too expensive for diversionary measures, and the Germans would pursue the Spaniards far too acutely. Hitler, moreover, demonstrated again on 1 August that in his eyes the key to defeating Britain still lay in direct attack. His War Directive 17 of that day called for intensified air and sea warfare against England itself to create the preconditions for Great Britain's "final defeat."[73] The participation of Spain was not important here. Spain was important because the *Wehrmacht* in May 1941 would turn its back to the West, and Northwest Africa would lie vulnerable to a British or perhaps an American attack. Germany would have to gain its foothold there *before* the attack on the Soviet Union.

The German Foreign Ministry now began to move. On 2 August, two days after Hitler's announcement of the eastern campaign and a week before the High Command even had a sketch plan for an attack on Gibraltar, Ribbentrop cabled Stohrer with the confidential message "What we want to achieve now is Spain's early entrance into the war." The foreign minister intended to travel to Madrid himself to make final arrangements with the Spaniards. For now, he summoned Stohrer to Berlin to discuss the Spanish *démarche* of 19 June, now six weeks old.[74] Yet Spain was still quite ready to enter the war at the price stipulated on 19 June.[75] At the same time, the German military began its own considerations. German army intelligence rated the Spaniards poorly. With an army of 500,000, poorly trained officers, and serious material shortages, the Spaniards could do little more than defend their homeland and colonial possessions, and even this task would demand aid if it were for any duration.[76] These handicaps did not seem overly significant for the Rock's capture. By 9 August, the staff of General Walter Warlimont, Jodl's immediate subordinate and the chief of *Abteilung Landesverteidigung*, had sketched a plan for Gibraltar's capture that called for a primarily German overland operation.[77] Hitler approved the sketch, and then the finished plan, on 24 August.[78] The full purpose of the Gibraltar plan was clear during its drafting, when Keitel ordered the military attaché in Rome to press for quicker French demobilization in Africa.[79]

If the military aspect to Spanish participation offered few problems, the economic burden that Germany was to assume was enormous—much more than Hitler would have accepted for a diversionary operation. Estimates in early August of Spain's needs were hardly optimistic, and when Ribbentrop pressed for more exact information, the answers were staggering.[80] Spain would need a minimum of 300,000 tons of grain, 400,000 tons of gasoline, 200,000 tons of coal, 200,000 tons of fuel oil, and a further list that included diesel fuel, manganese, hemp, cotton, and much more. Halder, who had always been cool toward an alliance with Spain, lamented, "We will have an ally for whom we [will] have to pay dearly."[81] Göring found the list outrageous and argued that Germany would be able to fill only a small part. Yet Hitler ordered the High Command to examine the extent to which Germany could fill the list.[82] He also warned the Italians not to stir up the political situation in the Balkans, for although Germany could survive without Rumanian oil, Spain could not.[83] On 2 September, Hitler told Jodl that Madrid's economic demands could not be allowed to impede the Gibraltar operation. By mid-September Berlin had agreed, albeit in principle, to all of Spain's economic demands, and it was Hitler who had insisted that the German purse be pried open.[84]

By the end of August, Berlin had worked out the political arrangements as well. The Germans would not inform the Spaniards of their decisions for another few weeks, but the draft protocol by Stohrer of 27 August, based on discussions with Ribbentrop, would remain the basis of German aims.[85] Germany accepted the Spanish ownership of Gibraltar, Tangier, and the Oran district outright but expected tremendous economic and strategic concessions in a united Spanish-controlled Morocco. The Germans expected the lion's share of mineral rights, and it should be remembered that the Schellert commission would travel to French Morocco in late September to gain closer look into these possibilities. Germany would gain certain harbors in French Morocco and also wanted the Spanish island of Fernando Po. Moreover, although it was apparently not mentioned to Stohrer, Hitler still wanted one of the Canary Islands, and within a few days he would order the Luftwaffe to examine the occupation of air bases at Casablanca. All transfers of French territory were, due to the danger of colonial secession from Vichy, to come officially in the peace treaty. Yet the meaning was clear. The burdens assumed by Germany would pay for themselves with a major German foothold in Northwest Africa for *after* the war.

In early September the Gibraltar issue would become even more urgent in Hitler's eyes, and the Führer would expand the concept of the Gibraltar operation to include the Portuguese island groups as well. The impetus for this development came from Washington, D.C. The German embassy in Washington attributed to Roosevelt a "fanatical hatred" for the Germans due to his Dutch-English ancestry and his supposed association with Jews, and argued that his ultimate aim lay in leading world democracy in the struggle against Germany.[86] No one in Berlin feared a major American impact in the war any time soon. American neutrality legislation and the sorry state of its rearmament prevented it. Hitler said in mid-September that American rearmament was the biggest bluff in world history and that the United States could play no important military role until 1945, by which time the war would have ended.[87] Still, the United States could create difficulties for the postwar world order. Most bothersome was Roosevelt's apparent intention to acquire strategic bases in the Western and perhaps even the Eastern Hemisphere. In mid-August, the paranoid military and air attaché, General Friedrich von Bötticher, whose reports Hitler read with great interest, saw the establishment of an American consulate at Dakar and newspaper tales of German aircraft arriving there as the start of an American scheme to push eastward across the Atlantic. "These," said von Bötticher, were the "familiar American tactics of mixing in the poison."[88] A few days later, Chargé d'Affaires Hans Thomsen reported that the Americans were also displaying a keen interest in Morocco and the Spanish and Portuguese island groups, and the Naval Command shared similar concerns.[89]

These concerns increased with the British-American Destroyer-Base Deal, which was announced on 3 September. Berlin had monitored the question throughout August, and once it became clear in mid-August that the destroyers were linked to British bases in the West Atlantic, uneasiness increased in all German agencies. Hitler prohibited negative public statements on the issue, recognizing that they would only ensure the deal's consummation.[90] The deal's completion brought greater consternation. Ironically, the embassy in Washington accused Roosevelt of assuming dictatorial powers by sending the destroyers illegally.[91] The deal disturbed the Naval Command even more, mainly due to America's acquisition of eight bases from British Guiana to Newfoundland. Already in mid-July, the navy had speculated that after the war the United States and Britain would enter into a closer relationship and become Germany's future enemies, and in August they predicted that Roosevelt's reelection in November would mean American entry into the war.[92] After de Gaulle's coup in central Africa, Raeder and his cohort noted that Washington would be very tempted by the French West African colonies. It was this prospect that in part had led them to advocate concessions to the Vichy regime and German supervision rights in Africa.[93] Now with the Destroyer-Base Deal, the picture seemed clear, and it was a grim one for German aims in Northwest Africa:

> *The Naval Command sees . . . imminent collaboration of*
> *England with the USA of the closest kind. England recognizes*
> *that it is no longer strong enough alone to emerge victorious in*
> *the great fight for its world empire, and it sees the only possibility*
> *in an ever-closer connection with the USA. . . . The [British] Em-*
> *pire will indeed undergo the most intense alterations, yet will . . .*

reemerge as an Anglo-Saxon World Empire. *In the interest of the USA's own power position one can hardly reckon with decisive . . . aid to the British. . . . Yet the possibility of . . . American action looms in the occupation of the Spanish and Portuguese islands . . . and . . . the occupation of the French Colonies of West Africa.*

The preparatory USA propaganda is accusing Germany of advancing against the French West African colonies and points to the possibilities of the German Luftwaffe *to attack America from West Africa via the South Atlantic.*

It is essential to recognize the special dangers which lie in an occupation of the Azores and Canary Islands or in an establishment in French West Africa (Dakar) by the USA or England. . . . The Naval Command feels itself duty-bound to bring the above considerations to the attention of the Führer . . . and to point out the necessity of immediate assumption of appropriate counter-measures.[94]

In answering a series of questions by the Army Command, the navy also said that American landings in Casablanca or Dakar would meet no serious resistance due to the poor economic situation there, and that such a move would bar the Axis from Northwest Africa. "[An] American landing," concluded the Naval Command, "would doubtless lead to [the] permanent establishment of the USA in [this] area which allegedly is important for the defense of all of America. Thus . . . after the British defeat, the Anglo-Saxon world would maintain strategically important positions while making the desired German establishment there difficult if not impossible!!"[95]

Hitler did not leave to posterity such lengthy considerations, but he agreed with the navy on certain points. His racial theories spared him the concern that Britain and the United States would meld politically. Still, he had believed since the French armistice that Germany should avoid a long war with Britain lest the British Empire devolve to the United States rather than Germany.[96] Now this very development appeared to be unfolding. He did not fear decisive American intervention, but the possibility that Washington would steal the strategic areas that Germany coveted loomed as ominously in Hitler's considerations as in those of the Naval Command. Berlin would thus need to take steps to prevent such an occurrence.

One such step lay in the inclusion of Japan into an alliance to threaten America's Pacific flank. In June the German embassy in Tokyo had been reprimanded for suggesting that Berlin would approve Tokyo's aims in Southeast Asia if the Japanese would pledge to attack the United States should the latter enter the war against Germany.[97] Yet as the Destroyer-Base Deal reached fruition, Hitler suddenly became more interested in a tighter relationship with Tokyo, and on 7 September Heinrich Stahmer, a special envoy from the *Dienststelle Ribbentrop*, arrived in the Japanese capital.[98] On 9 and 10 September on direct orders from Ribbentrop, he pressed Japanese foreign minister Yosuke Matsuoka for a quick decision regarding America's neutralization. The German arguments, which came directly from Ribbentrop, are revealing indeed. Germany, said Stahmer, "is taking a long view of carrying on the stupendous struggle against the British Empire, not to [mention] . . . America . . ." The present war, he said, would end soon, but the larger struggle against Anglo-Saxondom would continue "for tens of years yet, in one form or another."[99] These comments rang true with Matsuoka, who felt that one could deal with the Americans only from a position of strength.[100] Within the month, Germany and Japan would be allied. The more immediate steps that Hitler considered dealt with the Portuguese island groups themselves. On 5 September, two days after the announcement of the Destroyer-Base Deal and two days before Stahmer's arrival in Japan, Hitler stated for the first time that the Azores and the Canary and Cape Verde Islands would have to be taken in timely fashion by German and Italian forces to prevent such seizure by the British or the Americans. Jodl ordered Warlimont's staff to begin the planning.[101] Hitler thus added an important supplement to the Gibraltar operation, molding it into a general program for the East Atlantic.

It is at this point that a split becomes apparent between Hitler and the Naval Command, both on general strategy and their reasons for advocating the capture of Gibraltar. The German navy by the end of August had become uncomfortable with the tack that Hitler's strategy was taking. The navy viewed *Seelöwe,* and thus Britain's defeat, as a dead issue for the winter of 1940–41, while its concern over Washington's supposed aggressiveness was growing. The navy also had deep misgivings over Hitler's intention to invade the Soviet Union in the spring. A campaign in the East did not guarantee victory in the West and the movement of German forces to the East would strengthen Britain's strategic position, especially should the United States enter the war. The navy thus developed an alternative winter strategy that focused on the Mediterranean.[102] The capture of Gibraltar and Suez would provide the Axis with numerous advantages, including the elimination of Gibraltar for British escort and blockade operations; the use of bases in Spain for the battle of the Atlantic; freedom for Italian submarines to pass into the ocean; free transport in the Mediterranean for Axis vessels, the exertion of greater pressure on the Balkans, Turkey, and Arabia; the creation of a land connection from Egypt to East Africa; and the ability to monitor political developments in French North Africa. A shift to the Mediterranean would, in short, keep London on its heels throughout the winter and could possibly oblige Great Britain to quit the war, in which case the threat of American intervention would vanish as well.[103]

On 6 September, Raeder presented the Mediterranean strategy to Hitler, at the center of which stood the Gibraltar operation. Raeder argued that the capture of the Rock was not an interim action, but rather a key component in the war against Great Britain, and that Germany would have to execute it "before the USA intervenes." Hitler, who had already advocated an operation against Gibraltar for weeks, told Raeder that he agreed. Hitler and Raeder also agreed that Germany would need to occupy the Canary Islands on Spain's entry into the war, since the British would seek a new base there and since the United States might attempt to seize one as well.[104] Hitler commented that the Luftwaffe could and would execute this operation. Yet fundamental agreement between Hitler and his navy on the broader issue of the Mediterranean strategy and the *reasons* for the capture of Gibraltar did not exist. Hitler's interest in the Rock lay mostly in the connection of Europe with Northwest Africa, and Raeder did not change the Führer's mind. Two days after the meeting with Raeder, Hitler ordered the Luftwaffe Command to study the development of bases in Casablanca and Dakar and stated that these areas would be occupied by German troops. The discrepancy between Hitler and the navy on the significance of Gibraltar was subtle, yet key. It meant that if the possibility of German dominance in Northwest Africa were to vanish, or if it could be attained without Spanish help, Hitler's interest in Gibraltar would wane despite the navy's arguments.

In the early autumn of 1940, then, Hitler's designs for Northwest Africa looked as follows. For the French Northwest African colonies, Hitler for the most part ignored the advice of his aides and allowed the Italians to handle the French as they wished. This reticence on the Führer's part was due to the fact that the Italians were following the hard line that he preferred. The French North African forces would disarm, and if France seriously wished to win Equatorial Africa back from de Gaulle, it could send whatever forces it liked from North Africa. In the meantime Germany would, without harming Italy's sensibilities, assert a larger presence in Northwest Africa. Germany would send military and political observers and even air force specialists to scout the air bases in Casablanca that Pétain had denied Hitler in July. This policy was supplemented with the participation of Spain. After taking Gibraltar, Germany would be able to eliminate any threat the Anglo-Saxons could muster by stationing ground, air, and naval forces in the Azores, the Cape Verde and Canary Islands, and in Morocco. The Germans could also make an effort to occupy Casablanca and Dakar. In the meantime, the Japanese would restrict Washington's freedom of action in the Atlantic by maintaining pressure in the Pacific. In the spring of 1941, then, Germany would be able to turn east without worrying about the southwest, and after the defeat of bolshevism and the concurrent elimination of British resistance, Germany would continue to develop its bases and its fleet in preparation for the great struggle for global supremacy. Yet everything hinged on Spain. Without the cooperation of Franco, the Germans would continue to find the door to Northwest Africa and the Atlantic islands bolted by the Royal Navy. In mid-September, Franco's brother-in-law and interior minister, Ramón Serrano Suñer, arrived in Berlin to discuss Spain's all-important cooperation in this scheme.

Chapter 5

September Shifts

❦

The world is big enough so that Spain need not
suffer any mortgage on its territories
or on its economy. . . .
—Generalissimo Francisco Franco

September 1940 was a pivotal month for Hitler's designs for Northwest Africa. On the sixteenth, Franco's brother-in-law and interior minister, Ramón Serrano Suñer, arrived in Berlin for talks concerning Spain's entry into the war. The talks bogged down, but not due to Spain's economic situation or any presumed Spanish propensity for stalling the issues. The talks ran aground because the German desire for the strategic development of Northwest Africa was inconsistent with Spain's own territorial aims in that region. As the Spanish talks deadlocked, a new factor entered into Hitler's considerations—de Gaulle's failed landing at Dakar of 23 September. To Hitler, Dakar was confirmation that the Anglo-Saxon powers were determined to steal Germany's future bases in Northwest Africa. Moreover, the stiff French defense brought him reluctantly to the conclusion that he could perhaps trust the French to defend their African holdings for the time being. An arrangement with Vichy became more valuable, and an alliance with Spain began to lose its luster.

In the summer and fall of 1940, the German embassy in Madrid viewed Serrano Suñer as Spain's most influential political figure. As minister of the interior he controlled the press, as president of the political council of the *Falange,* he controlled the state party, and as Franco's brother-in-law, he had the ear of the chief of state. Military and monarchist figures in Spain feared Serrano's aim of a true falangist state and cared little for him. One of his enemies might have been Beigbeder himself.[1] Yet both ministers agreed on expansion into

Africa, and if it was Serrano whom Franco chose to deal directly with the Germans, the choice sprang in part from the alarm that a trip by the foreign minister to Berlin would have caused in London—alarm that Franco, for fear of a tightening British blockade, wished to avoid.

Serrano had wanted to travel to Germany since early July, but the Germans were uninterested at the time.[2] Yet Spain's eagerness to divide the spoils of the war remained when the Germans did become interested in August. The Germans and Spaniards began talks on Spain's economic and military needs in mid-August, and shortly afterward Ambassador von Stohrer reported that Beigbeder and Franco saw Spain's entry as imminent and that Franco was even willing to accept the risks of a longer war.[3] This willingness was evident elsewhere. Beigbeder again raised with Stohrer on 20 August the concern about the slow pace of disarmament in French Morocco, and Franco wrote Mussolini personally to gain his support for Madrid's claims in Northwest Africa.[4] Madrid would deal directly with the Germans soon enough, for the first week of September saw the planning of Serrano's long-awaited trip. The Spaniards reiterated that they would indeed enter the war if their military, economic, and territorial demands were met, and at 9:10 P.M. on 13 September, Serrano, together with a Spanish economic delegation and von Stohrer, boarded a special German train at Hendaye bound via Paris for Berlin.[5]

It was at this point that the French attempted to fit a wedge between Germany and Spain over Northwest Africa. The French Foreign Ministry had thought in June about ceding back to Spain the Beni Zerual and two other tribal regions of Morocco that the French had occupied counter to the border agreement of 1925 but Noguès had rejected the scheme and cut the proposal down to a truncated version of the Beni Zerual.[6] Baudouin and his general secretary, François Charles-Roux, still hoped that this small offer would start a dialogue that would forestall any drastic Spanish action. On 28 August, Baudouin met with the Spanish ambassador, José Felix de Lequerica, and told him that the French government would soon present Madrid with proposals concerning the Moroccan frontier. Lequerica launched into a lengthy historical treatise on France's transgressions against Spain in Morocco since the turn of the century and expressed the fervent hope that France would recognize Madrid's legitimate aims for the good of the new European order. "Besides," Lequerica added ominously, "Germany would always be able to implement more radical remedies to the old French-Spanish injustice in North Africa." Baudouin got the point. On 29 August, he and Charles-Roux rejected Noguès's scheme on the grounds that it would cause more problems than it would resolve and proposed full implementation of the French-Spanish Moroccan border agreement of 1925. Pétain accepted this idea two days later.[7]

Baudouin knew of Serrano's trip to Berlin and assumed that the talks there would concern Morocco due to rumors that Asensio was part of the Spanish delegation. He already had a 14 September appointment with Otto Abetz, the German ambassador in Paris, and he hoped to meet Serrano as well when the special train from Hendaye passed through Paris on the same day.[8] When Baudouin met Abetz, the latter expressed great concern over Morocco as well as regret that Germany did not occupy the area as a part of the armistice. Baudouin assured Abetz that Vichy would defend Morocco against all possible enemies. Yet Baudouin never met Serrano. According to Baudouin's information, the Spaniard had hoped to meet him but was convinced over lunch at the German embassy that he should not do so.[9] Thus at 11:00 P.M., Serrano's train left Gare d'Est for Berlin without the French foreign minister having spoken to him.

The Germans wanted no trouble from Serrano in the acceptance of the German demands on Spain. Serrano was met at Berlin's Anhalter Bahnhof at 10:00 A.M. on 16 September by von Ribbentrop, Interior Minister Wilhelm Frick, Chief of Protocol Baron Alexander von Dörnberg, and a host of other functionaries with appropriate fanfare. The Germans allowed him no time to collect himself after the eleven-hour train ride from Paris, taking him immediately to his hotel and then straight to the Foreign Ministry for a high-pressure discussion with Ribbentrop at 11:00. With no diplomatic experience, Serrano then had the unenviable task of facing Ribbentrop alone for three hours. The new Spanish ambassador, General Eugenio Espinosa de los Monteros, was barred from the meeting by von Dörnberg.[10] Still, Serrano was focused enough to concentrate his remarks on Morocco.[11] Madrid knew of the German Casablanca demand of mid-July, thanks to Baudouin's shrewd leak of that information to Lequerica at the time.[12] Now Serrano complained that Madrid had heard nothing from Berlin on the Spanish *démarche* of 19 June, while insisting that a united Morocco was the "natural and historical objective of Spanish expansion." Serrano also based the Spanish demand for 56,000 tons of fuel per month on the possibility that French forces in Morocco could return to action, revealing again that Franco saw Northwest Africa as Spain's theater of war. Ribbentrop accepted the Spanish demands "in principle" and then moved on to German thinking on larger issues. Victory against Great Britain, he said, was "absolutely certain," and the United States would refrain from intervention while trying to become the heir to the British Empire. After the German triumph, the task would be to reorganize Europe and Africa. Germany would claim central Africa for itself. Yet what Germany won it would have to protect, and it was "the Führer's wish" that Spain allow permanent German bases in French Morocco at Agadir and Mogador and that Spain cede to Germany one of the Canary Islands. The latter request hit Serrano like ice water. He strongly objected on grounds of Spanish national feeling, but Ribbentrop pursued the issue. Germany, Italy, and Spain would have to defend what they had won, and thanks to the increasing speed of airplanes, America was "moving closer and closer to the European-African area. In ten years," said the Foreign Minister, "the distance from Africa to America would possibly be no greater than today the distance from Germany to England."[13]

Serrano's refusal of German demands determined the character of his meeting with Hitler the following morning. Again Espinosa was intercepted at the door by von Dörnberg and prohibited from aiding Serrano during the meeting, the subsequent protests of both Spaniards notwithstanding.[14] Hitler presented Serrano with the broad strategic principles rather than concrete demands. He affirmed that the war was "already decided" but noted with some uneasiness the remaining British option of alienating French Africa from Pétain and using it as a base for continuing the war. Once Gibraltar had fallen, continued Hitler, "no serious danger from French Morocco either could any longer threaten." For the postwar world, Europe would need to integrate Africa in order to confront the bloc of North and South America effectively, and the entire area would demand a defensive perimeter on which Germany would need to begin work as soon as possible. "For under certain conditions," continued Hitler, "a great danger could threaten . . . the whole new order." England and France could entice to the Azores the Americans, who, thanks to "certain imperialistic tendencies . . . now coming to the fore," would gladly occupy the islands. Since Africa would be dependent on whoever controlled the islands off its coast, it was "necessary to set up defensive strong points on the islands" as soon as possible. Serrano agreed with Hitler's principles but not his remedies. He noted that that the defense of the Euro-African area could come within the framework of a more general alliance in which each partner did its share rather than with a cession of territory to Germany. Hitler decided not to pursue the matter further with Serrano and suggested a meeting with Franco himself.

Following Hitler's failure with Serrano, Ribbentrop had another try with the Spaniard in an unscheduled discussion later on the seventeenth. Ribbentrop promised that in the peace settlement Germany would give French

Morocco to Spain, with the exception of Agadir and Mogador. He then pressed Serrano anew for one of the Canary Islands, repeating Hitler's concerns in light of Roosevelt's recent aggressive policy. He asked Serrano to relay these concerns to Franco, along with the addendum that the Atlantic islands "must be equipped for defense immediately." With his unique tactlessness, the foreign minister said that the islands would need advanced technical installations that the Spaniards were "perhaps not in a position to provide." Serrano held firm. He again suggested a general alliance and attempted to steer Ribbentrop's eye toward Madeira and Saint-Louis. On Ribbentrop's suggestion that Spain would not receive Morocco at all without German aid, Serrano testily noted that Spain would gladly conquer Morocco with its own blood, and when Ribbentrop proposed that Spain hand Germany Fernando Po and Spanish Guinea instead, Serrano broke off the discussion, blandly noting that he would raise the issue with Franco.[15]

The German failure with Serrano was evident. Immediately the German Foreign Ministry overhauled the itinerary of Serrano's trip with the aim of pressing him again after he could correspond with Franco. In the original itinerary, Serrano was to have one meeting each with Ribbentrop and Hitler, then tour Bavaria and leave Germany on 21 September, enjoying a tour of the battlefields in the West en route to Hendaye. The Germans now changed the schedule. On the evening of the eighteenth, they sent Serrano off to the battlefields so that his tour there would correspond with Ribbentrop's earlier-scheduled talks in Rome with Mussolini. Serrano would then return to Berlin for more discussions.[16]

Hitler remained optimistic that Franco would understand Germany's position and also remained willing to meet Spain's economic and military prerequisites despite Ribbentrop's inclination to haggle, and a letter to Mussolini reflected this optimism. France was finished, Hitler said to Mussolini, but there was still the danger of secession in North Africa, and there was "no assurance that such secession might not even occur in secret agreement with the French government." Yet as soon as "a reliable bridge to North Africa via Spain" was created, the danger of secession would recede. Franco, he predicted, would cooperate. Meanwhile, the impending tripartite alliance with Tokyo would help restrain Roosevelt's Atlantic ambitions. "I believe in principle," said the Führer, "that in spite of all other misgivings a close cooperation with Japan is the best way either to keep America entirely out of the picture or to render her entry into the war ineffective."[17] The following day, Hitler wrote Franco to convince him of the validity of his aims. The present war, he said, would "for centuries" decide the future of Europe and

Spain. Once Gibraltar was in Spanish hands, "a sure connection will have to be brought about between Spain and North Africa (Spanish Morocco)." Once Britain lost Gibraltar, he cautioned, the British would attempt a landing in the Canary Islands, so German dive-bombers or long-range fighters would need to set up in Las Palmas *before* the start of the Gibraltar operation. In all, Gibraltar's fall would help assure that "North Africa would be delivered up to seizure by Italy, Spain and Germany. . . . The danger that a North African area detached from France might unite with British forces would thereby be definitively eliminated."[18]

Franco in fact remained far from disenchanted with the idea of cooperation with the Germans. Yet cooperation would be on Franco's terms only. As Serrano had hinted in Berlin, Franco wanted a partnership wherein a fully independent Spain aided by a rejuvenated German-financed armaments industry would defend the southwest on its own.[19] Yet Spain would cede no territory to Germany. The Canary Island demand was a ludicrous and insulting concept not even open to discussion, and the idea of German bases in French Morocco was also highly unattractive, for as Franco wrote to Serrano on 21 September, "we must avoid enclaves in our territory." Franco rather viewed the arrangement with Germany in the following terms: "Our presence in the Axis offers . . . the security and the domination of the western Mediterranean and the possibility of defense of our continent including North Africa, making it invulnerable to Anglo-American attacks. . . . In this it is necessary to [raise] what an alliance is; in . . . war, the bases of one become eventually the bases of the other. If we are to defend a European front, *we* will prepare our bases with one [joint] accord."[20] Franco expressed similar thoughts to Hitler. Apparently he felt that Serrano's indignation over the Canary Island demand had settled that issue, and he focused on Agadir and Mogador. "In our view," reasoned Franco, "these [bases] are unnecessary in peacetime and superfluous in wartime, because in this case you could not only count upon these harbors but on all that Spain possesses, since our friendship is to be sealed firmly for the future. . . . The advantages which these bases could offer would counterbalance neither the difficulties which this type of enclave always produces nor the harm which they would cause. . . ."[21] For the rest Franco, again thinking the Canary Island issue was settled, accepted Hitler's offer of German fighters and dive-bombers for Las Palmas to supplement the augmented Spanish defenses of the island group. He also commented that once at war, Spain would mass troops in Spanish Morocco to counter the danger of a Gaullist revolt in French North Africa, thus hinting that German troops in Spanish Morocco were neither necessary nor desired. Many an analyst of Franco's wartime policy has argued that he intended a pragmatic entry into the war "at the time of the last cartridge," and that he then retreated into firm nonbelligerency once the war looked as if it would drag into the winter.[22] In fact, Franco was thinking of a permanent alignment with Germany, whereby Spain would defend the southwest with German material and financial aid but without deference to Berlin. Franco was moreover willing in September 1940 to accept the possibility of a longer war. He mentioned to Serrano on the twenty-first that the value of Spain's participation could only increase with a lengthening of the conflict with Britain, and two days later he ordered measures in the Canary Islands for the storage of drinking water with exactly this possibility in mind. Provisioning in Spain did not loom as a major problem for Franco, for although Ribbentrop had haggled with Serrano over Spain's economic demands, Hitler himself had sounded much more agreeable on the issue. Naturally, Franco still hoped and believed that the German bombing of London would destroy the British spirit, and he left unused no opportunity to have the British embassy in Madrid informed that Britain's best option lay in surrender.[23]

While Franco was ostensibly smoothing over the German-Spanish differences from Madrid, Ribbentrop was whining about them in Rome.[24] The foreign minister went to Rome for discussions with Mussolini and Ciano to bring the Italians into line with new developments regarding Tokyo and Madrid. On the issue of Japan, Ribbentrop updated the Italians on the recent German efforts and noted that "the Führer was very favorably disposed toward the conclusion of this alliance," for though one could not discern whether Roosevelt would intervene in the conflict or not, the Japanese threat in the Pacific would oblige the Americans to "ponder a hundred times before participating."[25] The *Duce* readily agreed, and Ciano planned to go to Berlin the following week for the formal signing. On the issue of Spain, Ribbentrop communicated Hitler's desire to give French Morocco and Oran to Spain in the peace treaty with France, minus German bases and mineral concessions. Mussolini confirmed that Madrid's territorial demands did not clash with Rome's and commented that Spain's entry offered a counter to the de Gaulle movement in North Africa. Ribbentrop announced that he would sign a protocol with Serrano that recognized Spain's demands and the concessions to be made to Berlin. Averse to exclusion, Mussolini preferred a full three-power alliance with Spain as opposed to a bilateral protocol between Spain and Germany, and Ribbentrop gave his agreement to a more formal arrangement. Yet Ribbentrop remained uncomfortable with Spain's refusal of the Canary Island demand. On 20 September he complained, "The Führer had had this request presented to the Spaniards in order—looking far into the future—to counteract, through a series of naval bases, dangers which could arise for the European and African Continents . . . from the Western Hemisphere under the leadership of the United States. The Spaniards were surely loyal friends. . . . But on specific points, such as the one just mentioned . . . they were somewhat difficult."[26] Thus, the Germans had not given up on the idea of a naval and air base network in the Northwest African region. Moreover, it seemed to Hitler and Ribbentrop that the Spaniards could be brought around with a little extra persuasion. Success would have brought Spain into the war and would have cost the British Gibraltar, because for the present Hitler was willing to promise the Spaniards most of their territorial demands in Northwest Africa and was willing to support the Spaniards economically and militarily for the duration of the war. Yet two days after Ribbentrop's final meeting in Rome, a pivotal event occurred that ruined the arrangement and, although not appreciated at the time, contributed to the rescue of Britain's position at Gibraltar. This was the Anglo-Gaullist raid on Dakar.

One of Paul Baudouin's fears in the months after the armistice concerned Great Britain's support of de Gaulle and British propaganda in French Africa. The French foreign minister believed that such intrigues would bring into the empire the Germans and Italians, who would then combat dissidence as permanent guests. In August and September, Baudouin sent warnings to this effect to London via the French embassy in Madrid and supplemented these efforts with numerous overtures to Berlin on Vichy's determination to defend the empire, especially Casablanca and Dakar. With Pétain's approval, Vichy even staged a wild goose chase for de Gaulle in Morocco for German consumption. Such overtures were not without reason. As Baudouin told colonial minister Admiral Charles Platon on the eve of the British attack on Dakar, "Germany [will] judge our attitude by our capacity to defend Dakar and Casablanca." At the time, there seemed little reason for worry. In Madrid, British ambassador Sir Samuel Hoare communicated his assent with Baudouin's warnings.[27] Vichy remained militarily confident as well. Huntziger told General von Stülpnagel that Vichy would have a firm hold in French West Africa with the arrival of the six Senegalese battalions requested from the *Metropole,* and that in Morocco, British and Spanish propaganda made the situation difficult but not alarming.[28]

In fact, there was cause for alarm. Both Churchill and de Gaulle had been interested in Dakar since early July. Dakar offered the best port facilities in the central East Atlantic, and was located in a spot from where the

British could protect (or the Germans could threaten) the northern and southern Atlantic sea routes. Dakar also harbored the new 35,000-ton battleship *Richelieu* and 65 billion francs in French, Polish, and Belgian gold. Dakar would also offer the British a chance to do something right somewhere, while giving de Gaulle an important city to use as the Free French capital. The possibility also existed that the fall of West and Equatorial Africa would lead to the secession of the more valuable North African holdings from Vichy. The plan that became Operation *Menace* emerged with constant prodding from Churchill by mid-August, and the seizure of Dakar was to proceed as follows: Free French naval and military forces would approach Dakar while a more sizable British naval force waited on the horizon. At dawn, British carrier-based airplanes would drop leaflets over the city appealing to the town and garrison to join de Gaulle. A motorboat bearing de Gaulle's envoys would enter the harbor with a message from de Gaulle to Governor-General Pierre Boisson announcing the arrival of the Free French leader and his intention to deliver Dakar from German aggression. If Boisson were to resist, the British would land de Gaulle by force, and once de Gaulle was master at Dakar, the British would withdraw. This plan was flawed. It banked heavily on the presumption that Boisson would receive de Gaulle with open arms, for the British force lacked the firepower to execute a landing against serious resistance. Nonetheless Force M, featuring the British battleships *Barham* and *Resolution* and the carrier *Ark Royal*, left Gibraltar for Freetown on 6 September in preparation for the coup attempt.[29]

It was at this point that the three cruisers and three destroyers that the Axis had approved earlier in the week for service against de Gaulle's adherents in French Equatorial Africa put to sea from Toulon.[30] Thanks to a British foul-up, the ships cleared Gibraltar unmolested on the morning of the eleventh and the cruisers reached Dakar on the fourteenth. The cruisers had each brought to Africa eighty Senegalese infantry, and on 18 September, oblivious to the impending British action at Dakar, they sailed for Libreville, the main port of Vichy's equatorial enclave at Gabon. The cruisers were preceded in this journey by a loaded fuel tanker, escorted by yet a fourth cruiser, *Primauguet*. At noon on the nineteenth, the British intercepted *Primauguet* and escorted it back to Casablanca. On learning *Primauguet*'s fate, the three Toulon cruisers turned about and dashed for Dakar to avoid interception themselves. Two reached Dakar, but the British caught *Gloire*, which had engine trouble, and led it to Casablanca to join *Primauguet*. The French noticed that the British had presented each cruiser with the choice of bearing for Casablanca, but not Dakar, which the British argued had fallen under German influence. The French thus realized that London had designs on Dakar and placed the harbor on alert.[31]

On 20 September, the French delegation to the German Armistice Commission in Wiesbaden, still in the dark regarding the fate of the four cruisers, informed the Germans that France would defend its territories in Africa against any British attack. They asked to send the battleship *Strasbourg*, three cruisers, and a destroyer to West Africa from Toulon.[32] The French expected a positive response and had begun sailing preparations on the *Strasbourg* group the day before.[33] Yet French optimism was ill-founded. By the time the German Naval Command received the request on the twentieth, the fate of *Gloire* become clear, and since *Gloire* had chosen not to fight a suicidal battle, the Naval Command rejected the French request, based on the assumption that the French navy lacked the will to resist.[34] The following day General Paul Doyen, who replaced Huntziger as the chairman of the French delegation on the latter's promotion to the post of war minister, renewed the request in a personal talk with Stülpnagel and included a far-reaching addendum. The French request, argued Doyen, had by itself demonstrated that Vichy was willing to defend French Africa. France, through its present measures, was in a state of virtual armed conflict with Britain and virtual cooperation with Germany. Germany was thus also to recognize this cooperation with a statement that the French Empire would remain French.[35] Doyen's *démarche* received little response other than Weizsäcker's indignation that Vichy could dare make such a request.[36] The Naval Command continued its wait-and-see approach.[37] On the eve of Operation *Menace*, the Germans had contributed little to French defense save anxiety.[38]

The British and Gaullist forces arrived off Dakar at 5:30 A.M. on 23 September and soon began a three-day operation worthy of the apocryphal Murphy. Visibility was nonexistent due to haze, de Gaulle's envoys were either captured or chased off with machine guns, and aircraft from *Ark Royal* dropping leaflets were chased off by *Richelieu*'s antiaircraft guns. Subsequent Allied ultimatums and bombardments amounted to little, and Vichy forces effortlessly repulsed de Gaulle's feeble landing attempt at nearby Rufisque. Early on 25 September after their two battleships had taken serious hits, the British retired to Freetown. Two French submarines were lost and a French destroyer was damaged seriously, but the British dealt no serious harm to *Richelieu* or the French shore batteries. *Menace* had been a fiasco.[39]

The activity that *Menace* had triggered in Europe was more interesting than the battle, for the flaws in the British planning were unknown to Vichy or to Berlin, nor was the outcome assured. The French cabinet received the news of the fighting on the twenty-third at 2:50 in the afternoon. Baudouin, who thought he had reached an understanding with the British on the issue of the African colonies, was particularly dismayed and feared imminent German intervention. "If Dakar falls," he wrote in his diary, "North Africa will soon be invaded by the Germans. This means a campaign in Africa, and certainly the occupation of Marseille and Toulon. The whole structure of the Armistice will collapse. . . . Dakar will and must hold out."[40]

At 4:00 P.M. on the twenty-third, Pétain called an emergency cabinet meeting wherein the cabinet decided unanimously that France would hold Dakar at all costs, and that the French air force would take reprisals against Gibraltar.[41] Later on the evening of the twenty-third, Baudouin told a distraught Pétain that France had to profit militarily and politically from the Dakar raid. France needed the military means to defend the French colonies and a statement that West Africa would not suffer German or Italian presence.[42] On the same evening at 8:15 P.M. in Wiesbaden, Doyen reported to Stülpnagel that Vichy meant to hold Dakar and had dispatched three submarines and a number of bombers there from French Morocco. Yet France wanted more, namely the release of the *Strasbourg* group from Toulon, and the release of the eight aircraft groups in North Africa recently scheduled for disarmament that had not yet disarmed. These airplanes would serve to replace aircraft permitted by the Axis but lost in Dakar's defense. Doyen continued with the hope that the German government would trust the French at this critical time, arguing that the loss of Dakar from a strategic, economic, and political standpoint would be insurmountable for Vichy. Doyen finished his appeal with the request for a quick German decision.[43] At 10:00 P.M., Stülpnagel relayed the French government's requests to Hitler's headquarters in Berlin, adding his own position that the military requests be approved. Berlin, said Stülpnagel, had told the French on 11 September that they were to restore order in their African empire, and now was the time to allow them to do so.[44]

Hitler was unconvinced. He rejected both requests shortly before midnight due to his fundamental mistrust of the French and perhaps to the suspicion expressed earlier that de Gaulle and Pétain were cooperating.[45] In this decision the Führer found the support of Ribbentrop, though General Jodl had agreed more with Stülpnagel.[46] In a frantic late-night exchange with the embassy in Rome, Weizsäcker secured Italian agreement with the German line, which was not difficult since Ciano viewed the Dakar affair as a trick.[47] Weizsäcker then informed Wiesbaden at 3:00 A.M. that the French requests were refused.[48] Stülpnagel was furious. He wanted a reversal of the decision at least as it concerned the French aircraft. He phoned Weizsäcker that the German note to the French of 11 September had already allowed the French disposal over eighteen combat aircraft groups, and that a German rejection of the French request to keep that number up to strength would result in an embarrassing contradiction of a policy decision handed to the French only two weeks previously.[49] Jodl took the matter to Hitler at noon on the twenty-fourth, and Hitler upon reconsideration agreed. In Africa the French would be allowed disposal over all twenty-six combat aircraft groups then available for service. Nonetheless, Hitler remained firm on the issue of the *Strasbourg* group.[50] At 6:10 P.M., almost twenty-four hours after Doyen's original request, Stülpnagel gave the French chairman the German decision.[51]

Now it was Vichy's turn to be angry. The Germans had taken a full day to deliver an equivocal answer to Doyen's requests, and the government felt that now was the time to clear the air. Early on 24 September, the marshal's cabinet had decided that they wanted two things from the Germans. The first was the release of every military facility needed for a strong defense of the colonies. The second was a solemn declaration by Berlin that Germany would not occupy the colonies in West Africa during the war or after the peace.[52] The following night, after receiving the negative German reply, Doyen communicated these thoughts to Stülpnagel. The blood spilled at Dakar, argued Doyen, was only the beginning, for the British would not leave things as they stood. Meanwhile, he continued, "We find ourselves in a situation which is without precedent in history. You are making war on England, we are doing the same, and we are in a state of war with you." Doyen stated that German trust and help were essential, both militarily and morally. Materially, Doyen renewed the request for the *Strasbourg* group and also asked for the use of aircraft stocked in North African storage depots to keep the permitted twenty-six combat groups up to strength, as well as bombs and munitions from the *Metropole*. For French morale, Doyen insisted that the men fighting in the French colonies know that the places they were defending would remain French. Admiral Emile Duplat, the chairman of the French delegation to the Italian Armistice Commission at Turin, presented the Italians with a similar note the same evening.[53] The French government also pressed the Germans in Paris. On the morning of 24 September, Vice Premier Pierre Laval and War Minister Charles Huntziger traveled to the occupied capital to make the French case with Ambassador Abetz and the German army commander in chief, Field Marshal Walther von Brauchitsch.

Laval emphasized to Abetz that a German declaration on the colonies would deflate British and Gaullist propaganda, which claimed that Vichy was acting as caretaker for future German colonies.[54] On the twenty-sixth Huntziger, especially concerned about French Morocco, renewed his pitch to Brauchitsch for a larger army in North Africa than the Italians had allowed. He added that Badoglio himself had recently agreed that the Italian restriction of the French army to 30,000 troops in North Africa meant the abandonment of the region, and that Badoglio had assented to an army of 100,000. Huntziger preferred more, but this number would be enough for emergencies if France could keep the troops mobile and well equipped. The war minister continued that he wished to move the bulk of the troops to western Morocco because he expected a landing there.[55]

The German response to the French overtures was mixed. The German Armed Forces High Command and Naval Command were in fundamental agreement with French material requests. Raeder argued to the High Command that a British capture of Dakar had to be avoided at all costs and that Berlin should answer all French requests affirmatively, since the French had shown good faith in rejecting the Allied ultimatums.[56] Jodl and Warlimont agreed with Raeder and felt that French cooperation in the war against Great Britain meant important advantages, particularly where the British threat to North Africa was concerned. Jodl on 24 and 25 September had used "every opportunity to convince the Führer" of these advantages, and Warlimont on the twenty-fifth ordered a full examination of French military strength and the communications conditions between North and West Africa. Warlimont was especially interested in the use of Northwest Africa as a springboard for Hitler's scheme for occupying the Atlantic islands.[57] Yet Hitler came around only slowly and halfheartedly for now, unable to bring himself to trust Vichy. All the French would receive at present was permission to move bombs and munitions from the *Metropole* to North Africa and to keep their air squadrons up to strength with airplanes stocked in North Africa.[58] The political concession of a colonial guarantee was as out of the question now as ever, and the Foreign Ministry remained noncommittal with the French on this point.[59] Laval dejectedly reported on 27 September that the Germans were unbending and that neither Axis power wished to see France become an associated power.[60]

The French were successful in one aspect of their endeavors—the issue of the German control commission in Africa. It will be recalled that the Germans in late September were setting up the mixed control commission for the French African Atlantic coast and French Equatorial Africa, and that Berlin had sent two preliminary commissions for a tour of Morocco and Senegal. The economic commission, headed by Consul-General Schellert, arrived in Casablanca on 23 September, and the other commission under Luftwaffe lieutenant colonel Erdmann, whose secret task it was to evaluate the possibility of German air bases, arrived unannounced three or four days later.[61] Both were to continue to Dakar after their missions in Morocco were complete. The French authorities were suspicious of the Erdmann commission from the start due to inconsistencies in German lies concerning its function. Stülpnagel had told the French delegation in Wiesbaden that the Erdmann commission's charge lay merely in making contact with Schellert's group and the Italian inspectors in Morocco and that it would consist of no more than three men. Yet Erdmann told Noguès upon his arrival in a Focke-Wulf 200 with a commission of six officers that his job lay in examining the extent of the British political influence in French Africa. The chances appeared good that neither German agency was telling the truth, especially since Stülpnagel was very quick to reaffirm the mission's innocuous nature when the French confronted him with the inconsistency.[62] Baudouin, Noguès, Boisson, and Weygand, now delegate-general of the French government in Africa, were all determined after the Dakar raid that both commissions return to Europe immediately without going to Dakar due to the political effect that the trip would have there. The French Foreign Ministry cabled Wiesbaden on 25 September that the German officials in Casablanca could not go to Dakar.[63] In Morocco, Noguès had a difficult time with both commission heads and especially Erdmann, who was determined to take his reconnaissance mission to Dakar. On 27 September, Erdmann insisted on flying to Dakar immediately, even offering to go in civilian dress in a French airplane if need be. Yet Baudouin and Huntziger held firm. Noguès was ordered to prohibit the trip, and on 27 September the German Foreign Ministry and Armistice Commission ordered both commissions to return to Europe. Erdmann's group reluctantly returned to Europe from Casablanca on the morning of the twenty-ninth, and Schellert's followed soon after.[64] The Germans, also at the request of the French government, postponed the dispatch of the mixed control commission indefinitely.[65] Although Stülpnagel would continue his preparations for the mixed control commission well into October 1940, it would never travel to Africa in that form due to the French arguments during and after the Dakar incident.[66] Still, the Germans did not leave Morocco empty-handed. The Erdmann commission had garnered much information on the airfields near Casablanca and judged very favorably the possibilities for the stationing of Luftwaffe units there.[67]

On the whole, however, the French had gained little from Germany. Permission to send some munitions from the *Metropole* to replenish depleted stocks and the delay in German visits to French Africa did not mean a fundamental policy shift, and though the German High Command wanted to go further, Hitler remained skeptical. Hitler would soon move closer to the idea shared by his military subordinates that Germany should allow the French to defend their empire. Yet this shift in view came less from the French defense at Dakar than from the intransigence of Franco's Spain. To Hitler, the Dakar episode had been orchestrated in Washington as a ploy to gain bases in West Africa. It was too late to do anything about Dakar for the time being. It would have to stand or fall on its own. However, German bases in the Atlantic islands, particularly the Canaries, would protect the next presumed target, Morocco, while allowing Germany the possibility to reach the Portuguese archipelagoes as well. Dakar's immediate significance meant renewed approaches to Spain.

Madrid's ardor to enter the war on Germany's side had become stronger, not weaker, as a result of Dakar. Franco, Beigbeder, Serrano, and any other Spaniard with an eye on Northwest Africa held a pathological fear of de Gaulle ever since the coup in Equatorial Africa. Should de Gaulle succeed with a coup in Morocco, where French land, air, and sea power still outweighed that of the Spaniards, Spain would face not only the evaporation of its imperial dream but a possible threat to the Spanish zone as well. In the first week of September, Beigbeder had nervously predicted to Stohrer that French Morocco would fall to de Gaulle within two weeks. He pushed Italy and Germany for accelerated French disarmament and pushed Vichy for measures against British propaganda, noting that events there could bring Spain into the war at any time.[68] The British stance toward Madrid during the Dakar attack did little to assuage Spanish nerves. On the second day of the attack, Ambassador Hoare handed Beigbeder a note, which stated that the attack on Dakar was a self-contained operation that would not continue toward French Morocco, but the note was quick to point out that "if General de Gaulle establishes himself at Dakar . . . a spontaneous and successful Free French Movement in Morocco may automatically follow, which neither His Majesty's government nor General de Gaulle himself could check."[69] The latter possibility alarmed Franco's government. The government-controlled press blasted the British and de Gaulle while labeling Vichy's position in Africa as untenable. The press also rejected the notion that Vichy was now a participant in the war. The drift was that Spain itself should undertake the security tasks that Vichy could not fulfill.[70] Franco was now thinking of a ten-year Spanish alliance with Germany, whose value to Berlin would increase with recent events. "There is no doubt in the alliance," he wrote to Serrano on 24 September after discussions with his council of state, and he reckoned that the current war could be a long one. Serrano was to continue negotiations in Berlin and reach written agreements on mutual obligations regarding equal partnership between Germany and Spain, with the latter responsible for the defense of the southwest and with German aid arriving only as requested. Madrid, meanwhile, would keep London in the dark as long as possible.[71]

Yet when Serrano met with Ribbentrop on 24 September, it was clear that the Germans had other ideas.[72] Ribbentrop said that Berlin was watching the situation in Dakar closely and "with the necessary mistrust," and agreed that an alliance treaty could be signed while Serrano was still in Berlin, with separate protocols dealing with German aid, the date of Spanish entry into the war, and the promise of Morocco to Spain, "with certain reservations." The issue of bases, however, remained the sticking point. Serrano repeated Franco's arguments: Germany could trust Spain. Franco's loyalty was born not of opportunism but was rather an "eternal reality," and he would always share his bases with an ally. Spain, meanwhile, would defend its own bases as it was doing with the Canary Islands, which had recently received fighter planes and artillery from Spain's battleships. Ribbentrop commented that there was no mistrust involved; the issue was simply one of future German needs. Germany would have an empire in central Africa and would need to protect the entire area against the Americans—a foe that had made "extraordinary progress." The Reich had to make thorough defense preparations as soon as possible, and "with all respect for the Spanish army's bravery, present wars are won by those who have the best technical equipment and who . . . have prepared materially for the struggle for decades." The sharing of the Northwest African bases in the context of an alliance that Franco had suggested would not work in the transatlantic struggle that Hitler foresaw. If the Spaniards were to keep the bases and then call on German help at the moment of attack, too much time would already have passed. Germany needed its own bases; the "construction of ports, buildings, airport installations, and similar material preparations for defense would have to be completed long in advance, during peacetime." Ignoring Serrano's suggestion of joint preparation of the bases under continued Spanish ownership, Ribbentrop now moved from the abstract to the concrete. What had Franco said with regard to the cession of one of the Canary Islands to Germany? Serrano answered that it had not been within his authority to ask Franco such a question. Still, he had done so in an unofficial way, and in the same unofficial way, Franco had refused. Ribbentrop then pressed Serrano on the possibility of ceding to Germany Fernando Po and Spanish Guinea. Serrano refused and then raised the Spanish counterclaim in Spanish Guinea. Ribbentrop then moved on to Agadir and Mogador. Serrano stated that although mineral concessions in Morocco to Germany were negotiable, German enclaves were not. The German foreign minister was beside himself. Clearly disappointed over his lack of success, he noted testily that there remained much for Berlin and Madrid to iron out. He suggested that Madrid reconsider its position, since Spain's recent opportunities had come only due to German success and because, "a great Spain can only be made possible through final German victory."

Ribbentrop's failure sat poorly with Hitler, whose disappointment likely increased with the 25 September receipt of the latest tirade by von Bötticher in Washington. The United States, warned the military attaché, was pursuing a "large-scale imperialist policy in the Atlantic" and the "intention [was] to bring the western parts of Africa under the influence of the United States." Here, Washington was calling the tune and London was dancing. "It is characteristic of the conceit of the Americans," wrote von Bötticher, that "the United States pushes the interpretation of the Monroe Doctrine [while claiming] the right to look around for bases in West Africa."[73] If Germany wanted bases in the East Atlantic for the future, events seemed to suggest, it would have to move soon.

Hitler had one last try with Serrano later on 25 September. He again explained his theories, this time under the cloud of the Dakar episode, the outcome of which was still unknown in Berlin and which to Hitler underscored the need for bases in the Atlantic islands. Britain, he said, was acting as the agent of American imperialism, and anything the British conquered would devolve to the United States. Such a development could occur not only with Dakar but with the Moroccan coast and the all-important island groups as well, and one could not count on the French and Portuguese troops in these areas to fight a British takeover. "If England could somehow get a foothold on these island groups," warned Hitler,

> there was the danger that it would then invite America to establish itself there. Lately, the English had given up so many bases of their own that it would be easy for them to give away territories of other countries. . . . England alone was not to be feared anymore. . . . The British Empire possibly would disintegrate, and its

*parts would drag America into the conflict. Here, however, was
the problem which was decisive beyond the present war for the
whole future, whether and to what degree it would also be possible in the future to keep the Anglo-Saxon world coalition from
Europe and Africa. This was also a question of principle, for if
the Anglo-Saxons gained a foothold on any one point (for instance on the islands located off Africa and Europe) the European Monroe Doctrine would be finished. But this very thing was
the important counterpart to the American Monroe Doctrine
and must include Europe and Africa. From this point of view
of the outcome of the struggle for Dakar was of decisive importance.*[74]

Hitler cursed the French for not accepting his "offer" in July for German air
groups stationed in the area of Casablanca, which would have made that
area invulnerable to British threat. He then demonstrated to Serrano the
defensive possibilities offered by German dive-bombers if stationed on the
African coast and on the offshore islands. Here, perhaps due to the negative
stance of the Spaniards on a German base in the Canary Islands, Hitler
began to focus entirely on the Portuguese islands. Serrano suggested that
the Berlin-Rome-Madrid Axis could perhaps include Lisbon, but Hitler skep-
tically noted that the British would seize the Portuguese islands once talks
between Berlin and Lisbon began, and that Germany could solve the issue
only by military operations.

    Little changed before Serrano left Berlin. Later on the twenty-fifth in a
meeting with von Stohrer, Serrano allowed for tremendous mining concessions to the Germans in French Morocco and even on the Spanish mainland. But Madrid would not budge on the issue of bases. Spain, he said,
would make defensive preparations in Morocco itself and share them with
Germany when necessary. Stohrer's argument that Spain could not expect a
new empire for free fell on deaf ears, and the ambassador reported to Ribbentrop that German territorial aims in Spanish colonial areas could be
won only by force.[75] Serrano's only territorial concession was the waiver of
Madrid's claim to the extension of Spanish Guinea, but the remainder of the
Spanish territorial demands remained on his departure on 27 September,
including the entirety of Morocco.[76]

    In the next two days, Hitler would lose his taste for an exclusive ar-
rangement with the Spaniards and slowly adopt the idea of greater collaboration with France. As late as his final meeting with Serrano on 25 September,

Hitler still hoped for an arrangement with Spain. He remained willing in this meeting to hand the Spaniards Oran and French Morocco, minus bases there. His continued distrust for Vichy was clear in his comment to Serrano that the Atlantic islands were essential because "France would never forgive the territorial transfers to Spain, Italy, and Germany which would be imposed on her, and would be willing to act with any non-European power against her conquerors." Hitler also mentioned to Serrano on the twenty-fifth that he wished to take up the issue of Northwest Africa with Franco personally. Spain was still to be Germany's junior partner in the southwest. The idea of working more closely with France was suggested by the Naval Command, which had been impressed with the defense of Dakar, and which suddenly viewed France as a crucial junior partner in the ever-lengthening war against Britain. Gibraltar and Suez both remained key objectives, and the Luftwaffe would still have to secure the Canary Islands to keep the Royal Navy away. Yet Raeder and his cohort now called for an African addendum to their Mediterranean strategy. By working with Vichy, Germany could deprive Britain of a foothold in Northwest Africa. Germany could set up air bases in Casablanca, and the French with the *Strasbourg* group could even push the British from Freetown, which would eliminate convoy activities in that region. This step would facilitate the "great operative aim" of expelling the British from the Mediterranean. The navy, in a complete reversal of their stance after Mers-el-Kebir, was willing to overlook future political complications. Germany could fix the peace terms in advance and shove aside any problems caused by Italy in this regard. But there was "no more time to lose. . . . Whatever can be done by Germany to strengthen the will to resist and the defense preparedness of the French in their colonies should in the opinion of the Naval Command be done. . . . The attack on Dakar is only the beginning of a far-reaching English political plan for Africa which is possibly being executed in agreement with Roosevelt. . . . The prevention of the English and possibly the Americans from establishing themselves in the West and North African areas must now stand in the foreground of German considerations."[77]

Raeder brought up the issue with Hitler on 26 September, the day after Hitler's final meeting with Serrano. The grand admiral advocated an early territorial settlement with Vichy, with Berlin playing honest broker for Spanish and Italian claims in Morocco and Algeria.[78] Hitler agreed with Raeder's wish to keep the British and Americans from Northwest Africa but was not yet ready to accept the grand admiral's drastic political remedies. In fact the Führer, taken aback by Spain's inflexibility and France's apparent loyalty, was in a brief state of flux. For now, he did not believe, as Raeder did, that a modus vivendi could arise between France and Spain that would allow participation by both. He would have to choose between Spain and France, and for the first time he began to lean toward France because, as he put it, "Spain demands much (French Morocco) and offers little." The Führer mentioned that in such a case Germany and Italy would have to discuss peace terms and territorial cession in advance. Yet at the same time, Hitler could not bring himself to trust the French or write off the Spaniards completely. He stated that the *Strasbourg* group would remain in Toulon, he still felt that a meeting with Franco was a strong possibility, and he mentioned that Spanish cooperation would mean the securing by the Luftwaffe not only the Canaries, but the Azores and Cape Verdes as well. Hitler remained firm on the need to beat the Americans in the race for the strategic pearls of the East Atlantic, but his means of fulfilling this need were in a brief yet confusing time of transition.

The problem of supposed American aggression in the Atlantic received a partial solution on 27 September when Ribbentrop, Ciano, and Japanese ambassador Saburo Kurusu signed the Three Power Pact in Berlin. The agreement's aim was obvious from its terms. It would present the United States with a threat to its Pacific flank and thus discourage American intervention in the Atlantic theater. Article 3 stated that Germany, Italy, and Japan would "undertake to assist one another with all political, economic and military means when one of the three contracting parties is attacked by a power at present not involved in the European War or in the Sino-Japanese Conflict." Since Article 5 contained a disclaimer with regard to the Soviet Union, the meaning of the published treaty was entirely clear.[79]

An immediate solution in the Atlantic to the problem of America was much stickier. Two days after the signing of the Three Power Pact, Hitler held a long discussion with Ciano in which he revealed his latest thoughts on the matter. He had now begun to lean more toward Vichy than toward Madrid, for he had clearly become disgusted with the Spaniards in the span of the past few days. He cynically listed all of the Spanish demands, and then noted that all Germany would gain in return was Spain's "friendship" and "good graces." Hitler had now decided that he might not bother to meet Franco for a face-to-face discussion after all, since he was not sure if the Spaniards had "the same intensity of will for giving as for taking." And what if the French were to learn that they would lose Morocco to Spain? Would the French not then make an arrangement with the British, with North Africa falling into the hands of the latter? Such a contingency would make necessary Axis military involvement in French North Africa via the Iberian Peninsula, in which case Madrid might pull back into its shell of neutrality. Moreover, if the Spaniards were to occupy French Morocco and the British then attacked, continued Hitler, Madrid would only call for German and Italian aid, and the Spaniards would no doubt "let the tempo of their civil war prevail in their military measures." All in all, an arrangement with Spain could cost the Axis a great deal in money, materials, and blood, without reciprocity coming from Madrid. "It would be more favorable for Germany," he continued, "if the French remained in Morocco and defended it against the English." Yet despite his resentment toward Madrid, Hitler had for now arrived at no firm decisions on how best to proceed. He wished to speak with Mussolini on these issues. Ciano, who had also grown cynical with regard to Spain, concurred that the matter needed close discussion.[80] Thus, the stage was set for the 4 October meeting at the Brenner between Hitler and Mussolini, in which the Führer would finally unveil a scheme for bringing Vichy and Madrid under one roof for his aims in Northwest Africa. This very scheme would take Hitler to Montoire and Hendaye later in that month.

What was the meaning then, of Serrano Suñer's journey to Berlin? Nearly all of the prerequisites for an agreement between Spain and Germany existed in principle. Franco might have preferred to enter the war at the moment of the "last cartridge," but he was prepared to accept a long war and a long commitment for the sake of Morocco. The Germans, meanwhile, were willing to give the Spaniards almost everything they wanted. Ribbentrop mentioned on more than one occasion a written protocol that promised Gibraltar, French Morocco, and Oran to Spain, and Berlin was also willing to go a long way toward meeting Madrid's sizable economic demands. True, there existed the normal haggling by Ribbentrop over fuel and grain deliveries, and the German economic experts made certain adjustments in quantities for certain goods after an examination of the Spanish demands. Yet Hitler, as he had stated in late August and early September, was determined that economic issues form no obstacle to an arrangement, and the German Foreign Ministry accordingly promised the Spanish economic commission then in Berlin that Germany would fill Spain's most urgent requirements, as defined by mutual agreement. The Spanish figures from August had been, by Madrid's own admission, maximum demands anyway.[81]

It would appear, then, that the *major* problem in the prospective alliance was the issue of bases. The statements by Franco and Serrano in the second half of September 1940 show that they were willing to buy German goodwill with ten years worth of military responsibilities on Europe's south-western flank and with tremendous mineral concessions in French Morocco and Spain as well. The Spaniards were not pleased with this latter concession but accepted it as the price of empire. Yet Franco drew the line at the cession of Spanish territory, present or future. It was primarily on this issue that the German-Spanish alliance tumbled. To Franco, an alliance meant that the Germans could share Spanish bases in wartime. To Hitler, Germany needed bases of its own for future global struggle, which it could develop to the technological state of the art. Here there could be no sharing.

This analysis of Serrano's Berlin trip delivers the focus back to the fundamental reason for Hitler's interest in Spain. Was it Gibraltar's maritime significance for the elimination of Great Britain from the western Mediterranean? After the failure of the September negotiations with Serrano, Hitler became fond of complaining that the Spaniards were offering Germany nothing but their good graces in return for the sacrifices Berlin was to make. Hitler spoke with such conviction that it is easy to overlook the absurdity of his argument. Economically, Spain offered the Germans ownership of all French mining businesses in French Morocco and joint ownership of nearly twenty British and French mineral concerns in Spain, with all production not necessary for Spanish consumption to go to Germany. Moreover, the Spaniards said that they would be able to pay the civil war debt to Germany in five or six years.[82] Most important, Franco offered to Hitler something so obvious that it was easily forgotten in the face of everyone's postwar planning—the chance to take Gibraltar and eliminate the British from the western Mediterranean! Here was an offer of far more than Spain's good graces alone. For Hitler, however, such was not the case. His reason for including the Spaniards was less the maritime aim of expelling the Royal Navy from the Mediterranean and more a settlement over Northwest Africa. Gibraltar was still a component of this picture, but the necessity of Gibraltar's capture would wax and wane depending on Hitler's degree of trust in the French. If Germany could work with Vichy in Northwest Africa, then Gibraltar's importance would fade in Hitler's eyes. A diversionary, peripheral move against Great Britain was never enough by itself to pull Hitler into the Iberian Peninsula. This reading of the facts explains Hitler's complaints on the lack of Spanish reciprocity.

Probably in full recognition of the reaction of the armed forces should they become aware of his priorities in the matter of Spanish cooperation, Hitler excluded the military establishment from the discussions with Serrano. The Naval Command, which had been the most fervent advocate of the

Gibraltar operation, had little idea how the talks were progressing and at one point even blamed Spanish hesitations on economic factors alone.[83] Yet Jodl sensed that Spain's entrance into the war would hinge on politics, and in an astute analysis of the situation on 25 September, he noted the following: "The discussions with Spanish Minister of Interior Serrano Suñer . . . were devoted to general political questions. . . . Direct questions of joint conduct of the war were not discussed . . . so that the foundation for close military cooperation with Spain and Italy in the Mediterranean do not yet exist."[84] Though the issue of Spanish participation and an assault on Gibraltar would remain alive into the following year, Jodl's statement would one day make a fitting obituary for German-Spanish military cooperation in the Second World War.

Chapter 6

October Illusions

❧

Nothing can be done with these people.
—Adolf Hitler

These people are intolerable. . . .
—Francisco Franco

October 1940 witnessed the climax in Hitler's design for a base network in Northwest Africa. In the first week, he devised a scheme for the region into which he hoped German, Italian, French, and Spanish claims could all fit together. German and Italian aims would remain untouched. France would still lose territory in Africa but would receive some compensation from the British Empire after the peace. Spain would receive no more than Germany could take painlessly from France. Neither Spain nor France would learn the full extent of their compensation until after the war. Here was the "grand deception" by which Hitler hoped to forge a solution to the African jumble that his aims in the southwest had created. But could Hitler convince Pétain and Franco to cooperate? In mid-October he traveled to Montoire and Hendaye to find out. The results of the western rail journey were, in Hitler's mind, favorable. Yet there were fundamental problems with the Führer's settlement of affairs, primarily because his would-be allies winced at plunging into the unknown without concrete assurances on their futures. In the end then, it was the grand deceiver who deceived himself.

In the days following Serrano Suñer's disappointing visit to Berlin and the French defense of Dakar, there was much to recommend an arrangement with France to the exclusion of Spain. In his meeting with Ciano of 29 September, Hitler hinted that he would rather have the French defend Morocco than the Spaniards and that Germany's future in the southwest might be

better protected by the former for the time being. The French had promoted
this notion for months and amplified their efforts after Dakar. The German
commissioners who had met Noguès in Morocco during the Dakar attack
came away convinced that the French armed forces stood prevailingly behind Pétain rather than de Gaulle and that even though Noguès was anti-
German, he would fight any British or Gaullist transgressions.[1] The French
also took what measures they could to reinforce Northwest Africa. The six
Senegalese battalions that the Italians had approved in early September re-
sumed their transport to Dakar via Casablanca after the British raid and
were joined by three further colonial battalions from North Africa.[2] The
French also moved considerable airpower from Algeria to Morocco in the
days following the attack and received permission from the Germans to
replenish *Richelieu*'s munitions from stocks at Brest.[3]

This French stance during and after the Dakar episode struck German
command agencies in a very positive way, and the possibility of military
cooperation with the French seemed promising. The most thorough petition
came from General von Stülpnagel in a lengthy personal report to Warlimont.[4]
Stülpnagel had become convinced by the navy's argument for a peripheral
strategy against the British Empire and by the navy's concern that an extension of the war in time frame and geography would make American intervention more likely. The war, said Stülpnagel, would become a struggle
between Europe and the Anglo-Saxons. Here the Mediterranean and Africa
would play decisive roles, and the disposition of French Africa would be
pivotal. If the region were to join Britain and de Gaulle, a new and difficult
theater of war would open. Yet if it remained loyal to Vichy, there were
numerous possibilities. At worst it would remain neutral. At best, it would
add offensive options to the German war effort. Casablanca and Dakar
offered tremendous advantages in the supply war against Britain, and the
capture of Gibraltar, Malta, Bathurst, and Freetown would become possible
as well. Stülpnagel believed that Pétain would actively aid the German effort in French Africa if France were to receive assurances regarding its postwar imperial fate. The territorial bill for the war would then be assumed by
London after Britain's defeat. Warlimont received these ideas with favor.
Only a few days before, armed with maps and charts on France's military
strength and logistical capabilities in Africa, he had enthusiastically raised
similar possibilities with Jodl. French military involvement in the *Metropole,*
said Warlimont, was out of the question. But active cooperation in Africa
and Syria was possible, and a new political and military relationship with
Vichy was thus desirable. The Armistice Commission could move to Paris

for tighter liaisons with the French military, and the previously planned control agencies for Africa could become liaison staffs, which would retain their supervisory functions in a circumspect manner.[5]

The High Command dismissed Italy's wariness of collaboration with France. Mussolini, as he would soon tell Hitler at the Brenner, felt that de Gaulle had played his last card at Dakar and that Vichy was attempting to stumble onto the winning side of the war.[6] The Italian Armistice Commission in Turin mirrored Mussolini's views, particularly on the issue of French Mediterranean naval disarmament. It will be recalled that on 1 September the Italian Armistice Commission in Turin reinstated naval disarmament for their supervisory areas. They set a deadline of 30 September, and the Germans maintained the suspension of naval disarmament in their own control areas. During the Dakar crisis, the Italians extended their deadline to 15 October. The French wanted general resuspension of naval and air disarmament along with permission to keep the *Strasbourg* group battle ready and to conduct naval exercises around Toulon.[7] Although the Italians were working on a plan for a 100,000-man French army in North Africa in early October, a decision on the French navy did not follow until the twelfth of that month— three days before Turin's disarmament deadline, and the Italians exempted only the *Strasbourg* group from disarmament.[8] The episode irritated the German military agencies, which complained that Rome was trying to destroy France's Mediterranean power so that Italy could take Corsica and Tunisia.[9] In his pitch for German-French cooperation in the Mediterranean and Africa, Warlimont pointed out that Italy would have to refrain from their irritating demands for French disarmament.[10]

The German military's desire for cooperation with the French discussed the exclusion of not only the Italians but the Spaniards as well. Here was a difficult problem, since German military and naval circles still valued an attack on Gibraltar and feared a British occupation of the Canary Islands. Stülpnagel shied away from the complicated issue of how Berlin could bring Madrid into an arrangement with France, and the Naval Command blithely hoped that Germany could play "honest broker" in Morocco between French and Spanish objectives. The High Command was not sure that an arrangement was possible at all. By the first of October, Jodl had become aware of the unsatisfactory results of the Serrano mission to Berlin and noted that due to Madrid's lofty demands, Germany could shelve the plans for Gibraltar for the time being. Should the capture of Gibraltar become necessary later, continued Jodl, a joint German-Italian-French air strike on the Rock would be preferable.[11]

Yet solutions that favored France exclusively did not sit well with Hitler. Though Vichy's willingness to defend Northwest Africa and the offensive possibilities that French cooperation offered there were attractive, Hitler could not bring himself to trust Vichy completely, especially in North Africa where its armed forces were strongest. Italy, despite its weakness, was an ally whose desires would not be ignored. Franco, despite Hitler's irritation with him, was also needed, for the Strait of Gibraltar offered the quickest route to Africa, from where Germany could monitor French activities from Spanish Morocco. Hitler also wanted bases in Northwest Africa and in the outlying islands for after the war. Vichy had rejected this idea in July and Spain had rejected it in September, but cooperation with Vichy combined with a German presence in Spanish Morocco could change the disagreeable nature of both. Yet all expected rewards in Africa. France wished to keep its empire while Italy and Spain hoped to expand theirs. Hitler would thus have to cajole Vichy into defending French Africa, while maintaining Italy's claims, while also bringing Spain into the war in order to secure the easiest route to Africa. A reconciliation of everyone's aims in Africa was no easy matter. Hitler predicted that it would be possible only by means of a "grand deception."[12] Actually, the solution to the colonial problem that emerged was a rather careful mixture of truth and silence, as the Führer would explain it to Mussolini on 4 October in a crucial meeting at the Brenner, which Ciano would label "the most interesting of all that have taken place so far."[13]

Hitler opened the discussion by noting that the Axis had already won the war against Britain and that the United States could furnish the British with nothing more than modest material deliveries. The Three Power Pact with Japan would keep the possibility of active American intervention at a minimum, and victory was a matter of time. Still, cautioned Hitler, a swift end to the war was desirable "for various reasons." One can assume that these "various reasons" concerned Hitler's oft-stated worry that in a long war, Britain's empire and possible conquests in Northwest Africa would devolve to the United States. Here was an uncomfortable thought, given Hitler's intention to turn his back on the region during the eastern campaign. A swift peace with London was needed, said Hitler, and to this end the Axis needed to reconsider its relationship with Madrid and Vichy. He then announced to Mussolini that a European bloc involving Germany and the Latin states would force the British to the peace table. This comment deserves a close analysis. Although Hitler clothed his argument in the need to fight England with a "European coalition," his objectives indeed spanned beyond the present war. No sooner had the Führer proclaimed the need for a coalition than he berated the capabilities of the Spaniards while warning that one could never trust the French, who were of Gallic blood and had attacked Germany twenty-nine times in the last three centuries. Did Hitler really believe that a coalition with these countries would lead to a fruitful result? Or were the roles of Spain and France in this "coalition" to be confined to more limited tasks which served particular German aims? The fact remained that Hitler was still convinced that Germany could defeat Britain alone by direct attacks on England, whereas at the Brenner, Hitler was completely consumed with the issue of Northwest Africa, both in regard to its protection from a British or American strike in a prolonged conflict and in regard to its development for global warfare following Britain's defeat. French and Spanish cooperation were important for *these* issues. Hitler's proposal, then, was not so much for a coalition but rather for a temporary arrangement that would settle the issue of Northwest Africa in Germany's favor.[14]

Hitler assured the apprehensive Italians that Axis claims on France would remain unaffected by any arrangement with Vichy. Germany would still presumably have Alsace-Lorraine and central Africa, and Italy would still get Nice, Corsica, Tunisia, and French Somaliland. Spanish claims, however, would have to suffer. If the French were to learn that they would lose Morocco and Oran to their nonbelligerent neighbor, the French army there would join de Gaulle and necessitate an Axis reconquest, which would stand or fall on Madrid's questionable willingness to allow German troops through Spain. Public knowledge of the cession of Morocco could moreover prompt a British occupation of the Canaries before Germany could occupy them. In short, promises to Madrid could lead to an Allied takeover of the strategic areas that Hitler wanted. Thus, Germany could make none. At best, a German promise could come only if Germany could station dive-bombers within 350 kilometers of possible British landing points. How, then, could the Axis gain Spain's cooperation for Gibraltar's capture *while* convincing the French that they should continue to defend Northwest Africa? Hitler reasoned as follows: It would perhaps be possible to convince Vichy to cede a *portion* of French Morocco to Spain if France were to receive a prize such as British Nigeria in return. The Spaniards would simply have to be told that they would receive but a part of French Morocco for their troubles and that they would not receive Oran at all. Here was a territorial arrangement that Hitler felt could satisfy everyone, especially Germany. The French would continue to guard the Northwest African coast, and Hitler did not exclude the possibility that they could also reconquer the areas lost to de Gaulle. Germany, meanwhile, could monitor the French from vantage points in Spain or in Spanish Morocco after taking Gibraltar. Hitler was vague on the possibilities left open should he not be able to bring Spain and France under the same tent, but he inferred that Germany would work with France instead of Spain, and thus forgo an attack on Gibraltar. The stability of Northwest Africa was for now the paramount objective.[15] As for the *postwar* developments in Northwest Africa, Germany would attain the bases that it wanted regardless of who kept which part of Morocco. Hitler mentioned Agadir and Casablanca and announced that Germany would build drydocks, repair shops, oil stations, and fortifications. He ridiculed Franco's earlier argument that Germany would be able to share Spanish bases in the postwar world. "Germany," sneered Hitler, "was not interested in Spanish harbors . . . [it] needed bases of her own, already developed and equipped [by Germany] in peacetime." Mussolini and Ciano were rather surprised by Hitler's new policy as it touched France but were willing for the present to go along, so long as Italian claims remained untouched. The Duce warily emphasized that the Axis powers should never allow France to regain its strength, and he promised to remain vague with the Spaniards on the postwar disposition of Morocco. Thus, Hitler and his entourage left the Brenner in high spirits, and the Führer thereafter went to the Berghof from 5 through 9 October to think out the mechanics of the implementation of his arrangement.[16] Soon Hitler would take the "Brenner scheme" on the road to Montoire and Hendaye.

In the meantime, the concepts discussed at the Brenner were already receiving preliminary implementation with the French and the Spaniards. With France, this meant a slow yet perceptible strengthening of Northwest Africa. Immediately before and after the Brenner conference, the German Armistice Commission received orders from the High Command to avoid unpleasantness with the French delegation, since the issue of French defenses in Africa would soon receive a fundamental reevaluation favorable to Vichy.[17] The Italian Armistice Commission also demonstrated a shift in attitude after Mussolini's return to Rome.[18] Near the end of the month, the French Delegation in Turin submitted plans for a North African army of 100,000 men to a receptive Italian audience and received authorization for a number of light armored vehicles and medium-caliber artillery pieces for the 40,000 men in French Morocco.[19] Finally, the idea of the mixed control commission for Casablanca slowly became a dead letter. In the middle of

October, the German High Command postponed the issue indefinitely with the agreement of the German Armistice Commission and the restrained enthusiasm of Mussolini himself.[20]

The Spaniards were less happy with the new arrangements. On 1 October, Serrano Suñer had arrived in Rome for discussions with Mussolini and Ciano and wasted no time in blasting the Germans for their stinginess regarding Madrid's territorial demands. His comments had been damning enough for Ciano to delete them from the copy of the discussion record handed to Hitler at the Brenner a few days later.[21] Serrano waited in Rome while the Duce and Ciano traveled to meet Hitler at the Brenner, but the news from the conference on their return, such as Ciano was willing to give, only disappointed the Spaniard more. "Why," Ciano asked himself afterward, "hasn't he yet seen that the Germans have had an eye on Morocco for a long time?"[22] In spite of these disappointments, Franco remained hopeful that he could find an arrangement with Berlin that would bring Spain into the war and fulfill his territorial aims. Serrano wrote Ribbentrop on 10 October that he and Franco had discussed the Berlin negotiations extensively and that they would soon send economic counterproposals as well as proposals for a ten-year alliance between Madrid and Berlin.[23] Meanwhile, Spain strengthened its forces in the Canary Islands and in Spanish Morocco. Serrano mentioned on 10 October that Spain had installed in the Canary Islands four batteries, machine-gun nests, and fighter aircraft to preclude an Allied landing.[24] In the first days of October, the Spaniards moved two additional divisions to Spanish Morocco, bringing the troop strength there to more than seven Spanish infantry divisions.[25] One can gauge Franco's aims from these moves. First, he meant to strengthen the Canaries against an Allied landing attempt for the event of Spain's entry into the war while simultaneously showing Germany that its help in protecting the islands—help that Franco by now had reason to fear—was unnecessary. Second, Franco hoped to be ready for a variety of contingencies in Morocco. One might have been the protection of Ceuta or Tangier against a British strike. Another might have been a movement into the French zone should the Allies land there or should de Gaulle launch a coup. When Serrano announced to Ribbentrop the additional two divisions on 10 October, he stated in the next sentence that Franco suspected de Gaulle of preparing a revolt in Oran.[26]

The French, who were demobilizing their forces in North Africa, were alarmed by the Spanish buildup, especially given the absence of positive diplomatic contact with Madrid. On 30 September, Foreign Minister Baudouin had his ambassador in Madrid, Robert de la Baume, present to Beigbeder his proposal to settle the Moroccan border issue by implementing the border agreement of 1925. Baudouin also gave formal recognition to the Spanish fait accompli in Tangier. He had sensed correctly that Serrano's visit to Berlin had dealt extensively with Morocco and was determined, as he told Lequerica, that the Germans never have a hand in Moroccan affairs.[27] For good measure, on 5 October Baudouin appointed the Hispanophile François Piétri as the new ambassador to Madrid.[28] Yet the Spaniards made no response to Baudouin's overtures until mid-October, and even then Beigbeder rejected the French offer.[29] Perhaps more unsettling than Beigbeder's rejection of the French offer was the ouster of Beigbeder himself on 16 October and his replacement at the Foreign Ministry with Serrano Suñer, who was openly unfriendly to France.[30] The French used the only option still available. They complained to Berlin on several occasions about the Spanish buildup in Morocco, claiming that a Spanish advance into the French zone would be difficult to halt given French disorganization and would have incalculable effects elsewhere in the French Empire.[31] Although the French asked Berlin to use its influence with Madrid to bring a halt to whatever the Spaniards were planning, the Germans did nothing here to ease Vichy's concerns. Hitler, after all, believed he had found a political settlement that would obliterate such problems between the French and the Spaniards and was about to try and implement it.

Arrangements for Hitler's rail journey to meet with the French and Spaniards were made quickly. Hitler mentioned after the Dakar episode that he wanted to meet the ex–French ambassador to Berlin, André François-Poncet, or General Huntziger or even Pétain himself to discuss possible German-French cooperation.[32] On 12 October, the German ambassador in Paris, Otto Abetz, visited Hitler in Berlin and apparently convinced him that the best course lay in meeting the chief French officials, namely Laval and Pétain. Thus, Hitler would meet the French statesmen both on the way to and from a planned meeting with Franco at Hendaye.[33] On 20 October, Hitler's special train *Amerika* left Berchtesgaden, while Ribbentrop and his staff left from Berlin on the special train *Heinrich*. The journey that followed would cover over 6,000 kilometers. It truly speaks volumes for the importance of Northwest Africa in Hitler's eyes that, despite his narrow provincialism and despite his current dominance of the European continent, he would nonetheless undertake a journey of this scale to meet with the leaders of the comparatively weak Latin states, the trustworthiness and efficiency of which he so openly questioned.

The diplomatic preparations for the meetings with the French were slight,

presumably because Hitler wished to reach quick agreement on broad principles. There are certain clues to what Hitler wanted, however, in two memoranda prepared en route by Ribbentrop's staff: the first, a draft of a letter
from Ribbentrop to Laval, which the Germans never presented; the second,
a secret protocol draft postdated 24 October, which the Germans also did
not present.[34] Both emphasized a French contribution to the German war
effort in Africa, while containing vague assurances on France's future on
that continent. The French were to resist attempts to seize their territories
and were to allow Germany to use certain military resources for the prosecution of the war, which, since the Germans already controlled the Atlantic
coast of France, likely meant bases in Africa.[35] The demand that France
formally declare war on Britain in the draft letter was dropped in the protocol draft in lieu of a softer requirement that France would support Axis
measures aimed at the swift defeat of Britain within the scope of available
resources. In return, France would be allowed to deploy forces in Africa
over and above the stipulations of the armistice. France would also receive,
in the scope of an African colonial redistribution between itself, Germany,
Italy, and Spain, territorial compensations from the British Empire in Africa
so that, in terms of area, their African empire would remain essentially un-
changed. It has been argued, since these draft agreements were composed in
Ribbentrop's train and not Hitler's, that Hitler had nothing to do with the
drafts and that they lack significance.[36] Yet the authors of these drafts received their ideas from somewhere, and since the provisions of the drafts
closely mirrored Hitler's aims as discussed in the presence of Ribbentrop
with Mussolini and then with the French and Spaniards, one must assume
that Hitler had decisive influence.

Hitler held the initial discussion of his journey with Pierre Laval on the
evening of 22 October, fifty kilometers north of Tours in the rail station of
Montoire-sur-Loir.[37] He was less interested in detailed agreements than in
communicating his principles to Pétain. Laval, who was driven to Montoire
not knowing that he would speak with Hitler himself, did his best to steer
the latter toward a lenient peace, particularly in French Africa, which France
considered "an inalienable part of her own flesh and blood." Hitler countered that the colonial question would receive a more "European" solution
that would satisfy everyone's interests while providing for defensive preparations. In other words, France would sacrifice territory to nations that had
interests in Africa, and Germany would have bases on the northwestern
coast. The Führer stated cryptically that a solution would have to be found
that would "do justice" to the interests of all and would guarantee coopera-

tion in the "possible defense of [Africa] even in peacetime." And yet Hitler held out a thin thread of hope for France. Someone would have to pay for the war, and France could limit its own postwar suffering by adopting a firm line against Britain rather than a wait-and-see policy. Should Britain pay the territorial bill for the war, France could conceivably avoid "considerable diminution" of its African holdings, even if the aims of "third countries" were fulfilled at the peace. Laval correctly presumed that the "third countries" to which Hitler referred were Italy and Spain, and he stated the hope that territorial cessions could be avoided and French pride spared. France's pride, stressed the Führer at the end of the interview, could be spared only at Britain's expense. Hitler took pains with Laval to dance around the fact that France would lose considerable territory in Africa regardless of its stance and that British territory would serve to replace but a portion of the French territory lost to the Axis. Instead, he tried to lead Laval to believe that Britain would suffer most or all colonial losses if Vichy were to adopt the correct policy and that French holdings would remain essentially untouched. Yet Hitler's statement to Laval that France would "receive consideration commensurate with her importance, both in Europe and Africa," would have a different meaning in Berlin than in Vichy. Hitler wanted to put the French in a position whereby they could easily delude themselves, and Laval was willing to be deluded.

The German stop at Hendaye was a stickier affair than was the first Montoire meeting. The Spaniards, unlike the French, were not facing a Carthaginian peace and were less willing to clutch at straws. Since June, Madrid had wanted firm assurances rather than vague allusions for the future. Still, Franco was by most indications still willing to enter the war. He had moved Serrano to the Foreign Ministry on 16 October in a gesture that, if not purposely designed to impress Berlin, could not have had a negative effect.[38] He had also just rejected France's offer to adjust the Moroccan border according to the 1925 border agreement, assuming that he could get a better deal from Berlin. Finally, he had reinforced Spanish troops in the Canaries and in Spanish Morocco. He had become more, not less eager for a settlement with the Germans. Yet previous to the Hendaye meeting, neither he nor Serrano appreciated in the least that the Germans were interested in bringing France into the picture at Spain's expense. This ignorance persisted despite reports from Lequerica that the French rumor mill was speaking of a close Franco-German collaboration that would mean France's de facto entry into the war.[39]

Hitler's only face-to-face meeting with Franco was a tedious affair, beginning roughly at 3:30 P.M. and lasting three hours.[40] The Führer explained the situation that had made it necessary to bring Vichy and Madrid under a common roof. Britain's collapse was inevitable, he predicted, for Germany was pursuing the war against the English homeland with the utmost vigor. A threat from the United States was unlikely, for American military power would lack any teeth at all for eighteen months to two years. And yet, cautioned Hitler,

> There would arise a considerable danger if America and England established themselves on the islands lying off Africa in the Atlantic Ocean. The danger was all the greater because it was not certain whether the French troops stationed in the colonies would under all circumstances remain loyal to Pétain. The greatest threat existing at the moment *was that a part of the colonial Empire would, with abundant material and military resources, desert France and go over to de Gaulle, England, or the United States.* . . . The great problem to be solved at the moment *consisted in hindering the de Gaulle movement in French Africa from further extending itself and thereby establishing in this way bases for England and America on the African coast.*[41]

It was thus essential to strengthen the position of the Pétain government in the French colonies. The Axis needed to give some hope to the French regarding their empire, and this hope would have to come at the expense of Spain's territorial demands.[42] Spain would have to face the reality that its territorial rewards would not be as great as they would have been had there been no de Gaulle. Hitler went into no specifics on the issue of what Spain would get but the general meaning was clear. France was to be brought into the African equation to the detriment of Spain's future in Africa.[43]

Franco, who had opened the meeting with the statement that Spain would gladly enter the war, was shocked. He fully appreciated the Gaullist threat but had assumed that Spain would fight it rather than sacrifice its territorial future to it. He argued that his troops in Spanish Morocco could neutralize the Gaullist threat from Algeria or Tunisia, then launched into a lengthy discourse on Spain's historical claims in Morocco and Oran, while insisting on a formal agreement regarding these claims before Spain's entry into the war.[44] Hitler was visibly irritated, noting privately to Ribbentrop that "nothing can be done with these people."[45] Five days later, he would angrily state to Mussolini that he would prefer to have three or four teeth removed rather than suffer another interview with Franco.[46]

Ribbentrop did not fare much better with Serrano in a subsequent meeting of the foreign ministers, also on 23 October.[47] The new German policy had taken the Spaniards aback to such a degree that Ribbentrop, at the request of Franco and Serrano, had to explain once again the German position. He repeated Hitler's argument that the new solution was the only alternative to the possibility of French colonial secession and an expensive Axis reconquest of French North Africa. Serrano acidly noted that "evidently" Berlin was viewing the African issue in a new way. Franco, he said, had a plan for the eventuality of a French colonial secession. Ribbentrop ignored Serrano's arguments and presented him with a draft of what would become known as the Hendaye Protocol, a document that Hitler had already shown to Franco. The document consisted of six articles that covered the mechanics of Spain's entry into the war, as well as Madrid's adhesion to the Three Power Pact and the Rome-Berlin Alliance and Friendship Treaty of 1939. Serrano had few problems with most of the protocol, but raised strong objections to Article 5, which dealt with Spain's territorial rewards. It was vague in the extreme, stating that although Spain would get Gibraltar, it would receive parts of French Africa only to the extent that France could be compensated elsewhere.[48] Serrano noted aloud that France's aims in Africa were receiving a more sypathetic treatment than were Spain's. Yet Ribbentrop gave Serrano little comfort. Germany was trying to avoid a French colonial secession, which would harm everyone's interests, and the Spaniards would have to go along.

No firm agreement was reached. Hitler gave a dinner for Franco in his railroad car, during and long after which the dictators haggled over the same issues as before, with neither giving an inch.[49] An aggravated Hitler left Hendaye the same night. Ribbentrop remained, hoping to reach agreement with the Spaniards the next morning.[50] The Spaniards retired to San Sebastián for the night, reaching Franco's headquarters there around 2 A.M. Franco was angry and disappointed, having noted to Serrano earlier in the evening that the Germans were intolerable for expecting Spain to enter the war with no guarantees. "This new sacrifice of ours," he said privately, "would only be justified with the counterbalance of that which is to be the basis of our imperium. After the victory they would give us nothing if it is not agreed to now, despite what they are saying."[51]

The next morning, Serrano did what he could with Ribbentrop. To the latter's indignation, Serrano stayed in San Sebastián and sent Ambassador Espinosa to the German train with a supplementary economic protocol, which Serrano and his staff had written the night before. This document ostensibly dealt with the disposition of the French mineral resources in Morocco after the war, but these issues were not the important aspect of the document. The salient point was a statement that prescribed that Germany and Spain would begin negotiations as soon as possible on the raw material deposits in French Morocco—which according to this economic protocol was "later to belong to Spain." Ribbentrop took the copy of the document with him when he left Hendaye but did not sign it, thanks to the last phrase.[52] After Ribbentrop's departure, Serrano accepted a new and still-vague version of Article 5, which did not differ in principle from that presented by the Germans on the twenty-third.[53] Yet the Spanish position had not changed. The Spaniards held back official approval for the Hendaye Protocol as a whole, and since Article 4 of the protocol left the date of Spanish entry into the war to the joint agreement of Berlin, Rome, *and Madrid,* it was not a binding document for Spain anyway.[54] Moreover, the Spainiards wanted the Germans to agree to the supplementary economic protocol, which contained a promise for French Morocco. Serrano communicated his acceptance of Article 5 in a letter to Stohrer delivered by Espinosa and added an angry postscript that expressed, "the bitter feeling produced in both the *Caudillo* and myself by the fact that in spite of our friendship the trivial changes which we had suggested . . . which, without encroaching at all on the core of the problem or on the Führer's possibilities for negotiation, gave us a somewhat greater measure of security . . . were rejected."[55] Stohrer argued to Espinosa that the changes that the Spaniards had suggested on 23 October were hardly insubstantial. Espinosa simply expressed the hope that the Germans would sign the supplementary economic protocol without changes. The Spanish moves following the Hendaye meetings, which were augmented by unmistakable acrimony, should have been clear to the Germans. Spain insisted on a guarantee for French Morocco, and the chances of Spanish entry into the war were slim without it. Yet Hitler and Ribbentrop believed, as will be seen, that Serrano's hollow acceptance of Article 5 of the Hendaye Protocol, which seemed the chief bone of contention, had created the fundamentals of an agreement with Spain.

Hitler's meeting with Marshal Pétain on 24 October at Montoire would be far more harmonious than were the Hendaye meetings, for each leader had something that the other wanted. Pétain was determined to protect French Africa, and Hitler for the time being wanted it protected. Hitler meanwhile had opened a window on France's imperial future, and Pétain, the evening before his talk with Hitler, had demonstrated agreement with the principle of collaboration beyond the parameters of the Armistice Convention when he decided at Laval's behest not to bring Foreign Minister Baudouin to Montoire. How far Pétain was willing to go down this road was not yet clear, but Baudouin, who wished to hold to the letter of the Armistice Convention rather than plunge blindly into cooperation with the Germans, decided on the eve of the Montoire discussion that he had lost the struggle with Laval for the marshal's ear. A few days later he would resign his post, leaving Laval as foreign minister. In the meantime, it was Laval who would triumphantly accompany the marshal to Montoire.[56]

Hitler opened the discussion with Pétain at Montoire with an important and revealing statement that analysts of the meeting have completely ignored.[57] He said that he considered the meeting with Pétain as an answer to the marshal's letter of 17 July 1940—the *very same letter* that rejected the German demand for bases in Casablanca as beyond the Armistice Convention, and hinted that the demand could be resolved only through negotiation.[58] More than three months after the Casablanca demand, Hitler snatched the thread of negotiation that the marshal's letter had left hanging. Dakar, de Gaulle, and Franco had changed Hitler's mind, yet he was shrewd enough to abstain from specific demands. He mentioned nothing of a German presence in French Africa, and he remained cryptic on the issue of the territorial losses that France would suffer. The details could come later. Still, the Führer's meaning was clear throughout the conference—the visit to the marshal was about Northwest Africa. Hitler expected the French government to defend the area *and* to allow German bases there.

The Führer opened with the now-standard assurances that Germany would defeat the British on their own soil and that the United States could not save the British. Yet continuation of the war was costly, and France could lessen its heavy share of the costs by joining a "continental community" aimed at hastening London's defeat. Pétain, like Hitler, was more willing to discuss broad principles than specifics, yet he did state that he was in favor of cooperation, particularly if it could open a window for France on its empire. He cursed de Gaulle while stating that the French would never forget the attacks on Mers-el-Kebir and Dakar. The marshal gave no details but pledged that France would do everything to secure the empire, and noted that it was indeed in the colonies that "a field might be found where [cooperation] between [Germany and France] was a practical possibility." Laval happily chimed in with an analysis of Pétain's decision. France could not declare war, Laval said, but France could cooperate with Germany in the larger field of Africa by defending against British aggression. Such cooperation, argued Laval, was the same as active cooperation in the German war effort. Pétain confirmed that Germany and France could settle the details of cooperation on a case-by-case basis and noted that cooperation with Germany would mean a better future for France. Hitler agreed. Moreover, as will be seen, he understood Pétain's comments to mean that France would not only defend Northwest Africa, *but would allow German bases there as well.*[59]

Hitler and Ribbentrop left Montoire quite satisfied with the results of their western excursion. The French, it seemed, would go along with Germany's aims in Africa once the French government agreed on the line of cooperation announced by Pétain.[60] No one expected problems in this regard, especially after Laval's statement to Abetz on 26 October that those ministers opposed to the marshal's line would simply resign their posts. Laval also informed the German ambassador that he would soon meet with the French armed services chiefs to gather information on relative French and British strength in Africa and that the following week he would go to Paris with Huntziger to discuss military cooperation in Africa in greater detail.[61] The Germans were also satisfied with what they understood to be the results of the Hendaye meetings. Hitler and Ribbentrop believed that they had convinced Franco and Serrano that Spain alone could not halt a British-Gaullist incursion into French Morocco, and they also believed that Serrano's acceptance of Article 5 of the Hendaye Protocol had created the principles of cooperation between Madrid and Berlin.[62]

The German trains headed for Berlin after leaving Montoire but made an unexpected detour for Florence, where on 28 October Hitler and Ribbentrop met once again with Mussolini and Ciano.[63] Hitler had already planned to meet with the Duce, probably in early November, to discuss his rail journey. The reason for the detour was word of the imminent Italian attack on Greece and Hitler's hope to halt the ill-fated project. Hitler arrived in Florence at 11:00 A.M. on 28 August—five and a half hours after the Italians, without informing Berlin, attacked from their bases in Albania. The Italo-Greek war would soon bring disaster for the Italians in the eastern Mediterranean, which in turn would lead to German intervention in the region in the spring of 1941. Yet for the present, Hitler accepted the Italian step with poise.[64] He was far more preoccupied with selling his Northwest African scheme to Rome.

Hitler had to be especially persuasive in Florence, for the positions of

Mussolini and Ciano toward collaboration with France had hardened since the Brenner meeting, thanks to the fear that Rome's territorial demands on France would suffer should Berlin collaborate with Vichy. In a long letter of 19 October, the Duce had argued to Hitler that Vichy was in secret contact with de Gaulle and London and would only present the Axis with an expensive bill for its collaboration in the war. "With this attitude," cautioned Mussolini, "one cannot think of their collaboration. Nor should we seek it." Mussolini continued that the time had arrived for a separate peace with France, with Italy acquiring its "modest" territorial claims of Tunisia, Nice, Corsica, and French Somaliland. The Duce also raised doubts in his letter as to the wisdom of Spanish entry into the war, noting that the Spanish economy was still poor and that Spain was a card to be played only at the most opportune moment. Hitler received Mussolini's letter on 25 October, the day after the meeting with Pétain at Montoire, and thus doubtless realized that he would have to win Mussolini again to the scheme enunciated at the Brenner.[65]

Hitler's comments in Florence on the subject of Northwest Africa were thus extensive.[66] A difficult situation would emerge, he said, if Britain, "possibly as the vanguard of America," were to establish itself in Morocco, especially since Britain would possibly hand Morocco over to the United States. "The important thing now," said Hitler, "is to prevent the secession of Morocco from France, for since Spain could not on its own resources take a stand against it, such a procedure would force the Axis Powers, despite insufficient preparation, to press for Spain's immediate entry into the war, since that country was needed as a bridge to Africa in order to conquer Gibraltar, protect Spanish Morocco, and, if possible, anticipate the English there with such celerity that they could not seize any more air bases."[67] Cooperation with the French in Northwest Africa was essential, as was the provision of Vichy with some incentive to defend their territory. Spain, despite its hubris, would not be able to conquer the French zone should it break with Vichy and could conceivably lose Spanish Morocco as well. Hitler told Mussolini that he did not plan to ask the French to declare war, but he did want them to defend their African colonies. He also voiced the expectation that the French would make their air bases in Northwest Africa available to Germany. Hitler dismissed Mussolini's argument about French duplicity. He conceded that although he had once suspected a link between Pétain and de Gaulle, he now felt, after viewing the films of the fighting at Dakar and on hearing firsthand the marshal's invective against de Gaulle, that there was no such link. He had also been very impressed with Pétain

personally. Unlike Laval, whom Hitler saw as a "dirty democratic politi-
cian" who had steered toward collaboration out of opportunism, Pétain
had a decent and reliable character.[68]

Hitler did not bother to refute Mussolini's argument that the Axis should
place Spain's entry into the war on hold. Spain's participation was an inher-
ent part of the Moroccan question. Hitler told the Italians that he had been
unimpressed with Franco, who, though of stout heart, was of mediocre ability
and who had no sense for the limits of his own military strength. The Spaniards, he agreed, were unprepared for a war.[69] In addition, Franco's demand
for a guarantee for French Morocco and Oran could not be met by Germany without the risk of French colonial secession. Hitler stated confidentially
that Spain would receive no more than a "substantial enlargement of Spanish Morocco" and that, in the meantime, Madrid could receive no concrete
promises as to the final Northwest African territorial settlement, lest any
information leak to the French. Yet these obstacles were minor to Hitler.
The Gibraltar operation, executed by special German troops, would occur
with ease. Moreover, he and Ribbentrop were firm in the belief that they
had made the Hendaye Protocol fly. Thanks to his arrangements, Hitler
said, Germany would have its bases on the African coast, although he wist-
fully noted that he would still prefer one of the islands. The Führer noted
with confidence that Ribbentrop, Ciano, and Serrano could tie up the loose
ends of Spain's entry into the war and that the three dictators could then
meet in Florence to announce Spain's accession to the Three Power Pact and
the Rome-Berlin Axis. Mussolini was obliged to accede but still wanted a
peace settlement with Vichy to safeguard Italian claims on France. Hitler
promised that no settlement with the French would leave Italy's demands
unfulfilled, but he rejected the idea of a separate peace, since it would kill
French incentive to collaborate. As will be seen, Mussolini had not finished
arguing. The Germans would have a difficult time forcing the Italians to
cooperate with the French in North Africa.

For now, however, Hitler viewed his rail journey as a success. France
would defend Northwest Africa, Spain would allow Germany to attack
Gibraltar, and Germany would have bases on and off the Northwest African coast. A few days after his return to Berlin, Hitler gave to the High
Command the guidelines for his War Directive Number 18. General Warlimont's staff composed a draft by 7 November, and on the twelfth, Hitler
signed the final version of the directive.[70] The directive as it touched the
Northwest African region represents the apex of Hitler's expectations regarding German objectives. It contained a role for each of Hitler's prospec-

tive partners in the southwest. France would assume the role of a nonbelligerent. Its main task lay in the "defensive and offensive protection" of its holdings in Africa. France would also accept German military measures on French territory, and especially in its African colonies. This latter statement can refer to nothing but the bases in Northwest Africa that Hitler had wanted to create since July. The follow-up discussions to the Montoire meeting with Pétain, continued Hitler, would be the domain of the Foreign Ministry, which would work in close cooperation with the High Command. Once these discussions with Vichy were further under way, more detailed directions regarding cooperation with the French would follow.

Spain's role, according to the directive, would lie in cooperation with Germany in the military elimination of the British from Gibraltar, now codenamed Operation *Felix*. Spain's military role was clearly subordinate to that of the *Wehrmacht*. Germany's intelligence personnel would conduct the necessary reconnaissance of the area, the Luftwaffe would attack the British fleet at Gibraltar from bases in France, and German troops would cross the Spanish border, move through the Iberian Peninsula, and then take the Rock. Spanish cooperation in the assault on Gibraltar, then, would consist primarily of watching the Germans. All-important, however, was Spain's cooperation in securing the Canary Islands before the attack on Gibraltar. Here Hitler ordered that the naval and air force commands would study ways in which Germany could support Spanish measures.

Portugal had a role to play as well in Hitler's directive, although this role lay primarily in acquiescence with the German larceny of its Atlantic islands. Hitler was circumspect during his western trip with regard to his aims in the Portuguese archipelagoes, but he had certainly not forgotten their value, and with German projects turned toward the southwest for the winter, he fully meant to take the most important islands. The directive called for reports from the Naval Command and the Luftwaffe on the occupation of the Azores, the Cape Verde Islands, and Madeira. In order to choke off any complaints from Lisbon during such an operation, German mobile units would follow those designated for the Gibraltar assault into Spain and would execute a swift occupation of Portugal if need be.

The eighteenth war directive represented the high point of Hitler's expectations for Northwest Africa, and the notion that his aims in the region were part of a broad global strategy is not simply a matter of conjecture. Hitler was in fact quite vocal with regard to his aims. On the same day on which he signed the directive, he met with Soviet foreign minister V. M. Molotov and revealed a great deal. The United States, he argued, was helping Britain simply in order to grab the British Empire and to acquire bases for itself. He declared:

> *In the distant future it would be a question of establishing a great solidarity among those countries which might be involved in case of an extension of the sphere of influence of this Anglo-Saxon power, which had a more solid foundation, by far, than England. . . . It was not a question of the immediate future; not in 1945, but in 1970 or 1980, at the earliest, would the freedom of other nations be seriously endangered by this Anglo-Saxon power. At any rate, the Continent of Europe had to adjust itself now to this development and had to act jointly against the Anglo-Saxons and against any of their attempts to acquire dangerous bases.*

Therefore, Hitler stated, he was attempting to create a "Monroe Doctrine" of sorts for the whole of Europe and Africa between Germany, Spain, France, and Italy, wherein each would claim for itself only as much colonial territory as it could really use.[71] The next day, Hitler told Molotov that, to his mind at least, he had reconciled the colonial claims of all four interested parties, despite the difficulties. It had been especially trying, he said, to reconcile Spanish and French claims in North Africa, but "recognizing the greater future possibilities, both countries finally had given in."[72]

Yet in fact, Hitler had built the German position on the Northwest African coast on the loose sand of weak diplomacy. Within the month, all facets of Hitler's southwestern planning—the Portuguese, the Spanish, and the French—would erode, leaving the Germans with nothing to show for their grand projects of 1940 but scrap paper, unexecuted plans, and an unresolved situation in Africa. The following chapters will analyze the erosion.

Chapter 7

Winter Collapse I: Iberia

*The Führer is engaged with the question of
the occupation of the Atlantic Islands in
view of a future war against America.*
—Major Sigismund Freiherr von Falkenstein

The eighteenth war directive represented the zenith of Hitler's schemes for
the southwest. Yet it was based on the incorrect belief that he had reached
agreement with France and Spain and could strong-arm Portugal. German
diplomacy was faulty, and the desire to begin the eastern campaign the following spring placed a time limit on rectifying its shortcomings. In an as-
tonishingly short time, the house of cards Hitler built in Northwest Africa
would collapse. The next two chapters will cover the erosion of Hitler's
scheme, first by looking at Portugal and Spain, then by looking at France.

German thinking concerning the Portuguese Atlantic islands—Madeira,
the Cape Verde Islands, and the Azores—has received little scholarly attention. Those who claim that German war aims were exclusively European in
nature have written it off as a pipe dream that was fundamentally defensive
in nature.[1] Those who view Hitler's aims as global argue otherwise; that
Berlin thought seriously about occupying the islands and that German interest in the islands was offensive.[2] German thinking regarding the islands was
indeed serious, thanks to Hitler himself. Ever interested in Northwest Africa, Hitler became particularly concerned about the islands after the Destroyer-Base Deal of 3 September 1940. It was two days later that Hitler
first mentioned to Jodl that Germany would have to take the Azores, Cape
Verdes, and Canary Islands in order to forestall Britain or America.[3] German thinking on the issue was military, not diplomatic. Though willing to
accept a political arrangement with Lisbon if one were to fall from the sky,

Hitler never placed much faith in the possibility. Instead, he pressured the navy and the Luftwaffe against their better judgment to plan a strike. If such a strike never occurred, it was not for lack of interest.

Despite the authoritarian leanings of Dr. Antonio de Olveira Salazar, Portugal's chief of state, no one in Berlin seriously considered the possibility of recruiting Lisbon to the Axis. Portugal had an alliance with Great Britain dating to 1386 and had declared neutrality the day after war erupted in Europe. Hitler believed that any serious pressure from Berlin would prompt the British to occupy the Portuguese islands immediately.[4] A slight possibility seemed to exist during the summer of 1940 that Madrid could woo Lisbon into an Iberian alliance and away from Britain—a pet project of Serrano Suñer, which Franco supported. In March 1939, Spain and Portugal signed a treaty of friendship and nonaggression, which stated that neither government would allow the use of its territory by a third party against the other.[5] Although the preamble to the treaty said that it would not circumvent previous commitments, Serrano took the German victories of 1940 as the cue to sever Lisbon from London. Serrano and Franco pressed Portugal's ambassador, Dr. Pedro Teotónio Pereira, for a military alliance in late June and early July, suggesting that Britain or Germany could soon decide to occupy Portuguese territory.[6] Yet Salazar wanted no more than Iberian neutrality and presented the Spaniards with a draft protocol to the 1939 treaty that promised only mutual consultation to protect common interests.[7] Beigbeder acknowledged the offer on 2 July but was too occupied with French Morocco to engage in more than basic courtesies.[8]

The Germans became interested in a Luso-Spanish alliance once it appeared that a chance existed for one. On 3 July, Serrano informed Stohrer of his efforts and of a statement by Salazar that Portugal would resist any British encroachments.[9] Stohrer became intrigued when Serrano optimistically informed him that Portugal was ready to denounce its alliance with Britain. He reported Serrano's endeavors to Berlin on 12 July along with Serrano's request that Germany push Beigbeder and Lisbon to more energetic efforts.[10] Ribbentrop was interested. Germany was starting its attempt to branch out into the Atlantic, and Portugal could not help but play an important part, passively or otherwise. He thus launched onto a path of what was, for him, rather subtle diplomacy. On 16 July 1940, the day after the Germans made the Casablanca demand on Vichy, he told Stohrer that a Luso-Spanish alliance that ended the Anglo-Portuguese alliance "would certainly lie in the German interest," and ordered him to promote the idea with Serrano and Beigbeder.[11] Ribbentrop gave more discreet directions to the chief of the German legation in Lisbon, Baron Oswald von Hoyningen-Huene. Huene was to say, if the issue of a Luso-Spanish alliance were to come up, that Portugal could protect itself from British encroachments, and possibly unpleasant Spanish and German reactions, if it were to ally with Madrid and break with London.[12] Yet nothing came of these efforts. All Madrid received from Lisbon was the protocol to the 1939 treaty that Salazar had offered in July.[13] Spanish policy as described to Huene by Nicolás Franco, the Spanish ambassador to Lisbon and brother of the generalissimo, remained to separate Portugal from Britain, but for the moment Madrid had to take what it could get.[14] General Franco made similar representations to the Germans, adding that Madrid would keep trying to break the Anglo-Portuguese alliance.[15]

The Germans would not be fooled again. In early September 1940, Nicolás Franco pointed out to Salazar that according to the new protocol, Portugal had to inform Spain of any perceived threat to the Atlantic islands. Salazar acknowledged the argument, and the ambassador promised Huene that he would keep him apprised of anything Salazar might say on this issue.[16] Yet Berlin was unimpressed. Hitler ordered planning for the seizure of the Azores, Cape Verdes, and Canaries only two days after Huene's report.[17] He mentioned the Atlantic islands repeatedly to Serrano during the latter's mid-September visit to Berlin, and when Serrano insisted to Hitler on the twenty-fifth that Spain could bring Portugal into the Axis, Hitler and Ribbentrop were openly skeptical. The issue, they said, would be solved by military action.[18]

Such a solution was already under way. Hitler's order of 5 September for a study of the occupation of the Atlantic islands was relayed by Warlimont to his naval liaison officer, Captain Rolf Junge, who completed a lengthy study by the twenty-second.[19] Junge examined the problem in two scenarios. The first was the current war, in which the islands could serve as either mid-Atlantic British replacement bases for Gibraltar or as German supply raiding bases. In this context, the Azores and Canary Islands were highly desirable while the Cape Verdes and Madeira were of lesser value due to location and limited harbor facilities. The second scenario went beyond the present war into a future conflict wherein the British, driven from Europe, would pursue a transatlantic struggle with active American support. Here Junge agreed with Hitler that the Atlantic islands and the French West African coast would be of "inestimable value" for both sides, and especially as blockade bases against Europe. Yet could Germany occupy the islands first? To Junge, the Spaniards would defend the Canaries against the Anglo-Saxons and would need only logistical support. The Portuguese islands, he felt, could be easily occupied from the Atlantic coast of France, given the weakness of their defenses.[20] The problem lay in holding the islands after taking them. Regular sea or air supply would be impossible, given Britain's supremacy in the Atlantic. Moreover, Germany would be able to seize only the primary islands in the Azores and Cape Verdes. The Royal Navy and Air Force could then use the lesser islands for attack or blockade. "The defense of the occupied islands," continued Junge, "would collapse under its own weight in a relatively short time."

Major Sigismund Freiherr von Falkenstein, Warlimont's Luftwaffe liaison in the High Command, worked simultaneously on an aerial occupation of the Azores; an important study given Hitler's belief that Germany could occupy the Atlantic islands by air and maintain them by sea.[21] Falkenstein saw no problems in the occupation and defense of the Canaries, which lay relatively close to the European continent and which enjoyed satisfactory ground facilities. Such was not the case in the more distant and more poorly equipped Portuguese islands, which lacked even satisfactory airfields. Falkenstein believed that Junkers 52 pontoon-equipped transports could deliver occupation troops to the Azores so long as enough could be made available.[22] Bombing was possible with the Focke-Wulf 200 reconnaissance bomber, but such operations were possible only from Lisbon and with small payloads, and Falkenstein assumed that these planes would not land in the Azores but return to Europe.[23] The only aircraft that could perform combat in the Azores given the distance and lack of airfields were the Dornier 18 and Blohm and Voss 138 flying boats, neither of which had much fighting capability.[24] Holding the islands against a well-equipped enemy would be problematic. Germany could defend only the main islands, while the British could make life miserable for German forces. Flying boats could provide reconnaissance but little else. Raeder, at this time pressing the Mediterranean strategy, saw the Junge and Falkenstein reports on 24 September and met with Hitler two days later.[25] In discussing the Gibraltar operation, Hitler and Raeder agreed that the Canaries would have to be occupied beforehand by the Luftwaffe. Hitler's additional desire to occupy the Cape Verdes and Azores by air in the course of the Gibraltar operation, however, brought no response from Raeder.

Despite the technical difficulties of an operation against the Portuguese islands, the issue refused to go away, thanks to the September attack on Dakar. The attack confirmed to Hitler that Washington, through London, was attempting to establish a strategic presence in the East Atlantic, but the possibility of cooperation with Vichy in Northwest Africa made an Atlantic islands operation theoretically easier. Warlimont, eager for collaboration with France, ordered Junge to create a new study, this time factoring in the possibility of French cooperation.[26] Junge concluded in a 2 October study that French help would revolutionize the issue.[27] German use of Casablanca and Dakar would provide the navy with a tremendous advantage, particularly if the French were to push the British out of their bases at Freetown and Bathurst. Such a scenario would increase the value of the Atlantic islands to Britain as well, for the Royal Navy, robbed of Freetown, Bathurst, and presumably Gibraltar, would have no bases between the home islands and Capetown, while the Germans and French would have several. Yet from the French African coast, Germany would find it easier to occupy and hold the Atlantic islands. The Canaries, which Junge saw as already well defended by Spain, would enjoy steady maintenance from the Moroccan ports. Madeira and the Cape Verdes, due to their proximity to the African coast, could easily be reached through the air. Occupation and maintenance of the Azores would still be chancy, but German control of the West African coast and the other islands made the Azores less important.

The idea of using French African bases to occupy the Atlantic islands was not lost on Hitler. He doubtless considered it even before leaving on his trip to Montoire and Hendaye. On 14 October, he asked Raeder if the navy could transport men and material to the Azores, Cape Verdes, and Canaries should Germany find it necessary to occupy them by air. Raeder, though enthusiastic for greater cooperation with the French in Africa and familiar with Junge's enthusiasm for such a project, remained cool. The navy, he said, could make the transports only *before* aerial occupation, since Britain would still control the sea lanes. Hitler ordered a thorough examination of the entire issue, and the next day the Naval Command on Raeder's orders began looking into the occupation of the Azores and Canary Islands.[28]

Hitler's October rail journey convinced him that he had won Spanish and French support, and his enthusiasm about the Atlantic islands grew. On 23 October, the day of Hitler's meeting with Franco, Jodl reported that the Führer had become more interested in the Azores and had ordered a new study of their occupation.[29] Later in the week, Jodl reported that Hitler had again raised the issue of the Atlantic islands after the meeting with Pétain and that he was confident Vichy would allow use of the African coast for such an operation. Jodl and Warlimont ordered a more detailed examination than ever before. The new study was to examine logistical and defense issues concerning the different island groups with regard to sea and air operations. It was also to assume Spanish readiness for war, Portuguese neutrality despite territorial losses, and far-reaching cooperation from France, including German use of French bases and cargo ships.[30] Junge and Falkenstein went back to work immediately. "The Führer," wrote Falkenstein to the Luftwaffe operations staff when requesting data, "is engaged in the question of the occupation of the Atlantic Islands in view of a future war against America." The Luftwaffe's task lay in the seizure and maintenance of air bases, along with general supply questions.[31] Everything else was apparently left to the navy. Junge and Falkenstein completed the new study on 11 November and submitted it to Warlimont.[32] No copy exists today, but one can assume that its tone was as positive as that in Junge's study of 2 October, if not more so.

In the meantime, the Naval Command was working on its own study concerning the occupation of the Atlantic islands, which Raeder had ordered in mid-October. Rear Admiral Kurt Fricke, the naval command operations chief, was responsible for the lengthy treatise that emerged on 31 October as an in-house naval memorandum.[33] The striking characteristic of the study was its completely negative attitude toward the entire project. Although the Naval Command had in the summer insisted on control of the Atlantic islands while proposing bargains with Spain and Portugal for their acquisition, they sang a new tune when Hitler called upon them to take the islands by force in a hostile sea.[34] Fricke omitted all of the variables that everyone else had been factoring into the island issue. Suddenly absent from consideration was the need to protect Germany's connections with the future empire in central Africa, the need to deal in the future with the great Anglo-Saxon threat from across the Atlantic, cooperation with the Luftwaffe, and the possibility of using French African bases to reach the islands. Fricke examined the problem in the narrowest possible context of the current supply war against Britain and concluded that none of the island groups was worth the effort, for either Britain or Germany. Britain would not need the islands, since the Royal Navy already enjoyed dominance in the Atlantic, and Germany would not benefit significantly even if it were to take the islands. For the sake of argument, Fricke drafted a possible operation, presumably in order to demonstrate its vain nature—Operation *Dwarsläufer*, a project that clearly demonstrated the navy's aversion for such an undertaking. Fricke did not draw this operation against the Cape Verdes, an objective that in October 1940 could presumably have benefited from the use of Dakar, or against Madeira or the Canary Islands, operations that could have benefited from the use of the Moroccan coast. *Dwarsläufer* was aimed at the Azores—

precisely the group that Junge himself had declared the most difficult to control, and which the Naval Command doubtless knew would incite the least enthusiasm. *Dwarsläufer* was extremely unattractive. In Fricke's estimation, the navy could do no more than drop the troops at the main islands of Fayal and São Miguel, then leave them there. They would be on their own for the rest of the war, with only the slightest possibility of support from Europe.

Hitler meanwhile pressed forward. After returning from his rail journey, he met with Jodl, Brauchitsch, and Halder on 4 November. The Gibraltar assault, he said, would proceed as planned. German forces would simultaneously provide support for the Spaniards in the Canaries and would occupy the Cape Verdes. The use of Casablanca and Dakar would support these operations. As for protests from Portugal, Hitler would justify the Cape Verdes occupation with the argument that Germany was anticipating a similar British seizure. Motorized German infantry would follow the Gibraltar assault troops into Spain and would occupy Portugal if it were to provide any support to Britain.[35] Absent from this consideration were Madeira, which had no satisfactory port facilities, and the Azores, which were presumably too far for Hitler to consider at the moment. Hitler was apparently willing for now to settle for that which appeared to lie within reach.

Later the same day, Jodl presented Hitler's orders to Fricke. The rear admiral agreed with all of Hitler's points except one—the Cape Verdes occupation. He argued to Jodl that the operation would depend on French support at Dakar, that it would be difficult to execute, that there would be problems maintaining the islands, that the value of the islands was slight, and that the violation of Portugal's neutrality would prompt the British and the Americans to occupy the Azores and perhaps Portugal itself. It would be better, he said, to keep Portugal neutral while pressuring them to defend their own islands. Jodl brushed these objections aside, noting that Berlin was counting on France's "far-reaching support," that three German divisions on the Portuguese border would counteract a hostile attitude from Lisbon, and that above all, the Führer was very much in favor of the Cape Verdes operation. He ordered Fricke to examine the problem and noted that the issue would call for a definitive settlement between Raeder and Hitler.[36] In the meantime, Hitler's interest in the other island groups was rekindled. By 12 November when he signed the eighteenth war directive, he still maintained that the Canaries and Cape Verdes would increase in value after Gibraltar's fall and ordered Raeder and Göring to study the support of Spanish defenses on the former and the forcible occupation of the latter. Yet he also now ordered naval and air force studies on the capture of Madeira and the Azores.[37] All of the Atlantic islands were to come under German control.

Yet shortly after the eighteenth war directive, the island project died. The Luftwaffe rejected the Atlantic island project out of hand in the days following the Directive. Little is known concerning the considerations, but Göring seems to have had the decisive voice.[38] Even Falkenstein, who had once stated that operations against the Portuguese islands were possible, now demurred on all of the island groups except for the Canaries, where Germany presumably enjoyed political advantages.[39] The navy also refused to be pushed. They were determined to prosecute the war in the Mediterranean, thanks to their belief that it was the backbone of Britain's world position and thanks to Italy's recent disasters in the eastern Mediterranean.[40] Gibraltar still provided the key to the navy's objectives, and distant islands were no longer as important as they once appeared. Anglo-Saxon encroachment in the Atlantic and Africa was still a heavy concern, but the navy wished to remain within the limits of its strength, hoping to end the war with the British in the Mediterranean first, while worrying about more distant projects later. On 9 November, the Naval Command reaffirmed the opinions expressed by Fricke to Jodl five days earlier. The forceful violation of Portuguese neutrality would only give Britain an excuse to occupy the Azores, thus allowing the Royal Navy to mitigate the advantages Germany would gain in the Atlantic through Spanish entry into the war. Such a move would in addition push Brazil and the South American states closer to Washington. The best course lay in pressing Portugal to reinforce its own island defenses.[41]

Raeder and Hitler held their showdown on 14 November in the presence of Keitel and Jodl.[42] Hitler discarded all of Raeder's arguments. Britain, he said, would occupy the Azores once German troops took Gibraltar in any event and then cede them to the United States. Germany would have to get there first. Besides, argued Hitler, the Azores offered the chance to bomb America with the then-prototypical Messerschmidt 264 with its 12,600-kilometer range. Such a threat, he said, would force the Americans to look to their own defenses while curtailing aid to Britain. The capture of the Azores, he concluded, would forestall American intervention, while providing valuable services *after* the peace as well. Raeder held firm, repeating that Britain would not occupy the Azores when German troops crossed the Pyrenees. Germany, he argued, could possibly seize the Azores with luck in a high-risk operation, only to lose the islands afterward to concerted Anglo-

Saxon efforts. The burden of defending the Azores with submarines, continued Raeder, would also detract from the supply war in the Atlantic, which the navy still saw as paramount. It would be best, he said, to press Portugal to defend its own islands. Hitler listened, then ordered the necessary reconnaissance for the Azores operation. Raeder then tried to dissuade Hitler from the Cape Verdes and Madeira, contending that neither would be of much use for either side. The Cape Verdes in particular had poor harbor installations, low water supplies, and an unfavorable climate. Air support for an occupation would be problematic even with the use of Dakar, supply afterward would be impossible, and the occupation would be a political disaster.[43] Hitler gave no answer but remained undissuaded.

In the days that followed, the argument between Hitler and the navy over the island project continued. The High Command on Hitler's orders organized reconnaissance missions to the Canaries and Azores with both naval and Luftwaffe officers.[44] In the meantime the Naval Command, in a lengthy memorandum from chief of staff Admiral Otto Schniewind, attempted to convince the High Command that the island project was not worth the risk. Schniewind's report was a near-exact copy of the study completed by Fricke on 31 October, complete with the sketch of Operation *Dwarsläufer*. The one difference between the Schniewind report and Fricke's lay in the evaluation of the Canary Islands. Fricke had declared that the Canaries, like the Portuguese islands, had little practical merit. Yet now that the navy in late November was working with the Spaniards to reinforce the islands, Schniewind declared the Canaries to be of great value. Such a statement, given the perceived state of German-Spanish relations, cost nothing.[45]

For the moment the navy would win its point, not due to their arguments but because the calendar was running out. The islands were to be taken as part of the Gibraltar operation. As will be seen, Gibraltar had to fall by late February 1941 if the forces in Spain were to be readied for the eastern campaign in the spring. Hitler realized, as he said on 18 November, that the passage into Spain would have to begin within eight weeks at the most.[46] The timing had grim implications for the island project, since the High Command had yet to do the reconnaissance. On 18 November, Hitler still pushed the operation.[47] Yet the next day, Jodl conspicuously omitted any mention of the Portuguese islands in his report to Warlimont on the status of Operation *Felix*.[48] On 30 November, Brauchitsch heard that the political leaders had dropped their planning for the Atlantic islands and had opted instead for closer diplomatic ties with Lisbon.[49] In a 5 December briefing on *Felix*, Hitler made the revealing statement during the discussion of the

Army divisions earmarked for Portugal that he no longer considered a British landing there likely. In short, he was placing the Portuguese island project on hold, since the reason for the extra divisions lay in the intimidation of Salazar after a German occupation of the Cape Verdes.[50] The following day, 6 December, Jodl confirmed that the island operation had been postponed due to the impossibility of gathering the necessary intelligence in time for the assault on Gibraltar.[51] For the present, the operation against the Portuguese islands entered dormancy.

The hibernation of the Portuguese island idea in December 1940 did not mean that Hitler had changed his mind. He would return to it in the middle of the following year, shortly before the attack on the Soviet Union. For now, one can say the following. Hitler's predilection toward eventual war with the United States and his concern that the Americans might get the key bases first led him to press consistently in 1940 to occupy the Portuguese islands. His hesitance in November was not due to a lack of determination or even to the navy's argument that such an operation could not occur without risking heavy losses. The problem was simply a shortage of time. Later, when Germany seemed to have more time, Hitler would return to this very important scheme.

The evaporation of the Portuguese project on 6 December was followed the next day by Franco's refusal to enter the war. Thus, Hitler would watch disappear his illusory chance not only to seize the Portuguese islands but also to reinforce the Canaries and to put mobile troops in Spanish Morocco via Gibraltar. The reasons for Madrid's decision not to enter the war on 7 December 1940 are several. First, Spain's economy, already in a shambles, took a drastic downturn in November. Though willing to provide substantial aid, Berlin was unwilling to start deliveries until Spain entered the war. Such stinginess did not encourage Madrid. Second, Hitler refused to guarantee Madrid's colonial aims in Africa, and the chance that Franco would enter the war without certain rewards was slim. Finally, and most important, Spain became very wary of *German* aims in Morocco once they became clear in November. Before Franco even gave his refusal, German-Spanish friction there had become manifest. Even with economic aid and colonial guarantees, Franco would still have been loath to provide the Germans with a route to Africa.

Hitler and Ribbentrop fallaciously believed after the Hendaye meetings that Spain was ready to enter the war on Berlin's terms. From the days following Hendaye down to Franco's refusal on 7 December, they insisted on this erroneous reading of the facts, despite clear signals to the contrary.

Spain's unhappiness after Hendaye was evident. After Ribbentrop left, Serrano Suñer made clear to him the bitterness that he and Franco felt over the German refusal to alter Article 5 of the Hendaye Protocol to Spain's liking. Serrano's acrimony was lost on the Germans, who believed that his hollow acceptance of Article 5 of the toothless protocol had created the fundamentals of a working arrangement.

Franco did not give up at first. In a letter of 30 October, he tried again to convince Hitler of Spain's just cause. He focused on Hitler's argument that French Northwest Africa would defect if word of the transfer of French territory were to leak. Franco argued that this contention was inaccurate. Based on natural right and history, the lands in question were not French. It was natural *Spanish* territory, which France had stolen at the time of the Entente Cordiale. "It is not French territory that we want," claimed Franco, "nor do we claim to profit from French blood. We want only that which a clever liberal diplomacy . . . wrested from us in complete injustice. . . . I thus repeat the Spanish aspiration to the Oran district and to the part of Morocco which is in French hands and which links our zone of the North with the Spanish possessions of Ifni and the Sahara."[52]

The attempt to prove that French Morocco was not French failed. Hitler in fact saw the letter, due to Franco's opening proclamation of loyalty to the Axis, as confirmation of Franco's intention to enter the war.[53] In his 4 November meeting with Jodl, Brauchitsch, and Halder, he stated confidently that Franco would join the conflict. Berlin would conclude political negotiations with Madrid and proceed with the Gibraltar operation.[54] Possible British reactions to the loss of Gibraltar were landings in West Africa, Morocco, or the Atlantic islands. France, said Hitler, would defend its own territories, but he also hinted strongly that it might become necessary to send German forces to Spanish Morocco.[55] Germany would likewise help the Spaniards defend the Canaries and occupy the Cape Verdes.

Ribbentrop, hunting with Ciano in the Sudetenland, acted later the same day. After speaking with Hitler, he produced the Hendaye Protocol for Ciano's signature, which he obtained after changing Article 5 to guarantee Italy's colonial claims. Since time was short, Ribbentrop planned to send the protocol to Madrid for Serrano's signature rather than having a signing ceremony in Vienna. He also said that a meeting with Laval in the near future was possible.[56] According to Ciano, Ribbentrop defined the new association with Spain and France as follows: "He made a point of stressing that this huge program must not be regarded as exclusively directed against England. As far as England is concerned, the war is already won; it is a question of reaching a rapid conclusion. The program has more of an anti-American character."[57]

Yet would Spain cooperate? On 6 November, Ribbentrop sent the protocol to Madrid for Serrano's signature. Serrano was willing to sign,[58] for the protocol committed the Spaniards to nothing. The date of Spain's entry into the war was left to Madrid's discretion. Ribbentrop understood these shortcomings, and on 11 November he summoned Serrano to the Berghof for final discussions of Spain's entry into the war. The visit, he said, could occur only on 18 November due to a full schedule. Serrano thus had an easy excuse to refuse the invitation should Spain not have wished to enter the war. Yet he accepted the invitation as soon as he received it, showing that both he and Franco still hoped for an arrangement based on Franco's letter of 30 October.[59] The Germans seem to have taken Serrano's immediate acceptance of the invitation as a sign of Spanish acceptance of German terms, for Hitler signed the eighteenth war directive the same day.

Hitler and Serrano met at the Berghof on 18 November. Hitler's stated aim lay in making the political arrangements so that the Gibraltar operation could begin in six to eight weeks.[60] Militarily, he said, there were no problems. Yet should Spain decide to enter the war too late, the German troops would be needed elsewhere. Serrano refused to be pushed. His most immediate concern at the Berghof seems to have been the recent economic downturn in Spain. Stohrer had already reported in the middle of the month that conditions had worsened in the past few weeks and that some parts of Spain were experiencing famine.[61] A week before the Berghof meeting, Serrano and Spanish minister of commerce Demetrio Carceller had devised a scheme whereby 100,000 tons of grain then located in Portugal that was bound for Switzerland would be diverted to Spain, with Germany filling the grain deficit for the Swiss. Yet Berlin insisted that Spain receive no economic aid until it entered the war.[62] Hitler and Ribbentrop maintained this course while insisting that Spain's economic situation would improve if Spain were to fight. Serrano, whose expected wheat shipments from Canada and Argentina would have been halted should Spain have done so, was naturally unconvinced.

More disturbing was Hitler's treatment of the fundamental issue of Northwest Africa. In his impatience, the Führer revealed more to the Spaniard than he might have intended, showing not only that Madrid's claims would receive no assurances, but also that he viewed the Gibraltar operation as a way in which to build a *German* presence in Morocco. If there was a time when the Spaniards decided definitively not to enter the war, it was after this revelation. Serrano reiterated to Hitler his complaints on Article 5 of the Hendaye Protocol, commenting that Germany was sacrificing its loyal Spanish friends for its hereditary French enemies. Hitler stated that he did not trust France but a more specific protocol could, should it become known, trigger French Morocco's defection. This fluid state would end, said Hitler, once Gibraltar had fallen and German divisions had moved into French Morocco. Hitler wryly commented that he would be pleased if any arrangement with France were to last until that time. After further argument by Serrano that the protocol gave Spain only general guarantees that Madrid would not be able to defend in a public forum, Hitler showed his hand completely. The protocol, he stated, could under no circumstances become public knowledge, nor could Germany embark now on an exact delineation of future territorial settlements in North Africa. "Otherwise," said Hitler, "Morocco would immediately break away and the conquest of Gibraltar would have *no sense anymore*. [A specific written agreement] would lead to the loss of the object of the agreement. . . . He [Hitler] would then prefer that Gibraltar remain in English hands and Africa with Pétain."[63] Spain would simply have to trust Germany with its imperial future. After the peace, Spain would receive justice in Morocco, *and* Germany would have a base on the coast. For now, however, it was important that Gibraltar fall quickly, for the sooner the Rock was in Axis hands, the sooner the war could end and the less effect American intervention would have. Besides, revealed Hitler, the troops held for the Gibraltar operation would likely be needed elsewhere by the spring of 1941. Yet before the conquest of the Rock could begin, the Spanish defense of the Canary Islands would need reinforcement. Hitler helpfully offered artillery, antiaircraft guns, munitions, and dive-bomber squadrons. None of Hitler's disclosures at the Berghof could have comforted Serrano. He gave no encouragement to Franco's letter of 30 October. Worse, he revealed that he would use Spain to place German troops in Morocco. Over lunch with Ribbentrop and Ciano, who was also at the Berghof, Serrano complained openly but only irritated the Germans.[64] His farewell meeting with Ribbentrop the next day determined nothing. Serrano brusquely excused himself after noting several disagreements.[65]

Inexplicably, Hitler remained optimistic that Spain would enter the war. Two days after meeting with Serrano, Hitler noted to Hungarian minister president, Count Pál Teleki, that Rumania's oil would be used in part to supply Spain's needs.[66] In a letter to Mussolini on the same day, Hitler stated that he would prevail upon the Spaniards immediately for their entrance into the war, which could occur in six weeks. This move, he said, would help Italy by relieving British pressure in the eastern Mediterranean, but primarily it would resolve the Northwest African question. For Germany, wrote Hitler, "the purpose of Spain's entry must be to seize Gibraltar and close the Straits and to bring at least one or two divisions to Spanish Morocco in order to guarantee against a possible defection of French Morocco. . . . This must be avoided and it cannot therefore be left in any circumstances to hope, much less to chance."[67] Hitler was more explicit in a later letter. As will be seen in the next chapter, Vichy's apparent level of willingness to cooperate with German aims in Africa had left the Germans suspect after a disappointing French-German military conference in Paris on 29 November. On 5 December, Hitler wrote Mussolini that

> . . . one cannot have full security regarding the attitude of the
> Vichy government. I have always believed that there does not
> exist a put-up game between the French government and General
> de Gaulle. Nevertheless the circumstances require great prudence.
> Already the slightest counterstroke could cause North Africa and
> West Africa to become insecure and—separating themselves from
> Vichy—they would offer England dangerous bases of operations.
> The name of General Weygand, who has been sent there to main-
> tain order, does not have a very tranquilizing effect on me. In
> such circumstances the possession of the Strait of Gibraltar is one
> of the greatest importance. From that moment only can the situ-
> ation in Northwest Africa be considered as definitely resolved in
> our favor.[68]

Military preparations under General Halder had already reached an advanced state. Exercises against a site resembling Gibraltar in Besançon had begun in the first week of November and had become efficient by the end of the month. On 20 November, Halder issued orders for the organization of Operation *Felix*. Command went to Field Marshal Walter von Reichenau, commander of the Sixth Army, beneath whom stood an army corps charged with the assault on the Rock, an army corps for flank protection, and two motorized divisions for a possible march into Portugal. The attacking corps would assemble at Bordeaux at the last possible moment before crossing into Spain. Once air attacks on the British fleet at Gibraltar had begun, the corps would cross into Spain, then move to Burgos to Valladolid to Salamanca to Seville to Gibraltar.[69] The troops for Spain were ready to march by 29 November.

It was Hitler more than the army who insisted that a large contingent travel to Spanish Morocco following the Rock's capture. On 4 November, he had hinted that Germany would send troops there. The army operations staff thus prepared a long study on the forces necessary to close the Strait from the African side. They determined that the ports opposite Gibraltar in Spanish Morocco, Ceuta and Tangier, were not worth taking due to their inefficiency, and that even if the British did decide to move to Ceuta or Tangier after the loss of Gibraltar, the seven Spanish divisions in Spanish Morocco could prevent them from doing so without German help. The only German task in Spanish Morocco would lie in helping the Spaniards close the Strait from the southern side with coastal artillery. The study recommended that three German artillery detachments with the necessary antiaircraft pieces set up between Cires Bay and Ras es-Samar, an area spanning the four-kilometer Moroccan coastal stretch closest to the Andalusian shore. The Spanish infantry was strong enough to defend these coastal guns, and if German infantry were to become necessary, Germany would need no more than one regiment with enough trucks to give one battalion of that regiment some mobility. The rest of the regiment was superfluous and could quarter in Tangier. Fully motorized regiments or special troop units, continued the study, were too valuable to be employed in a *Nebenaufgabe* such as this.[70] To Hitler, the purpose of placing German troops in Spanish Morocco was greater. On 25 November, he told Jodl that two full divisions including the Third Panzer Division, once earmarked to support the Italians in Egypt, would go to Spanish Morocco.[71] The decision to send more troops to Spanish Morocco, where there was no war in progress, than to Egypt, where there *was* one, shows that Hitler was interested in more than defending four kilometers of undesirable coastline. It also confirms that the Gibraltar operation was hardly part of a comprehensive Mediterranean strategy in his eyes. Halder had in fact already completed the problem of moving the divisions across the Strait.[72] Meanwhile, the Germans placed a rush order to the National Institute of Geography in France for five hundred staff maps of Morocco and Algeria.[73]

Yet there were time limits. On 5 December, von Brauchitsch told Hitler that if German troops in Spain were to participate in the eastern campaign, *Felix* would have to be complete by the end of February. Thus, ground operations at the Rock would have to commence at the start of that month. Hitler answered that the air attack on Gibraltar and the crossing into Spain would start on 10 January 1941, so that the ground assault on the Rock could begin in the first week of February. Hitler further ordered that one motorized and one armored division would cross into North Africa, and noted that Vichy's scare tactic of citing the chance of colonial secession would end once a few German divisions were in Morocco.[74] Hitler held the final discussion on Operation *Felix* on 7 December 1940 and approved the assault plan, from which Warlimont drafted War Directive 19.[75] Already on 4 December, Hitler had ordered the chief of military intelligence, Admiral Wilhelm Canaris, to Madrid. An old acquaintance of Franco, Canaris would seek on 7 December the *Caudillo*'s approval for the operation.[76]

The tale of Franco's refusal is well known. Canaris met Franco and Vigón at 7:30 P.M. on the seventh and informed them of Hitler's wish that Spain enter the war on 10 January. Economic aid from Germany, he said, would begin with the passage of German troops into Spain. Franco said no. Spain, he said, was not ready economically, thanks to a grain deficit exacerbated by infrastructural problems. Franco also cited the concern that the British would seize the Canaries, Spanish Guinea, and the Portuguese islands. Spain was doing what it could to prepare, but for now, war was impossible.[77] There were more vital reasons that Franco did *not* mention that night. Spain's original *démarche* of 19 June had made clear the price for entry into the war—economic assistance and territorial rewards in Africa—and the latter was wholly missing. Franco was irritated over the lack of a reply from Hitler to his 30 October letter, and Serrano, on his return from the Berghof, voiced great dissatisfaction to Stohrer over the issue of compensation.[78] Not only did the chance of extending Spain's empire seem slim, but there was also the danger, apparent after the Berghof meeting, that German aims would eliminate what little Spain already had. Spanish concerns focused on Spanish Morocco and the Canaries, where the Spaniards, beginning in November 1940, fought to limit or exclude German activities. The friction in these areas suggests that even had Spain's economy become solvent, and even had Berlin rewritten the Hendaye Protocol to Madrid's liking, the cooperation that Berlin sought in Northwest Africa would still have been difficult to realize.

Spain's possessiveness toward Morocco increased in early November when Spain incorporated the Tangier zone into Spanish Morocco. On 3 November, Spain formally dissolved Tangier's international institutions—the international control commission, the legislative assembly, and the mixed information bureau. Spanish officers filled these positions, and Colonel Antonio Yuste, commander of the June occupation, became military governor of Tangier, replacing the French head of the control commission. The Spanish press announced that Tangier was now Spanish, while warning the French not to protest. Extra artillery in the zone punctuated the warning.

On 28 November, Franco would proclaim unity of law between Tangier and Spanish Morocco.[79] The fact that these moves came a few days after Hendaye with no warning to Berlin or to Rome was not lost on the Germans. Stohrer commented that it was "due to a certain feeling which has spread [in Madrid] after Hendaye that [Spain] should act independently in order to assure itself of 'Tangier at least.'"[80] Serrano said nothing to dispute this theory.[81]

It was also no coincidence that Spain began to combat the German position in Morocco in late November 1940, after Hitler revealed at the Berghof that he wished to place troops there. Sources on German activity in Spanish Morocco during the war are scarce, yet the number of Nazi Party, SD, and Abwehr agents in Spanish Morocco was not insignificant.[82] German print, radio, and film propaganda was quite lively, and effective connections existed between the German consulate in Tetuán and Moroccan nationalists.[83] Spanish apprehension began to increase in June 1940, when the Spaniards saw a chance to realize their aims in French Morocco. In late June the high commissioner, General Carlos Asensio, told the German consul, Herbert Georg Richter, that Spain was displeased both with German propaganda in Spanish Morocco and with German contacts with the nationalist underground in the French zone. He tried unsuccessfully to reach agreement with Richter that German propaganda function under Spain's supervision.[84] Remaining cooperation between Berlin and Madrid in Morocco disintegrated after Hitler's statements at the Berghof. On 30 November, Ambassador Espinosa slapped Ribbentrop with blistering indictments of German propaganda in Morocco, noting that German agents disregarded Spanish interests and had brought complaints from the High Commissariat for some time.[85] Spanish authorities in Morocco acted accordingly. By the end of the year Richter, who once held up the High Commissariat as a Germanophile body, complained bitterly:

> *The sympathies of the natives for us are well known to the Spaniards and drive them to a morbid jealousy of any German influence in the country. The Spanish effort to exclude us systematically from Morocco has been evident in the course of the year on unimportant occasions as well as in matters of principle. The greatest obstacles were placed in the way of exhibiting German war films; permission for Germans to enter Tangier, which could be occupied by Spain in June only as a result of the German victories in France, was delayed for months; the return of the former*

German Legation property in Tangier is being postponed beyond reason.

In the French zone, too, which certainly does not belong to the Spaniards, they do not want any German influence. A shipment from the Madrid Embassy to the Consulate containing Arabic propaganda material, which by reason of its text and sense could only be used in the French zone, was confiscated by the High Commissioner in a way that I consider to be contrary to international law . . . The Spanish policy here in this country is a bad sign for the future, if Spain should really succeed in gaining possession of the French zone entirely or even in part. Spain would have only one aim: she would never rest until the last German had left the country—the heart's desire, openly expressed, of the Secretary General [Tomás Garcia Figueras] of the Alta Comisaria *here. . . .*[86]

Symptomatic of German-Spanish friction was the issue of the German legation building in Tangier. The property had been confiscated from the Germans during the First World War and given to the *Mendub,* the sultan's representative in the city.[87] Berlin requested its return soon after Spain occupied Tangier in June 1940. This was no small issue of protocol. The return of the legation would have boosted German prestige in Morocco, and the General Consulate in Tangier, once set up in 1941, would be the German espionage hub for Northwest Africa.[88] Moreover, German agents suspected the *Mendub* of financially backing Britain's war. On 28 June, Richter requested that the German Armistice Commission press France on the issue,[89] and from early September Stohrer pressed Beigbeder for the building's return. Yet the *Mendub*'s eviction would have insulted the Sultan, which Beigbeder was not about do.[90]

Spain's legal incorporation of Tangier into the Spanish zone of Morocco in early November created a ticklish situation. Since it came on the heels of the Hendaye conference, Berlin feared that Moroccan natives would see the incorporation as the result of a Spanish-German agreement.[91] Moreover, Spain's possessive attitude seemed to bode ill for German interests. Thus, the legation issue became more acute. Ribbentrop had Serrano informed that Germany still had a "considerable interest" in Tangier and Morocco and expected a restoration of its pre-1914 status and the return of the legation.[92] At first the request presented few problems. Serrano told Stohrer before leaving for the Berghof in mid-November that Spain would see to the legation's return, and the German embassy planned a large ceremony to celebrate the restoration and to impress the Moroccan natives.[93] Spain's attitude changed after the Berghof conference. On 4 December, three days before Franco's refusal to enter the war, Serrano told Stohrer that the legation's return was postponed indefinitely due to anger among Spanish authorities in Morocco over subversive German activities. Berlin denied all charges and pressed for the legation's return. But when Stohrer challenged Serrano to prove the allegations, the latter produced a list of German agents in Spanish Morocco and repeated that he could not give a date for the return of the legation to Germany.[94]

Madrid would finally bend to Berlin's wishes, but not until March 1941, after the heaviest pressure from Hitler for Spanish entry into the war had already passed. The *Mendub* was evicted on 16 March, and the next day in a grand ceremony with thousands of spectators, the German legation was restored, with the German consulate in Tangier opening soon after.[95] Yet the Spaniards were not to be outdone. Four days after the German celebration, Madrid staged its own festivities to commemorate the caliph's official entry into the city. Tangier's streets were adorned with Spanish and Moroccan flags, and military parades followed the caliph. In a touch of irony, Spain invited a surprise guest to add an anti-French luster—Abd-el-Aziz, the sultan deposed in 1908 during France's conquest of Morocco.[96]

The German-Spanish relationship that would emerge in Spanish Morocco would be a strange one indeed. On the one hand, a bitter propaganda battle between the two would persist. The Germans would complain about Spanish propaganda that assumed an anti-German slant, while Spanish authorities would raise objections to German propaganda in the Spanish zone; each watched the other with the utmost care.[97] In the meantime, the Tangier consulate would work to the German advantage for the next three years as an espionage hub for the charting of Allied Mediterranean traffic. In the beginning of 1942, it was removed from the purview of the embassy in Spain and was made directly answerable to Berlin, and the official personnel grew from fifteen to fifty. British protests included demands that Spain expel German agents, together with a list of 116 names in December 1943. Yet it was only in May 1944 that the Spanish government closed the Tangier consulate, thanks to economic pressure from London and Washington, and even afterward, German agents remained on Spanish territory through the end of the war. Whatever their suspicions about the Germans, Spanish authorities remained reluctant to take orders from the Allies even after the defeat of the former.[98]

Madrid was also determined to prevent a German presence in the Canary Islands. In mid-September of 1940, Hitler and Ribbentrop had made a tremendous issue of Spanish cession of one of the Canaries, and Hitler and the navy agreed that regardless of ownership, the islands would be an inviting target for the Anglo-Saxons after the Gibraltar operation and would have to be protected.[99] Franco had asked in June for German help in defending the islands, and even after Serrano's first two discussions in Berlin, he wrote Hitler that Germany could share Spanish bases in wartime. Yet Ribbentrop's bludgeoning of the cession issue in the last week of September, even after Franco's earlier refusals, ended the desire for German aid here. Rather than ask for German help, the Spaniards took their own measures to strengthen the main islands.[100]

Although these efforts were weak, Madrid still rejected German aid. Franco's comment at Hendaye that the defenses in the Canaries might not be enough to prevent an Allied landing brought Hitler's offer of coastal batteries with engineers to install them and to train the Spanish troops in their use. Yet Franco remained mute on the offer.[101] Hitler noted with irritation to Mussolini on the twenty-eighth that Spain could not enter the war until the Canaries were more aptly defended and that he wished to place dive-bombers, long-range artillery, and special troops there.[102] In his meeting with his military commanders on 4 November and in the eighteenth war directive that followed, Hitler ordered that the navy and Luftwaffe help the Spaniards.[103] At the Berghof in mid-November, Hitler again raised concerns while offering artillery and aircraft, but Serrano sharply rejected the offer. Spain, he said, had artillery and seasoned commanders and was assembling fighter aircraft and installing machine gun nests in the Canaries. He promised—or warned—that Spain would defend each island as if it were the Alcázar.[104]

In spite of these comments, Berlin planned to strengthen the islands against an Allied landing. The task fell primarily to the navy, which was agreeable enough as far as the Canaries were concerned.[105] Raeder told Hitler on 14 November that adding defenses to the islands was tricky but possible. The German navy would need an exact accounting of what defenses were in the Canaries, and German reinforcements would have to arrive in the islands before Spain's entry into the war. French cooperation with transport shipping from Casablanca would be helpful but perhaps undesirable, given recent French-Spanish acrimony.[106] On 16 November, the navy dispatched Captain Hans-Erich Voss to Spain and the Canaries for a ten-day reconnaissance mission. Also traveling to Spain was Captain Hermann Menzell of the

Abwehr, whose responsibilities included arranging transport of German artillery batteries from Hamburg to the Canaries. Both traveled in civilian clothing, and their trips were arranged by Canaris.[107] In Berlin, Schniewind began to arrange shipment of four midsized fixed artillery batteries and four midsized army motorized artillery batteries to Gran Canaria and Tenerife. Personnel, munitions, and tools were also to travel to the Canaries, with enough provisions for three months.[108]

Fricke, meanwhile, worked on the details. On 30 November, he informed Warlimont, Canaris, and army transport chief General Rudolf Gercke that the deployment of the fixed batteries in the Canaries would present problems due to the two weeks needed to set up the batteries after their arrival. Fricke suggested sending only the mobile batteries, on the assumption that they alone could bolster Spanish defenses. These batteries would have to remain in the Canaries for the remainder of the war, said Fricke, but they would be of good use in defending the coasts. He asked Warlimont to see to the preparation of the batteries for shipping and promised that the navy would get them to the islands. Fricke included a scheme whereby the batteries would travel by sea from Germany to France to the Canaries, arriving at their final destination on the day of Spain's entry into the war. Should the transport be intercepted en route to the tropics, the story would be that Berlin was selling the weapons to the Spaniards.[109] At the same time, Fricke prepared a list of naval personnel to travel to the Canaries, pointing to the need for information specialists and men who had experience in dealing with the Spaniards.[110]

Yet there were already dark clouds threatening the transport. Captain Voss returned to Berlin on 26 November with a pessimistic report. The Spanish navy, he said, was a motley collection of vessels, and the coastal guns in the Iberian Peninsula were old and small. The Canaries had but twenty 15-centimeter artillery pieces. More disturbing was the Spanish attitude. Voss, who had talked often with Generals Juan Vigón and Agustín Muñoz Grandes, had the feeling that the Spaniards had cooled toward Germany, that they were displeased with the German visits, and that they resented German help.[111] Meanwhile Menzell, who had been in Spain since mid-November, had made no headway with the Spaniards over the weapons shipment to the Canaries. On 3 December, Raeder told Hitler that the navy was ready for its tasks in the capture of Gibraltar but that the island fortifications were still being negotiated.[112] This news was no surprise to Hitler, who had expected problems with the issue of German help in the defense of the islands.[113]

On the following day, the Naval Command received a report from Spain that Menzell had finally reached an agreement with the Spaniards for the artillery to move to the islands. He gained Spanish assent by offering to *sell* the batteries to Spain, thus allowing them to transport the artillery themselves without German assistance.[114] This had not been Berlin's first choice, but the navy was willing to take what it could get. Fricke informed Warlimont, Canaris, and Gercke that the Spaniards would purchase the batteries at the French-Spanish border and ship them themselves, hoping to place the batteries in the islands before the German attack on Gibraltar. A small German support staff would travel in disguise to the Canaries for the setup of the batteries, but the army units originally envisioned would not.[115] The news of Menzell's breakthrough also affected Canaris's mission; Canaris now received additional orders to expedite with Franco the movement of the batteries.[116] On 7 December, shortly before Canaris's meeting with Franco and Vigón in Madrid, Fricke informed his subordinates that the newest report from the High Command said the preparation of the batteries for shipment had to begin immediately, so that they could be set up in the islands by 10 January.[117] The German efforts with regard to the Canary Islands came to naught, with Franco's negative response to Canaris on 7 December.

Despite the problems over Morocco and the Canaries, Franco's refusal brought a shock when it arrived in Berlin on 8 December. One Foreign Ministry official complained that the refusal stood "in flagrant contradiction" to the Hendaye discussions and recent reports by Stohrer himself on Franco's position. Ribbentrop himself wanted answers, and Stohrer received orders to refrain from approaching the Spaniards for the time being.[118] The Spanish answer also surprised the High Command. Jodl had already begun preparations to travel to Madrid to brief Franco on the Gibraltar operation.[119] On the receipt of Franco's answer, such preparations were placed on hold, and Keitel, with some irritation, ordered Canaris to press Franco for a time when Spain *would* be prepared to enter the conflict.[120]

Hitler's own position evolved over a span of some forty-eight hours. On 8 December, while Berlin was waiting for an answer from Canaris's new *démarche* with Franco, Hitler spoke to Keitel about the possible consequences of Franco's refusal, which the Führer viewed entirely in terms of the present situation in French Africa. If Franco were to refuse, brooded Hitler, then Germany would not be able to get into Morocco. Here was a disturbing problem, given recent reports pointing to the unreliabilty of General Weygand and to unsteady political developments in North and West Africa. Should disaffection truly take root there, said Hitler, Weygand would set up a countergovernment. In such a case, German troops, unable to move from Spain into Morocco, would have to occupy the unoccupied zone of France. On the same afternoon, Warlimont began the preparations for what would become Operation *Attila*—the occupation of unoccupied France together with the seizure of French air and naval units stationed there.[121] On 10 December, Hitler would sign War Directive 19, which embodied *Attila* and which began with the comment that it was for the specific contingency of an African colonial secession under Weygand.[122]

In fact, Hitler's worries calmed considerably after his statements of 8 December. It was at this very time, in spite of Hitler's suspicion of Weygand, that the possibility of cooperation with Vichy against separatism in Africa seemed to be at its height. At noon on 9 December, Warlimont flew to Paris for discussions with Laval and Huntziger—discussions that Laval had all but promised would lead to active French-German cooperation in Africa.[123] Thus on 9 December, when Canaris reported that he had asked Franco for a date of entry into the war and Franco had replied that he could name no such date, Hitler took the news with the utmost tranquillity. He told Halder that Spain's final refusal had actually given him greater latitude in dealing with the French than he had previously enjoyed. Without Spain in the colonial equation, he could win Vichy's cooperation by assuring the French to a greater degree that they could keep their African holdings intact.[124] On 10 December, the day of the Warlimont-Laval-Huntziger meeting in Paris, Hitler coolly canceled Operation *Felix,* noting that the reconnaissance missions now in Spain and in the Canary Islands would complete their missions, but that all other facets of the operation were to be discontinued, and that the German artillery destined for the Canary Islands would not be delivered.[125] The war directive for Operation *Attila,* signed the same day, bore the same number, 19, that the directive for *Felix* had once borne. *Felix,* in other words, was dead at least until the completion of the eastern campaign the following year. Yet the hope that Hitler had attached to cooperation with France would very shortly be terribly disappointed. Hitler would surprise himself with how quickly *Felix* would rise from the grave.

Chapter 8

Winter Collapse II: France

❧

The day 13 December will be
a black date for France.
                    —Otto Abetz

Two months have been lost which otherwise might
have helped to decide world history.
                    —Adolf Hitler

The main pillar to Hitler's designs in Northwest Africa in late 1940 was France. France was to defend its holdings there from the Allies while flushing de Gaulle from Central Africa. The French were also to provide Germany with bases from which to occupy the Atlantic islands. After the Montoire meetings in late October, it seemed as though the French would willingly accept this role. Vichy and Berlin discussed issues ranging from the release of French prisoners to the reconquest of French Equatorial Africa even at the risk of Franco-British war. The arrangement appeared solid enough for Hitler to write off Spanish participation in the war after Franco's refusal of 7 December, with the comment that Spain's absence would help the relationship with Vichy.

Yet Hitler's suspicion of France had always run deeper than his hope for an arrangement. Pétain's dismissal of vice premier and foreign minister Pierre Laval on 13 December 1940 sent a signal to Hitler, albeit an incorrect one, that Vichy was no longer interested in cooperation. Hitler blamed General Maxime Weygand, since September France's delegate-general in Africa, as the perpetrator of the Laval affair and feared that Weygand would swing French Africa over to the Allies. All projects in the southwest now collapsed. The only avenue of salvage lay once again through Spain and Gibraltar, and once again, Hitler turned back to Madrid, this time with a fury the Spaniards had yet to witness.

In Vichy, Montoire signaled the triumph of Pierre Laval in the French government over those such as Baudouin who wished to conduct relations with Germany within the confines of the armistice treaty. Cooperation with Berlin in Africa, thought Laval, could bring France numerous advantages not only for its imperial future but also in the conduct of the German occupation at home. He embarked after Montoire on a hunt for concessions, and if he did not act as a "lone wolf," he still led the pack. On 31 October, the German embassy in Paris hosted Laval, War Minister Huntziger, and Finance Minister Yves Bouthillier at a large lunch meeting that included Ambassador Abetz, Hans Richard Hemmen, and the new commander of the German occupation forces, General Otto von Stülpnagel.[1] Laval announced that the cabinet was firmly behind cooperation as discussed at Montoire and that he had come to Paris to discuss details. He wanted the following: Germany would release the forces needed to strengthen French Africa, and France would prevent the spread of dissidence there while winning back the lost areas. Since this would serve Germany's interest as well as France's, Laval wanted political concessions for the *Metropole,* such as the loosening of the demarcation line, the reduction of occupation costs, and a fair exchange rate between the mark and the franc. Huntziger presented several long memoranda on military needs in Africa. Vichy, he added, aimed not only to prevent further British meddling in French Africa; it would attack the British if necessary to reconquer the lost areas. He urged that the memoranda receive speedy approval, for, as he warned, "England and perhaps others will not wait."

Huntziger's requests of 31 October were extensive.[2] In North Africa, he wanted the number of troops allowed raised from 100,000 to 120,000. The extra men would form light mobile units for the Moroccan-Algerian border.[3] Since ground forces would focus on Morocco, he also asked for the release from captivity of officers with experience there. For West Africa, Germany had already allowed the transfer of nine supplementary battalions from the *Metropole* and North Africa. But Huntziger noted that since a British attack or Gaullist sedition were likely, more were needed for counterthrusts and for the reconquest of Equatorial Africa. He wanted a large mobile detachment and the release from captivity of officers and NCOs with experience in West and Equatorial Africa.[4] Huntziger also requested greater freedom of movement for the navy and an elimination of Italian stinginess on naval issues. For the air force in Africa, Huntziger requested a fourth bomber group for West Africa, a boost in French bomber and reconnaissance groups from thirteen to seventeen aircraft, and the resumption of production of the Lioré 45 bomber, the Dewoitine 520 fighter, and Hispano-Suiza engines in the unoccupied zone.[5] Additional material for the army, navy, and air force would come partly from North African stocks but partly from the *Metropole*.

Berlin was unwilling to consider any of the political concessions for which Laval hoped. Ribbentrop mentioned in early November that he would meet Laval to "water down his wine." Germany would not make what he saw as one-sided concessions.[6] Hitler, against Abetz's advice, proceeded immediately after the 31 October meeting to expel 100,000 French citizens from Lorraine. Germany, the Führer said, should complete the procedure *before* beginning new relationships with France.[7] Even on the issue of Germany's postwar African empire, Berlin was willing to surrender nothing, as the studies emerging at this time from the German Foreign Ministry clearly indicate.[8] Hitler was not exaggerating when he told Serrano Suñer on 18 November that he would be happy if an arrangement with France were to last until the capture of Gibraltar.

Yet Germany's desire for military collaboration in Africa was positive, due partly to German aims there and partly to de Gaulle's current success in Gabon, the last Vichy enclave in French Equatorial Africa.[9] The German Armistice Commission advocated Huntziger's memoranda, which seemed modest enough to present no danger to the Axis.[10] The High Command agreed on 1 November, since France was to become a benevolent neutral that would fight for German interests and permit German measures on its territory.[11] Warlimont, ever the advocate of collaboration, hoped for full approval of France's requests and pressed to start talks with the French to the exclusion of Italy.[12] It was the expectation of success with the French that prompted Hitler to insist on the occupation of the Portuguese islands in early November.

Talks moved slowly but surely. On 1 November, the more suspicious Ribbentrop was entrusted with the French talks while the more enthusiastic High Command received but a consultative function.[13] Hitler meant to have counterconcessions for each military concession to France, and the Armistice Commission began a list of counterdemands that featured German air bases in North and West Africa and French cooperation with German armament production.[14] On 9 November, Hitler contacted Laval through Göring in Paris.[15] Laval pressed Göring for the same concessions mentioned to Abetz on 31 October, as well as a halt to expulsions from Lorraine, but to no avail. Göring jumped straight for the African issue, stating that France must remain master in the colonies. If France were to expect any concessions, it would have to dislodge de Gaulle while taking action against any British encroachments, though a formal declaration of war was unnecessary. Germany might demand even more, he said, all of course for the common effort against Britain. "If Germany," postulated Göring, "today demanded bases on the West coast of Africa there was no intention to seize the colonies but only a desire to broaden the bases of operations against England. This was a sphere in which the idea of having England as the common enemy could be best expressed, and in that case accommodation could be shown by Germany." Laval was eager to defend the colonies, but he warned that active German participation in Africa would fuel Britain's public argument that de Gaulle was defending the French Empire from Germany. France, he suggested, would act alone in the empire. He concluded with the vague statement that Germany and France would need to find common agreement over the means to be employed there.

Yet time for common agreement was running out, in part due to de Gaulle's conquest of Gabon and in part due to the change of seasons in the tropics, which brings dry weather in the autumn and winter, and rain in the spring and summer. On 5 November, General Doyen briefed Stülpnagel in Wiesbaden that the outlook was bleak in Libreville and Port Gentile—the final Vichy strongholds in Gabon. France, he said, intended to reconquer Equatorial Africa, beginning with the key position of Lake Chad. Yet due to the rainy season, the best time to begin was January 1941, less than two months away. Thus, Germany would need to reach a decision on the French requests of 31 October immediately.[16] Doyen managed to shake a few concessions from the Germans, mainly for West Africa. On 9 November, Keitel ordered on Warlimont's urging that the Armistice Commission obtain information on all French requests to which Germany would presumably agree, with regard to the exact extent of the requests and the extent to which the French would need materials from the *Metropole* and officers from prison camps. The High Command also ordered Wiesbaden to open discussions on the operations that France had in mind, without discussing political concessions.[17]

Hitler took the most decisive steps himself. He was primarily concerned at this point with Vichy's ability to hold West Africa. Libreville, the capital of Gabon, fell to de Gaulle on 10 November, and Hitler was counting on the use of Dakar to take the Cape Verdes. On 12 November, the day he signed the eighteenth war directive, which stated that France would allow German measures on its soil, Hitler granted Huntziger's request for the mobile detachment and the fourth bomber group for French West Africa. Materials were to come from stocks in Africa unless unavailable there. Wiesbaden would inform the Italians of the decision summarily.[18] As will be seen, Hitler also approved of some degree of leniency in *North* Africa, although he was as yet unwilling to wrest decision-making power in the area from Rome. Germany hoped it could nudge the Italians in the right direction.[19]

Yet the spirit of Montoire never pervaded in Italy. Mussolini opposed it despite Hitler's belief that the Florence meeting of 28 October had changed the Duce's mind. Rumor in Turin had it that Germany was offering France a separate peace that ignored Italy's territorial claims, and Colonel Frido von Senger, the German liaison in Turin, reported in mid-November that French-Italian relations were worsening daily.[20] In November the Italians suspended French Mediterranean transport and rescinded approval already granted for two fuel tankers to go to West Africa. Worse, the Italians demanded the immediate disarmament of the North African ports of Oran and Bizerte. French protests in Turin, which pointed out Vichy's determination to maintain its Mediterranean position, went for naught.[21]

The German military worked to strengthen the French in Africa despite the Italian authority granted by the Roatta Agreements. In the first week of November, Warlimont and Böhme recommended against showing the French memoranda of 31 October to the Italians, and Böhme even told the French to refrain from mentioning it in Turin.[22] In mid-November Warlimont took up the issue with Ambassador Karl Ritter in the Foreign Ministry. The German aim, he said, was to have Rome unconditionally accept German leadership concerning French military activity in Africa. At the very least, Rome would have to halt the measures it was now taking. Ritter agreed with the general's stance and noted that Ribbentrop would discuss such issues with Ciano soon.[23] Hitler hoped to coax the Italians painlessly. At the same time as Warlimont's talk with Ritter, Keitel held a two-day session with Marshal Badoglio in Innsbruck. It was Berlin's policy, Keitel said, to have France defend its overseas possessions. French sea transport in the Mediterranean would thus have to resume, and Oran and Bizerte would have to remain capable of defense. Keitel even hinted that Italy could allow the French army in North Africa to exceed 120,000 men. Badoglio was friendly and gave Keitel to understand that Italy would be more lenient and that Turin would check with Wiesbaden before implementing measures that concerned the French forces in Africa.[24]

Italian intransigence remained nonetheless. In December Italy would grudgingly grant the 120,000-man army for French North Africa while accepting the French plan for the mobile force at the Algerian-Moroccan border.[25] Yet Turin insisted that Oran and Bizerte disarm, prompting complaints from Wiesbaden and nonresolution of the issue.[26] The Italians also protested German approval of coded radio contact between Vichy and French colonial authorities until German annoyance obliged Turin to agree.[27] Finally, in a move perhaps inspired by Madrid, Turin demanded the dismantling of the French mountain fortifications along the Spanish-French Moroccan border.[28] Rome's unwillingness to cooperate only harmed its interests. When the time came for the Axis to exercise greater surveillance in Northwest Africa, Berlin would act unilaterally.

In the meantime, the French were trying to implement collaboration in Africa. Diplomatically, Laval did his best to claim the empire as an exclusive French responsibility. On 15 November, he had Abetz informed that General Noguès in Morocco was fully behind the new policy and that Vichy was determined to expunge de Gaulle from the empire, even at the risk of armed conflict with Great Britain. Earlier in the week, he had attempted to wave the Spaniards away from Morocco as well, complaining to Ambassador Lequerica that the 150,000 Spanish troops on the French Moroccan border were hardly conducive to stability.[29] Militarily, preparations for reconquest were under way. On 14 November, the French reported in Wiesbaden that de Gaulle had only 3,500 men and twelve aircraft for immediate action, and that with the end of the rainy season in early December, Vichy could launch an operation against Chad through the West African colony of Niger via Niamey and Zinder, just north of Nigeria. Yet Hitler's grant of the mobile detachment for West Africa had come just two days before, and as a result the government had only two battalions in the Niger region.[30] By 23 November, Huntziger, Darlan, and air minister General Jean Bergeret had, on Pétain's orders, devised an operational plan for the reconquest of French Equatorial Africa. Laval doubtless hoped to present the plan to Ribbentrop, but the Germans did not bite. A foreign ministers' meeting might have devolved into a discussion of the Lorraine deportations, the demarcation line, and other political issues. Thus on 27 November, Hitler decided that Warlimont would go to Paris and receive the French plan.[31] The German aim as described in a Foreign Ministry memo was as follows: France would reconquer Gaullist Africa and defend the empire against Great Britain while attempting to take Britain's West African coastal bases. France would also allow the German navy and Luftwaffe the use of French bases in Africa.[32]

A German delegation headed by Warlimont and Abetz received Laval,

Huntziger, Darlan, and Major Paul Stehlin of French Air Force Command in the German embassy on the evening of 29 November.[33] The results were discouraging. Huntziger argued that Vichy could not initiate action in the Gulf of Guinea due to British naval superiority, and commented that the alternate approach to Lake Chad along the weakly defended Niamey-Zinder route lay exposed to British attack from Nigeria. Preparations for an attack on Chad could not be complete before April 1941. Worse, because the rainy season begins in May, operations could not start until November 1941—almost an entire year in the future. Huntziger said that in the meantime the recently released general Maurice-Emile Falvy would strengthen the Niamey-Zinder route with the mobile detachment that Hitler had granted, and that Vichy would send emissaries into Equatorial Africa to win back those troops that had strayed from the marshal. More irritations followed. Darlan argued that if his navy were to defend the key route from Toulon to Dakar, munitions production would need to resume in occupied and unoccupied France. He also complained that merchant shipping with the colonies remained unsatisfactory. Stehlin added that in a few months France would have no reserve aircraft. Aircraft production for French needs would have to resume despite the recent acceptance of German contracts. Huntziger added that Italy was still creating problems with the French military in North Africa. Turin had not permitted the 120,000-man army requested almost a month earlier, and was trying to water down the 100,000-man army by counting naval and air force personnel in the total number. Warlimont's main concern lay in a speedier advance on Chad. He suggested attacks on Freetown and Bathurst to allow French transports to the Gulf of Guinea, which would open an easier route to Chad via Gabon. Yet although Laval had few inhibitions about direct attacks on the British, Huntziger inclined toward patience.

The Germans were disappointed. Abetz told Huntziger that action in November 1941 would come after the war had ended and would thus be useless.[34] Warlimont was more inclined to see the glass as half full. On his return to Berlin, he reported to Ritter, Keitel, Jodl, and Hitler himself that even if offensive operations had to wait, France remained willing to defend the empire—no small favor to the Axis war efforts. Germany, he said, should expeditiously grant all of the requests of the 31 October memoranda. Otherwise the dry season would pass and delays in offensive operations would increase.[35]

Hitler understood this argument when he heard it on 3 December. He had wanted France to defend the empire since the September attack on Dakar.

Yet he seems to have been very concerned by the apparent French backslide on reconquest. If France lacked the will for offensive action, then perhaps it lacked the will to defend the empire, to say nothing of allowing German bases there. Thus, the day after Warlimont's briefing, Hitler told his military commanders that Germany needed to take Gibraltar as soon as possible while placing armored and motorized infantry divisions in Spanish Morocco. This move would end what the Führer understood to be the French black-mail of colonial secession.[36] On 5 December, Hitler wrote Mussolini, con-cerned that "one cannot have full security regarding the attitude of the government of Vichy" and that "the slightest counterstroke" could send French North and West Africa into the Allied camp. For the first time, Hitler also voiced his deep suspicion of General Weygand in Algiers and empha-sized that the control of the Strait of Gibraltar was paramount, for it would allow Germany to counter a French African defection. "From that moment only," he wrote, "can the situation in Northwest Africa be considered as definitely resolved in our favor."[37] After Franco refused to enter the war on the night of 7 December, Hitler became more concerned. He told Alfieri the next day, "The present situation [is] exceedingly serious," for "Spain is hesi-tating [and] France becoming refractory."[38] On 9 December, he told Keitel that, if Weygand were to defect, Germany would be unable to put troops in Morocco. From this anxiety Operation *Attila,* the occupation of unoccu-pied France, quickly emerged.[39]

Yet at the same time, there was reason to hope that Germany could still forge an arrangement with France. On 4 December, while Hitler was order-ing the placement of two divisions in Spanish Morocco, Laval met with Lieutenant Colonel Hans Speidel, Otto von Stülpnagel's chief of staff. Laval stated that both he and Pétain had been unhappy with Huntziger's 29 No-vember presentation. He promised to tell Huntziger and Darlan the next night that France needed a plan that could run immediately, not in a year. He added that once Germany granted the requests in Huntziger's 31 Octo-ber memoranda, fuel supplements alone would be needed to reconquer the lost territories.[40] Abetz soon reported that the French government would also discuss air attacks on Fort Lamy from southern Algeria and that Laval wished to report on the issue. He recommended that Warlimont return to Paris. Ribbentrop and Hitler were amenable.[41] Thanks to Laval, then, there was reason to believe in a Franco-German arrangement and on 9 December when Warlimont's plane left for Paris, Hitler commented to Halder that perhaps Franco's refusal to enter the war had been a blessing in disguise. Germany would have greater latitude in dealing with the French.[42] On 10

December, the day of Warlimont's meeting in Paris, the Führer canceled Operation *Felix*.[43]

The true course of Vichy cabinet discussions in the week preceding 10 December may never be known. Baudouin's diary paints Laval as the sole advocate of aggression in Africa, with Huntziger and Pétain appearing more cautious. The official record, however, suggests that Pétain and Huntziger had indeed concluded, at least temporarily, that an offensive against Chad, even at the risk of war with Britain, lay in France's interests.[44] Why the French became more eager at this point is not entirely clear. The desire to fight de Gaulle had never been lacking, nor had the resolve to retaliate against British strikes. Laval's hope, expressed since 31 October to the Germans, that such an action could win domestic concessions and territorial guarantees surely played a part. It would appear that for the moment, Pétain had decided to see what magic the unscrupulous foreign minister could create.

The same group that gathered in the German embassy on 29 November met on the evening of 10 December.[45] Laval said that the news would please Berlin, and Huntziger soon confirmed this statement. The reinforcement of the Niamey-Zinder route, he revealed, was under way with the sea transport of six to eight battalions from North Africa to West Africa. In Niamey, General Falvy was making preparations and overseeing political operations against Equatorial Africa. Extra war materials for West Africa were being gathered for shipment. By February 1941 the reinforcement of the Niamey-Zinder route would be complete and two to three bomber groups could from that time begin attacks on Fort Lamy and other Chad bases from Zinder and perhaps N'Guigmi.[46] French parachute units would then take the Gaullist bases in Chad. Should the British seek to disrupt French operations, added Huntziger, France would respond with air attacks on the northern Nigerian city of Kano. There were also plans, said Huntziger, for an attack on Bathurst from Dakar, and plans for an attack on Freetown were in progress. A surprised Warlimont had Huntziger confirm the last statement. Laval added that France was sincere in the desire to reconquer its lost colonies and fully accepted the possibility of war with Britain.

Yet the French wanted consideration. Militarily, Huntziger wanted the colonial officers and NCOs needed for the mobile detachment granted on 12 November released from prison camp.[47] He also needed more than a million liters of airplane fuel—a difficult problem in light of Italy's recent request for 30,000 tons of fuel. Laval had a political agenda as well. Primarily, he hoped that Berlin would declare that the French Empire would remain French. This, he said, would unmask de Gaulle not as the defender of

France's imperium but as a British stooge whose job lay in holding open the overland route to Egypt. Laval said he wanted to discuss the issue in greater detail with Ribbentrop, but Abetz refused to bite, noting blandly that Germany would surely demand the return of the Cameroons. When Laval conceded this point and tried to pursue the issue further, Abetz refused to talk politics. Laval's comment that the issue was of greater importance than the smaller one of releasing colonial officers only angered Huntziger. Still, Laval's closing words left no mistake that the French were still willing to take active measures in Africa. The marshal, he said, had emphasized repeatedly that the rebel areas had to be reconquered as soon as possible and that France had to counter English attacks as effectively as it could. "If you help us," Laval said, "we are ready to act. France is ready to act . . . to act immediately." After the meeting, Major Stehlin went to North Africa, Dakar, and Niamey to inform the commands there of the Paris discussion.

The German reaction was positive. Warlimont and Abetz agreed that Vichy's willingness to act had "received a decisive impetus since the first conference, and that there [could] be no doubt about the sincerity of the political and military intentions of the Pétain government."[48] Accordingly, the Germans began to meet Huntziger's military requests. Keitel studied the issue of airplane fuel immediately and on 12 December decided that Germany would provide half of the Italian demand for 30,000 tons of French airplane fuel. On the same day the High Command initiated steps for the release of French colonial officers, NCOs, and soldiers. Keitel ordered the Armistice Commission to examine the French personnel requests so that Germany could reach a decision on numbers simultaneously with political arrangements, which Keitel evidently expected soon. Keitel also planned to implement Abetz's suggestion that Germany reduce prisoner releases by finding trustworthy colonial soldiers from the occupied zone for service in West Africa.[49]

German-French collaboration in Africa was under way and Hitler's prophecy that Spain's absence would ease arrangements with France was about to be tested. Since the political discussions that Keitel and Laval had expected never occurred, one can only speculate as to what they would have entailed. Certainly, Vichy was prepared to attack de Gaulle and Berlin was prepared to give it the means to do so. The possibilities were also very strong that Germany would have demanded the bases on the Northwest African coast that Hitler had wanted since June. Whether Germany would have granted the type of political concessions for which Laval hoped is doubtful, but the question would become moot. All possibilities raised by the talks of 10 December ran aground on 13 December—a date that must be seen as one of the most pivotal in the Second World War. It was on this date that Hitler's schemes in Africa fell to pieces thanks in part to the fall of Pierre Laval.

At midday on 13 December 1940, Laval returned to Vichy from Paris. He brought an invitation from Hitler for Pétain to go to Paris for a special gesture. Germany was bringing the remains of the duke of Reichstadt, the son of Napoleon, from Vienna for reinterment in the Hôtel des Invalides. Here might have been the backdrop of the political meeting which many in Berlin and Vichy had been expecting.[50] At 8:00 P.M. Laval was summoned to an unscheduled meeting of the council of ministers. Pétain requested a letter of resignation from each minister, and upon receipt of the letters, kept only those of his minister of education, Georges Ripert, and the vice premier and foreign minister, Pierre Laval. Under police escort, Laval was taken to his country home in nearby Châteldon and placed under house arrest.[51]

The truth regarding the reasons for Laval's dismissal remain mysterious.[52] French memoir literature suggests that it concerned his policy of reconquest in Africa, which tied France to Germany while risking war with Britain.[53] Scholars have assailed this theory, since Huntziger, Darlan, and Pétain were also behind reconquest and none had qualms about firing on Allied forces later in Syria, Madagascar, or North Africa. Many argue that Pétain's explanation—that the affair was a domestic issue with no importance for Vichy's German policy—is more likely.[54] The marshal had never liked Laval personally, as numerous entries from Baudouin's diary show.[55] Laval's irritating style included the monopolization the negotiations with Germany without keeping the remainder of the Cabinet fully informed. The truth probably lies in the middle. Laval's problem was not his policy of collaboration; it was his failure to gain counterconcessions. Before his dismissal, Laval had made humiliating concessions to the Germans, particularly in the financial realm, without easing the ordeal of the occupation.[56] The Chad expedition was another concession—a potentially disastrous one—that lacked compensation. Vichy did not back away from collaboration as such. When it again raised the possibility of the Chad operation in the spring of 1941, it attached numerous counterdemands so that France would not be, as Pétain and Darlan would say, "marching in the dark."[57] In the meantime, Pétain was not lying when he wrote to Hitler on 13 December that Laval's methods lacked the national confidence or on the eighteenth when he wrote that differing views on the machinery of government had been one of the main difficulties with Laval.[58]

Of greater immediate importance was Berlin's reaction, which was stormier than anyone in Vichy had anticipated. To Hitler, Laval had come to embody France's willingness to cooperate with German aims in Africa. The affair thus confirmed to the Führer the truth of his past anti-French invective. Especially significant would be Hitler's unshakable conviction that Laval's dismissal and the fate of the French Empire in Africa were tied together and that it was General Weygand who had extorted Laval's removal with the threat of colonial defection. Hitler would never again trust the French in Africa as he had in the weeks after Montoire. From 13 December 1940 to 8 November 1942, France would receive next to no concessions for North Africa. Since simultaneous German efforts to extend influence into the region would be counterproductive, Northwest Africa would not only fail to become a springboard for German policies but would lie vulnerable to invasion.

The French sensed that Laval's dismissal would need damage control. Marshal Pétain's letter of explanation to Hitler of 13 December pledged that the affair meant no retreat from the spirit of Montoire and that "I want to make this collaboration more effective with each day."[59] In Wiesbaden on 16 December, Doyen passed Huntziger's message that France still adhered to the 10 December discussions.[60] But these efforts had no effect in Berlin, which replied that Abetz would go to Vichy to relay Hitler's answer and that the French had best make no changes in the meantime.[61]

Against the protests of Darlan and Stehlin, who were in Paris for the reinterment of the duke of Reichstadt, Abetz left for Vichy on 16 December, arriving at 9:00 P.M. with an SS escort. On the morning of the seventeenth, he told Pétain and Darlan that the Führer saw the Laval affair as a personal affront and presented them with several demands. First, France could keep the new foreign minister, Pierre-Étienne Flandin, but would have to make Laval minister of the interior. Second, Vichy was to replace its representative to the German occupation force, General Benoit La Laurencie, with the cooperative Ambassador Fernand de Brinon, hitherto Laval's personal representative in Paris. Finally, Pétain was to replace the vice-premiership with a multiheaded directorate consisting of Huntziger, Darlan, Flandin, and of course Laval.[62] Despite Abetz's threat that failure to comply would bury the spirit of Montoire, Pétain held firm. Laval's removal was irrevocable, he said, and if Germany were to insist on his reinstatement, then he would resign rather than become "the laughingstock of the country."[63] Darlan threatened resignation as well. Abetz fumed that France had thrown off the mask and that Vichy's attitude, which came from Italy's recent setbacks in Albania and North Africa, would prove disastrous.

Abetz's attempt later in the day to reconcile Pétain and Laval failed. Laval was brought back to Vichy, but there was only acrimony between Pétain and himself. A letter that Pétain had composed in the meantime to Hitler also struck Abetz as unsatisfactory, since it rejected the German demands concerning Laval.[64] Pétain had a new letter drafted and presented it to Abetz in the afternoon. It swore that the present situation had no effect "as to my firm determination to continue, in the spirit of our conversation at Montoire, the cooperation agreed upon between our two countries." It accepted the idea of the directorate and the appointment of Brinon. Yet Pétain could not reinstate Laval, for "my dignity and my authority would be seriously compromised if I should immediately take M. Laval back into the government." Pétain left a small opening, however. There would be an investigation into the reasons for Laval's removal. Should it throw a benign light on Laval, then he would return to the government. Here was the seed of future misunderstanding. Abetz thought that a sham investigation would be a face-saving formality and reported this assumption to Berlin as fact. Pétain had other ideas.[65] In the meantime, Abetz rejected the argument that the dismissal had been of domestic significance alone and informed Ribbentrop, who needed little convincing, that the real motive in removing Laval had in fact been France's "traditional hatred" of Germany. Vichy, he said, was making a show of cooperation while preparing to resume the struggle against the Reich.[66] Abetz asked for and received the sealing of the demarcation line to all French government officials as a punitive measure until Laval's reinstatement.[67] In a private talk with Spanish ambassador Lequerica on 17 December, Abetz revealed his indignation and that of Hitler. "The Führer," stated Abetz, "is furious with the affair, which he considers as a personal affront . . . I am indignant for my own part as well about this insult against Germany . . . during the moment of our very close dealings with the Minister of Foreign Affairs. The day 13 December will be a black date for France. The French have revealed themselves at a critical moment. During an insignificant failure by our Italian brothers, inflated by English propaganda . . . they have shown their true sentiments."[68]

Hitler was furious indeed. By 18 December he was again talking about a peace with Britain at France's expense.[69] For the moment he refrained from rash action, due to his unique assessment of the reasons for 13 December. He would soon reveal the belief that General Weygand was the true culprit in the matter. Weygand, who became delegate-general of French Africa on 6 September and set up his headquarters in Algiers in early October, was not deserving of such mistrust. Although determined to prevent a German presence in French Africa, he also viewed de Gaulle as a traitor, and he had no intention of joining the Allies. He was anti-encroachment, not necessarily anti-German.[70] Yet the Germans had been suspicious of him since he left for Algiers. His role, if any, in Laval's dismissal remains shrouded, but his aversion to Laval was well known in German circles. In mid-November the German Foreign Ministry demanded an official French denial of American press reports on the hatred between the two and the possible defection of Weygand.[71] Weygand's views on the plans to reconquer Gaullist Africa are unclear, but the Germans had reason to be concerned. On 30 November, the day after the first disappointing talks in Paris, Brinon told Speidel that Weygand was opposed to Laval and was anti-German, though also anti-Gaullist. The government, said Brinon, would remove him from his post in Africa.[72] Yet Weygand remained, and the Germans continued to receive disturbing reports. Hitler was concerned enough about the creation of a countergovernment in Algiers to order plans for Operation *Attila* after Franco refused to enter the war.[73] Yet the Vichy government seemed likely to remove Weygand. Huntziger commented to Warlimont on 10 December that Weygand was being watched and that his command would be broken down into three parts. He was to be summoned to Vichy soon for the news.[74] This removal of Laval then, whom Warlimont had said was the prime mover for the Vichy reconquest of Africa vis-à-vis Vichy's generals, came as a shock in Berlin, and there was reason for Hitler to believe that Weygand was somehow involved.[75]

More circumstantial evidence appeared after 13 December that seemed to implicate Weygand. Most disturbing was the report that the new American ambassador to Vichy, Admiral William Leahy, would soon arrive there to foster French resistance, and that his counselor of embassy, Robert Murphy, would establish personal contact with Weygand.[76] Ribbentrop had Huntziger pressed on the nature of Murphy's mission but received no answers.[77] By mid-December Hitler was more convinced that the recent breakdown in German-French relations was Weygand's work, and he told Jodl that if for no other reason, *Attila* would be maintained.[78] Hitler's suspicions would become firmer after Berlin learned that Pétain did not intend to reinstate Laval after the promised investigation. On 21 December, Brinon told Abetz that German insistence on Laval's reinstatement would only damage relations, and that Pétain hoped that a directorate of Darlan, Huntziger, and Flandin could promote the spirit of Montoire alone. Hitler, he promised, would soon receive a letter from Pétain on the matter. Abetz himself was willing to endorse these comments. He cabled Ribbentrop that Darlan would

continue an Anglophobe policy, while Brinon would purge the French administration and Paris police of undesirables. Both men were also on good
terms with Laval. Abetz continued that Pétain's resignation and the consequences that it might have brought in Africa had been avoided. He suggested that Berlin be content while keeping a low heat under the Laval affair
in order to ensure his reinstatement later.[79] Yet Ribbentrop lacked patience.
Shocked that Pétain's investigation had not brought the expected result, he
ordered Abetz to say that Germany could only note "with the utmost aston-
ishment" that Laval was still outside the government and that Berlin would
withhold comment until it had learned the contents of Pétain's letter.[80]

Hitler learned the contents when Darlan delivered the letter in a tense
meeting northwest of Paris on Christmas Day. The investigation, said the
letter, validated the grievances against Laval, but the affair was purely inter-
nal and would not affect French policies.[81] Hitler was thoroughly unconvinced.
Instead, he gleaned from the letter one sentence that confirmed his suspicions. Pétain had commented that should he bring Laval back into the government, "I would be inflicting a dangerous blow to the unity of the empire."
Here, Hitler pointed out, was the key. *Weygand* had caused Laval's fall with
the threat of defection. Stehlin, who was present, wrote that Hitler mentioned Weygand's name twice, accompanying it with a fit of wrath.[82] France,
Hitler said, was following the path that had led the country to disaster and
would live to regret it. Moreover, he noted ominously, cooperation with
France was over. Darlan's protests that France still supported Montoire fell
on deaf ears.[83]

Abetz offered numerous reasons for Pétain's stiffening policy in the Laval
affair, with numerous possible solutions.[84] Yet Hitler had seen all that he
needed to see. His conviction that he had traced the Laval affair to Weygand
would remain. On the last day of 1940, he wrote Mussolini:

> *The reasons communicated to me officially [for Laval's dis-*
> *missal] are untrue. I no longer doubt for a second that the reason*
> *is that General Weygand is sending extortionist demands from*
> *North Africa to the Vichy government and the latter does not feel*
> *able to proceed against General Weygand without assuming the*
> *danger of losing North Africa. I consider it possible that in Vichy*
> *itself quite a number of persons are covering the Weygand policy*
> *at least secretly. I do not believe that General Pétain personally is*
> *acting disloyally. However, one cannot be sure of that either. This*
> *forces us to maintain a sharp scrutiny of what is going on.*[85]

These ideas shaped Berlin's future policies toward Northwest Africa, which were designed to prevent the defection of Vichy-controlled Africa, but were steeped in counterproductivity. A three-pronged scheme developed. First, Germany would turn a "cold shoulder" to the French overtures for cooperation in Africa. Montoire was dead. Second, Germany would monitor the situation in French Northwest Africa as best it could by sending observers to Morocco. Finally, Germany would return to the plan to take Gibraltar so that German troops could move into French Morocco if need be. These issues will receive coverage in order.

Hitler commented to his military commanders on 9 January 1941 at the Berghof that Italy's problems in Albania had created a shift of mood in unoccupied France and the French Empire. The French hoped for a reversal of fortune while following a policy of watchful waiting. This was especially the case with Weygand, who had certainly threatened defection should Vichy act against Great Britain. Hitler's solution was that Germany no longer had any obligations to France, and he added that this state of affairs was a good one for Germany.[86] France would receive a "cold shoulder" from Berlin.[87]

This was not the preferred policy of Germany's more insightful diplomats and strategists, who saw more need than ever to work with France. Leahy was on his way to Vichy, and on 17 December Roosevelt announced a program of increased aid for Great Britain, which would eventually become the Lend-Lease Plan of March 1941.[88] Meanwhile in the eastern Mediterranean, the British were pounding the Italian fleet while beginning their rout of the Italians in North Africa.[89] Grand Admiral Raeder and his associates flatly announced that the United States had entered the war, albeit without a formal military alliance. The Axis, they admitted, could no longer decide the war in the Mediterranean, but they still hoped to attack Gibraltar to cripple British transport in the Atlantic while relieving pressure on the Italians. Gibraltar would also create a connection between Europe and Northwest Africa for the movement of goods and troops.[90] Cooperation with France thus remained key. The navy blamed the sudden absence of cooperation partly on the recent American diplomatic initiatives in Vichy and on the recent Italian setbacks, but primarily on German policy. Laval's dismissal, they said, should have been met differently, for the French remained willing to cooperate.[91] The navy also felt that Berlin overestimated the specter of Weygand. Raeder planned to raise this issue with Hitler at the Berghof meeting of 9 January, but never did so due to Hitler's furious invective against the French delegate-general.[92] State Secretary Ernst von Weizsäcker shared the navy's view. In the second week of January, he argued to

Ribbentrop that the cold-shoulder policy was counterproductive. "Our present almost complete reserve toward the Vichy Régime," argued Weizsäcker, "can in the long run lead to a political vacuum between ourselves and the French, which is advantageous to English and American propaganda."[93] Carl-Heinrich von Stülpnagel agreed. The Armistice Commission had long maintained that the rumors regarding Weygand had been unfounded and that Weygand stood firmly behind Pétain.[94]

Yet Hitler maintained his course. The navy's arguments were ignored, as were those of Weizsäcker. Stülpnagel, meanwhile, would be removed from his post on 12 February and replaced as chairman of the Armistice Commission by General Oskar Vogl, previously chief of military inspection in Bourges, who had a penchant for strictness if not insight.[95] On 8 February, Keitel sent new directives to Wiesbaden. The Laval affair, Keitel said, had destroyed German trust in France and, until further notice, the armistice treaty would be the sole criterion for German-French relations. Military concessions which Germany had hitherto granted would remain in place and would receive the sharpest inspection. All future French requests would be denied. Existing forces in Africa were enough to combat de Gaulle, and unless France were to show that reconquest was their true objective, "there exists only the danger that each military concession by us [will] one day work against our ally and thus also against ourselves."[96]

The second response to the Laval affair was the dispatch of German observers to French Morocco. It will be recalled that the Germans in September 1940 had already made plans for a mixed German-Italian control commission for French Morocco and West Africa. The project had slipped into abeyance at Vichy's request following the Anglo-Gaullist attack on Dakar. Now Berlin would exhume the idea despite French protests. Observers would go to French Morocco and remain until the American landings in November 1942. Moreover, there would be nothing "mixed" about their presence. Italian officials in Morocco would be sent packing.

An official German presence in French Morocco began in the third week of December with the arrival of a Dr. Theodor Auer and a small economic staff to Casablanca. Auer's group served under Hemmen's economic delegation in Wiesbaden, but their functions also involved political and military information gathering with the occasional cloak-and-dagger episode involving the protection and support of German spies.[97] After the Laval affair, General Noguès spoke to Auer twice, assuring him that Vichy had not changed its policy toward Germany and that he and Morocco, despite rumors to the contrary, stood firmly behind the marshal.[98] Auer was convinced and reported his observations on 30 December 1940. "Presently in [French Morocco]," he said, "there is no reason for worry concerning the interests of our war effort." He continued that there was no Gaullist movement to speak of and that Noguès's political leanings harmonized well with Vichy's. In addition, there was no reason to expect any initiative against the government from the French army in Morocco or from the Moroccan natives. Though the French often invoked the threat of a native uprising, Auer said, the independence movement was feeble. The true wielders of native power, the tribal leaders, had no reason to revolt against France, which defended their positions and bought their loyalty with gifts. Morocco, Auer concluded, would remain calm as long as the French felt that it would remain French, the natives had a steady flow of green tea and sugar, and French prestige there remained unbruised.[99]

Hitler was less optimistic. Despite Auer's comments, planning for a full German inspection commission went forward in late December. The new commission began officially as an armament and fuel inspection commission under the wing of the high command's War Economy and Armaments Office in Berlin and under the direct command of Wiesbaden. The exact origins of the armament and fuel commission are not completely clear. German and Italian officials had talked in Munich in mid-November about Axis use of French fuel stocks. It was agreed that Italy would create fuel inspection commissions in North Africa with German liaison officers attached, and that one of these Italian commissions would be in Casablanca. Wiesbaden, invoking the Roatta Agreements of June 1940, protested that the Atlantic coast of Morocco was a German sphere of responsibility. The protest was submitted to Hitler, who agreed on 10 January 1941. Mussolini would be informed that a German commission in Casablanca would replace the Italian one there.[100] For the moment, the Italians would retain their military control commissions in Fez and Rabat, but in fact their days were also numbered, for the German commission, as Wiesbaden learned on 11 January, would grow by degrees.[101] With the French African empire seemingly near defection, Hitler was no longer concerned with Rome's feelings or the Roatta Agreements.

After Hitler's decision, events moved quickly. On 14 January, the German Armistice Commission's armaments department under Colonel Hünermann informed the French delegation that Germany would form in Casablanca a commission to inspect armament and fuel stocks *for all of French Morocco save the Mediterranean coast*. Details on the size of the commission were to come later. The French were told to provide a liaison for a small preliminary group that would travel to Casablanca in a week.[102] Vichy protested immediately. The next day, Doyen expressed to Stülpnagel his "profound surprise" given the "delicate situation" in the French colonies. A few discreet civilian observers under Auer were bad enough. An official military inspection group was a different matter with potentially explosive results.[103] Huntziger protested to the German embassy in Paris the same day. Rumors of Vichy treachery in Africa, he said, were a Gaullist ploy to deceive Berlin, and he vouched for the loyalty of Noguès and Weygand. Moreover, the German commission could cause the natives to lose respect for France. He asked to discuss the issue with Warlimont or another high German military figure before Berlin implemented the decision.[104]

French overtures were unsuccessful. Huntziger's complaints were taken directly to Hitler, who deduced that Weygand and Huntziger simply "did not want the Germans and Italians to look at their cards in North Africa."[105] On 16 January, Stülpnagel told Doyen that the German armament and fuel commission would only supplement the Italian commissions already in Morocco, and that the French government thus had no grounds for complaint. As for the fear that the Commission could cause political problems, Stülpnagel wryly noted that Noguès had made no indication to this effect on the arrival of Auer's group.[106] On the same day, Hünermann informed the French that the preliminary group, consisting of four officers and an interpreter, would start from Wiesbaden for Casablanca on 22 January.[107] When the twenty-second arrived, the French tried again to stop the German mission, this time with the desperate argument that thunderstorms had destroyed the airfield at Casablanca. The Germans decided to take their chances.[108] On 26 January, the preliminary group arrived in Casablanca, and the leader of the group, Major Battre, visited Noguès with Auer the same day. Noguès was noticeably disturbed with even this small German military presence, and he voiced the hope that for the sake of order, the commission would not grow in size.[109]

Yet the remainder of the armament and fuel commission was set up in the final week of January. It would amount to forty-eight men in all under the command of Lieutenant Colonel Pietri and would leave for Casablanca on 5 February. Its charge was to inspect armament and fuel stocks *while paying particular attention to possible French political or military intentions as reflected by the disposition of these stocks.* Moreover, the commission was to make general military observations and to this end had members of the Abwehr, army, navy, and Luftwaffe attached, as well as a courier staff with two airplanes. Finally and perhaps most irritating to the French, its members would be uniformed, at least when on duty.[110] Auer protested vehemently. In his report to Wiesbaden after the meeting with Noguès on 26 January, he argued that the commission should grow very gradually without giving the impression of occupation, and preferably should not grow at all.[111] He further warned that the dispatch of some fifty German officers to Casablanca—Italy had but twelve inspection officers in all of French Morocco—could risk the peace by undermining French authority. Rather than feed the British propaganda that warned of a German occupation of Morocco, he advised, Berlin should win Morocco's natives over with goods.[112] Yet Auer failed to persuade. On 6 February 1941, the remainder of the armament and fuel commission arrived. Noguès pledged his cooperation to Pietri and asked that the Germans remain discreet.[113] Time would tell if the Germans would indeed honor the resident-general's request.

No sooner had Wiesbaden created the armament and fuel commission than the High Command began work on a full-scale military control commission for all of French Morocco. The first definite mention of such a commission, which was to be under the command of General Schultheiss, came on 2 February 1941, the same day Auer's advice reached Berlin.[114] In presenting his new guidelines to Wiesbaden on 8 February, Keitel had noted that Germany would take over inspection functions in French Morocco, that the Foreign Ministry had given its agreement to this intention, and that Wiesbaden would work out the details with the Italian Armistice Commission.[115] In April, against French protests, Schultheiss and his commission of roughly two hundred men would arrive in Morocco, and the Italian commissioners would leave. That which the French had attempted to prevent since the armistice would finally occur. A German presence in North Africa, in the form of German control in French Morocco, would become a reality. Yet Hitler had wanted even more, and this he demonstrated when he turned back toward the route via Spain to Northwest Africa.

Hitler's turn back toward Madrid in January and February 1941 has been described as a *Nachspiel* to earlier German efforts to get Spain in the war—an aftershock caused by the December 1940 intensification of British pressure on Italy in the Mediterranean.[116] There are other possible interpretations, however. Operation *Felix*, after all, was canceled on 10 December 1940, the day *after* the commencement of General Archibald Wavell's North African offensive, and since the directive number used for *Felix*, 19, was given to *Attila* on the same day, one can assume that Hitler did not plan to return to the Gibraltar operation any time soon. The reason for the turn back to Spain and for the new intensity of German pressure on Madrid might well have been the situation in France. Hitler's conviction that General Weygand had been behind the Laval affair and his fear that Weygand could defect either in the near future or during the eastern campaign made it all the more essential for Germany to gain control of the Strait of Gibraltar as soon as possible.

On 18 December 1940, Hitler signed War Directive 21, Operation *Barbarossa*—the centerpiece of his continental war. The Soviet Union's destruction would give Germany its all-important Lebensraum. The army would need all available units, and all preparations were to be complete by 15 May 1941.[117] Von Brauchitsch had told Hitler in early December that if Germany were to employ the forces in *Felix* in the eastern campaign, then *Felix* had to be complete by late February. Hitler agreed; German forces were to enter Spain on 10 January and attack the Rock by 5 February.[118] In December and January, then, little time remained to take Gibraltar and settle the real and imagined problems in Northwest Africa. Hitler told Raeder on 27 December that *Barbarossa* would proceed as planned and that Germany would build up the navy and Luftwaffe afterward.[119] Yet could the Führer leave Germany's future bases of operations to chance during *Barbarossa*? With French loyalty in doubt and American interest in Africa increasing, he could not. He would try to force a settlement of the issue before *Barbarossa*.

Through most of December 1940, Hitler accepted Franco's refusal with the calm assurance that Spain's absence would make German arrangements with France easier. Even after Laval's dismissal, he refrained from turning back to *Felix*. This restraint was due partly to Abetz's expectation that Pétain's investigation into the Laval affair was a formality that would bring Laval back. Hitler had also yet to convince himself fully that Weygand had been behind the intrigues at Vichy. Thus on 20 December, the day before Pétain revealed that his investigation confirmed the correctness of Laval's dismissal, Hitler wrote Mussolini about Franco in a tone that was irritated at most, noting simply that the Axis might have expected a stronger show of gratitude from Franco and that Germany and Italy "would have to remember [Franco's] attitude."[120]

After Darlan brought Pétain's letter on Christmas Day, which "revealed" that Weygand was holding the French Empire hostage, Hitler's stance toward Spain changed. In speaking with Raeder on 27 December, he again noted Gibraltar's importance in terms of a German move into French North

Africa and said that he would have Ribbentrop push Ambassador Espinosa on the issue.[121] In his 31 December letter to Mussolini, which connected Weygand to the Laval affair, Hitler heightened his invective against Franco. He noted without uncertainty the connection between Gibraltar and the threat posed by Weygand and damned Franco for ruining a well-planned operation. "From the moment the Strait of Gibraltar was in our hands," bemoaned the Führer, "the danger of any kind of untoward behavior on the part of French North and West Africa would have been eliminated. For this reason I am very sad about this decision of Franco's which does not take into account the help which we—you, *Duce,* and I—once gave him in his hour of need. I have only a faint hope left that he will become aware of the catastrophic nature of his own actions and he will after all—even though late—find his way to the camp of the front whose victory will also decide his own fate." He noted with a certain malevolence, "I fear that Franco is committing here the greatest mistake of his life."[122]

With the new year, Hitler moved toward an attempt to change Franco's mind. On 9 January, at a conference at the Berghof that included Ribbentrop and the *Wehrmacht* chiefs, Hitler reviewed Germany's situation. The end of the Soviet Union would bring helpful results in its wake. It would free Japan's rear flank, thus allowing Tokyo to threaten America in the Pacific. It would convince Britain that its cause was hopeless, thus forcing London to make peace. It would end all continental threats to Germany, thus allowing it to pare down its army while preparing for the next enemy with augmented naval and air force production. The war, he said, was won, but one problem remained. The French, thanks to Italian mishaps in Greece and in Libya, had adopted an attitude of watchful waiting, especially in Africa. Weygand was especially dangerous, for he had undoubtedly threatened to defect with North Africa if Pétain took up the fight against Great Britain. Germany could need to implement Operation *Attila* at any time. Hitler said that events could not go sour for Germany even with the loss of North Africa, but in truth he could not bring himself to leave the area to chance. Thus, even though he said early in the meeting that the *Wehrmacht* could cancel *Felix,* he noted near the end that, even though it hardly seemed possible, he would try once more to win Spanish entry into the war.[123]

Little changed in military circles for a few days, despite the High Command's willingness to pursue the Gibraltar operation with or without Spanish help. The day after the Berghof meeting, Jodl told Warlimont that *Attila* had to remain ready and that *Felix* was still in a state of suspension. This irritated Warlimont, who agreed with Raeder on the need to take Gibraltar for the Mediterranean's sake and who felt that Hitler had badly misjudged the stance of Weygand. French Africa, he believed, was in no danger unless the British were to take action there. In Warlimont's eyes, as in Raeder's, Germany could attack Gibraltar *and* cooperate with the French in Africa.[124] The navy had in fact worked on a scheme in late December whereby German submarines would attack the Royal Navy at Gibraltar despite Spain's nonbelligerence. Yet studies demonstrated the tremendous difficulties of this scheme, and Submarine Commander Karl Dönitz demurred at weakening the supply war in the Atlantic.[125] The idea would not have won Hitler's approval anyway. A sea assault on Gibraltar would not have guaranteed the land route through Spain that Hitler wanted. On inquiry from Warlimont in mid-January, Jodl said that an attack on Gibraltar without Spain's agreement was against the Führer's wishes and that *Felix* was thus still abandoned.[126]

Yet in the political realm, Hitler was taking steps to gain Madrid's agreement. On 19 and 20 December, Mussolini, Ciano, and General Alfredo Guzzoni, deputy chief of *Commando Supremo*, visited the snow-covered Berghof for pivotal meetings with Hitler and his top aides. To the Italians, the main issue was German aid in Greece and in Libya where their fronts were crumbling daily. These Berghof meetings were, as one historian has stated, "Italy's end as a Great Power," for Italy's war effort was in many ways handed over to Germany.[127] German troops, Hitler said, would attack Greece in March, and German support would go to Libya as soon as possible. Yet with their ally collapsing, Hitler and Ribbentrop spent considerable time on the issues of Weygand and Franco. On the nineteenth, Ribbentrop lectured Ciano of the need to take Gibraltar to paralyze French sedition in North Africa. He announced that German efforts to bring Franco into the fray were exhausted and expressed the strong hope that Mussolini would try his own luck.[128] Later the same day, Hitler made more forceful overtures.[129] His long tirade against Vichy and Weygand now included the note that even declarations of loyalty from Pétain and Weygand would not bring him to trust France. Huntziger was suspect due to his Alsatian background, and though Darlan's Anglophobia was sincere, he was but one man in a rotten government. Hitler wanted Laval back in the government but feared forcing the issue. Germany could do nothing more, said Hitler, since decisive steps against Vichy could result in the defection of North Africa. And yet, said Hitler, if the Axis held Gibraltar, "it would extraordinarily ease the situation relative to North Africa and would put an end to the whole de Gaulle magic, especially if two

German divisions could be transferred to Spanish Morocco and a few air bases could be set up there. Unfortunately Franco had failed to recognize this situation. He was only an average officer who, because of an accident of circumstance, had been pushed into the position of Chief of State. He was not a sovereign, but a subaltern in temperament." He chronicled Franco's ingratitude to the Axis, damned him again for pulling the plug on *Felix*, and then asked Mussolini to meet Franco in a last attempt to change his mind. The Duce reluctantly agreed to do so at the end of the month.

In the discussion of the following day, Hitler underscored the same themes. According to recent reports, Hitler said, the French had left only a small troop contingent on the Tripolitanian border, and were moving their forces in Morocco west. From the Strait of Gibraltar, Germany could cut the rail connections between Morocco and Algeria and thus end all black-mail by Weygand, while easing the situation to the rear flank of Tripoli. In the meantime, Italy had to hold Tobruk so as not to encourage the French, and because the Italian position might be needed as a point of departure to solve the Moroccan question. There were, said Hitler, two danger spots for Germany at present—Russia and Algeria—and the latter threat would vanish as soon as Gibraltar fell into Axis hands.[130]

Later on the twentieth, the German High Command began to act. Jodl telephoned Warlimont that Germany would send a support force to Libya in mid-February under the code name *Sonnenblume*. Jodl also informed Warlimont that *Felix* was, thanks to Mussolini's upcoming efforts, to be maintained.[131] The next day, Warlimont relayed Jodl's orders to the service branches and ordered his own staff to examine the extent to which *Felix* had been dismantled.[132] The navy began preparing anew. On 23 January, Fricke had the coastal batteries destined for the Canary Islands placed on fourteen-day alert. Transport vessels were to remain available.[133] It was all a wasted effort. At the same time, Ribbentrop was destroying any possibility that the Axis could bring Spain around. The jackhammering attempted by Ribbentrop at this time remains a mystery, especially given his comment to Ciano on 19 January that German efforts with Madrid were exhausted and that the time for an Italian effort had come. Perhaps the foreign minister could not admit failure. Perhaps he truly believed that a bullying approach could shake Franco from what Hitler believed was a lack of resolve.[134] Whatever the reason, the verbal assault now launched on Madrid would not have the desired effect.

Before the Berghof meeting with the Italians, Ribbentrop met with Ambassador Stohrer in Salzburg and instructed him to make a forceful *démarche* with Franco upon his return to Spain. This, according to what Ribbentrop told Ciano on 19 January, was to be Berlin's last try. On 20 January 1941, while Hitler and Ribbentrop were meeting with the Italians, Stohrer was meeting with Franco and Serrano. Equipped with written notes that he had made in Salzburg, Stohrer explained "with ruthless candor" that the Führer was very disappointed by Franco, who had reflected a lack of faith in a German victory. Since Germany would provide economic aid and since German troops would do most of the fighting, Berlin rejected the excuse that Spain could not wage war. Spain's hour, he said, had struck. Franco had forty-eight hours to decide, a deadline intended not to pressure Madrid but rather to reflect Germany's need to use the troops elsewhere soon. Franco and Serrano were astounded. Spain intended to fight, argued Franco, but only once it had become economically solvent. Present negotiations with the United States and Great Britain for grain would cover no more than Spain's peacetime needs, and German economic aid would come too late if Berlin were to wait until Spain was already at war. Stohrer brushed this argument aside. Germany might choose not to help Spain later, and Spanish aspirations would be jeopardized. Franco raised the possibility of advance German aid to relieve Spain's most acute economic needs. Stohrer said that it could be possible if *Germany* could set the date for Spanish entry. Franco and Serrano requested time to discuss the matter and Stohrer agreed.[135]

Franco might have been stalling for time. The two-day deadline, coupled with the statement that German forces would be needed elsewhere afterward, tipped the German hand. During the next two days, Stohrer received no answers from Serrano on the pretext that Franco's defense council had not reached a decision.[136] Ribbentrop sought to solve the impasse on 21 January with an especially pugnacious oral message for Franco. Without Hitler and Mussolini, it said, there would be no Franco, and the fate of Nationalist Spain was bound to that of the Axis. The Gibraltar operation would be of value only if it were to be executed within a few weeks, and after this period, other operations would take priority. Ribbentrop ended with the ominous prophesy that "unless the Caudillo decides immediately to join the war of the Axis Powers, the Reich government cannot but forsee the end of Nationalist Spain."[137] Franco, on hearing the message on 23 January, was visibly furious. Spain's entry into the war would come, he protested, but economic recovery was a prerequisite. He launched into a treatise on Spain's economic woes, while Stohrer tried unsuccessfully to bring him back to the immediate point at hand. Spain, said the ambassador, had to act in the immediate future. Franco said that he would answer later.[138]

Ribbentrop responded with a second oral message on 24 January, again demanding a "yes or no" answer. He grudgingly included a promise for the 100,000 tons of Swiss grain then in Lisbon, which the Spaniards had requested back in November.[139] Yet this concession was too little and too late. By early February, Stohrer would report a lack of bread in several sections of Spain and the expectation of food riots. Franco would comment later to Mussolini that the Swiss shipment would barely suffice for twenty days.[140] Moreover, Ribbentrop's messages made no attempt to solve the colonial issue of Article 5 of the Hendaye Protocol, and although the Spaniards would not mention this omission to the Germans, they would indeed mention it to the Italians in February. Finally, the Germans were still talking about the use of the Strait of Gibraltar as a route for German troops into Africa.[141] Thus Franco, on receiving the new message on 27 January, was no closer to entering the war. On the contrary, he pointed out the logistical problems that would face his army in Morocco and complained for the first time that the fight for Gibraltar would not be short. He requested a visit by economic experts and asked if Keitel could visit as well. Stohrer tried several times to push Franco for a definite answer but failed. The result was that a week after receiving a forty-eight-hour deadline, Franco had given no answer. Ribbentrop chided von Stohrer for allowing Franco to digress, while asking if he had read the messages verbatim. Surely, he felt, such abrasive language could not have failed to bring Franco into the war.[142]

Ribbentrop's failure left Hitler in a dilemma. Would he cancel *Felix* again or would he take the chance that *Felix* would intrude on the timing of *Barbarossa*? He opted for the former alternative at first. Despite the fact that Warlimont's staff had been preparing *Felix* anew since 21 January, Hitler told Jodl on the twenty-eighth that Germany would have to discard the plan, since the political conditions could not be created. He reasoned that even if preparations were to commence on 1 February, the attack on Gibraltar itself could not begin before mid-April. In such a scenario, the troops there would not be available for *Barbarossa* by mid-May.[143] Yet in spite of the primacy of *Barbarossa*, Hitler could not bring himself to let Northwest Africa hang. In his letter to Mussolini of 5 February, Hitler again voiced hope that the Duce could convince Franco of the urgency of the situation. Spain's latest proposal for entry into the war in the autumn or winter of 1941, he said, was not good enough. Had Franco entered the war in December, he lamented, Germany could have attacked the Rock on 1 February. "It is a shame," Hitler muttered, "to see . . . a great chance . . . lost simply through irresoluteness."[144]

While waiting for Mussolini, Hitler tried a personal letter to Franco on 6 February.[145] He bluntly informed Franco that he gave no credence to his excuses. He, Franco, and Mussolini were linked by history. If Germany and Italy were to fall in their struggle against Jewish democracy, Nationalist Spain would follow. Yet Hitler was most upset at the delay that Franco had created. "It is my conviction," declared Hitler, "that time is one of the most important factors in a war. . . . Two months have been lost which otherwise might have helped to decide world history." Franco remained unimpressed with the importance of time. Hitler would not receive a reply for a month— an answer that again gave no solid assurances.[146]

Mussolini's turn came at the Italian Riviera town of Bordighera. Although Hitler wanted this meeting to occur by late January, Serrano did not receive Ciano's invitation until the twenty-sixth and did not reply until the twenty-ninth.[147] Thus, a rather skeptical Duce greeted Franco and Serrano on 12 February.[148] Possibly due to the ease that Franco and Serrano felt with the Italians, they spoke more freely than they had with the Germans. Franco dropped the bombshell that although Spain intended to enter the war, it would take Gibraltar by itself. In short, Franco wanted German troops neither in the Iberian Peninsula nor in Morocco. Before Spain entered the war, however, there were two conditions that Germany would have to meet. First, Germany would have to supply Spain with enough grain to last the duration and with the equipment that Spain would need to fight effectively.[149] Second, there would have to be a revision of Article 5 of the Hendaye Protocol that would guarantee French Morocco to Spain. Franco and Serrano talked extensively on this point. The Hendaye meeting, they said, had been a tremendous disappointment. The Germans understood neither Spain's needs nor its aspirations. The Spaniards also voiced great irritation with Berlin's willingness to work with Vichy to Madrid's detriment, and with the seemingly lax German attitude toward possible French treachery in Morocco, where Weygand, according to Franco, was maintaining daily contact with the United States. Having vented their spleens, Franco and Serrano left for Spain the same day.

On the way back to Spain, Franco and Serrano paid a courtesy call on Marshal Pétain and Admiral Darlan at Montpellier on 13 February. The prearranged meeting hinged mainly on ceremony. The participants spent much time amidst great pomp, discussing the extradition of republican refugees to Spain. Yet Pétain and Franco also agreed that close cooperation between their respective countries in North Africa was desirable, as was the need to keep the Germans out of western Mediterranean region.[150] On his return to Madrid, Serrano wisely denied to Stohrer that this issue had come up.[151] Still, the Spaniards had to have felt pleased. Vichy had already offered the previous autumn to implement the Moroccan border agreement of 1925 while recognizing Spain's actions in Tangier, and on the eve of the Hendaye meeting, Madrid had rejected this offer. In February 1941, with the possibility of an arrangement via Berlin dead, Vichy was still willing to talk. An agreement with the French could leave Spain with something for its trouble without obliging Spain to deal further with the Germans.[152] In fact, Spain would receive nothing definite from Vichy either. Until the time of Operation *Torch* Madrid would continually press Vichy for a generous new arrangement in Africa, but without the tiniest success.[153] In the meantime, friction continued between Noguès and the Spanish High Commissariat concerning any public statements concerning Spanish colonial claims, even when Spanish speeches were made as far away as Barcelona.[154]

In Berlin, the Germans read Franco's comments to Mussolini as a final refusal to enter the war. Perhaps Franco meant it that way. His material conditions practically demanded that Germany create a new country where Spain was located.[155] On 22 February 1941, Ribbentrop cabled Stohrer that Spain had not the least intention of entering the war, and he ordered the ambassador to maintain reserve in Madrid.[156] Hitler echoed this sentiment in a letter to Mussolini of 28 February, regretting once more that the Spanish stance wrested from Germany "the best opportunity for putting an end to the French seesaw policy."[157] Hitler voiced the same regrets to Ciano the following day, noting that the German expedition to Libya and the consolidation of the desert theater now presented the sole means of keeping pressure on French North Africa. As for the idea of a solo Spanish expedition against the Rock, Hitler was cynical indeed, grumbling that, "they would probably not obtain their objective in ten years."[158]

All that remained was the final dismantling. On 14 February the navy ceased all preparations for *Felix*.[159] Three days later, Raeder ordered that the coastal batteries that had been reserved for the Canaries be moved to Narvik to help defend the north flank during *Barbarossa*.[160] On 22 February, the High Command reported that *Felix* and the conquest of Malta would be projects for the coming autumn.[161] Germany would not move into North-

in March, would not harmonize the contradictory aims of helping the British while arming themselves until 1942, and even then, the Americans would have to respect the Japanese threat in the Pacific.[2] Hitler fully shared this optimism, noting in the same month that American help to Great Britain would produce no tangible results until 1942 and that by that time, increased German industrial output would dwarf such aid.[3] Still, the concern remained that Roosevelt would seize key bases while Germany was busy in the East. Hitler thus wanted peace with Washington, at least until after the eastern campaign. Through the spring and summer of 1941, he repeatedly warned the navy away from incidents in the Atlantic, despite Raeder's attempt to shift Germany's focus west and the navy's anger at the privileged position of American shipping.[4] Berlin also worked on clumsy public relations gestures. In meetings with the former American ambassador to Belgium John Cudahy in May 1941, Hitler and Ribbentrop emphasized that Germany's position was unassailable, that American entrance into the war would be sheer folly, and that Germany had no designs on the United States.[5]

At the same time, Berlin was working to create a greater Japanese threat in the Pacific. In early March, Keitel proclaimed that the service branches would cooperate fully with their Japanese counterparts in order to bring the latter into active operations against the British in the Far East. If Germany could move Japan to attack Singapore, he said, British forces would be tied to the Pacific, London would surrender more quickly, and the United States, fearing for its Pacific flank, would remain neutral.[6] Later in March, Hitler and Ribbentrop welcomed Tokyo's foreign minister Yosuke Matsuoka to Germany. The Three Power Pact's aim, said Ribbentrop to his guest on 27 March, lay in neutralizing America through intimidation. Japan could best contribute by attacking the British in Singapore. With Great Britain near defeat and America unprepared to help, added Hitler later in the day, the Axis could end the war against the former while isolating the latter. Yet the time to act was now. Inaction would witness the American inheritance of the British Empire, after which Washington would remain hostile to the Axis while growing stronger. The Germans assured Matsuoka that they would attack the Soviet Union if the latter created trouble on the Japanese flank, without sharing the secret that Germany would soon attack the USSR anyway. The Germans *also* promised to join Japan if the latter, by attacking Britain's Far Eastern holdings, were to become involved in a war with the United States. The risk of an earlier war with the United States, in other words, was fully acceptable to Hitler if the Japanese were willing to bring *their* considerable power to bear against the Anglo-Saxons as well. The alternative to this promise in Berlin's eyes, after all, might have been a Japanese-American rapprochement, the consequences of which would have been even less preferable for Germany. The willingness to risk war sooner rather than later with the Americans would of course remain agreeable in December 1941, when the Japanese would attack Pearl Harbor on the seventh and Germany would respond on the eleventh with a declaration of war on the United States. Yet for the spring, the Japanese balked. Though sympathetic to German arguments, Matsuoka commented that some in Tokyo still feared a long war with the Americans. For the moment, Tokyo would decide for itself and Germany would have to wait, accepting what seemed like a real possibility that the Japanese could reach accommodation over its political and economic differences with Washington.[7]

Though events in the Pacific were beyond Germany's reach in the spring of 1941, hope remained that the Reich could still influence events in Northwest Africa. Part of the solution was purely military. Hitler gave orders in late February for the execution of *Felix* immediately after victory in the East was assured. The resulting plans for Operation *Felix-Heinrich* called for Germany to pull the troops necessary for Gibraltar's capture from the eastern front once the army had reached the Kiev-Smolensk-Opotchka line, reoutfit the troops for service in the Iberian peninsula, and then send them to Bayonne for the crossing into Spain. It was hoped that the men would withdraw from Russia by 15 July and would attack the Rock by 15 October. Halder was a bit skeptical. *Felix-Heinrich* would demand from the eastern front two armored divisions, 29 of 111 artillery battalions, and enough transport vehicles and fuel to hinder seriously Germany's forward movement. The chief of general staff dryly noted that *Felix-Heinrich* could not occur until victory in the East was definitely assured.[8]

Hitler was uncomfortable with waiting until October anyway. He thus made one final grand attempt in May 1941 to sway the French into allowing German bases in Northwest Africa. The attempt had its genesis as early as February 1941 with the new ascendancy in Vichy of Admiral Darlan. On 9 February, Flandin resigned as foreign minister, and within the week Darlan assumed the portfolios of foreign affairs, information, interior, and vice premier as well.[9] This concentration of power, for which Darlan had angled since mid-January, meant that he had the marshal's approval to restore relations with Germany if he could. Darlan wished to thaw German policy while finding a place for France in the new European order. An early compromise peace, he hoped, would allow France to assume colonial and maritime duties in keeping with its prior experience.[10] Thanks to Laval's continued ab-

sence, Darlan's climb had but a measured effect on Hitler.[11] Still, Berlin had
not lost interest. On 11 February, Ribbentrop asked Abetz for his opinion
on several questions. He wished to know the chances for the creation of a
new French government with Laval as premier and including Darlan. He
wished to know if such a government would allow German bases in French
Africa as well as other favors there in return for a peace settlement. Finally,
he wanted to know if General Weygand in Algiers would unconditionally
accept such a French policy. Abetz answered each question in the affirmative,
and Ribbentrop presented his findings to Hitler.[12] Hitler was skeptical at
first. In mid-March 1941, Raeder argued to Hitler that Germany, with Vichy's
help, needed to secure Northwest Africa to prevent the domination of the
East Atlantic by the Anglo-Saxons. Germany, added Raeder, would also
need bases for attacks on Britain's West African holdings and on Anglo-
Saxondom in general. Yet Hitler remained unwilling to make new diplomatic overtures. He stated that no arrangement with France was possible at
present and once again cursed the Spaniards for killing the Gibraltar operation. He agreed only that the French and Spanish issues would receive a
swift and decisive solution after *Barbarossa*.[13]

Darlan, meanwhile, remained persistent. On 4 April, he handed a long
memorandum to Abetz that described his vision for France's future. Abetz
sent the memorandum to Berlin and recommended that it receive a serious
look, lest Darlan follow Laval into the political abyss without Berlin reap-
ing any advantage.[14] At the end of April, Abetz was summoned to Hitler's
headquarters. He arrived on the twenty-fifth with a list of possible concessions to France, such as a reduction of occupation costs, which the ambassador felt would bolster the anti-Gaullist, anti-British line in Vichy. He also
suggested that Ribbentrop and Darlan meet soon.[15] Abetz's arguments had
their effect. The next, day Hitler decided that he would meet Darlan.[16]

What had changed Hitler's mind? Abetz thought that the answer lay in
Iraq.[17] Since 1930, Baghdad had been bound by a mutual assistance treaty
with London and had allowed two British bases within Iraqi territory. On 3
April, the pan-Arab leader Rashid Ali-al-Gailani placed himself at the head
of an anti-British National Defense government and soon after asked for
German and Italian aid, which could have arrived most quickly through the
French mandate of Syria.[18] Yet these events might not have been the primary cause for Hitler's new interest in France. Berlin had not particularly
wanted a coup in Iraq, and once the takeover by Rashid Ali occurred, German political and military circles were skeptical about supporting it. Only
after Hitler had decided to receive Darlan did the idea of using Syria to

supply the Iraqis get more than theoretical discussion.[19] Another possible motive for a meeting with Darlan lay in the use of Tunisia to support General Erwin Rommel in Libya. Rommel had opened the German offensive in the Cyrenaica on 31 March, and since 11 April the Afrika Korps had stood before Tobruk. Yet the Afrika Korps was hampered by poor Libyan port facilities and lengthy supply lines. On 25 April, the Germans asked to purchase French trucks in North Africa. The French agreed in principle, and further talks concerned the use of Bizerte as a supply base for the Afrika Korps.[20] Yet Bizerte might not have been the main reason for Hitler's interest in meeting Darlan either. The course of negotiations would show that the most compelling reason for Hitler's change of heart lay in his desire to control the Northwest African coast before turning east. Hopeful that Berlin could work with Darlan, he decided to try once again.

Political and military negotiations with the French began in Paris in the first week of May, and the Germans emphasized their aims in Africa. The original agenda, as explained by Ribbentrop to Keitel on 28 April, featured French removal of unreliable officers in North Africa, West Africa, and Syria. It also featured German submarine and cargo bases on the West African coast. Aid for the Iraqis was merely something "that ought also to be demanded," and Tunisia was not mentioned at all. In return for the French gestures, Germany would allow the rearmament of six destroyers and seven torpedo boats.[21] On the same day, Hitler expressed concern over Northwest Africa and the Atlantic islands to Spanish ambassador Espinosa de los Monteros and added the corrosive comment that Germany would already have had troops in Spanish Morocco had Gibraltar fallen in February. "The current objective of the British," Hitler warned, "was to establish themselves in North Africa, to occupy the Portuguese islands, and to overthrow Franco."[22] It is true that Ribbentrop later changed the priorities of his 28 April agenda to emphasize aid to Iraq, but not until 3 May, the day after Iraqi-British hostilities opened at Habbaniya.[23] On the same day as Ribbentrop's shift toward the Middle East, Abetz offered Darlan the prospect of new arrangements on the demarcation line, occupation costs, and French prisoners in return for a quick agreement on Syria.[24] Vichy accepted Germany's requests on the seventh in return for the rearmament of seven torpedo boats, some slight relaxations of the demarcation line, and the promise of discussions on occupation costs.[25] With the Iraqi question solved, Hitler and Ribbentrop could concentrate on Africa when they met Darlan the next week. The most striking facet of Darlan's visit to the Bavarian Alps in May 1941 was the constant German emphasis on the American threat to Africa and the need to meet it. The German arguments were *identical* to those used with Serrano Suñer the previous September. Ribbentrop opened talks on 11 May with the comment that Great Britain had lost the war and would soon find itself driven from the Euro-African land mass.[26] Although America would be foolish to try to change the new order, Roosevelt was driven by "the biggest and stupidest imperialism in world history" and would doubtless make a play for Northwest Africa. Since France alone would be unable to withstand the threat, the Eastern Hemisphere needed to pool its efforts, and Germany would play the decisive role. "We had to reckon," counseled Ribbentrop,

> with the Americans' trying to undertake a move against Europe, even though, viewed within the larger picture, such a move would be of no consequence for the outcome of the war. One must realize that it would be undesirable, for instance, if America gained a foothold in Africa. It was essential that France should recognize that henceforth the European-African hemisphere could conduct but one common policy. . . .
>
> The Führer was no random conqueror, without a plan. . . . He was sober in his calculations and was accustomed to think in long periods of time. . . . [He] held that it was not enough to think of Germany alone, but that if a still greater catastrophe were to be averted in the future, consideration had to be given to the organization and security of Europe and Africa, i.e., our hemisphere.
>
> France . . . had to understand that she had to live with the Greater German Reich in the future. By virtue of the size of her population, it was Germany's task to guarantee the security of Europe and the European-African hemisphere. . . . If other hemispheres [sic] attempted to establish themselves, say, in Africa—if, for instance, America were to attack Africa—France by herself would not be strong enough to conduct that struggle, and a collaboration with Germany would have to come into being.
>
> These were new questions, to be sure, but owing to . . . rapid technological advances, they were already of immediate interest and so close to the thinking of German statesmen that the latter had all but ceased to pay attention to intrigues in Europe, and were rather concentrating on securing the entire Continent against other hemispheres [sic].

If France were willing to contribute by standing against Great Britain and America, said Ribbentrop, it would enjoy a place of honor in the new Europe. He could not be exact, of course, but France would emerge with a considerable colonial empire. The British would presumably pay the largest colonial bill.

Hitler stressed the same themes with Darlan later the same day. No one on the Continent could rejoice, he warned, if Germany as the primary defender of Europe were to lose the war. The long-term threat to the New Order, he continued, was not Great Britain but rather America, and France needed to adjust. An American imperialism was emerging that increasingly focused on French Africa, said Hitler, and Vichy would have to defend its empire, especially Dakar. At present, Germany was doing everything possible to end the war by fighting the British. The fate of France, he stated, would be decided by Vichy's stance. Would France watch and wait, or would France help?[27]

The next day, Ribbentrop put the key question to Darlan. He reiterated that the dominant issues no longer concerned German-French relations in isolation but rather the entire European-African hemisphere, in which Germany held the dominant position. France could have an honorable place only after making the fateful choice of "war with England."[28] What had Ribbentrop meant? Berlin was not interested in full French belligerence so much as in cooperation over Africa. Ribbentrop told Darlan on 12 May that Germany would do almost all of the fighting and that the French would render but a "certain kind of assistance." The next day in Palazzo Venezia, Ribbentrop told Mussolini that Germany primarily wanted naval bases in Morocco and that, beyond this request, Germany wished no assistance besides support in Syria and the sale of trucks for the Afrika Korps. Even French naval support against Great Britain was not wanted.[29] On 14 May, moreover, Abetz prepared a list of proposals for negotiations that revealed that the Germans indeed wanted ports in French Morocco and French West Africa.[30]

Darlan agreed in principle with "war with England" but wanted substantial concessions in return to win over the French people. Only later would he reveal that this meant a full overhaul of the armistice regime. On 20 May, Warlimont arrived in Paris for a weeklong round of negotiations with Darlan and Huntziger. His instructions from Hitler and the High Command focused on the use of French facilities in Syria, Tunisia, and West Africa. In return, Hitler was willing to allow some degree of rearmament in

Africa and was also amenable to minor concessions for the *Metropole*.[31] The discussions on Syria and Tunisia presented few problems, and the talks on West Africa began on a positive note as well.[32] Warlimont reported on 22 May that the French were ready in principle to put Dakar at Germany's disposal. Darlan apparently wanted only an advanced reinforcement of Dakar, with the release of 2500 men from German camps. Warlimont, who correctly viewed the reinforcements also in the context of the reconquest of Equatorial Africa, thought that the negotiations would conclude on the following day.[33] His optimism was contagious. At the Berghof on the same day, Hitler spoke with Ribbentrop, Keitel, Jodl, and Raeder, and all were pleased. Keitel said that the French requests could be met and that the French would be able to defend North and West Africa against the Anglo-Saxons. Raeder, who had already called for the use of Dakar, was thrilled. He now renewed the call for German artillery to defend the Canaries. Hitler was even more ambitious. With an arrangement on French Africa seemingly near, he again raised the issue of the capture of the Azores with Raeder. Despite the latter's continued coolness toward the idea, Hitler maintained his interest, noting that in the autumn the islands could base the new German long-distance bomber, then in its early stages of production, for use against the United States.[34]

Over the next few days, German-French cooperation in Africa seemed on the verge of realization, even though the French augmented their demands for reinforcements for West Africa. On 23 May, Abetz reported that the French were willing to make Dakar available in mid-July, but that they were concerned over British or American countermeasures and wanted the defenses there augmented *before* German vessels arrived.[35] The following day, Darlan's intermediary, Jacques Benoist-Méchin, added that France was willing to meet British countermeasures with an attack on Freetown and that France also wanted to be ready to reconquer Equatorial Africa by the end of the rainy season. This meant, he said, that Germany would have to release *all* of France's interned colonial soldiers. Warlimont was ecstatic. "The decisive step [in] negotiations over [the] particulars for large-scale, far-reaching joint planning," he reported, "has now occurred." He received permission to continue negotiations along these lines and also received orders to request the use of Dakar as an air base as well.[36]

Yet German euphoria would melt over the next week as the French began increasingly to qualify their terms. The hardening of the French position in late May is a mystery. Perhaps Darlan always intended to raise the stakes once the talks reached a favorable point. Perhaps the French flinched, thanks to Britain's attack on Syria, which began with the bombing of airfields there on 14 May. In any event, Huntziger and Colonial Minister Admiral Platon took a hard line in late May. Huntziger pointed out on the twenty-third that German favors for the French military in Africa mainly served German interests. If Dakar was presently quiet, why should France ask for trouble?[37] On the twenty-sixth, Platon added that Vichy would need to prepare the West African population for the arrival of German forces, which were now to be in the visible form of airplanes. He wanted four mobile infantry detachments like the one Hitler had granted in November 1940 for the operation against Equatorial Africa, plus the accompanying air cover and fuel supplies. Benoist-Méchin added that a German declaration of French imperial sovereignty would be in order.[38] The next day, Darlan arrived in Paris with more counterdemands. German use of Dakar, he said, would throw France into worldwide conflict with Britain and meant full orientation toward the Axis as an associated partner. France thus needed substantial political favors for the *Metropole,* which would amount to a full revision of the armistice treaty. This statement caught Warlimont and Abetz off guard, and the issue of Dakar suddenly plunged into a clutter of conditions and counterconditions.[39]

Thus the so-called Paris Protocols, signed on 27 and 28 May 1941, were an indecisive anticlimax. The first protocol, regarding support in Syria, contained nothing new and was already outdated when it was signed. The British had already bombed Syrian airfields on 14 May, and on 8 June British and Gaullist forces would invade Syria, forcing Vichy forces to surrender on the fourteenth. The second protocol concerned the use of Bizerte in return for the transfer of some 15,000 army and air force officers and soldiers to North Africa from the *Metropole* and prison camps. The third protocol, which dealt with Dakar, was meaningless. France granted the use of Dakar in principle, but German use was to come in two stages, each conditioned by counterdemands. In the first stage, beginning 15 July 1941, German submarines could use a tender in the harbor for resupply and cargo ships could stay in the harbor for a limited period. In return, France expected numerous military concessions for West Africa, including the release of the men needed to fill out the mobile infantry detachment that Hitler had granted in November, added stocks of munitions and motor vehicles, increases in airpower and antiaircraft defenses, and the rearmament of nine destroyers, seven torpedo boats, two submarines, an aircraft carrier, and the battleship *Provence.* Moreover, if Germany expected a reconquest of Gaullist Africa, it needed to release an additional four motorized detachments, ten combat air groups, and the requisite motor and aircraft fuel. In the second stage, the timing of which was left open, German naval and air units would have full use of use Dakar, but the French first wanted approval of an attached supplementary protocol, which demanded in unspecified form economic and political concessions necessary to convince the French public that the impending hostilities with Great Britain and the United States were worth France's while.[40] In short, the protocol on Dakar had devolved into a vague basis for further negotiation.

Military agencies in Berlin remained hopeful. The Naval Command, which had lost four tankers in the Atlantic in a week and which had wanted to operate against the high-traffic area of Freetown, was pleased to take what it could get. In the second week of June, Fricke requested that the High Command reach an agreement with Vichy as soon as possible. Rear Admiral Gerhard Wagner, the naval command's first admiralty staff officer, ordered the immediate movement of a German tanker from the Canaries to Dakar and for a cargo ship loaded with torpedoes, spare parts, and provisions to make for Dakar from Nantes. He hoped that Germany could begin using Dakar on the prescribed date of 15 July.[41] On 6 June, the High Command had ordered the Armistice Commission to resume talks with the French, and on the tenth General Vogl and Colonel Böhme arrived in Paris to do so.[42]

Yet the French position was not as pliable as the Germans had hoped. Weygand appeared in Vichy on 2 June, complaining bitterly over Darlan's proposed concessions and threatening resignation if they were implemented. Only the strictest neutrality, he said, would preserve the empire. Governor-General Boisson from Dakar and Admiral Jean Estéva, the resident-general in Tunis, joined Weygand in condemning the protocols.[43] The cabinet remained prepared for collaboration in Africa despite these objections but maintained the desire for heavy concessions when Vogl and Böhme arrived. Although the Germans approved the reinforcements that the French had requested for the defense of West Africa, they were prepared to grant neither the four motorized detachments for the reconquest of the equatorial region nor substantial political concessions.[44] On 12 and 14 July, as Vichy was losing Syria, Darlan would slow matters more by making the second protocol regarding Tunisia contingent on the same kind of broad political settlement on which the third protocol had been based.[45] Negotiations would continue in a halfhearted way throughout 1941. The High Command and the Foreign Ministry bickered briefly in June over possible concessions to the French over occupation costs and the demarcation line.[46] Yet in truth, the protocols were dead.

Hitler had in fact become disgusted with the entire process. On 2 June, he met with Mussolini at the Brenner and renewed his invective against the French. Vichy, he complained, was constantly presenting Berlin with new demands. He gave new voice to his suspicion of a Vichy-Gaullist connection and noted that had Germany not maintained pressure from the occupied zone, Vichy would likely have adopted a Gaullist stance already. Yet German pressure would have to remain restrained, said Hitler, lest North Africa defect. He returned to his frustration with Franco, noting that if Germany had taken Gibraltar early in the year, "the French government could not have conducted a two-faced policy." Hitler continued that he "felt all the worse from the French blackmail as he was continually telling himself that if Gibraltar had been taken in February, two armored divisions would have been stationed in Africa. He then could have taken a firm line with the French government and demanded from the French . . . Agadir and bases on the Moroccan coast. He would have demanded Dakar, also. . . ." The most difficult part of the war was over, said Hitler. The *single* danger remaining was the defection of French North Africa. "One must try to prevent that," he said, "by skillful diplomacy."[47]

In the coming weeks, the High Command on Hitler's order would draft a new directive that reflected the realization that the problems of Northwest Africa would be solved *after* the eastern campaign. War Directive 32, "Preparations for the Period after *Barbarossa*," appeared on 11 June and was circulated as a basis for further study on the nineteenth—three days before German troops rolled over the Soviet border.[48] It contained a list of objectives for the period after continental hegemony had been established, which aimed at the next step—global supremacy. *Barbarossa,* it said, would crush the USSR and leave Germany and Italy as the primary continental powers. Germany would then reduce the army and place industrial emphasis on the navy and Luftwaffe, while taking several swift actions to wring Britain's surrender and preparing for conflict with the United States. In the Atlantic and on the Channel, Germany would continue the siege of England and prepare anew for a landing there. In the Near East, Germany would launch a new push on Suez. The most ambitious projects, however, were in the southwest. First, Germany would resume preparations for Operation *Felix* during *Barbarossa*'s wind-down. After bullying Spain into the war, Germany would take Gibraltar and move troops into Spanish Morocco. The Germans would then employ bases in West Africa and launch operations against the Atlantic islands. Meanwhile the French, who would presumably become more pliable after *Barbarossa,* would defend the Atlantic coast of

North Africa while eliminating Britain's positions in Freetown and Bathurst. Final directives would come while the eastern campaign was still in progress. Nonetheless, Hitler was still uncomfortable leaving issues in Africa hanging for so long. In late June, he played briefly with the reduction of France's occupation costs.[49] On 21 July 1941, the day before the attack on the USSR, he commented in a letter to Mussolini that "France is, as ever, not to be trusted. Absolute surety that North Africa will not suddenly desert does not exist."[50]

Hitler's discomfort over Africa faded as the Russian campaign began with extraordinary success on the twenty-second. Now it was no longer necessary to bargain with France, since Germany would soon be able to impose its will. On 2 July, Keitel informed Ribbentrop that Hitler had decided for the moment to forgo the use of Dakar "for political reasons" and that the High Command would press France to defend West Africa. The navy would be able to use Dakar as soon as political circumstances permitted.[51] Raeder voiced the navy's disappointment with this arrangement on 9 July after the American occupation of Iceland two days earlier. Yet his argument to Hitler, that Germany needed to cooperate with Vichy in Northwest Africa, brought only the comment that the Hitler did not trust the French and that Vichy's conditions were overblown.[52] Besides, felt Hitler, the success of the eastern campaign would restrain the United States, since it would encourage southward expansion by the Japanese.[53]

Barbarossa's early success affirmed the expectation that the Soviets would collapse soon, and it seemed that the projects described in the thirty-second war directive would soon be realized. On 3 July 1941, Halder stated that Germany would complete the campaign within two weeks, and on the same day, the army dusted off the plans for Operation *Felix*.[54] The navy was even more confident. Already in the spring, Hitler had approved their plans for their new mammoth wharf at Trondheim while emphasizing the urgent nature of its completion.[55] In late July, Fricke composed a new study on what the navy would build at its new wharves in the next twelve to fifteen years. His projected fleet included 25 battleships, 8 aircraft carriers, 50 cruisers, and 400 submarines, and these extravagant numbers did not even include escort or home defense forces![56] Of particular note were the design proposals for the postwar fleet. The new aircraft carriers, for example, would junk the design of *Graf Zeppelin* in favor of one that allowed a larger action radius with higher speeds for increased "Atlantic capability."[57]

Hitler was confident meanwhile regarding the race for naval bases. He had already stated that success in the East would restrain the Americans by clearing Japan's rear flank[58] and that after *Barbarossa* Germany would move into Northwest Africa "with an offensive stance against America."[59] Whatever the Americans were able to take in the interim—and this would not amount to much—they would have to disgorge. Referring to the American occupation of Iceland, Hitler informed Japanese ambassador Hiroshi Oshima in mid-July 1941: "We cannot get around the reckoning with America. One should not think that [the Führer] has accepted the American occupation of Iceland because he is not acting at the moment. . . . If he, the Führer, is silent at this moment regarding Iceland, this does not mean that he has given it up. The Americans would have to get out, even if he would have to fight for years."[60] In the meantime, he repeated to Raeder that he wanted no incidents with the Americans for another month or so and commented that after the eastern campaign he would take the sharpest measures against America. For now, an American occupation of the Spanish or Portuguese islands would bring the German occupation of Spain and Portugal, as well as German armored and infantry divisions into Northwest Africa.[61] Actually, the degree to which Hitler took such a threat seriously in the heady days of July 1941 might well have been quite slight.

Yet as time would show, *Barbarossa* would *not* conclude in the autumn and Germany would be unable to take decisive action in Northwest Africa or in the Atlantic islands. Questions regarding the area's security would thus hang in suspension due to Germany's commitment in the East, Hitler's distrust of France, and the Iberian distrust of Hitler. Berlin in the end would simply have to watch Northwest Africa as closely as possible and hope that nothing unfavorable happened there. Until the Allies settled the Northwest African issue for themselves, Germany's attempts to monitor the area constituted the final attempt for a favorable outcome to an issue on which Hitler and his subordinates had worked since the summer of 1940. It is to these last efforts that this study will now turn.

The Germans could take no measures concerning Portugal's islands except watch events unfold. After the American occupation of Iceland in July 1941, the German Foreign Ministry heard many reports of an imminent American occupation of the Azores. Reports from South America added that Washington was pressuring Brazil to join in an operation. Ribbentrop ordered Baron von Hoynington-Huene to ask Salazar what Lisbon planned to do. Huene gained few answers on his own. Salazar tersely noted that he had no official knowledge of any American schemes.[62] The best-informed German in Lisbon was the military attaché, Colonel Freiherr von Esebeck, who had built a good working relationship with the undersecretary of war,

Captain Fernando dos Santos Costa. In May 1941, Esebeck reported that the Portuguese were indeed determined to defend the Azores and that their best troops were there.[63] In late May, German army intelligence reported that Lisbon had strengthened the contingent in the Azores to 10,000 men, and in July this estimate reached 17,000.[64]

Yet the Portuguese were unwilling to let the Germans observe any activity in the Azores. Since the outbreak of the war, Germany had in Ponta Delgada an honorary consul, Leo Weitzenbauer, who served the German navy by observing the comings and goings of British vessels. Yet as an honorary official, Weizenbauer was not entitled to diplomatic immunity, nor could he communicate in cipher with the German legation in Lisbon. He depended on the Italian consulate in Ponta Delgada to send his reports. In the second half of 1941, the German Foreign Ministry decided to send a full consul, a certain Herr Sakowski, to the Azores. He arrived in Lisbon at the end of 1941, probably a short time after America's entrance into the war. Yet Sakowski never made it to the Azores. The Portuguese would not allow him to go to the islands, and while the German legation did its best to force Portugal to allow the trip, Sakowski remained in Lisbon in November 1942, nearly a year after his arrival.[65]

The Spaniards were more forthcoming. Serrano Suñer in November 1941 had already boasted to Hitler that Spain would attack the Azores should the Allies try to occupy them.[66] Once the United States entered the war, Franco strengthened the Canary Islands while placing the Spanish colonial administration directly under his own supervision.[67] Spain maintained its seven divisions in Spanish Morocco as well.[68] In 1942, Madrid was willing to assume even larger commitments. Franco and his two foreign ministers that year, Serrano Suñer and Count Jordana, all told Stohrer throughout the year that Spain would consider an Allied landing in French Morocco as a casus belli, and officers in Spanish Morocco agreed.[69] Yet Spain could not act effectively without German material aid. Franco made a personal appeal to Stohrer for arms on 1 April 1942, and the Germans heard similar requests throughout the year from the Spanish Foreign Ministry. In the first week of November 1942, Jordana correctly noted that the Allied buildup in Gibraltar was aimed at French Morocco. Stohrer supported Spain's requests and proposed that Berlin maintain the Spanish resolve as much as possible.[70] Yet Berlin was unwilling to act; German weapons were needed for German troops in the East.[71] The concern also existed that a Spanish advance into French Morocco during an Allied landing would prompt the French to join the Allies and fight the Spaniards.[72] Only *after* American troops had already taken French Morocco did the German Foreign Ministry begin to think seriously of supplying Spain with materials to defend Spanish Morocco, and by then it was too late.[73]

Germany's relationship with Vichy concerning the defense of Northwest Africa was more complex but also unsuccessful. The Germans had more official observers in French Morocco than in any other area of Northwest Africa. Theodor Auer's station in Casablanca was raised to the status of General Consulate at the end of 1941.[74] In addition, there were a substantial number of Admiral Wilhelm Canaris's Abwehr agents disguised as civilian businessmen. Responding to a Foreign Ministry complaint that the cover used by Abwehr agents harmed legitimate German business interests in Morocco, Canaris commented that "Morocco is one of the most important operational areas for the offensive and defensive tasks assigned to me."[75] Yet the largest German surveillance agency in French Morocco was *Kontrollinspektion Afrika (KIA)*, which would assume complete official military supervisory functions in the spring of 1941. Plans for *KIA* had begun in Wiesbaden on Göring's orders in January 1941, even before its predecessor, the German Armament and Fuel Commission, arrived in Casablanca in February. By 7 March, the order for *KIA* was complete. Composed of some two hundred men, *KIA* would become the sole military inspection agency in French Morocco.[76] *KIA*'s headquarters were in Casablanca, but *KIA* also commanded several subcommissions. A subordinate control commission located in Fedala monitored the French army in Morocco, and this army commission had its own subcommissions in the French divisional command centers of Fedala, Meknes, Marrakech, and later in Fez. *KIA* also included control commissions for the French navy, for the air force, and for armaments and fuel stocks. *KIA* as a whole had the official function of supervising French demobilization while inspecting French military installations. It was also to observe political and economic developments while cooperating with Auer's group in Casablanca. German commissioners were in uniform while on duty. Yet *KIA* was not to be a subversive force. Officers were to refuse gifts and invitations from the French and to refrain from meddling in domestic affairs.[77]

KIA's setup in French Morocco represented a new policy turn, which brought objections from Italy, France, and some Germans as well. Yet with Northwest Africa at stake, Hitler was determined to leave as little as possible to chance. *KIA*'s replacement of Italian inspectors in Morocco came not a moment too soon for the German military, which had never approved of the ambiguous Roatta Agreements anyway. The old argument that Italy was not doing its job in French Africa received new confirmation in February 1941, when the new German liaison delegation to the Italian control commission in Algiers discovered that the Italian chief, General Boselli, had yet to meet with General Weygand.[78] Earlier in the month, the Germans drew up a new delineation of inspection responsibilities in the French Empire, and talks in Wiesbaden with the Italians began on 10 February with Stülpnagel and Böhme representing the German position. To the embarrassment of the Italians and Mussolini himself, the Italians accepted Germany's proposals in March, and the new delineation was made official in April.[79] Germany would assume inspection responsibilities for all of French Morocco (minus the Oudja district on the Mediterranean coast), French West Africa, French Equatorial Africa, Madagascar, Indochina, and the French Antilles. Germany would also create permanent liaisons with the Italian bodies in Oran, Algiers, and Tunis, and would participate in the hitherto exclusive Italian control of military-related shipping from French Mediterranean ports. In return, the Italians would send liaisons to *KIA* in Casablanca and to any future German commissions in West Africa, Madagascar, and the Indies.[80]

The French put up a stronger fight but fared no better. Vichy had yet to reconcile itself to the relatively small Armament and Fuel Commission in Morocco and had demonstrated its ill temper by hampering German radio and courier contact between Casablanca and Wiesbaden and by delaying the shipping of German equipment to Morocco.[81] In mid-March, Germany's intention to send the future *KIA* to Morocco became known in Vichy, likely through an Italian leak in Casablanca. Noguès warned Vichy that "If France is to be held out of the war, it is necessary to stand against the German maneuvers unequivocally, which inevitably would bring about war in Morocco in a short time."[82] Pétain meanwhile feared political infiltration with expanded German control.[83] On 17 March, Brinon delivered an official statement to Abetz, which argued that the few visible German inspectors already in Morocco risked ruining the delicate political balance there, and that the dispatch of more officers would substantially increase this risk.[84] General Doyen made similar arguments to Vogl in Wiesbaden on the twenty-first, reminding Vogl of Stülpnagel's statement that the Armament and Fuel Commission was a mere supplement to Italian agencies and relaying warnings from Weygand and Noguès that the expansion of German control could have disastrous effects.[85] The Germans answered with a note of their own, which ignored all objections while officially announcing that Germany would assume inspection responsibilities in Morocco with a new commission of two hundred men.[86] Doyen responded on 31 March with warnings of a stoppage of American economic aid to Morocco and native unrest, and the statement that the French government could not agree with expanded German control.[87] That night, Doyen and Darlan converged on Paris to argue the point with Abetz. On the High Command's request, Abetz refused to receive Doyen and stonewalled Darlan. He brushed aside Darlan's argument that German officials were meddling with the Moroccan natives and commented that if France truly had nothing to hide, it would greet the new German presence.[88] The next day, the French delegation in Wiesbaden assented to the German demand, with the proviso that Germany send no more than fifty new commissioners and that the commissioners not be uniformed. Vogl rejected these conditions.[89]

A series of protests came from Auer's group in Casablanca as well. Consul Klaube, an expert in North African affairs, warned that the French authorities and population viewed the German officials already in Morocco as a harbinger of occupation. The dispatch of three times that number of uniformed Germans as part of a more comprehensive commission, he said, would trigger disastrous consequences that would only aid Germany's enemies. Currently, said Klaube, the French were ready to combat an Anglo-American landing, but the arrival of a larger commission would kill this resolution. Germany, he suggested, could guarantee the French will to defend Morocco with economic aid, propaganda, and diplomacy, but not with augmented control. "If we do not intend a total occupation of Morocco," cautioned Klaube, "then every additional German soldier that arrives here is detrimental to our interests."[90] None of these arguments were effective in Berlin, which surely had eventual occupation in mind. On 14 April, the French delegation in Wiesbaden gave its unconditional assent to the German demands, and two days later Germany officially assumed military inspection functions in French Morocco. By the end of April 1941, half of the new German officials had arrived in the French protectorate.[91]

The Germans were never successful in placing observers in Dakar. Ever since the raid of September 1940, the French were able to stave off a German presence with the argument that German observers would cause political convulsions. Berlin never pressed the point, especially since Governor-General Boisson had already proven his reliability. Though the German General Consulate in Casablanca technically included French West Africa in its area of competence, there were no journeys to Dakar by any of Auer's staff. In the first half of 1942, Berlin tried without success to create an observation post in the French West African capital, much to the disappointment of the Abwehr and the Foreign Ministry itself.[92] News from French West Africa thus remained sparse. The only information Berlin received came from the occasional interview between Auer and French businessmen and citizens of third countries who traveled between Casablanca and Dakar for commercial or personal reasons.[93]

The German military task in Morocco was no small one. The Germans and Italians had allowed the French an army in North Africa of 120,000 men. The army in French Morocco comprised roughly 47,000 men divided into four full divisions and a small independent group in the area of Agadir. The divisions were broken down into twelve infantry regiments, four cavalry regiments plus two smaller detachments, and three artillery regiments. In addition, the French had under their command 16,000 Sherifian riflemen divided into small units called *goums*. The Germans also allowed a small number of troops over and above the numerical limits for special tasks. These troops included extra coastal defense forces of four rifle companies, eight Atlantic mobile coastal defense platoons, and six coastal artillery batteries. The Germans also permitted the French to maintain the twenty-two small mountain posts along the Spanish Moroccan border. Finally in late 1941, four thousand motley Levantine troops began to arrive in Morocco with Germany's permission, fresh from their defeat in Syria.[94] The French navy in Morocco was stationed primarily at Casablanca, where in 1942 the French kept the battleship *Jean Bart* as a floating fortress, as well as a cruiser, eight destroyers, eleven submarines, and eight sloops.[95] The French air force in Morocco in 1942 included two fighter groups of 26 aircraft each, four bomber groups of thirteen aircraft each, and two reconnaissance groups of thirteen aircraft each. The French navy had a fighter and a bomber group as well.[96] The function of German inspectors lay in keeping the French to their prescribed limits in men and material. Everything above these limits was to be discharged or stocked. Periodic inspections of individual units were announced a few days in advance, and surprise inspections were exceptional, occurring only in cases of suspicion of hidden armaments or other violations.[97]

Relations between the German inspectors and French officers were tense, due to the German desire to see everything with any bearing on French military strength combined with the French desire to minimize the German presence in Morocco. Noguès's objections to the German presence was already known. Weygand compounded matters by appointing General Maurice-Emile Béthouart as the chief liaison officer to *KIA*. Béthouart was a germanophobe who would later make secret preparations to receive the Allies in

North Africa.[98] In the meantime, he was determined that the Germans see as little as possible of Morocco and that Morocco see as little as possible of the Germans. Thus, German inspectors ran into numerous irritations. Often the troop units that the Germans inspected would be on an exercise or work detail on the inspection date.[99] The French also tried to keep German inspectors out of the Rif region in an attempt to hide the German presence from the more unruly tribes there.[100] French authorities endeavored on several occasions to keep the German inspectors from viewing any installation that did not have a direct bearing on troops and arms. In November 1941, for instance, they temporarily prevented German inspectors from examining food stores and military clothing stocks, with the argument that these installations were not truly military.[101] French liaison officers on inspection visits interrupted questions by German inspectors that pertained to training, with the argument that such questions went above the scope of German authority.[102] The Germans usually got their way in such disputes. In late November 1941, Vogl told General Paul Beynet, who had replaced Doyen as chief of the French delegation in Wiesbaden in June, that the German commissioners would determine the military significance of any given installation.[103] With regard to French training, the Germans were patient. In October 1941, *KIA* chief Inspector-General Schultheiss ordered that the French would answer questions on unit composition, movement from the base, and the use of weapons, munitions, and motor vehicles. In this way, the Germans could gain some insight into French training.[104] In March 1942, the new *KIA* chief, General Heinz-Helmut von Wühlisch, eliminated all limitations on inspection questions.[105]

The Germans were also irritated by the French harassment of their information sources. Auer and his staff complained to Berlin throughout 1941 and 1942 that Noguès's officers were searching German dispatches and that French police in Casablanca were harassing and arresting local informants who approached the consulate building or spoke to German officials.[106] *KIA* encountered the same sorts of problems, which was especially galling given the augmented American representation in Morocco. As a result of the Murphy-Weygand economic agreement of February 1941, the United States placed twelve "vice consuls" in North Africa, half of whom were in French Morocco. Their official job lay in monitoring the movement of American goods, but they also had general observatory functions.[107] In May 1942, Auer demanded of Noguès the creation of German consulates in Marrakech and Fez, and Abetz demanded in June that France limit American representation to its prewar level and to proper consular functions.[108] Noguès himself was displeased with American actions, but the Germans were un-convinced of his sincerity.[109] Auer wished to have Noguès replaced but real-ized that Noguès, who always emphasized his indispensable relationship with the natives, had firm support in Vichy. Since Noguès's support in Vichy grew after Laval returned to form a new cabinet in April 1942, the Germans had to live with him as best they could.[110] *KIA* responded to the harassment of informants in 1941 with the order that German commissioners would wear their uniforms off duty as well as on, would carry sidearms at all times, and would use the sidearm if they encountered any trouble in the course of their activities.[111]

The Germans handled French violations summarily. A fine example of this process came with the disbandment of four companies of the Sixth Senegalese Rifle Regiment. The Italians had ordered the companies demobi-lized while still responsible for French Morocco. The Germans, on learning of the continued existence of the units in July 1941, demanded their imme-diate dissolution. The French delayed in disbanding the units, with the ar-gument that many of the soldiers came from Gaullist-controlled Africa and could not return home on political grounds, and the excuse that the primi-tive African troops needed to remain in a military setting for disciplinary reasons. *KIA* reported the French violation to the German Armistice Com-mission in Wiesbaden in October, and Wiesbaden rejected all French argu-ments. The troops from West Africa would have to return there, and those from Equatorial Africa would serve in work camps. The French command in Morocco continued to stall, but the Germans finally won the argument with the threat to retract permission for troop movements. The French de-mobilized the four companies in November.[112]

Yet German inspectors never saw their mission as successful. The French could create hidden arms stores in civilian warehouses, places of worship, or in private homes, and despite the help of informants, the Germans were usually unsuccessful in discovering hidden arms stocks. In June 1942, Ma-jor Seelisch, leader of the army subcommission in Fedala, complained that information on the location of hidden weapons was generally too vague to be of use, that equipment was too easy to hide, and that wild goose chases only made German inspectors look foolish.[113] Announced inspection visits to French units had problems as well. The French could doctor inventory figures to conform with German limits and pass them as genuine, since the Germans could only perform spot checks. By August 1942, von Wühlisch was convinced that the entire inspection system was flawed and reported to Wiesbaden that more unannounced visits to the units were necessary.[114]

Although the Germans were firm on limits, they allowed French forces to reach a maximum effectiveness within permitted limitations. Noguès openly proclaimed his determination to fight an Allied invasion, and with the exception of Béthouart, who became the commander of Division Casablanca in January 1942, most commanders were of the same mind. Troop morale, for the most part, also seemed high.[115] French units were allowed to train as they wished, and during the summers of 1941 and 1942, when an invasion on the Atlantic coast was most likely due to calmer seas, they received clearance to move all troops thought necessary for defense to the coast. The Germans allowed the French to replace damaged equipment from their stocks, so long as the French stocked the damaged equipment in return.[116] This trend was especially true in the case of French air forces. The Italians in March 1941 had based flight training in French Morocco on the provisions of the so-called Turin Protocol, which limited training time to eight hours a month and training areas to a 15-kilometer radius around the home base of any given aircraft.[117] Since French air bases tended to lie in populous areas such as Casablanca or Marrakesh, these conditions fettered training. In the summer of 1941, the Germans doubled the training radius around air bases, providing a 100-kilometer area for low-flying exercises, and allowed special areas for instrument and night-flying exercises as well as for bombing and shooting practice. The Germans raised monthly training time to fifteen hours per crew.[118] At the same time the French received a tremendous reconnaissance zone for Morocco as far west as 25 degrees longitude.[119] In November the Germans removed all boundary restrictions for air training in Morocco.[120] In August and December 1941 the Armistice Commission approved additional weaponry for all French combat aircraft in Morocco.[121]

Yet it was obvious that the French would have problems resisting a large-scale attack. After the first German inspections of the French army in May and June 1941, a German report stated that "against the attack of a modern-equipped and motorized enemy, the four divisions could put up resistance for only a brief time."[122] By November 1942, this appraisal had changed very little. The army was more sharply drilled by the summer of 1942 than a year before.[123] Troop reinforcements moved to the Atlantic coastal areas for the summer and held alarm drills, some rather impressive, which presupposed a landing there.[124] But problems of inefficiency and imbalance combined with crippling supply shortages tempered German assessments. The French built concrete bunkers and artillery positions at all possible landing areas, but while some defenses such as in Port Lyautey were extremely impressive, others such as those in Safi had only primitive defense works. Local command often moved slowly to improve the situation. The Germans saw, for example, that the Second Battalion of the Third Moroccan Rifle Regiment, which had moved to Safi for the summer, was spending its days on the football field rather than improving its positions. Meanwhile, concrete bunker construction moved slowly due to cement shortages, while civilian building continued unabated thanks to a concrete factory in Casablanca.[125] Fuel supplies, meanwhile, were a nightmare. The Germans noticed in December 1941 that most permitted short-term exercise movements were not occurring due to fuel shortages and that the French were converting engines for alcohol consumption.[126] In April 1942, the vehicles in Division Casablanca had only a small fuel reserve and did little with their engines except start them. The same was true of the coastal defense platoons that were to patrol the shore.[127] In August 1942, the Germans learned that many of the motorized units that had moved to the coast for the summer had left 75 percent of their motor vehicles at their home bases due to fuel needs![128] The air force, meanwhile, was not using its increased training hours for lack of fuel, and effective Atlantic reconnaissance, by Darlan's own admission in October 1942, was not occurring.[129] The French also suffered from weapons and munitions shortages. Light and heavy machine guns were Great War leftovers, and the army had a 75 percent shortfall in munitions *under* the permitted amount for machine guns, rifles, and sidearms as of September 1942. At the same time, the French had no machine pistols, even though the Germans had granted their use months before.[130] In May 1942, when General von Wühlisch was asked about the possibilities of creating new units in Morocco, he answered that the French had enough manpower for at least five more infantry regiments but that they lacked the equipment for existing units, even counting the materials they had probably hidden.[131]

It was clear in 1942, then, that Morocco could not be defended against a large-scale landing. In May, Commander Wever of the German Armistice Commission commented after a plain-clothes inspection visit that French resolve notwithstanding, the only factor that favored the defenders was the small number of good landing spots on the coast. The fulfillment of French wishes to augment their forces, he said, would aid French defenses materially and morally. The French defenses would thus be sufficient for any reasonable task.[132] Von Wühlisch reached similar conclusions. Morale and resolve, though high, would not overcome supply shortages. Without additional antitank weapons, artillery, armored vehicles, munitions, and fuel,

Morocco would not hold out for more than a few weeks.[133] Nothing demonstrates this opinion better than the fact that *KIA* had standing plans to flee Morocco at the first sign of an Allied landing.[134]

Given the high importance that Hitler placed on Northwest Africa, it is curious that the Germans did nothing to improve the situation in Morocco. One reason for the paradox was a continued lack of trust by Hitler. The slow progress of the Paris Protocols negotiations prompted Keitel in September 1941 to give new directives to Wiesbaden that allowed flexibility for the reinforcement of West Africa, which had defended itself in 1940, while allowing little for North Africa, which was still suspect. For the western colonies, Wiesbaden could agree to French requests over and above the Paris Protocols for the possibility that Germany would want a French offensive against Gambia later. North Africa, meanwhile, would be confined to limited munitions, replacement parts, and fuel for permitted weapons. Further concessions were out of the question until the political and military leadership in North Africa had become reliable. In the meantime, *all* grants for North Africa needed Keitel's prior approval.[135] The Germans would stick to this policy down to November 1942, despite the French desire for greater cooperation in North Africa. Even the long-awaited removal of General Weygand from his post in Algiers in November 1941 failed to sway Hitler.[136] "There are so many Weygands in France," he told Ciano, "that any one of them could take over the role . . . tomorrow."[137] Hitler, already suspicious of Noguès, was also disappointed at the new commander of the armed forces in French North Africa, General Alphonse Juin, especially since Abetz had expected Darlan to assume Weygand's position as delegate-general.[138] The contrived return gesture for Weygand's removal, the release of the Levantine formations for service in French Morocco, changed nothing. Of the 13,000 Levantine troops in France in November 1941, only about 4,000 ever traveled to Morocco, and on the eve of the American invasion a year later, they remained improperly outfitted.[139]

A stern test for Hitler's policy came at the end of 1941. Operation *Crusader,* the renewed British offensive in North Africa, began on 18 November as the British under General Claude Auchinleck moved from Egypt to relieve German pressure on Tobruk. On 4 December, Rommel abandoned Tobruk, and by Christmas Axis forces had evacuated the port of Benghazi and continued a retreat toward Tunisia that would not halt until early January 1942. Worse, the British sank four Italian transports and two cruisers bound for Libya in early December. Suddenly the need for transport facilities in Tunisia had become acute.

On 1 December 1941, Göring met with Pétain and Darlan at Saint-Florentin to see about the possibilities.[140] The Frenchmen, true to Darlan's policies earlier in the year, brought a tremendous list of proposed German economic and political counterconcessions aimed at the normalization of relations. France, they said, was determined to defend North and West Africa against Anglo-Saxon encroachments, which would become more likely with the German use of Bizerte. Yet France needed military concessions in Africa and an easing of the general situation in the *Metropole* to win the population over. At the very least, France would need a guarantee of colonial integrity.[141] Göring refused even to consider French proposals that went beyond Africa's immediate military security and was barely prepared to discuss that much. Germany, he exaggerated, had proof that Weygand had wanted reinforcements in Africa in order to join the British at the right moment. Even with Weygand retired, there was no guarantee that others in Africa would not do the same. He expressed trust for Pétain and Darlan, but he added that not all Frenchmen were so reliable and that a coup could see German concessions work against Germany. For now, Göring advised the French to present exact plans for their proposed defense of North and West Africa. Only after learning such plans would Germany be ready to talk about concessions.

Meanwhile the Italians, whose transports were finding the bottom of the Mediterranean in increasing numbers, became impatient. General Ugo Cavallero, who had replaced Badoglio as the chief of the *Commando Supremo* in December 1940, felt that the entire North African situation depended on Bizerte, and on the night of 1 December, Mussolini argued to General von Rintelen that the use of Tunisia represented the last hope in North Africa. The situation, he said, called for significant concessions to France, so that the Axis could use Bizerte in the current month.[142] In a note of 5 December, the Italian Armistice Commission chided its German counterpart in Wiesbaden for moving too slowly. The Axis, it said, should grant Vichy all of the requested reinforcements. Turin also announced that Ciano would raise the issue in an upcoming meeting with Darlan.[143] On the same day, the German liaisons in Turin warned that Ciano would try to secure the use of Bizerte at any price and that Rome expected an accommodating stance from Germany.[144]

Hitler, restive over concessions to the French in North Africa, quickly squashed the Italian initiative. In accordance with his instructions, Keitel had the Italian High Command told that Germany would do everything it could to secure the route to Libya, primarily with the employment of the

Second Air Fleet. The supply situation would gradually improve. In the meantime, the Axis would forgo the use of Bizerte. Only *after* the route to Libya was restored could the Axis approach the French on the use of Tunisia. Premature use of the port and coastal facilities, added Keitel, would lead to a British attack in French North Africa without the French having the forces necessary to repel it.[145] Ribbentrop had Ciano informed of Hitler's view as well before he departed to meet Darlan.[146] Ciano, who had been pessimistic on the use of Bizerte anyway, denied that it was a main issue on his agenda and agreed not to raise it.[147] Darlan in fact raised the issue when he met Ciano at Turin on 10 December, and Ciano responded only briefly.[148]

On the same day that Ciano and Darlan met, Göring invited General Juin and the colonial minister, Admiral Charles Platon, to Berlin. They were to present France's plans for defending French North and West Africa.[149] Due to later German concerns that a visit by two high officials would trigger Allied suspicion, Juin arrived alone and in secret.[150] He met Göring and Warlimont for a three-and-a-half-hour meeting on 20 December. Göring wanted two concessions.[151] First, France was to allow the supply of the Afrika Korps through Tunisia. Second, France was to declare readiness to defend the southeastern Tunisian border should Axis forces need to retreat to Tunisia. Despite the heaviness of these demands, Göring was unwilling to make serious concessions, arguing, in exact contradiction to what Berlin had just told Rome, that Germany was demanding nothing which could trigger a premature Allied counterstroke. Once France agreed, he said, Germany would discuss counterconcessions. Juin was ready to meet both German demands, but only after receiving reinforcements to defend the Tunisian-Libyan border and North Africa as a whole. For North Africa, he wanted six divisions from the *Metropole*, excluding the moribund Levantine forces, and the release of armored vehicles and artillery stocked in North Africa. Ten thousand tons of fuel were also requested. For Dakar, Juin wanted air reinforcements and additional supplies. Finally, he raised the old French requests for political concessions. Göring was furious, proclaiming that France had to accept the German demands unequivocally. Then and only then would he take Juin's requests to Hitler, and even here, Göring referred to Juin's military requests alone. Juin gave no promises, and after Rommel launched his counteroffensive of January 1942, promises were no longer needed. Yet the series of talks sparked by *Crusader* demonstrated clearly the level of Berlin's mistrust for the French. The Germans simply refused to reinforce French North Africa, even with Rommel's desert campaign seemingly at risk.

Hitler's distrust was but one reason why North Africa was left vulnerable in 1942. The other concerned German intelligence miscalculations regarding Allied capabilities. Many reports reached Berlin in 1941 and 1942 from German embassies and consulates in neutral countries that the Allies were planning an attack on French Morocco. Yet there were also reports that the Allies would land in the Atlantic islands, in Spanish Morocco, in Spain, in Portugal, in West Africa, on the Guinea Coast, in France, in Norway, in Holland, in Belgium, and even in Yugoslavia.[152] The Germans did not discount this type of reporting. In June 1942, Ribbentrop directed his mission chiefs that "the most important task now . . . is the reliable and swift transmission of all news regarding the question, whether, when, and where England and America will make an invasion attempt."[153]

Yet Berlin never gained any hard evidence of Allied intentions through this sort of channel. The Germans mainly relied on assumptions about Allied capabilities. Hitler had long argued that the Americans were mere parade soldiers and that the Japanese threat in the Pacific would erase the possibility of American action in the Atlantic. The months following Japan's attack on Pearl Harbor on 7 December 1941 and the resulting German declaration of war on the United States on the eleventh seemed to bear out Hitler's prediction. By Christmas 1941 the Allies had lost the Gilberts, Guam, Wake, and Hong Kong. Malaya and Singapore would soon follow. Hitler felt vindicated in how easily the American "house of cards" had collapsed in the Pacific.[154] The German armed forces were also impressed. Raeder commented to Hitler on 12 December 1941—the day after the German declaration of war—that the Allies were too occupied with the Pacific to launch large operations against the Atlantic islands.[155] Warlimont reached similar conclusions two days later. Before the Japanese attack in the Pacific, argued Warlimont, Anglo-Saxon war planning had involved the securing of Atlantic sea lanes and the creation of a wide land and sea envelopment of the German power sphere so that a decisive land offensive could begin sometime in 1943. Yet the Japanese offensive, said Warlimont, had ruined this planning. At worst, there existed naval parity in the Pacific between the Japanese and the Allies, and the latter could not and would not abandon their Pacific interests without a fight. Warlimont acknowledged the possibility that the Americans in 1942 would realize their long-held aim of taking the Atlantic islands, Dakar, and eventually Morocco. But this possibility was an absolute worst-case scenario for Germany. Japanese success in the Pacific would surely prevent any strong Allied move in the Atlantic.[156]

The most careful and important study of this type emerged in March 1942 in a rare combined effort by German army and navy intelligence. It was entitled "British-American Operational Possibilities against Europe and Africa in 1942."[157] Hitler himself had ordered the study, and all copies of it were to be returned after perusal to the army's western intelligence department, where they were to be destroyed.[158] The study was an attempt to discern Allied options from available cargo shipping and manpower. In the autumn of 1941, the study said, the *Wehrmacht* had assumed that any Allied operations against the Continent would come in 1943 at the earliest. Now with Allied defeats piling up in the Pacific, such possibilities were less likely. The German navy reckoned that the Allies had just under five million tons of shipping available for troop transport. By adding projected construction and subtracting projected losses along with Allied needs in the Pacific and Middle East, the navy calculated that the Allies would have no more than 1.5 million shipping tons for a landing operation in the Euro-African area by the end of 1942. This, said the study, was not enough for a large-scale landing against a well-defended coastline or port. Thus, there would be no such landings in 1942. Against the well-defended European coasts of Norway and France, Germany could expect nothing more than commando raids. A landing in the Iberian Peninsula was conceivable but unlikely. The Allies' best options—and these were still not good ones—lay on and off the Northwest African coast. An attack on Morocco was improbable. The beaches were unsuitable for operations due to swells, and Casablanca, the only truly fine port in Morocco, was well enough defended to meet whatever the Allies would be able to muster. Juin's determination to combat an Allied landing was also a factor. Another frontal attack on Dakar was also unlikely. Dakar now had 15 infantry battalions, 4 artillery detachments, and 160 aircraft. If the Allies wished to take Dakar, they would have to land at Bathurst and approach it from the rear, and such a maneuver could not be kept secret. As for the Atlantic islands, the Canaries had 30,000 reasonably well equipped Spanish troops who would fight a landing attempt, thus making one fairly improbable. The Portuguese groups had weaker defenses and thus were the most likely target for the Allies should they attempt such an operation in 1942. The study concluded that although a large offensive in the Euro-African theater *could* come in 1943, preparations alone *would* come in 1942. In the case of Morocco, the French agreed with German assessments. In the spring of 1942, Juin and the French command in Morocco concurred that a large landing there was highly problematic. They expected no more than commando raids and felt able to repulse such actions. In addition, the most probable time for an attack was the summer due to post-September tide patterns.[159] Thus in early October, the additional

French forces that had moved to the shore for summer coastal defense began to travel back to their inland bases.[160] In fact, the Germans and their French collaborators were not far off the mark. Washington and London, after long negotiations, agreed on the North African landings in late July 1942.[161] The logistical problems of the operation were indeed formidable. Shipping and supply problems were largely responsible for the postponement of the original October target date to a landing date in November, and transport problems were not solved until the eve of the operation.[162] Operation *Torch* thus ran on a shoestring, and one can scarcely fault the Germans and French for doubting that the Allies would embark on such an undertaking.

The only measures the Germans took to augment French defenses in the autumn of 1942 focused on Dakar rather than Morocco. Germany's inclination toward additional defenses there was due less to the Allied deception campaign, which began in London in August 1942, than to Berlin's own assumptions.[163] The German idea that French West Africa was politically reliable remained intact in 1942. Auer's information from French West Africa confirmed that General-Governor Boisson remained firmly behind Vichy and more determined than Noguès to repel an Allied attack.[164] In October 1942, moreover, the possibility of an Allied move on Dakar seemed increasingly likely. Months before America's entry into the war, the British had been sending aircraft to Egypt via Takoradi, Lagos, Kano, Fort Lamy, and Khartoum, and in the Washington conference of December 1941, President Roosevelt assumed responsibility for maintaining the Takoradi route.[165] Thus, modest American contingents arrived in Liberia in June 1942 to build and defend airfields there, and in French Equatorial Africa in August with the same mission.[166]

Neither the augmented American involvement in western Africa nor the Takoradi route were unknown in Berlin. In fact, the German consul and his staff in Monrovia were expelled in November 1942 at Washington's behest.[167] The German Foreign Ministry was concerned that the Allies might attack Dakar from the land side, and these concerns grew in October as Berlin received more reports of such an attack. A retired French officer with ties to the Dakar intelligence network reported that French officers there expected an attack from an American contingent that numbered 400,000 men. Dr. Ernst Bielfeld, chief of the African section of the Foreign Ministry, correctly considered the manpower estimate to be exaggerated but still warned that the current American strength in West Africa was enough to realize "America's imperialistic plans in Central Africa" at least in part. He argued that an attack on Dakar from the land side from Gambia was "possible and likely."[168]

In October Keitel announced that the High Command also considered an Allied attack on Dakar likely but noted that Germany had recently been generous with French requests for reinforcements there.[169] Already in September, the German Armistice Commission approved long-standing French requests for heavy weapons and armored vehicles for West Africa. This included the shipment of 400 heavy machine guns, 30 antitank guns, 115 field cannons, 91 armored vehicles, and more. The weapons came not only from North African stockyards, but also from the *Metropole,* and began to arrive in Dakar in early October. Darlan told Vogl when the two men met in Rabat on 24 October 1942 that the troops in Dakar were indeed eager to use their weapons.[170] Unfortunately for the French troops and their German benefactors, the Allied attack that would come in two weeks hit 2,500 kilometers to the north. Thus began the cracks in Hitler's European fortress.

Allied command on the eve of Operation *Torch* noted two prerequisites for success—Spanish neutrality and a French resistance that was no more than a token struggle.[171] Yet German attempts to protect Northwest Africa ran aground on political and military miscalculation. Berlin had never built a cooperative relationship with Lisbon, and in 1942 was obliged to leave the Portuguese islands to their fate. The Spaniards had been willing to cooperate but needed additional equipment to do so effectively. Due to Franco's history as an associate and Germany's commitments elsewhere, Berlin chose not to take Madrid up on its offers. Spain, with 30,000 men in the Canary Islands and seven divisions in Spanish Morocco, would presumably be able to defend those areas against anything the Allies could muster. Spanish help in French territory, moreover, was deemed politically unwise. Vichy had been most willing to cooperate against an Allied attack, and the French *did* have the weapons stored in the *Metropole* to offer a long and determined resistance. Yet Berlin, though trusting of West Africa, could never bring itself to trust the North. The French were strong enough in Morocco to repel Allied commando raids in any case, which was the most either country expected. Given the decisions made in Washington and London in the summer of 1942, the fate of Northwest Africa was thus sealed. Despite Hitler's two-and-a-half-year quest for a German Atlantic springboard in Northwest Africa, the region would only serve his enemies.

Conclusion

⮑

Whoever counts on a pleasant welcome here
is in for a cruel disappointment.
　　　　　　　　　—General Charles Noguès

The introduction of this book posed several questions concerning German strategic interests in Northwest Africa in the Second World War. These questions sought to illustrate the necessity of the study by measuring the urgency of the Northwest African issue for Hitler's Germany. The questions were as follows: When, why, and to what extent did the issue of Northwest Africa surface in German discussions? Was the issue more offensive or defensive in nature? Did Germany take serious diplomatic steps with the colonial powers that controlled Northwest Africa and the outlying islands to win a permanent presence for itself in these areas? Did Germany have earnest military plans to seize such areas should diplomacy fail? What effect did opinions from within the German diplomatic and military hierarchy with regard to a German foothold in these areas have on Hitler's decision-making process? To what degree did Hitler follow or ignore the advice of his military experts? How did German aims in Northwest Africa affect the European war then in progress? How did the progress of the war affect the urgency of the Northwest African issue? Finally, why did Germany ultimately fail even to arrange for the creation of a strong defensive bastion in Northwest Africa when the strategic urgency of doing so in 1942 should have been obvious? Some answers are now possible.

　　Hitler's Germany made unwavering attempts following the armistice of June 1940 to procure enclaves in Northwest Africa for the construction of naval and air bases. These bases were to serve Germany in a transatlantic struggle with the United States. Hitler began forming his ideas on global struggle with the first volume of *Mein Kampf* in 1924. He began pressing ahead with the naval and air force design and construction necessary for global war in the mid-1930s. He began to think about the geographic prerequisites of the future global struggle with America immediately following the cease-fire with France. In expectation of a quick end to the war in the West, Hitler remained reticent concerning his territorial claims in the French Empire during the armistice process. Such claims were reserved for the peace conference that was to occur later in the year. Directly after the armistice, however, Hitler began to think of ways in which Germany could press into Northwest Africa even before the final peace settlement.

The conquest of Gibraltar was the most effective of these methods. Hitler's motive behind the capture of the Rock had perhaps less to do with the continuing war against Great Britain than has been assumed. Hitler, after all, began to speak of taking the Rock in the first week of July—more than two weeks before signing the directive for Operation *Seelöwe,* and more than two months before the German navy mentioned Gibraltar as a maritime objective in its peripheral Mediterranean strategy against the British. To Hitler, Gibraltar's fall would allow the extension of German power into Northwest Africa, so that Germany could prepare a strategic position there. Other methods of extending German power into the Northwest African region also appeared soon after the armistice of 1940. In mid-July 1940, Hitler mentioned a trade of French Morocco to Spain for one of the Canary Islands, and he demanded from the French eight airfields in the area of Casablanca. Again, Hitler pictured neither of these objectives with the immediate war against Great Britain in mind. In the Canaries, Hitler originally wanted one of the smaller, less-developed islands. In Casablanca, the Germans wished to construct brand-new airfields. The length of time necessary for the development of naval and military facilities in these areas, combined with the German assumption at the time that the war with the British would end in a matter of weeks, strongly suggests that these German schemes were directed against an entirely new Atlantic foe.

The German desire for bases in Northwest Africa was offensive, not defensive, in nature. Hitler began to work toward the creation of a strategic position there in mid-1940—literally years before the United States presented any military threat to the new order in Europe. Hitler himself had commented to his generals in September 1940 that the United States would present no threat to Europe before 1945, by which time he expected the current war in the West to have long ended. Thus, even in his own mind, he did not conceive the idea for bases in Northwest Africa due to an immediate threat from the Americans. It is true that after the Destroyer-Base Deal in September 1940 and the British-Gaullist Dakar expedition of the same month, Hitler became increasingly concerned that the Americans would steal a march on Northwest Africa and the Atlantic islands before Germany. He pressed more avidly for the conquest of Gibraltar and for Spanish cession of one of the Canary Islands. For the first time, he also ordered plans for the capture of the Portuguese archipelagoes. Yet even these maneuvers, though perhaps triggered in *timing* by action from Washington or London, cannot be portrayed as defensive. Not once in the early autumn of 1940 did Berlin offer to help Madrid or Lisbon to strengthen their own defenses on the islands. Not once did the Germans approach the French with a joint defense arrangement for French Northwest Africa. Rather, Germany wanted its *own* bases, which it would develop *after* the current war in the tranquillity of peacetime. The pattern of development of these installations—if the fifteen-year plan for the development of Trondheim can serve as a guide—eliminates the possibility that Hitler wanted these bases due to a perceived immediate American threat to the new order in Europe. One cannot, moreover, define Hitler's desire to steal strategically favorable positions before his future enemy could do so as defensively motivated. One may as well argue, as Hitler did, that the Germans were defending themselves when they attacked Poland, France, and the Soviet Union. One may as well argue as well that bombers and battleships are defensive weapons.

The diplomatic steps taken with the French and the Spaniards for the attainment of coastal enclaves in Northwest Africa were intense. The German demand on the French for the eight air bases in Casablanca led Vichy to believe that the total occupation of France was likely were the French government to refuse. The German Foreign Ministry had deliberately contrived Serrano Suñer's visit to Berlin in September 1940 in such a way as to bully quick consent from the Spaniard for permanent German bases in Morocco and in the Canary Islands. Hitler's "Brenner scheme" of October 1940 was as inspired a diplomatic arrangement as the Third Reich ever created, and the keen desire for its implementation was enough to take Hitler on a 6,000-kilometer rail journey through France, down to the Spanish border, and back to Berlin via Florence. The German policy of the cold shoulder toward France's defense needs in Africa from the winter of 1940–41 was in large part caused by the firm suspicion that General Weygand in Africa had been responsible for Pierre Laval's ouster in Vichy. This concern also triggered Berlin's fervent pressure on Madrid that same season for Spain's

entry into the war so that German troops could press into Northwest Africa. The melodrama of the Paris Protocols in the spring of 1941 received similar inspiration from the perceived need to set up German bases in Northwest Africa before the German campaign in the East. All the while, the Germans slowly wrested from the Italians the responsibility for military and political inspection in French Morocco. The pattern of German diplomacy in this period was as clear as the diplomacy itself was earnest. At times Berlin emphasized its relations with Madrid. At times Berlin concentrated on its relationship with Vichy. Yet the target was always the same—the Northwest African region.

German military planning concerning the possible seizure of points in the Northwest African region was never executed. Yet the reasons for non-execution were more political than military. In most cases, the military planning itself was quite thorough, and Germany could have implemented the planning had the political preconditions existed. The German troops earmarked for the Gibraltar operation were fully ready in December 1940 to move against the Rock when Franco refused participation on the seventh of that month. In addition, the German navy adeptly prepared the logistics for the transfer of German troops across the Strait of Gibraltar and into Spanish Morocco. The Naval Command also plotted with minuscule precision in December 1940 the operation to send motorized batteries to the Canary Islands for the defense of that archipelago. Finally, the navy readied the prerequisites for submarine refueling operations from Dakar in the spring of 1941. In each case, political failures made Germany's diligent military planning ineffectual. The only German military preparations that had not received such attention to detail were those concerning the occupation of the Portuguese Atlantic islands. Here the problem was primarily one of time. Hitler demonstrated on numerous occasions in the autumn of 1940 that he wanted to realize such an operation, and he manifested this interest again in the spring of 1941. Yet the proper reconnaissance of the islands was a prerequisite, and since Hitler wished to occupy the islands simultaneously with the conquest of Gibraltar, Germany lacked the time to study them properly. Hitler intended to return to the many German projects in the Northwest African region following the completion of the eastern campaign. The minute planning for Operation *Felix-Heinrich* and Hitler's thirty-second war directive both demonstrate this ambition. Unfortunately for Berlin, the eastern campaign did not run as planned, and Germany's post-*Barbarossa* planning gathered dust.

When assessing the importance of the issue of Northwest African bases for Hitler himself, one must also balance his interest in the region against that of his military and naval experts. Indeed, Hitler's zeal for a permanent German position in the East Atlantic outstripped even that of the German armed forces—the very organizations that were to benefit the most from such a position. During the period of the German-French armistice, Hitler and the German Naval Command were in full accord concerning the need to develop bases in the East Atlantic for a future conflict with the United States. Yet once the British demonstrated clearly that they would continue the war, a vital difference of opinion developed between Hitler and the armed forces. Hitler increasingly convinced himself that Germany had defeated Great Britain and that the British government was, in a final act of defiance, acting as the agent of Roosevelt's imperialist policy in the Atlantic. Hitler's aim, then, lay in beating the Americans to the points of future global strategic significance, even at the expense of the prosecution of the actual war against Great Britain. The German armed forces viewed similar problems but recommended different solutions. The Naval Command, for example, agreed with Hitler that the British and the Americans were in the process of forming an "Anglo-Saxon World Empire," but they felt that the best way to terminate this menace lay in forcing the British to surrender as soon as possible. Balanced against this pressing requirement, the need for outright German ownership of bases in Africa faded into the background for the time being. Germany's armed forces, and the Naval Command in particular, pressed instead for an augmentation of the Axis war effort in the Mediterranean, where Germany could fight the British without facing the risks of crossing the English Channel. They also recommended cooperation with the nations that owned the base sites. Germany was to provide aid to the Spaniards and Portuguese for the defense of their respective islands, while reaching a rapprochement with France over the defense of Northwest Africa. Hitler could never agree with such a solution, partly due to his global vision, partly due to his judgment of the war's progress, and partly due to his negative assessment of the nations in question. The British, in Hitler's eyes, were defeated whether Germany made a commitment to the Mediterranean or not. In the meantime, the Portuguese were tied too closely to the British to be trusted, the Spaniards were too weak, inept, and indecisive, and the French were, as Goebbels had said, still the French. Thus, the creation of a *German* position in the East Atlantic took precedence over all other potential aims in the general region, including the western Mediterranean. Instead of cooperating with the Portuguese, Hitler ordered the creation of a nearly impossible scheme to steal their islands. Instead of cooperating with the Spaniards, Hitler and Ribbentrop obnoxiously pressed them to allow German ownership of one of the Canaries and spoke openly of their desire to place German troops in Spanish Morocco. Instead of cooperating with the French, Hitler turned a cold shoulder toward Vichy due to his misplaced suspicions. One can only presume what the German position in Africa in 1942 would have been had Warlimont, Stülpnagel, or Raeder been in charge of German policy during the critical period in 1940 and 1941. In any event, Hitler was convinced enough of the correctness of his course to ignore the advice of those German officials who had long made the science of war their career.

The Northwest African issue for Germany, while an issue of constant concern in Berlin, underwent shifts in intensity owing to the ebb and flow of events in the Second World War. The problem was a living component of the world conflagration. The British attack at Mers-el-Kebir in July 1940 determined the timing of the German demand for air bases at Casablanca. The French refusal of that demand prompted Germany's shift toward Spain and Hitler's increased interest in Gibraltar. The Destroyer-Base Deal of 3 September 1940 prompted the timing of Hitler's order for the preparation of plans to take the Portuguese archipelagoes as well as the intensification of his pursuit of Madrid. The coup by de Gaulle in French Equatorial Africa began the long process by which Germany would wrest inspection duties in French Northwest Africa from its Italian ally while placing German officials in French Morocco. The stubbornness of Serrano Suñer in Berlin in late September 1940, combined with the failed British-Gaullist landing at Dakar, prompted the Brenner scheme, which the Germans spent the remainder of 1940 trying to implement. The Laval affair, combined with Hitler's determination to attack the Soviet Union by the spring of 1941, gave rise to the white-hot intensity with which Berlin pressed for Spanish entrance into the war in early 1941. The spring 1941 deadline for the eradication of the Soviet Union also prompted the timing of the Paris Protocols, just as Germany's overconfidence in the ease of its tasks in the East in the summer of 1941 prevented their implementation. Finally, the Japanese successes in the Pacific in late 1941 and early 1942 provided Berlin with a partially justified sense of security concerning the Allied ability to attack North Africa. The Northwest African issue in German political and strategic considerations thus forms a legitimate piece to the puzzle of the Second World War, and this piece contributes to an understanding of the entire picture.

This analysis regarding the integral nature of the Northwest African issue also works in reverse. Just as the course of the war affected German aims in Northwest Africa, so German aims in that region had a major effect on the German prosecution of the war. It is true that these aims had little impact on the eastern campaign, Hitler's foremost prerequisite for national survival. The Germans worked around the constant of *Barbarossa* when plotting the timing of their moves in Northwest Africa. Yet the Northwest African issue had a tremendous impact on the German war in the West. It is certain that Spain, from the summer of 1940 to Serrano's visit to the Berghof of November 1940, was prepared to enter the war on the German side. The loss of Gibraltar would have been devastating for the British both in the Middle Atlantic and in the Middle East. Had Hitler agreed with Franco's conception of a cooperative alliance between Berlin and Madrid, the Rock would have been Hitler's for the taking. Hitler also could have gained a much stronger measure of French cooperation in Africa against the British and the Americans. His unwillingness to make military concessions to the French in Africa, combined with his recalcitrance toward concessions for the *Metropole*, prevented the German use of Bizerte and French railway facilities in Tunisia, the use of Dakar, and a sterner resistance against the Allied landings. Yet Hitler felt he could have his bases on his terms. Following the annihilation of the Soviet Union, Germany was to return to make its own rules without concessions. Yet Germany never returned.

The question regarding the inability of Northwest Africa to defend itself in 1942 has already received an answer. The responsibility for Allied success there must rest largely with Berlin itself. Hitler clearly recognized the importance of the Northwest African region for the prosecution of a global war for either side. Yet Berlin, in its pursuit of a strong strategic position in the area, made two fatal mistakes. The first lay in diplomacy. Hitler, due to his conviction that the Spaniards were technologically inept and that the French would never change their intentions toward Germany, was determined to go it alone in the strategic development in the Northwest African region. The sharing of bases with the Spaniards or with the French, an option suggested by Madrid, Vichy, and the German armed forces, was out of the question. Imaginative diplomacy in the autumn of 1940 might have created a cooperative relationship for southwestern security that included both Madrid and Vichy. The Spaniards and the French had already been talking of a border adjustment in French Morocco in the summer of 1940, and Spain claimed from 1940 through most of 1942 that it would fight an Allied invasion of North Africa if it were to have the necessary means. Had Berlin been able to act as an honest broker in Morocco while agreeing to share Northwest African bases rather than insisting on ownership, Germany might have created a genuine security system for Northwest Africa. Yet such a scheme lay far beyond Hitler's imagination. The German answer to collective security in the Southwest was the Brenner scheme—a plan based on deceit that was doomed to failure. The second mistake lay in the German reading of the Axis military situation. The German political and military leadership believed that Germany would have the time to impose its will in Northwest Africa despite the broadening of the war in 1941 and the increase in German military commitments. The war in the East, Berlin had believed, would be complete by the autumn of 1941. The German army had already begun plans *before* the Russian campaign for pulling troops off the eastern front for a subsequent sprint across Europe to Gibraltar. Even after the eastern campaign proved to be tougher than Berlin had originally anticipated, and even after Germany and the United States were officially at war, there seemed small cause for concern. The American shipping shortage, combined with the failure of the Allies to halt the Japanese advance in the Pacific, would keep the enemy from any large-scale action in the Euro-African theater until 1943 at the earliest. The eastern campaign would surely have ended by that time, and Germany would be prepared to meet whatever threat the Allies could have made. This calculation was incorrect. Despite the trouble and sacrifices Germany had accepted in the name of German dominance in Northwest Africa, this key region would not serve Hitler's global aims. It served rather as the start for the global role that his enemies would one day assume.

Shortly after the American landings on the Atlantic coast, the Allied military situation in French Northwest Africa was a good one indeed. Algiers surrendered on 8 November on the authority of Darlan, who happened to be in the city visiting his ill son. Oran surrendered the next day. Following bitter resistance against the landings and against the American march toward Casablanca, Noguès officially surrendered French Morocco to General George S. Patton Jr. on the afternoon of 11 November. Patton, on Noguès's request, discarded the original armistice terms in French Morocco, which would have established an American military government there, and implemented a "gentleman's agreement" that left Noguès in control of the French armed forces in Morocco and allowed the Americans to occupy those areas deemed essential for security.[1]

The Germans countered the Allied landings of 8 November by landing in Tunisia the following day. They met the kind of French resistance for which the Allies themselves had hoped—none. With similar opposition, the Germans rolled across the demarcation line to occupy the free zone of the

Metropole on 11 November. In Tunisia, the Germans and Italians would hold a central position until May 1943. Yet even in November 1942, the Germans were far too late to save the situation in Morocco. Berlin had failed to use the Spanish and French trump cards that early success in the war had dealt it. Now the Germans attempted a new, futile appeal to the native population, thus revealing the sudden weakness of their position concerning Morocco. On 6 December 1942, the German-controlled Arabic language radio broadcast from Paris sent the following call to the Moroccan population, laced with the customary Nazi subtleties:

> *What do the Americans want, Moroccans? They want to help the Jews. . . . General Noguès supports the Jews in your country against you, Moroccans, in the charge of the Americans. . . . The Americans are still coming to you as false friends with small gifts, with tea and sugar, but with brutal soldiers, who do not know your ancient religion and culture, and who will place you on the same level with the blacks in America. . . . Proud, valiant Moroccans, believe in your own strength, act with all cleverness which you have always manifested in difficult times, for your religion, for your customs, for your children. You know that you have powerful friends in Adolf Hitler and his soldiers, who already in Tunisia are fighting against the traitors Noguès and Darlan and against the American intruders. Support this struggle with all your means. Take up arms wherever you find them. Do damage to the enemy wherever you can. Commit sabotage. Have patience until the German victory also brings the liberation of Morocco from Jewish-American slavery.[2]*

Yet it was too late for such appeals. No one in Northwest Africa was listening anymore.

Notes

Introduction

1. George F. Howe, *Northwest Africa*, 97–115.
2. Samuel I. Rosenman, *The Public Papers and Addresses of Franklin D. Roosevelt, 1942, Humanity on the Defensive*, 455–57.
3. Ibid., 456–57, n. 1.
4. Review essays include Meier Michaelis, "World Power Status or World Dominion?" 331–60; Milan Hauner, "Did Hitler Want a World Dominion?" 15–32; Jochen Thies, *Architekt der Weltherrschaft*, 9–31.
5. Alan Bullock, *Hitler: A Study in Tyranny*, 723; Martin Broszat, "Soziale Motivation und Führerverbindung des Nationalsozialismus."
6. Andreas Hillgruber, *Hitlers Strategie*.
7. Ibid., 583–84. See also idem., "Der Faktor Amerika in Hitlers Strategie, 1939–1941," 3–21.
8. Günter Moltmann, "Weltherrschaftsideen Hitlers," 225, 227.
9. Gerhard L. Weinberg, *Germany, Hitler, and World War II*, 30–56; idem., *World in the Balance*, 53–95. Alternate views which build on Moltman's and Hillgruber's thinking on German global strategy include Hans-Jürgen Schröder, *Deutschland und die Vereinigten Staaten, 1933–1939*; Detlef Junker, *Kampf um die Weltmacht: Die USA und das Dritte Reich 1933–1945*; idem., "The Continuity of Ambivalence: German Views of America, 1933–1945"; Philipp Gassert, *Amerika im Dritten Reich: Ideologie, Propaganda und Volksmeinung 1933–1945*.
10. See Thies, *Architekt*, 136–47 on the air contracts and Jost Dülffer, *Weimar, Hitler und die Marine*, on naval contracting.
11. For the effect of early Nazi ideologues on Hitler's ideas concerning Germany's proper global role, see Geoffrey Stoakes, *Hitler and the Quest for World Dominion*.
12. Adolf Hitler, *Mein Kampf*, I, 315.
13. Ibid., I, 300–329.
14. Ibid., I, 288.
15. Ibid., II, 689 and n. 1.

16. Weinberg, ed., *Hitlers zweites Buch*, 77.

17. Quoted in Thies, *Architekt*, 52–53.

18. Quoted in ibid., 55–56.

19. Hitler, *Mein Kampf*, I, 286.

20. Weinberg, ed., *Hitlers zweites Buch*, 131–32.

21. Ibid., 123, 130–31.

22. Ibid., 218.

23. Ibid., 128–32.

24. Ibid., 130.

25. Weinberg, *World in the Balance*, 59.

26. Edouard Calic, ed., *Ohne Maske*, 100–101.

27. Ibid., 99.

28. Hugh Trevor-Roper, ed., *Hitler's Table Talk*, 7 January 1942.

29. Weinberg, *The Foreign Policy of Hitler's Germany*, vol I, 133–58; idem., II, 249–55, 577–78.

30. James V. Compton, *The Swastika and the Eagle*, passim.

31. The notion that Hitler had no interest in naval affairs is effectively refuted by Dülffer, *Marine*, 205–25.

32. Ibid., 312–14.

33. Weinberg, *Foreign Policy*, I, 210–16; Dülffer, *Marine*, 279–390.

34. Dülffer, *Marine*, 455–56. For wharf construction, preparation on which began in April 1935, see idem., 314, n. 63, 383–86, 434, 438–39, 472, 479.

35. Germany, Auswärtiges Amt, *Akten zur deutschen auswärtigen Politik, 1918–1945* (hereafter cited as *ADAP* with series, volume, and document numbers), D, I, 19. Quotes in English translation below will, unless noted otherwise, come from the American edition, United States, Department of State, *Documents on German Foreign Policy*.

36. Dülffer, *Marine*, 469–71, 544–55.

37. Keith W. Bird, *Weimar, the German Naval Officer Corps, and the Rise of National Socialism*, 16–17; Holger H. Herwig, *The Politics of Frustration*, 151; Rolf Guth, *Die Marine des deutschen Reiches, 1919–1939*, 25–26; Dülffer, *Marine*, 67.

38. Erich Raeder's views on fleet configuration can be seen in his two-volume study of the naval aspects of the Great War, *Der Kreuzerkrieg in den ausländischen Gewässern*, summarized in Dülffer, *Marine*, 99–100. For discussions with Hitler on fleet configuration, see idem., 244–45, 435–36, 476–503, 569.

39. Thies, *Architekt*, 136–47; Richard J. Overy, "From 'Uralbomber' to 'Amerikabomber': The Luftwaffe and Strategic Bombing."

40. Percy Ernst Schramm, ed., *Kriegstagebuch des Oberkommandos der Wehrmacht (Wehrmachtführungsstab)*, (hereafter cited as *KTB/OKW*), vol. I, 6 December 1940.

41. Norman Rich, *Hitler's War Aims*, vol. II, 394, 416–19.

42. Thies, *Architekt*, 18.

43. Quoted in Hillgruber, *Strategie*, 22.

44. Dülffer, *Marine*, 370–76, 476–78, 514, 527–29.

45. Carl Axel Gemzell, *Organization, Conflict, and Innovation*, 278–79.
46. Robert H. Whealey, *Hitler and Spain*, 95–134, 117, 126–27.
47. Charles B. Burdick, "Moro," 256–59.

Chapter 1. The Window on the Atlantic

1. Hitler, *Mein Kampf*, II, 666. Italics in original. Hitler's views of the French in general are treated in Eberhard Jäckel, *Frankreich in Hitlers Europa*, chapter 1.
2. Hitler, *Mein Kampf*, II, 618–24.
3. Ibid., II, 674.
4. On Vichy in general, the best introduction is Robert O. Paxton, *Vichy France*.
5. Werner Jochman, ed., *Monologe im Führer Hauptquartier, 1941–1944*, 31 January 1942, 245.
6. On the armistice with France, see the scholarly account by the chief of the quartermaster group in Jodl's planning staff (*Abteilung Landesverteidigung*), Hermann Böhme, *Der deutsch-französische Waffenstillstand im zweiten Weltkrieg*, vol. I, 20–22; Jäckel, *Frankreich*, 32–33; Paxton, *Vichy France*, 7; idem., *Parades and Politics at Vichy*, 7–8.
7. Böhme, *Waffenstillstand*, 17, 22.
8. MacGregor Knox, *Mussolini Unleashed, 1939–1941*, 39–40.
9. See Mussolini's memorandum of 31 March 1940 in Italy, Ministro degli Affari Esteri, *I Documenti Diplomatici Italiani* (hereafter cited as *DDI* with series, volume, and document numbers), 9, III, 669; Knox, *Mussolini*, 88–89.
10. The text of the Italian draft is in *DDI*, 9, V, 45.
11. Weinberg, ed., *Hitlers zweites Buch*, 176; Ralf Georg Reuth, *Entscheidung im Mittelmeer*, 18.
12. The three Munich discussions are covered in Malcolm Muggeridge, ed., *Ciano's Diary, 1939–1943*, 18 and 19 June 1940; idem., *Ciano's Diplomatic Papers*, 372–75; *DDI*, 9, V, 65; Vittorio Zincone, ed., *Hitler e Mussolini*, 51–54; *ADAP*, D, IX, 479; Giacomo Carboni, *Memorie Segrete, 1935–1948*, 95–101.
13. Muggeridge, ed., *Ciano Papers*, 373–74. Böhme, *Waffenstillstand*, 29.
14. *ADAP*, D, IX, 456; chapter 4 below.
15. Burdick, "Moro," passim. The German navy reprovisioned its submarines 23 times in Vigo, Cádiz, El Ferrol, and Las Palmas between January 1940 and September 1942.
16. Werner Rahn and Gerhard Schreiber, ed., *Kriegstagebuch der Seekriegsleitung, 1939–1945: Teil A* (hereafter cited as *KTB/Skl*. with volume and entry dates), IX, 26 May 1940.
17. The study of 3 June 1940 is printed in Michael Salewski, ed., *Die deutsche Seekriegsleitung, 1935–1945*, vol. III, 106–108.
18. The undated Carls study is printed in ibid., 108–14. Fricke's initial of 14 June suggests that it appeared a few days earlier. See idem., n. 53, and Schreiber, *Revisionismus und Weltmachstreben*, 290, n. 189. It has been assumed that

the Carls study was requested by the operations section of the Naval Command, especially since Carls enjoyed the special trust of Raeder, having served as his chief of staff in the early 1930s, and was considered a possible successor to the commander in chief. See Salewski, *Seekriegsleitung*, I, 236; idem., III, 105–106; Dülffer, *Marine*, 486–87.

19. Salewski, ed., *Seekriegsleitung*, III, 109–10, n. 22, 27, 29.

20. No italics in the original.

21. Ibid., 110, n. 25, n. 26.

22. Gerhard Wagner, ed., *Lagevorträge des Oberbefehlshabers der Kriegsmarine vor Hitler, 1939–1945*, 106–108; Salewski, ed., *Seekriegsleitung*, III, 115–16.

23. Böhme, *Waffenstillstand*, 47–48.

24. The records of the German-French discussions are in *ADAP*, D, IX, 512, 513, 521, 522, 523, 524. See also Böhme, *Waffenstillstand*, 48–69; Jäckel, *Frankreich*, 38–42.

25. On Article 5, the Germans added at the requests of Generals Weygand and Huntziger that the French air contingents could disarm themselves under German and Italian supervision. Surely Huntziger's veiled threat of 22 June that the pilots would not obey a government command to hand over their aircraft, and the logical assumption that they would fly to British territory or North Africa instead, had its effect on the German thinking in this matter.

26. Paul Bauduoin, *The Private Diaries (March 1940 to January 1941)* (hereafter cited as *Bauduoin Diary*), 20 June 1940; Maxime Weygand, *Mémoires*, vol. III, 246.

27. Italy's demands were still unknown to Berlin. See Roland Krug von Nidda (Foreign Ministry liaison with OKW) to Foreign Ministry, Nr. 33, 23 June 1940, Politisches Archiv des Auswärtigen Amtes, Büro des Staatssekretärs, Friedensverhandlungen mit Frankreich (hereafter cited as AA, StS, FF, with volume and microfilm frame numbers), I, 206122.

28. *Baudouin Diary*, 21 and 22 June 1940.

29. Weygand to Huntziger, 1 July 1940, Anl. 1, Heydrich to Ribbentrop, C.d.S.P. B. Nr. 53382/40 GRs, 6 August 1940, AA, Abteilung Inland IIg, Frankreich: Wako Material Wako Berichte, Bundle 375.

30. Böhme, *Waffenstillstand*, 70–72; Knox, *Mussolini*, 130–33.

31. *ADAP*, D, IX, 508 and n. 1.

32. Knox, *Mussolini*, 130–33.

33. See the interpretation in Elke Fröhlich, ed., *Die Tagebücher von Joseph Goebbels*, Teil I: *Sämtliche Fragmente* (hereafter cited as *Goebbels Diary*), vol. IV, 24 June 1940.

34. *ADAP*, D, IX, 525.

35. Mario Roatta, *Otto milioni di baionette*, 102–104.

36. Knox, *Mussolini*, 128–30.

37. The Italian-French negotiations are covered in Böhme, *Waffenstillstand*, 69–80. The treaty text is printed in *DDI*, 9, V, 95.

38. José Felix de Lequerica (Spanish ambassador to France) to Colonel Juan Beigbeder (Spanish minister of foreign affairs) nos. 458, 59, 60, 24 June 1940,

Archivo General del Ministerio de Asuntos Exteriores (Madrid), (hereafter cited as AMAE, with Legajo and Expediente numbers), L 1190, Ex 97.

39. Knox, *Mussolini*, 133.

40. See Krug to Foreign Ministry, Nr. 33, 23 June 1940, AA, StS, FF, I, 206122; Mackensen to Foreign Ministry, unnumbered, 25 June 1940, idem., 206132.

41. *ADAP*, D, IX, 526; *DDI*, 9, V, 91.

42. *ADAP*, D, X, 23 and n. 1; StS Nr. 490, 27 June 1940, AA, StS, FF, I, 206162–63.

43. This point is emphasized in the postwar manuscript, "Der Waffenstillstand," by the German liaison officer to the Italian Armistice Commission, Frido von Senger und Etterlin, Institut für Zeitgeschichte (Munich), 10–11.

44. Muggeridge, ed., *Ciano Diary*, 24 June 1940. One should compare this comment on the length of the war with the more optimistic predictions that Ciano made to Ambassador von Mackensen earlier the same day. See Mackensen to Foreign Ministry, Nr. 1199, 24 June 1940, AA, StS, FF, 206127–28.

45. Keitel appointed Lieutenant Colonel Hermann Böhme to the post. Böhme, Waffenstillstand, 150–51.

46. Ibid., 95–97.

47. The mechanics of the setup of the two commissions are covered in ibid., 147–55, 201–206.

48. Ibid., 147–48, 207.

49. The signed protocol of the meeting no longer exists, but there is a detailed report on the meeting from the Foreign Ministry representative with the German Armistice Commission, Andor Hencke, in *ADAP*, D, X, 54. Böhme, who was present during the meeting in Wiesbaden between Stülpnagel and Roatta, interprets German restraint toward Morocco as a result of Spanish interests in the area. Yet if such were the case, Italian presence in French Morocco would have been just as annoying to Madrid as a German presence. It is more likely that the agreement over Morocco was the result of simple shortsightedness, especially since the protocol was written and signed in a very hurried meeting in which Stülpnagel did most of the talking. See Böhme, *Waffenstillstand*, 206–10.

50. The Hencke report and account by Böhme cited in note 49 above both suggest that the Roatta Agreements dealt with French West and Equatorial Africa. As will be seen in chapter 3 below, both are wrong on this point.

51. Böhme, *Waffenstillstand*, 206–10; Von Senger und Etterlin, "Der Waffenstillstand," Institut für Zeitgeschichte, 5–6, 19–20; memorandum by Krug, 19 July 1940, AA, StS, FF, I, 206346; memorandum by Krug, 22 July 1940, idem., 206373–75.

52. Quoted in Böhme, *Waffenstillstand*, 79.

Chapter 2. The Demand for Casablanca

1. The text is printed in France, *La Délégacion française auprès de la commission allemande d'armistice* (hereafter cited as *DFCAA*), I, 463–64.

2. Böhme, *Waffenstillstand*, 344–53; Karl-Völker Neugebauer, *Die deutsche Militärkontrolle im unbesetzten Frankreich und in Französisch-Nordafrika, 1940–1942*, 63–65; Paxton, *Parades and Politics at Vichy*, 76–77.

3. Hencke to Foreign Ministry, Nr. 15, 1 July 1940, AA, StS, FF, I, 206176; Böhme, *Waffenstillstand*, 293.

4. Philip Bankwitz, *Maxime Weygand and Civil-Military Relations in Modern France*, 333–34.

5. For Operation Catapult, see Arthur J. Marder, *From the Dardenelles to Oran; Hervé Coutau-Bégarie and Claude Huan, Darlan*, 238 ff.

6. Weygand to Huntziger and Duplat, 457/DSA, 6 July 1940, Anl. 3, Heydrich to Ribbentrop, C.d.S.B. Nr. 53382/40 GRs, 6 August 1940, AA, Inland IIg, Wako Berichte, bndl. 375.

7. *DFCAA*, I, 40–41; memorandum by Hans Kramarz, zu Pol. IM, 9477g, 4 July 1940, AA, StS, FF, I, 206197; unsigned memo, 3 July 1940, idem., 206192–93. *ADAP*, D, X, 93.

8. *DFCAA*, I, 41–42, 34; "Note concernant la suspension de clauses de la convention d'armistice," July 1940, Anl. 11, AA, Inland IIg, Wako Berichte DII 95 GRs, bndl. 377; Böhme, *Waffenstillstand*, 325–26 and n. 136.

9. Unsigned memo, 4 July 1940, AA, StS, FF, I, 206196; Böhme, *Waffenstillstand*, 325–26.

10. Hencke to Foreign Ministry, Nr. 29, 4 July 1940, AA, StS, FF, I, 206202; *ADAP*, D, X, 115.

11. Memorandum by Kramarz, 6 July 1940, AA, StS, FF, I, 206206–207.

12. Quoted in Paxton *Parades and Politics at Vichy*, 76.

13. See for example *DFCAA*, I, 39–40, 43, 51–52; memorandum by Grote, Pol. IM, 9920g, 12 July 1940, AA, StS, FF, I, 206264–65; memorandum by Grote, Pol. IM, 10 0047g, 15 July 1940, idem., 206292–93; *KTB/Skl.*, XI, 3, 4, 5, 8, and 10 July 1940. See also *Baudouin Diary*, 4 and 5 July 1940; Böhme, *Waffenstillstand*, 314–23.

14. Memorandum by Grote, Pol. IM, 9789g, 10 July 1940, AA, StS, FF, I, 206231–34; memorandum by Krug von Nidda, 19 July 1940, idem., 206349–52; Böhme, *Waffenstillstand*, 335.

15. *KTB/Skl.*, XI, 5 July 1940.

16. *DFCAA*, I, 43, 51–52.

17. *KTB/Skl.*, XI, 8 July 1940; Wagner, ed. *Lagevorträge*, 109–10.

18. Fröhlich, ed., *Goebbels Diary*, 6 and 7 July 1940; Böhme, *Waffenstillstand*, 335–39.

19. Fröhlich, ed., *Goebbels Diary*, IV, 8–14 and 19–20 July 1940.

20. *ADAP*, D, X, 129; Muggeridge, ed., *Ciano Papers*, 375–79.

21. Memorandum by Grote, Pol. IM, 9920g, 12 July 1940, AA, StS, FF, I, 206264–65.

22. Memorandum by von Kessel, Pol. IM, 10076g, 16 July 1940, ibid., 206298–89; OKW/Abt. Ausland Nr. 15436/40g Ausl. IIIa, 19 Aug. 1940, Bundesarchiv/Militärarchiv (Freiburg) (hereafter cited as BA/MA), RW 4/310.

23. Hans Richard Hemmen to Foreign Ministry, Nr. 19, 13 July 1940, AA, StS,

FF, I, 206283; memorandum by Krug von Nidda, 19 July 1940, idem., 206352–53; *ADAP*, D, X, 163.

24. OKW/Abt. Ausland Nr. 15436/40g. Ausl. IIIa, 19 August 1940, BA/MA, RW 4/310; Anl. zu Abw. II, Nr. 1261/40 gKdos., 17 Sept. 1940, idem., RM 7/255. See also the French memorandum, "Senegal (Mars–Août 1940)," Anl. 25, Heydrich to Ribbentrop and Martin Luther, Nr. 53 351/40, 6 Nov. 1940, AA, Inland IIg, Wako D II, 81 GRs 1940, bndl. 375a.

25. *KTB/Skl.*, XI, 10 July 1940.

26. Ibid., 12 July 1940.

27. See chapter 3 below.

28. *DFCAA*, V, 440–42; Böhme, *Waffenstillstand*, 326–27.

29. *KTB/Skl.*, XI, 3 July 1940.

30. *DFCAA*, V, 441–42.

31. *Baudouin Diary*, 6 July 1940.

32. "Note concernant la suspension de clauses de la convention d'armistice," Anl. 11, AA, Inland IIg, Wako D II, 95 GRs, bndl. 377; Weygand to Huntziger and Duplat, 457/DSA, 6 July 1940, Anl. 3, idem., bndl. 375.

33. *Baudouin Diary*, 6 July 1940 argues for the author's successful intervention with Pétain. Paxton, *Parades*, 73–75, argues that Vichy's reserve came from Duplat's initiative.

34. *DFCAA*, V, 442.

35. Ibid., 442–44.

36. Muggeridge, ed., *Ciano Diary*, 5 July 1940.

37. *KTB/Skl.*, XI, 5 July 1940; memorandum by Grote, Pol. IM, 9857g, 11 July 1940, AA, StS, FF, I, 206236–38.

38. *ADAP*, D, X, 129. Böhme, *Waffenstillstand*, 341–46, states that the idea of the bases in North Africa came originally from the Luftwaffe Command, and that this organization drafted the final version of the note that the Germans handed to the French. There is no surviving documentary evidence to prove the assertion.

39. Hans-Adolf Jacobsen, ed., *Generaloberst Halder: Kriegstagebuch* (hereafter cited as *Halder Diary*), vol. II, 8 July 1940; Böhme, *Waffenstillstand*, 340.

40. Memorandum by Grote, Pol. IM, 9833g, 10 July 1940, AA, StS, FF, I, 206226.

41. Memorandum by Grote, Pol. IM, 9833g, 10 July 1940, ibid., 206226; memorandum by Grote, Pol. IM, 9857g, 11 July 1940, ibid., 206236–38.

42. Memorandum by Grote, Pol. IM, 9789g, 10 July 1940, ibid., 206231–34. The command in full no longer exists and thus no more detail is available than the cited memo.

43. For comment on the 11 July draft, see memorandum by Krug von Nidda, 11 July 1940, ibid., 206253–36.

44. See for example Fröhlich, ed., *Goebbels Diary*, IV, 25 June 1940.

45. *ADAP*, D, X, 73, 166.

46. Fröhlich, ed., *Goebbels Diary*, IV, 25 June 1940, 3 July 1940.

47. Ibid., 27–29 June, 3, 4, 7, 9, 10, 13, 14, 15, and 17 July 1940.

48. Muggeridge, ed., *Ciano Diary*, 19–20 July 1940.

49. Fröhlich, ed., *Goebbels Diary*, IV, 3 July 1940.

50. Ibid., 9 July 1940.

51. Karl Klee, *Das Unternehmen "Seelöwe,"* 67–69.

52. Burdick, "Moro," passim.

53. *ADAP*, D, X, 73.

54. Ibid., 129; Muggeridge, ed., *Ciano Papers*, 375–79.

55. *ADAP*, D, X, 108.

56. On this issue, see ibid., 92, 127, 137, 178.

57. Wagner, ed. *Lagevorträge*, 108–20.

58. Ibid., 113–18. The original version of the study held that Great Britain alone would be Germany's primary enemy after the war. The change to a more general Anglo-Saxon threat was added by the Naval command chief of staff, Rear Admiral Otto Schniewind, and approved by Raeder. See Salewski, ed., *Seekriegsleitung*, III, 121–36.

59. Dülffer, *Marine*, 570–71.

60. On Hitler's ideas regarding future Anglo-German relations, see the contrary views in Hillgruber, "England's Place in Hitler's Plans for World Dominion," 5–22, and Weinberg, "Hitler and England 1933–1945: Pretense and Reality," 299–309.

61. Thies, *Architekt*, 136–47.

62. *ADAP*, D, XII, 584.

63. Wagner, ed. *Lagevorträge*, 108, 263; BA/MA, RM 6/74.

64. Paxton, *Parades*, 76–77.

65. Memorandum by Grote, Pol. IM, 9789g, 10 July 1940, AA, StS, FF, I, 206231–34.

66. *ADAP*, D, IX, 488, and chapter 4 below.

67. On German aims in the Spanish civil war, see Whealey, *Hitler and Spain;* Weinberg, *Foreign Policy*, I, 284–99; idem., II, 142–66; Hans-Henning Abendroth, *Hitler in der spanischen Arena;* Manfred Merkes, *Die deutsche Politik gegenüber dem spanischer Bürgerkrieg, 1936–1939.* The newest perspectives are in Christian Leitz, *Economic Relations between Nazi Germany and Franco's Spain, 1936–1945.*

68. The Germans would reveal to the Spaniards in September that they also wanted the French Moroccan ports of Agadir and Mogador. See *ADAP*, D, XI, 63; chapter 5 below.

69. See chapter 3 below on the issue of Axis spheres of interest..

70. *ADAP*, D, X, 151.

71. Ibid., D, X, 158, and n. 3. Mussolini's statement of 15 July, in which he declared without reservation his agreement with a German base at Oran, should be viewed as a sop to Hitler. He already knew that Hitler would not demand a base there.

72. Paxton, *Vichy France*, 61–63.

73. Michael B. Miller, *Shanghai on the Métro*, 54–63.

74. See chapter 4 below.

75. See the comments by Baudouin and Laval in Lequerica to Beigbeder, no. 860,

4 July 1940, AMAE, L 2295, Ex 4; Lequerica to Beigbeder, unnumbered, 18 July 1940, L 1190, Ex 97; Lequerica to Beigbeder, nos. 526–29, 20 July 1940, idem.

76. See *Baudouin Diary,* 16 July 1940; Böhme, *Waffenstillstand,* 347–48.
77. *DFCAA,* V, 438–40.
78. *Baudouin Diary,* 18, 22 July 1940.
79. Ibid., 25, 27 July 1940. Böhme, *Waffenstillstand,* 349, argues that Stülpnagel had in fact never made such remarks.
80. *ADAP,* D, X, 208 and n. 1.
81. See Stülpnagel's warnings in DWStK Chefgruppe Ia, Nr. 3/40 gKdos. Chefs., 12 August 1940, BA/MA, RW 34/9. Hitler's reply is in OKW/WFSt/Abt. L (III), Nr. 33 226/40 gKdos. Chefs., 17 Aug. 1940, idem. See also *KTB/OKW,* I, 12 August 1940 for Hitler's concerns on a possible British attack on Dakar.

Chapter 3. The Specter of de Gaulle

1. The best biography on de Gaulle during the war is Jean Lacouture, *De Gaulle,* vol. I.
2. *KTB/OKW,* I, 15 August 1940. The embassy in Madrid had reported to Berlin on 25 July that according to Spanish sources the de Gaulle movement was decreasing steadily in popularity and that "the failure of the de Gaulle movement is especially noteworthy in the colonies." See *ADAP,* D, X, 225. The official history of the Free French movement places the number of troops at approximately 2,600 in July 1940. See Jean-Noël Vincent, *Les Forces Françaises dans la Lutte contre l'Axe en Afrique,* 20–38.
3. Memorandum by Grote, Pol. IM, 10679g, 30 July 1940, AA, StS, FF, I, 206432–33; memorandum by Krug, 31 July 1940, idem., 206435–36; memorandum by Grote, Pol. IM, 10735g, 31 July 1940, idem., 206437; Foreign Ministry memorandum, 6 August 1940, idem., 206475; memorandum by Krug, 23 July 1940, idem., 206379–80; memorandum by Krug, 28 July 1940, idem., 206408–09; *KTB/Skl.,* XI, 25, 31 July 1940; idem., XII, 8 August 1940.
4. See for example John Kent, *The Internationalization of Colonialism,* 27–84.
5. On the blockade, see W. N. Medlicott, *The Economic Blockade,* vol. I., 549. The decision was announced in the House of Commons on 2 July 1940.
6. *KTB/Skl.,* XI, 12 July 1940; *DFCAA,* I, 61–62.
7. See the references to this issue in North Africa and in Senegal on pp. 20–21 above.
8. Memorandum by Grote, Pol. IM, 10176g, 18 July 1940, AA, StS, FF, I, 206312; memorandum by Krug, 19 July 1940, idem., 206352–53. *KTB/Skl.,* XI, 19, 20, 23, 27, and 28 July 1940; memorandum by Grote, Pol. IM, 10327g, 21 July 1940, idem., 206361; memorandum by Krug, 22 July 1940, idem., 206369–71.
9. See Darlan to Michelier, no. 1399 F.M.F.3/S.E.C.A., 25 July 1940, Anl. 8, Heydrich to Ribbentrop, C.S.P. & S.D., C.d.S., B. Nr. 53 351/40, 6 Novem-

ber 1940, AA, Inland IIg, Wako Berichte D II, 81 GRs, 1940, bndl. 375a; *Baudouin Diary*, 31 July 1940, 1–2, 20 August 1940. *KTB/Skl.*, XI, 25 July 1940; *DFCAA*, I, 100, 106–11.

10. *KTB/Skl.*, XI, 25–26 July 1940; Paxton, *Vichy France*, 66.

11. For the 105 Mediterranean voyages permitted by the Italian Armistice Commission between 25 July and 7 August 1940, see Mackensen to Foreign Ministry, Nr. 1434, 31 July 1940, AA, StS, FF, I, 206440; Mackensen to Foreign Ministry, Nr. 1460, 6 August 1940, idem., 206476; memorandum by Wiehl, *ADAP*, D, X, 267. On Hitler's order, see memorandum by Grote, Pol. IM, 10718g, 31 July 1940, AA, StS, FF, I, 206441.

12. Charles de Gaulle, *Discourses et Messages*, vol. I, 18–20. German reactions are in *KTB/Skl.*, XI, 31 July 1940.

13. *KTB/Skl.*, XII, 3 August 1940; memorandum by Grote, Pol. IM, 10940g, 5 August 1940, AA, StS, FF, I, 206461–63.

14. *KTB/Skl.*, XII, 19 August 1940. See also memorandum by Grote, 21 August 1940, AA, StS, FF, I, 206560–64.

15. *KTB/Skl.*, XII, 1 August 1940; *DFCAA*, I, 88.

16. *KTB/Skl.*, XI, 31 July 1940; memorandum by Grote, Pol. IM, 10768g, 1 August 1940, AA, StS, FF, I, 206443–44; memorandum by Krug, 2 August 1940, idem, 206453; memorandum by Grote, Pol. IM, 10870g, 3 August 1940, idem., 206459; *DFCAA*, I, 82, 91.

17. *DFCAA*, I, 101–106. French occupation costs as of 21 July were 20 million Reichsmarks per day at the inflated rate of 20 francs to the mark. See Alan S. Milward, *The New Order and the French Economy*, 58–64; Paxton, *Vichy France*, 53, 143–44.

18. Tupinier report of 12 August 1940, Anl. 4, Heydrich to Ribbentrop, C.S.P & S.D. 53531/40 GRs, 13 September 1940, AA, Inland IIg, Wako Material, bndl. 375. Tupinier to the secretary of state for the colonies in Vichy, 20 August 1940, Anl. 19, Heydrich to Ribbentrop, C.S.P & S.D., C.d.S., B. Nr. 53531/40 GRs, 4 December 1941, AA, Inland IIg, Wako Berichte, DII 95 GRs, bndl. 377; *DFCAA*, I, 121, 126, 141, 150.

19. For Huntziger's meeting with Stülpnagel, see *DFCAA, I*, 131–40. For Stülpnagel's report, see Hencke to Foreign Ministry, Nr. 140, 23 August 1940, AA, StS, FF, I, 206571–72. In a personal note by Huntziger found by the SD in French headquarters, Huntziger's used a much stronger tone. He accused the Germans of attempting to force a breakup of the French Empire through stifling economic contact, and he proposed that Germany declare the eventual fate of the colonies. Anl. 34, Heydrich to Ribbentrop, C.d.S. B. Nr. 53 351/40, 6 November 1940, AA, Inland IIg, Wako Berichte, D II 81 GRs, bndl. 375a. Whether Stülpnagel saw this piece of paper before his report of 22 August is unclear. Concerning the passage of French merchantmen through the Strait of Gibraltar, the Germans on 20 August 1940 did agree to a test run, which occurred without incident on 6 September. See *DFCAA*, I, 127–28, 130, 144, 174–225; *KTB/Skl.*, XIII, 4, 10 September 1940.

20. *DFCAA,* I, 41, 150, 174; memorandum by Grote, 27 August 1940, AA, StS, FF, I, 206586–67.

21. The numbers are taken from André Truchet, *L'armistice de 1940 et l'Afrique du nord,* 254–90. For analysis, see Böhme, *Waffenstillstand,* 123–29.

22. The raw figures, which do not include naval aircraft, come from a 25 July 1940 air ministry evaluation reproduced in Truchet, *L'armistice,* 116. Of this number, Truchet reckons that 523 fighters, 295 bombers, and 350 reconnaissance craft were capable of action. Böhme, in *Waffenstillstand,* 127, places the total number more in the neighborhood of 800.

23. Böhme, *Waffenstillstand,* 127–28; Bernard Destremau, *Weygand,* 645, n. 2. On French air and land power in Africa before and after the armistice, see also Martin Thomas, "Plans and Problems of the *Armée de l'Air* in the Defence of French North Africa before the Fall of France," 472–95; idem., "The Anglo-French Divorce over West Africa and the Limitations of Strategic Planning, June–December 1940," 252–78.

24. See the report of 16 August 1940 by the German liaison officer in Turin, Colonel Frido von Senger und Etterlin, in von Senger, "Auszüge aus den Wochenberichten," ED 61, Institut für Zeitgeschichte, Munich (hereafter cited as "Von Senger Reports"). See also MacGregor Knox, "Fascist Italy Assesses Its Enemies 1935–1940," in Ernest R. May, ed., *Knowing One's Enemies,* 351.

25. "Von Senger Reports," 16 August 1940, 29 August 1940; DWStK Chefgruppe Ia, Nr. 3/40 gKdos. Chefs., 12 August 1940, BA/MA, RW 34/9; Knox, *Mussolini,* 179–80.

26. Hencke to Foreign Ministry, Nr. 91, 1 August 1940, AA, StS, FF, I, 206448; memorandum by Grote, Pol. IM, 10870g, 3 August 1940, idem., 206459; Foreign Ministry memorandum, 5 August 1940, idem., 206471; *KTB/Skl.,* XI, 21 July 1940.

27. DWStK Chefgruppe Ia, Nr. 3/40 gKdos. Chefs., 12 August 1940, BA/MA, RW 34/9; memorandum by Grote, Pol. IM, 10679g, 30 July 1940, AA, StS, FF, I, 206432–33; memorandum by Grote, 14 August 1940, idem., 206517–19. On British propaganda, see memorandum by Grote, 20 August 1940, idem., 206541–43; Hencke to Foreign Ministry, Nr. 136, 21 August 1940, idem., 206552–53; *KTB/OKW,* I, 21 August 1940; *DFCAA,* I, 131–40. Although Stülpnagel trusted Noguès, many in Berlin distrusted his freemason background. See Foreign Ministry memorandum, 5 August 1940, AA, StS, FF, I, 206471; memorandum by Grote, 19 August 1940, idem., 206537–40.

28. Nr. 117/40 gKdos., 7 August 1940, BA/MA, RW 34/9; "Von Senger Reports," 16 August 1940; *KTB/OKW,* I, 8, 13 August 1940.

29. On these complex discussions, see memorandum by Grote, Pol. IM, 10 0047g, 15 July 1940, AA, StS, FF, I, 206292–93; memorandum by Grote, Pol. IM, 10358g, 22 July 1940, idem. 206363–64; memorandum by Krug, 22 July 1940, idem., 206369–71; memorandum by Krug, 22 July 1940, idem., 206373–75; memorandum by Grote, Pol. IM. 10768g, 1 August 1940, idem, 206443–44; memorandum by Grote, Pol. IM, 10823g, 2 August 1940, idem.,

206457–58; memorandum by Kramarz, Pol. IM, 13215g, 24 September 1940, AA, Büro Unterstaatssekretär, Äquatorial-Afrika (hereafter cited as UStS, AEF); enclosure 3 in von Senger to German Armistice Commission, Pr. Nr. 216/40, 26 September 1940, enclosed in DWStK Chefgruppe Ia, Nr. 6/40 gKdos. Chefs., 30 September 1940, BA/MA, RW 34/9; *DFCAA*, I, 72.

30. DWStK Chefgruppe Ia, Nr. 3/40 gKdos. Chefs., 12 August 1940, BA/MA, RW 34/9; *KTB/OKW*, I, 13 August 1940.

31. By 12 August 1,560,000 men had been demobilized in the *Metropole* and demobilization in the area was thus completed in its essentials. On Hitler's order, the army in the *Metropole* was to be limited to 100,000 men. See *KTB/ OKW*, I, 5 and 13 August 1940.

32. For Hitler's reply, as reported to Wiesbaden by Keitel, see OKW/WFSt/Abt. L (III), Nr. 33 226/40 gKdos. Chefs., 17 August 1940, BA/MA, RW 34/9; *KTB/ OKW*, I, 19 August 1940.

33. *KTB/OKW*, I, 15 August 1940. Hitler was certainly concerned by reports from German agents that the French were sending war materials from unoccupied France to North Africa. As of 15 August the Germans had already begun investigating. See memorandum by Grote, 16 August 1940, AA, StS, FF, I, 206523–26.

34. See chapter 4 below.

35. De Gaulle, *Mémoires de Guerre*, I, 89–90.

36. Ibid, 90, 268, 271–72, 290–92. Paxton, *Parades*, 37.

37. De Gaulle, *Mémoires*, I, 91–92, 285; Elie Castor and Raymond Tracy, *Félix Éboué*, 91–108.

38. On the coups, see Robert Bourgi, *Le Général de Gaulle et l'Afrique Noire, 1940–1949*, 49–69. See also the correspondence between de Gaulle and de Larminat printed in de Gaulle, *Mémoires*, I, 287–90.

39. *DFCAA*, I, 186–89; *KTB/OKW*, I, 29–30 August 1940; *KTB/Skl.*, XII, 30 August 1940; memorandum by Grote, 29 August 1940, AA, StS, FF, I, 206593–95; memorandum by Woermann, 5 September 1940, *ADAP*, D, XI, 20; Paxton, *Parades*, 78–79.

40. New Hebrides had already joined de Gaulle on 20 July 1940, but this initial defection did not cause concern in Berlin.

41. See the German sources cited in note 39 above.

42. *KTB/Skl.*, XII, 30 August 1940, my emphasis.

43. *KTB/OKW*, I, 30 August 1940; Hencke to Foreign Ministry, 31 August 1940, AA, StS, FF, I, 206604–45; *KTB/Skl.*, XIII, 1 September 1940.

44. *KTB/Skl.*, XII, 31 August 1940; *KTB/OKW*, I, 31 August 1940.

45. Hencke to Foreign Ministry, 31 August 1940, AA, StS, FF, I, 206604–605; Hencke to Foreign Ministry, Nr. 151, 30 August 1940, idem., 206600.

46. Hemmen to Foreign Ministry, Del. Nr. 88, 31 August 1940, ibid., 206606–10. The Germans at this time had indeed devised a plan for moving the French gold to Paris and the remainder of the gold to Berlin on German Condor airplanes. See memorandum by Woermann, 5 September 1940, *ADAP*, D, XI, 20; *KTB/Skl.*, XIII, 11 September 1940.

47. *ADAP*, D, XI, 25.

48. Hencke to Foreign Ministry, Nr. 156, 2 September 1940, AA, FF, II, 206856–57; memorandum by Kramarz, 2 September 1940, idem., 206854–55.

49. *KTB/OKW*, I, 2 September 1940. The report came from the OKW's officer for special issues, Lieutenant Colonel von Tippelskirch, and might have been written a day before it was submitted, since, as shown below, the Italians reconsidered their position on 1 September.

50. Protocol in Anl. 36, Heydrich to Ribbentrop, C.S.P. & S.D., C.d.S., B. Nr. 53 351/40, 6 November 1940, AA, Inland II g, Wako Berichte, D II, 81 GRs, bndl. 375a. See also *DFCAA*, I, 189; *KTB/Skl.*, XII, 30 August 1940; idem., XIII, 12 September 1940.

51. Tupinier to secretary of state for the colonies, 6 September 1940, Anl. 18, Heydrich to Ribbentrop, C.S.P. & S.D., C.d.S., B. Nr. 53531/40, 4 December 1940, AA, Inland IIg, Wako Berichte, D II, 95 GRs, bndl. 377.

52. On discussions concerning German economic advantages in French imports, see *KTB/Skl.*, XII, 30 August 1940; Tupinier to secretary of state for the colonies, 6 September 1940, Anl. 18, Heydrich to Ribbentrop, C.S.P. & S.D., C.d.S., B. Nr. 53531/40, 4 December 1940, AA, Abteilung Inland IIg, Wako Berichte D II 95 GRs, bndl. 377; Ministere des Finances, Secretariat General pour les Questions Economiques, Note au Sujet des Produits Coloniaux, 2 September 1940, Anl. 13, Heydrich to Ribbentrop, C.S.P. & S.D., C.d.S., B. Nr. 53531/40, 4 December 1940, idem.; *DFCAA*, I, 181–85. German participation in the French colonial economy would soon increase to 10% of French colonial imports until November 1942. See Paxton, *Vichy France*, 144.

53. The Foreign Ministry had first raised the issue of economic representation on 23 August, and according to a later report by Hemmen, he raised it with the French on 5 September. See Hemmen to Foreign Ministry, Nr. 111, 13 September 1940, AA, StS, FF, II, 206939–40. The Germans were especially interested in gaining information on iron ore deposits near Konakry. On this issue, see Hermann Friedrich Sabath to Otto Abetz and German Embassy in Paris, W II 5420, 22 August 1940, AA, Deutsche Botschaft Paris (hereafter cited as DB Paris), Westafrika; Rudolf Schleier (Deputy to Abetz) to Deutsche Handelskammer Paris, Nr. 479, 29 August 1940, idem.; Sabath to Abetz and DB Paris, W II 5607, 31 August 1940, idem.; German Embassy Paris to Foreign Ministry, W. Nr. 1914/41, 28 May 1941, idem.

54. Protocol in Anl. 36, Heydrich to Ribbentrop, C.S.P. & S.D., C.d.S., B-Nr. 53 351/40, 6 November 1940, AA, Abteilung Inland II g, Wako Berichte D II 81 GRs, bndl. 375a; Tupinier to Secretary of State for the Colonies, 6 September 1940, Anl. 18 of Heydrich to Ribbentrop, C.S.P. & S.D., C.d.S., B. Nr. 53531/ 40, 4 December 1940, AA, Abteilung Inland IIg, Wako Berichte D II, 95 GRs, bndl. 377.

55. Memorandum by Ernst Woermann, *ADAP*, D, XI, 20; memorandum by Weizsäcker, idem., 72; *KTB/OKW*, I, 4–5 September 1940.

56. Hencke to Foreign Ministry, Nr. 1566/1747, 4 September 1940, AA, UStS, AEF; *ADAP*, D, XI, 14, 20.

57. Memorandum by Grote, 3 September 1940, AA, UStS, AEF.

58. Mackensen to Foreign Ministry, Nr. 1455, 5 August 1940, AA, StS, Deutsch-Italienische Beziehungen, III, B 002118–19; *ADAP*, D, XX, 360.

59. *ADAP*, D, XI, 5, 20; memorandum by Grote, 3 September 1940, AA, UStS, AEF.

60. See his marginal exclamation points on Hencke to Foreign Ministry, 31 August 1940, AA, StS, FF, II, 206604–605. He ordered Hencke to inform Stülpnagel that events in French Equatorial Africa had passed into the political realm and were thus a Foreign Ministry responsibility. Stülpnagel agreed readily and stated that there was a written agreement with Italy from the time of the Roatta Agreements, which stated that the zones of disarmament supervision *did not* signify the delineation of political or economic interest spheres. See Hencke to Foreign Ministry, 2 September 1940, *ADAP*, D, XI, 5. If this written agreement ever existed, it does not exist now. There is no reference to it anywhere in the records, and the discussion on the Roatta Agreements in Böhme, *Waffenstillstand*, 206–10, contains no mention of it. Perhaps Stülpnagel was attempting to cover an earlier mistake. In any event, he prohibited the use of the word "Interessensphären" within the Armistice Commission on the same day as his discussion with Hencke, for fear of the political misunderstandings that such usage could cause. See memorandum by Kramarz, 2 September 1940, AA, StS, FF, II, 206854–55; memorandum by Grote, 3 September 1940, AA, UStS, AEF. In general, see Weizsäcker's later note to Keitel of 19 September 1940, *ADAP*, D, XI, 72.

61. *ADAP*, D, XI, 20, 72; *KTB/OKW*, I, 4–5 September 1940.

62. *KTB/OKW*, I, 2 August 1940; 25 August 1940; memorandum by Grote, Pol. IM, 11123g, 9 August 1940, AA, StS, FF, I, 206501–503; memorandum by Grote, 3 September 1940, AA, UStS, AEF.

63. *KTB/Skl.*, XII, 30 August 1940. Stülpnagel mentioned to Hencke on 2 September 1940 that Hitler had rejected the idea of sending German control commissions to Africa, and it is not known whether Hitler had repeated the order at that time or Stülpnagel was merely repeating the decision that Hitler had made before de Gaulle's coup. The latter is the more likely possibility, however, since, so far as is known, the issue of control had not been raised again with Hitler before 2 September. Stülpnagel said that the High Command would raise this and related issues with Hitler the following day, and that the navy was trying to get Hitler to reconsider its plan to send commissions to Casablanca and Dakar. See *ADAP*, D, XI, 5; memorandum by Kramarz, 2 September 1940, AA, StS, FF, II, 206854–55.

64. Weizsäcker's own retrospective memo of 19 September 1940 states that he and Jodl agreed on the idea of a mixed commission. See *ADAP*, D, XI, 72. Jodl apparently stated afterwards however, that the issue of control in Africa was still open while soliciting opinions on the matter from his work staff, from the Abwehr, and from Stülpnagel as well. See *KTB/OKW*, I, 4 and 5 September 1940. The Woermann memorandum on the Weizsäcker-Jodl meeting cited in n. 55 above has no mention of a commission of any kind.

65. On Italian steps, see memorandum by Grote, 3 September 1940, AA, UStS, AEF; memorandum by Grote, 12 September 1940, AA, StS, FF, II, 206934–37. See also Böhme's report of 2 September to OKW on his discussion with Pintor in Rome of that day, enclosed in Hencke to Foreign Ministry, Nr. 1566/1747, 4 September 1940, UStS, AEF. On the French response, see memorandum by Grote, 7 September 1940, FF, II, 206897–98. The six warships left Toulon on 9 September. See *KTB/Skl.*, XIII, 10 September 1940.

66. Mussolini had also written Hitler on 24 August 1940 with the argument that the French still did not see themselves as defeated and added that trends in North Africa were demonstrating that the French were hoping for continued British resistance and American intervention. See *ADAP*, D, X, 388. It should also be mentioned that after de Gaulle's coup, Badoglio had ordered planning for possible Italian actions against Tunisia and Corsica. See Knox, *Mussolini*, 180.

67. For his report to the High Command, see Hencke to Foreign Ministry, Nr. 161, 6 September 1940, AA, StS, FF, II, 206884–86; *KTB/OKW*, I, 5 September 1940.

68. *KTB/OKW*, I, 6 September 1940.

69. For Hitler's order, see *ADAP*, D, XI, 33.

70. Hitler's statement of 8 September did not say specifically that supplementary army troops would have to come from *North* Africa, but the transmission of this order to the French on 11 September, covered on p. 48, n. 80 below, *did* say so. This tacit rejection of Stülpnagel's proposal to allow the French to use African troops then stationed in France was not insignificant. The most recent German count of early September 1940 had placed 30,000 demobilized North African troops in the *Metropole* waiting for repatriation (50,000 had already been repatriated), and 70,000 Equatorial African troops demobilized and waiting for repatriation. See memorandum by Grote, 3 September 1940, AA, UStS, AEF. On 9 September, the French delegation in Wiesbaden presented a plan for the repatriation of 100,000 African troops. See memorandum by Grote, 9 September 1940, AA, StS, FF, II, 206909–11. With regard to additional aircraft, there is no clear statement in the Hitler order or the 11 September note that the French must deplete their forces in North Africa, but since the 18 combat groups allowed by the Italians and Germans at this time were for *all* of French Africa, the French could not reinforce central or West Africa without weakening the north.

71. The original draft of the policy order is discussed in Neugebauer, *Militärkontrolle*, 74, n. 20, yet that author, incorrectly in my opinion, assumes that the deletion meant that Hitler had given up the idea.

72. *KTB/OKW*, I, 6 and 10 September 1940, for a reference for the need to make preparations for the occupation of German bases.

73. Memorandum by Minister Emil von Rintelen of the Foreign Ministry's political department, 10 September 1940, AA, UStS, AEF.

74. This decision was reached by Weizsäcker and Jodl. See Weizsäcker to the German chargé d'affaires in Rome, von Plessen, Nr. 1231, 9 September 1940,

AA, StS, FF, II, 206901–902, and the memo by Weizsäcker in *ADAP*, D, XI, 33, n. 2.

75. On the change, see memorandum by Emil von Rintelen, 10 September 1940, AA, StS, AEF; memorandum by Plessen, 9 September 1940, AA, Deutsche Botschaft Rom (Quirinal) (hereafter cited as DB Rom), Geheimakten, Lage in Äequatorial-Afrika, Kontrolle in Nordafrika (AEF); memorandum by Plessen, 10 September 1940, idem.

76. *ADAP*, D, XI, 33 and n. 2; idem., 72. Weizsäcker to von Plessen, Nr. 1231, 9 September 1940, AA, StS, FF, II, 206901–902.

77. Memorandum by Kramarz, 11 September 1940, AA, StS, FF, II, 206927–28; memorandum by Weizsäcker, StS, Nr. 695, idem., 206929. See also Weizsäcker's memo of 19 September 1940 in *ADAP*, D, XI, 72.

78. See the reference to Woermann's memorandum of 7 October 1940, *ADAP*, D, XI, 154, n. 3.

79. See memorandum by Weizsäcker, StS, Nr. 695, AA, StS, FF, II, 206929; Weizsäcker to Mackensen, Pol. IM, 12 595g, 12 September 1940, idem., 206932–33; *ADAP*, D, XI, 72. See also the two memoranda by Mackensen of 12 September 1940 in AA, DB Rom, AEF.

80. The German note is in *ADAP*, D, XI, 47. The Italian note is included in memorandum by Kramarz, 12 September 1940, AA, UStS, AEF. The addendum was added on 9 September at Berlin's suggestion. Memorandum by Emil von Rintelen, 11 September 1940, idem.; Weizsäcker to German Embassy in Rome, Nr. 1234, 9 September 1940, AA, StS, FF, II, 206904–905.

81. *Baudouin Diary*, 2 and 12 September 1940.

82. *DFCAA*, I, 273–84; *Baudouin Diary*, 14 September 1940; Hencke to Foreign Ministry, Nr. 165, 12 September 1940, AA, UStS, AEF.

83. On the appointment, see Bankwitz, *Weygand*, 337–45. Vichy also sent senior officers to inspect French units in areas deemed politically unstable. See Paxton, *Parades*, 80; *DFCAA*, I, 273–84.

84. For detail on the Italian note, see memorandum by Grote, 13 September 1940, AA, StS, FF, II, 206943–45. The Italians also disallowed all armored vehicles, antitank artillery, antiaircraft artillery, and field artillery over 75 millimeters.

85. Hemmen to Foreign Ministry, Nr. 111, 13 September 1940, ibid., 206939–40; Hemmen to Foreign Ministry, Del. Nr. 119, 17 September 1940, ibid., 206975–76.

86. Ibid.; memorandum by Federer, 19 September 1940, ibid., 206990–91; Hencke to Foreign Ministry, 5 October 1940, *ADAP*, D, XI, 154.

87. *ADAP*, D, XI, 154 and n. 3; idem., 175 and n. 3.

88. Ibid.; Hemmen to Foreign Ministry, Del. Nr. 124, 20 September 1940, FF, II, 206997. On the naval officer, see *KTB/Skl.*, XIII, 17, 19 September 1940; *KTB/OKW*, I, 20 September 1940. The account in Neugebauer, *Militär-kontrolle*, 76, mentions Keitel's original refusal of the navy's request but fails to mention his later agreement.

89. The Spanish negotiations are covered in chapter 5 below.

90. The 13-page report by Schellert of 26 September 1940 on his commission's

trip to Africa is located in AA, Büro des Reichsaussenministers, Afrika, I, 66175–87.

91. *DFCAA*, I, 418, 434–35. See especially the personal letter from army captain Wilhelm Bürklin of 1 October 1940, BA/MA, RH 2/1519.

92. See chapter 5 below.

Chapter 4. The Riddle of the Rock

1. Donald S. Detwiler, *Hitler, Franco, und Gibraltar,* 27–36; Charles B. Burdick, *Germany's Military Strategy and Spain in World War II,* 16–130. The Mediterranean Strategy as a whole is covered in Gerhard Schreiber, "The Mediterranean in Hitler's Strategy in 1940: 'Programme' and Military Planning," in Wilhelm Deist, ed., *The German Military in the Age of Total War.*

2. Jochmann, ed., *Monologe,* 1 August 1942, 323.

3. Weinberg, ed., *Hitlers zweites Buch,* 217.

4. See especially Christian Leitz, *Economic Relations,* chapters 1 and 2.

5. Weinberg, *Foreign Policy,* I, 284–99; idem., II, 144, 158.

6. Detwiler, *Gibraltar,* Burdick, *Germany's Military Strategy.*

7. Stanley G. Payne, *Franco Regime,* 266 ff.; Paul Preston, *Franco,* 355 ff.; Denis Smyth, *Diplomacy and the Strategy of Survival;* Xavier Tusell and Genoveva García Queipo de Llano, *Franco y Mussolini.*

8. Preston, *Franco,* 1–373.

9. Ramón Serrano Suñer, *Entre el silencio y la propaganda, la historia como fue: Memorias,* 54–56. Payne, *Franco Regime,* 92.

10. Payne, *Franco Regime,* 171–79.

11. Quoted in Smyth, *Survival,* 16.

12. David S. Woolman, *Rebels in the Rif;* Preston, *Franco,* 35–68.

13. Quoted in Woolman, *Rebels,* 132.

14. Smyth, *Survival,* 45.

15. Serrano Suñer, *Memorias,* 285.

16. See Christopher Andrew, *Théophile Delcassé and the Making of the Entente Cordiale,* 191–93, 216–27; William A. Hoisington, *The Casablanca Connection,* 136–37. The official argument for Spanish claims in Morocco is in the contemporary Spanish account, José María de Areilza and Fernando María Castiella, *Reivindicaciones de España,* 267–501. The account is polemical but complete and with good maps. For Spain's problems in its zone, see Victor Morales Lezcano, *España y el norte de Africa,* 163–217.

17. Charles R. Halstead and Carolyn J. Halstead, "Aborted Imperialism: Spain's Occupation of Tangier 1940–1945," 53–55; Hoisington, *Casablanca,* 150.

18. See Hoisington, *Casablanca,* 153; Woolman, *Rebels,* 165–66, 208–209. De Areilza and Castiella, *Reivindicaciones,* 420–32, contains the documentation on the 1925 border agreement.

19. Charles R. Halstead, "A 'Somewhat Machiavellian' Face: Colonel Juan Beigbeder as High Commissioner in Spanish Morocco, 1937–1939," 46–66; idem., "Un africain méconnu: le colonel Juan Beigbeder," 31–60.

20. Reported by the German consul in Tetuán, Herbert Georg Richter, in his report to the Foreign Ministry, Nr. 707/Pol. III, 10 May 1940, AA, Deutsche Botschaft Madrid (hereafter cited as DB Madrid), Marokko-Allgemein, Bd. 5.

21. On the invasion scare, see Hoisington, *Casablanca*, 149. On the French request of 1939, which was one of the French government's prime criteria for normalization of relations between France and Spain, see Foreign Ministry (Berlin), to DB Madrid, Pol. III 359g, 18 February 1939, AA, DB Madrid, Frankreich und Beziehungen zu Spanien; Estado Español, SIPM, Nr. 10/8-390, 6 May 1939, AMAE, L 1065, Ex 5.

22. Richter to Stohrer, unnumbered, 24 June 1940, AA, DB Madrid, Marokko-Allgemein, Bd. 5; Richter to Foreign Ministry, Nr. 469/40, 15 April 1940, idem; Richter to Foreign Ministry, Nr. 915/Sekr., 26 June 1939, idem.

23. Richter to Foreign Ministry Nr. 1192/39, 11 August 1939, enclosed in Foreign Ministry to DB Paris, Pol. III 3318, 18 August 1939, AA, DB Paris, Spanien: Politische Akten, bndl. 1363.

24. Richter to Foreign Ministry, Nr. 1231/Pol III, 18 August 1939, enclosed in Foreign Ministry to DB Paris, Pol. III, 3380, idem; Richter to Foreign Ministry, Nr. 626/41, 10 May 1941, AA, DB Madrid, Marokko-Allgemein, Bd. 5. For the book by Tomás García Figueras, see *Marruecos: La Acción de España en el Norte de Africa.*

25. Morales Lezcano, *Historia de la no-beligerancia española durante la segunda guerra mundial,* 25–26.

26. Serrano Suñer, *Memorias,* 288.

27. Stohrer to Foreign Ministry, Nr. 1496/20, 20 May 1940, AA, DB Madrid, Entwicklung der allgemeinen Lage, Bd. 1.

28. Preston, *Franco,* 355.

29. Stohrer to Foreign Ministry, 3 June 1940, *ADAP,* D, IX, 380.

30. Quoted in Samuel Hoare (Viscount Templewood), *Ambassador on Special Mission,* 48. See also Smyth, *Survival,* 41–42. On Spanish press comments, see *ADAP,* D, IX, 380; Stohrer to Foreign Ministry, 7 June 1940, Nr. 1769, AA, StS, Marokko, I.

31. Morales Lezcano, "Las causas de la no beligerancia española, reconsideradas," 609–31.

32. On Tangier's administration, see Halstead and Halstead, "Aborted Imperialism," 54–55; Hoisington, *Casablanca,* 150–51. For Spanish irritation, see the newspaper articles by Beigbeder's press chief, Enrique Arquéz, "¿Ha sido Tánger neutral alguna vez?" *España,* 8 June 1939, and the prize-winning "Cómo perdimos Tánger," idem. *España,* a Tangier newspaper under the Arquéz's editorship, was generally recognized as Beigbeder's voice. Richter still called it "Das Blatt Beigbeders" even after Beigeder had become foreign minister. Beigbeder commented to Richter in June 1939 that he aimed to keep polemic over Tangier at a steady flow so that the question would remain open. See Richter to Foreign Ministry, Nr. 839/Pol. III, 12 June 1939, AA, DB Madrid, Tanger Zone, Bd. 3; Richter to Foreign Ministry, Nr. 30/Pol. VII,

10 January 1940, idem. Arquéz later wrote a polemic on Morocco entitled *El momento de España en Marruecos.*

33. Beigbeder to Lequerica, no. 330, 8 June 1940, AMAE, L 1217, Ex 69. Beigbeder argued to the French that sole Spanish occupation would be a better guarantee of Tangier's neutrality.

34. Hoisington, *Casablanca,* 151–52.

35. The principles of the agreement are in Beigbeder's note to the Portuguese embassy in Madrid, no. 56, 14 June 1940, AMAE, L 1217, Ex 69, and in his note of the same day to the French ambassador. See Beigbeder to Robert de la Baume, no. 324, 14 June 1940, idem.

36. Beigbeder to Asensio, no. 20 cif., 13 June 1940, ibid.

37. Manuel Amieva (Spanish consul in Tangier) to Beigbeder, no. 69, 14 June 1940, ibid.

38. Stohrer to Foreign Ministry, Nr. 1895/14, 14 June 1940, AA, DB Madrid, Tanger Zone, Bd. 3; Stohrer to Foreign Ministry, Nr. 2621/40, 17 June 1940, idem.

39. Of all Beigbeder's announcements of the occupation to the foreign missions in Madrid, the only announcements that made no mention of a previous agreement with the French government were those to the embassies of Italy and Germany. See AMAE, L 1217, Ex 69. On the convincing of Berlin that no contact had been made with the French, see Woermann to DB Madrid, Nr. 846/15, 16 June 1940, AA, DB Madrid, Tanger Zone, Bd. 3; Stohrer to Foreign Ministry, Nr. 1925/16, 16 June 1940, idem; *ADAP,* D, IX, 456.

40. For Beigbeder's statements to various European capitals, see AMAE, L 1217, Ex 69. Beigbeder explained to Stohrer that public mention of the sultan and the ephemeral nature of the occupation were purely to avoid hostile French-British reaction. See Stohrer to Foreign Ministry, Nr. 2621/40, 17 June 1940, AA, DB Madrid, Tanger Zone, Bd. 3. On the occupation regime, see Hoisington, *Casablanca,* 150–52; Halstead and Halstead, "Aborted Imperialism," 55–57; Smyth, *Survival,* 46, 133–72; Payne, *Franco Regime,* 268, and chapter 7 below.

41. The lack of clarity is due in part to the Servicio Historico Militar, which claimed during the research for this book that no records from the Army of Africa exist from the period of the Second World War.

42. Stohrer to Foreign Ministry, Nr. 1906, 15 June 1940, AA, StS, Marokko, I. Payne, *Franco Regime,* 270, states that there had been military plans for an advance in Northwest Africa since June 1940.

43. Richter to Foreign Ministry, Nr. 8, 15 June 1940, AA, StS, Marokko, I.

44. For the protocol, see *ADAP,* D, IX, 465. For Franco's letter to Hitler, dated 3 June, see idem., 378. Detwiler, *Gibraltar,* 23, argues that Franco's letter was more forthcoming to the Germans than I think might have been the case.

45. Asensio had told Richter on 15 June that the imminent Spanish advance into Morocco hinged on the outcome of the negotiations in Berlin with Franco's representative, which no doubt meant the talk between Hitler and Vigón. See Richter to Foreign Ministry, Nr. 8, 15 June 1940, AA, StS, Marokko, I.

46. Detwiler, *Gibraltar,* 24–25, states that the Germans were more forthcoming on Morocco's future than this interpretation argues.

47. Richter to Foreign Ministry, Nr. 725/40, 20 June 1940, enclosed in Foreign Ministry to DB Rom, Pol. III 1734, 4 July 1940, AA, DB Rom, Lage an der französisch-spanischen Zonengrenze. For Italian perspectives, see *DDI,* 9, V, 42.

48. *ADAP,* D, IX, 459 and n. 1.

49. Lequerica to Beigbeder, no. 824, 18 June 1940, AMAE, L 2295, Ex 4. Lequerica to Beigbeder, unnumbered, 16 June 1940, idem., L 1217, Ex 69.

50. Richter to Foreign Ministry, Nr. 725/40, 20 June 1940, enclosed in Foreign Ministry to DB Rom, Pol. III 1734g, 4 July 1940, AA, DB Rom, Lage an der französisch-spanischen Zonengrenze; Richter to Foreign Ministry, Nr. 732/40, 25 June 1940, enclosed in Foreign Ministry to DB Rom, Pol. III 1765g, 4 July 1940, idem.; Richter to Stohrer, unnumbered, 24 June 1940, AA, DB Madrid, Marokko-Allgemein. On Noguès, see Hoisington, *Casablanca,* 152, n. 53.

51. Stohrer to Foreign Ministry, 23 June 1940, *ADAP,* D, X, 3; see also Zoppi to Ciano, 22 June 1940, *DDI,* 9, V, 86.

52. For the above, see Hoisington, *Casablanca,* 150–55; François Charles-Roux, *Cinq mois tragiques aux affaires étrangères (21 Mai 1er Novembre 1940),* 224–48.

53. Stohrer to Foreign Ministry, Nr. 1971, 19 June 1940, AA, StS, Marokko, I. For the same note from the Spanish ambassador to Berlin, see *ADAP,* D, IX, 488. The Spaniards gave an analogous message in Rome omitting the requests for weapons and foodstuffs. See *DDI,* 9, V, 54. Detwiler, *Gibraltar,* 25, sees the offer as a logical follow-up to Vigón's discussion with Hitler on 16 June. As argued above, there may be intervening factors to consider.

54. Smyth, *Survival,* 32–33, 42–44, 47–49; Burdick, *Germany's Military Strategy,* 25.

55. For the reduction of the army, see Weinberg, *Germany and the Soviet Union, 1939–1941,* 104; Hillgruber, *Strategie,* 161–62. For the rest, see *ADAP,* D, X, 73; idem., XI, 41; chapters 1–2 above.

56. For the document, see International Military Tribunal, *Trial of the Major War Criminals before the International Military Tribunal, Nuremberg, 14 October 1945–1 October 1946* (hereafter cited as *IMT* with volume, document, and page numbers), XXVIII, 1776-PS, 301–303.

57. Klee, *Seelöwe,* 60–63.

58. Stohrer to Foreign Ministry, Nr. 2037, 22 June 1940, AA, StS, Marokko, I. Beigbeder's comment of 23 June that the Spanish *démarche* had been well received in Berlin and that he was planning to send Vigón to discuss the issues further was no doubt an attempt to force the issue, since no German answer had come as yet. See Stohrer to Foreign Ministry, 23 June 1940, *ADAP,* D, X, 3.

59. *ADAP,* D, X, 16. Weizsäcker's mention of North Africa only was no doubt due to the fact that Madrid's demand for an extension of Spanish Guinea

could have come only to the detriment of the former German colony of Cameroon according to its pre-1919 border. The Spaniards were fully aware of the fact but held to their claim in principle, citing the treaty of El Pardo with Portugal of 1788. In the Spanish government's authorized statement on the issue (in 1941) in Areilza and Castiella, *Reivindicaciones de España,* 264–66, the authors conceded that Madrid's aims in the region could defer to those of Berlin. Walter Zechlin, the African affairs expert in the German embassy in Madrid, here commented sardonically that "Spain is magnanimous enough to leave [Cameroon] to us." See Stohrer to Foreign Ministry, Nr. 2320/41, 15 May 1941, AA, DB Madrid, Kolonien.

60. Ginés Vidal (Spanish chargé d'affaires in Berlin) to Beigbeder, no. 288, 29 July 1940, AMAE, L 1083, Ex 10.

61. The Spaniards had paid special attention to the disarmament clauses at the time of the Italian-French armistice negotiations. See the undated memorandum containing Pétain's comments to Lequerica on this issue in AMAE, L 2295, Ex 4. Beigbeder's many complaints to the Germans and Italians in July and August regarding the pace of French disarmament in Morocco are in AA, StS, Marokko, I; idem., FF, I; *DDI,* 9, V, 323, 394, 539, 566, 577, 591. See also Vidal to Beigbeder, 31 August 1940, AMAE, L 1083 Ex 10.

62. See especially Stohrer to Foreign Ministry, Nr. 2089, 25 June 1940, AA, StS, Marokko, I; Erich Heberlein (German councillor of embassy in Madrid) to Foreign Ministry, Nr. 2746, 11 August 1940, idem.; *ADAP,* D, X, 88.

63. Vidal to Beigbeder, 31 August 1940, AMAE, L 1083, Ex 10.

64. *ADAP,* D, X, 73.

65. Ibid., 129. In fact, the German High Command had yet to consider Gibraltar in a serious way. See Burdick, *Germany's Military Strategy,* 22–23, n. 24.

66. Wagner, ed., *Lagevorträge,* 108–20. They demonstrated their confidence by their aversion toward French naval support in the Atlantic and their discussion over postwar battle fleet construction.

67. Jacobsen, ed., *Halder Diary,* II, 13 July 1940.

68. Detwiler, *Gibraltar,* 31; Burdick, *Germany's Military Strategy,* 30–31.

69. Hubatsch, ed., *Weisungen,* 61–65.

70. Detwiler, *Gibraltar,* 31–32; Burdick, *Germany's Military Strategy,* 22–27.

71. *KTB/Skl.,* XI, 21 July 1940; Wagner, ed., *Lagevorträge,* 120–21; Jacobsen, ed., *Halder Diary,* II, 22 July 1940.

72. For the meeting of 31 July 1940, see Wagner, ed., *Lagevorträge,* 126–29; Jacobsen, ed., *Halder Diary,* II, 31 July 1940; *KTB/OKW,* I, 1 August 1940.

73. Hubatsch, ed., *Weisungen,* 65–66.

74. *ADAP,* D, X, 274 and n. 1.

75. Memorandum by Stohrer, 8 August 1940, ibid., 313.

76. See the report of 10 August 1940 in ibid., 326.

77. The plan is outlined in *KTB/OKW,* I, 9 August 1940. For the definitive treatment of the technical planning, see Burdick, *Germany's Military Strategy,* 36 ff.

78. *KTB/OKW,* I, 20, 24 August 1940; Burdick, *Germany's Military Strategy,*

38–9; Militärgeschichtliches Forschungsamt, gen. eds., *Das deutsche Reich und der zweite Weltkrieg* (hereafter cited as *DRuZW*), vol. III, 187–88.

79. See p. 37, n. 28 above.

80. *ADAP*, D, X, 313, 329, 355; Jacobsen, ed., *Halder Diary*, II, 9 August 1940. See also Leitz, *Economic Relations*, 132–35

81. Jacobsen, ed., *Halder Diary*, II, 21 July 1940, 9, 27 August 1940.

82. Memorandum by Woermann, 27 August 1940, *ADAP*, D, X, 404 and n. 2.

83. Ibid., 407.

84. For Hitler's order, see *KTB/OKW*, I, 2 September 1940. For German agreement, see memo of 16 September 1940, *ADAP*, D, XI, 62. The German numbers on grain and gasoline are lacking in zeroes, so that they are equal to 1/100 of Spain's requests. This is a misprint, since the other requests are accepted in full, and there is no reference elsewhere to the German problems with grain and gasoline deliveries after the Hitler decision of 2 September.

85. For the text, see *ADAP*, D, X, 405.

86. See the memoranda by Ambassador Hans Heinrich Diekhoff of 21 and 29 July 1940 in ibid., 199, 252, and also those from Chargé d'Affaires Hans Thomsen and Military and Air Attaché General Friedrich von Bötticher from July and August in idem., 108, 195, 199, 287, 288. See also *KTB/Skl.*, XI, 24 July 1940. For the German embassy in general, see Compton, *Swastika*, 62, 110–12, 122–23 and Weinberg, *World in the Balance*, 60–63.

87. Jacobsen, ed., *Halder Diary*, II, 14 September 1940. Mussolini concurred that American intervention was a "reality of tomorrow." *ADAP*, D, X, 388.

88. *ADAP*, D, X, 342.

89. Compton, *Swastika*, 94; *KTB/Skl.*, XII, 21 August 1940.

90. For comments from the German embassy in Washington, see *ADAP*, D, X, 322, 342, 362; for those of the Naval Command, see *KTB/Skl.*, XII, 3, 5, 12, 14, 16, 17, 19, 22, 23, 25, 29, and 30 August 1940. Hitler's order is in the entry of the twenty-third.

91. *ADAP*, D, XI, 10.

92. *KTB/Skl.*, XII, 12 August 1940. Salewski, *Seekriegsleitung*, I, 277.

93. *KTB/Skl.*, XII, 30 August 1940.

94. Ibid., XIII, 3 September 1940. Raeder passed these views to Hitler in their conference of 6 September 1940, described below.

95. *KTB/Skl.*, XIII, 10 September 1940. See also Jacobsen, ed., *Halder Diary*, II, 23 August 1940.

96. See pp. 5–6 above; Jacobsen, ed., *Halder Diary*, II, 13 July 1940; See also Rudolf Hess's comments of 15 September 1940 in *ADAP*, D, XI, 61.

97. *ADAP*, D, X, 6 and n. 3.

98. Theo Sommer, *Deutschland und Japan zwischen den Mächten, 1935–1940*, 377–400; Jacobsen, ed., *Halder Diary*, II, 23 August 1940.

99. *ADAP*, D, XI, 44, n. 3.

100. Gerhard Krebs, *Japans Deutschlandpolitik, 1935–1941*, 438–87.

101. *KTB/OKW*, I, 5 September 1940.

102. For a summary of the navy's thoughts at this time, see Salewski, *Seekriegsleitung*, I, 274–84. Salewski's interpretations regarding the navy's benign views of the United States are not followed here. See also the manuscript by Kurt Assmann, the chief of the German navy's historical department, "Die Seekriegsleitung und die Mittelmeerkriegführung," (undated) 1–14, BA/MA, RM 8/1257.

103. The memorandum of 29 August 1940 by Operations Chief Kurt Fricke and First Admiralty Staff Officer Gerhard Wagner entitled "Kriegführung gegen England bei Ausfall der Unternehmung 'Seelöwe'" and its presentation to Hitler by Raeder on 6 September 1940 are printed in Wagner, ed., *Lagevorträge*, 134–41. On the authorship, see *KTB/Skl.*, XIII, 5 September 1940. See Schreiber, *Revisionismus*, 271–87, on German-Italian cooperation in the Mediterranean.

104. The Naval Command had already reasoned more than a week before that a capture of Gibraltar would lead the British to find a replacement base in the Canaries and that the British probably already had plans for such a landing. On 21 August, a German tanker in the Canaries was ordered to Bordeaux due to the possibility of a British strike, and on the twenty-ninth the navy also began to consider the fate of the seven freighters and six tankers in the Canaries and Azores. See *KTB/Skl.*, XII, 21, 28, 29 August 1940. On British plans to take the Atlantic Islands, see Smyth, *Survival*, 66–70, 142–47, 217–15, 231–33; Monika Siedentopf, *Die britische Pläne zur Besetzung der spanischen und portugiesischen Atlantikinseln während des zweiten Weltkrieges*.

Chapter 5. September Shifts

1. Stohrer to Foreign Ministry, 2 July 1940, *ADAP*, D, X, 87.
2. Ibid., XI, 250, n. 2.
3. Stohrer to Foreign Ministry, 20 August 1940, ibid., 369; Stohrer to Foreign Ministry, 21 August 1940, ibid., 373.
4. Stohrer to Foreign Ministry, 20 August 1940, ibid., 369. Franco to Mussolini, 15 August 1940, ibid., 346. Mussolini's answer was positive on the condition that Spain enter the war. Franco received Mussolini's reply with a true show of enthusiasm. See Mussolini to Franco, 25 August 1940, ibid., 392; Tusell and Queipo de Llano, *Franco y Mussolini*, 94–97.
5. Stohrer to Foreign Ministry, 6 September 1940, *ADAP*, D, XI, 30; Detwiler, *Gibraltar*, 37.
6. See p. 59 above.
7. Lequerica to Beigbeder, no. 1003, 28 August 1940, AMAE, L 2295, Ex 5; Charles-Roux, *Cinq mois*, 237–39; *Baudouin Diary*, 29, 31 August 1940.
8. *Baudouin Diary*, 12 September 1940. Asensio's general secretary, García Figueras, *was* part of the economic delegation en route to Berlin.
9. Ibid., 14 September 1940.

10. Espinosa to Beigbeder, no. 292, 29 September–3 October 1940, AMAE, L 1188, Ex 3. On Espinosa's appointment, see Payne, *Franco Regime,* 270.

11. *ADAP,* D, XI, 63.

12. Lequerica to Beigbeder, unnumbered personal telegram, 18 July 1940, AMAE, L 1190, Ex 97; Lequerica to Beigbeder, nos. 526–29, 20 July 1940, idem. Beigbeder had hinted to Stohrer in late July that a demand for German installations in Morocco could push the colonies into the arms of de Gaulle. See *ADAP,* D, X, 231.

13. It is likely now that Hitler, as opposed to 11 July, was interested in the main island of Las Palmas due to its more developed harbor and airfield facilities. With the increasing American threat, a less developed island would not have been adequate. For the High Command and navy appraisal, see *KTB/OKW,* I, 17 September 1940; *KTB/Skl.,* XIII, 17 September 1940.

14. For the protocol, see *ADAP,* D, XI, 66. See also Espinosa to Beigbeder, no. 292, AMAE, L 1188, Ex 3.

15. *ADAP,* D, XI, 67.

16. Ibid.; Espinosa to Beigbeder, no. 292, AMAE, L 1188, Ex 3; for the official itinerary, see idem.

17. Hitler to Mussolini, 17 September 1940, *ADAP,* D, XI, 68.

18. Hitler to Franco, 18 September 1940, ibid., 70.

19. On plans for a refurbished Spanish air force in particular, see Leitz, *Economic Relations,* 129–30.

20. Franco to Serrano Suñer, 21 September 1940, Serrano Suñer, *Memorias,* 331–40. On Morocco, the furthest Franco would go was a 99-year lease on Mogador.

21. Franco to Hitler, 22 September 1940, *ADAP,* D, XI, 88.

22. Beginning with Hoare, *Mission,* 92–93, and more recently Benny Pollack, *The Paradox of Spanish Foreign Policy,* 3–13. Taking a more nuanced view is Smyth, *Survival,* 85–88.

23. Franco to Serrano Suñer, 23 September 1940, Serrano Suñer, *Memorias,* 341–42. See also Hoare, *Mission,* 48 ff.; Smyth, *Survival,* 85.

24. Ribbentrop met with Mussolini and Ciano on 19, 20, and 22 September 1940. See *ADAP,* D, XI, 73, 79, 87; Muggeridge, ed., *Ciano Papers,* 389–93; Muggeridge, ed., *Ciano Diary,* 19–22 September 1940.

25. *ADAP,* D, XI, 73.

26. Ibid., D, XI, 79.

27. *Baudouin Diary,* 23 July 1940, 11, 18, and 28 August 1940, 2, 5, 12, 14, 16, and 18 September 1940.

28. Hencke to Foreign Ministry, Nr. 158, 4 September 1940, AA, StS, FF, II, 206879–80.

29. Marder, *Menace,* 6–48.

30. See above p. 39ff.

31. Marder, *Menace,* 92–98.

32. Memorandum by Federer, 21 September 1940, AA, StS, FF, II, 207003–7005.

33. Memorandum by Kramarz, Pol. IM, 13070g, AA, UStS, AEF.

34. *KTB/Skl.*, XIII, 20 September 1940. The Naval Command here even postulated that the French had staged *Gloire*'s engine problems.

35. *DFCAA*, I, 326–34; Welck to Foreign Ministry, Nr. 174, 21 September 1940, AA, StS, FF, II, 207009–10.

36. See his marginalia in AA, StS, FF, II, 207009–10.

37. *KTB/Skl.*, XIII, of 21–22 September 1940. The fate of the other two cruisers had become known by the twenty-second, and the navy hoped that the Schellert commission, which included a navy officer, would get to the bottom of the situation when it arrived in Dakar.

38. On 21 September, the Italian Armistice Commission on Badoglio's order also rejected the request to send the *Strasbourg* group. They permitted deployment of the eighteen allowed air combat groups in Africa for an emergency. See "Von Senger Reports," 26 September 1940, enclosure 1.

39. Marder, *Menace*, 100–59.

40. *Baudouin Diary*, 23 September 1940.

41. Marder, *Menace*, 175. The first attack on 24 September involved 40 bombers and dropped 150 bombs. The second on the twenty-fifth involved 100 aircraft, which dropped about 300 bombs. Damages were slight.

42. *Baudouin Diary*, 23 September 1940.

43. *DFCAA*, I, 384–87. Duplat made the same requests at Turin.

44. *ADAP*, D, XI, 92.

45. For this suspicion, see ibid., 68.

46. *KTB/OKW*, I, 24, 25 September 1940.

47. Memorandum by Rademacher, 24 September 1940, AA, UStS, AEF; Mackensen to Foreign Ministry, Nr. 335, 23 September 1940, idem. For further exchanges later that evening, see idem., passim; Muggeridge, ed., *Ciano Diary*, 24 September 1940.

48. Note by Foreign Ministry night service appended to Mackensen to Foreign Ministry, Nr. 335, 23 September 1940, AA, UStS, AEF. For the original draft reply, see von Senger to German Armistice Commission, Pr. Nr. 216/40, 26 September 1940, enclosure 2, BA/MA, RW 34/9.

49. Memorandum by Weizsäcker, StS Nr. 727, 24 September 1940, AA, StS, FF, II, 207022–23.

50. *ADAP*, D, XI, 96; Weizsäcker to Mackensen, Nr. 1340, 24 September 1940, AA, StS, FF, II, 20734–36; Mackensen to Foreign Ministry, Nr. 359, 25 September 1940, idem.; memorandum by Grote, Pol. IM, 13 236g, 24 September 1940, AA, UStS, AEF; memorandum by Kramarz, Pol. IM, 13215g, 24 September 1940, idem. On the Italian side, see von Senger to German Armistice Commission, Pr. Nr. 216/40, 26 September 1940, enclosed in Chefgruppe Ia, Nr. 6/40 gKdos. Chefs., 20 September 1940, BA/MA, RW 34/9; "Von Senger Reports," 26 September 1940 and enclosure 1.

51. *DFCAA*, I, 388–89; *KTB/OKW*, I, 25 September 1940; memorandum by Grote, Pol. IM, 13288g, AA, StS, FF, II, 207044–45. For the corresponding Italian note, see von Senger to German Armistice Commission, Pr. Nr. 216/40, 26 September 1940, enclosure 3, BA/MA, RW 34/9.

52. *Baudouin Diary,* 24 September 1940.

53. *DFCAA,* I, 389–92; *ADAP,* D, XI, 108; memorandum by Grote, Pol. IM, 13 3548, 26 September 1940, AA, StS, FF, II, 207046–48.

54. *ADAP,* D, XI, 102; *Baudouin Diary,* 24 September 1940.

55. *ADAP,* D, XI, 112. Huntziger stated that at this time the French had 180,000 men under arms in North Africa and were scaling the army down. The date of Badoglio's decision to allow the French 100,000 troops is not clear.

56. *KTB/Skl.,* XIII, 24 September 1940.

57. *KTB/OKW,* I, 24, 25 September 1940.

58. For the mechanics of this arrangement, see the memoranda in AA, StS, FF, II, 207046–55; von Senger to German Armistice Commission, Pr. Nr. 216/40, 26 September 1940, enclosed in Chefgruppe Ia, Nr. 6/40 gKdos. Chefs., 30 September 1940, BA/MA, RW 34/9.

59. On German reactions, see *ADAP,* D, XI, 98 and n. 1; idem., 102 and n. 2; *DFCAA,* I, 412–14.

60. *Baudouin Diary,* 27 September 1940.

61. See pp. 49–51 above. Charles-Roux, *Cinq Mois,* 333, mistakenly combines the two commissions and has them arriving as one in Casablanca on 25 September. Noguès reported Erdmann's arrival on the twenty-seventh. See *DFCAA,* I, 434–35.

62. *DFCAA,* I, 434–35; Captain Wilhelm Bürklin to OKH/GenStdH/Abt. Fremde Heere West, 1 October 1940, BA/MA, RH 2/1519.

63. Charles-Roux, *Cinq Mois,* 334; *DFCAA,* I, 432–33.

64. Charles-Roux, *Cinq Mois,* 334–7; *DFCAA,* I, 435; memorandum by Grote, 30 September 1940, AA, StS, FF, II, 207061–63.

65. The French delegation in Wiesbaden asked for postponement on 22 and 26 September. See *DFCAA,* I, 432–33. Duplat asked the Italians in Turin to postpone the project on the twenty-second or twenty-third. "Von Senger Reports," 26 September 1940, enclosure 1. The Germans answered on the twenty-sixth. See *DFCAA,* I, 435.

66. On Stülpnagel's work, see pp. 49–50 above.

67. Memorandum by Grote, 30 September 1940, AA, StS, FF, II, 207061–63.

68. *DDI,* 9, V, 323, 394, 539, 566, 577, 591; Stohrer to Foreign Ministry, Nr. 3041, 7 September 1940, AA, UStS, AEF. Beigbeder also pressed the Spanish ambassador to London for information on de Gaulle's whereabouts and passed any solid information from him to Vichy. See Heberlein to Foreign Ministry, Nr. 3101, 12 September 1940, idem.; *Baudouin Diary,* 8 September 1940.

69. Hoare to Beigbeder, 24 September 1940, enclosure 1 in Hoare to Jordana 9 November 1942, AMAE, L 5162, Ex 1.

70. Hans Lazar to Foreign Ministry, Nr. 3251, 25 September 1940, AA, UStS, AEF. Beigbeder also had repeated his warning to Hoare that revolt in French Morocco could provoke Spain's intervention. See *DDI,* 9, V, 637.

71. Franco to Serrano Suñer, 24 September 1940, Serrano Suñer, *Memorias,* 342–48.

72. Protocol in *ADAP,* D, XI, 97.

73. Ibid., D, XI, 99.
74. Protocol in ibid., 117. See also ibid., 184.
75. Ibid., 104.
76. Ibid., 116.
77. *KTB/Skl.*, XIII, 25 September 1940.
78. Wagner, ed., *Lagevorträge,* 143–46. Raeder also raised the complaint of the Naval Command that Germany, unlike Italy and the United States, had no official representation at Dakar.
79. For text, see *ADAP,* D, XI, 118.
80. Protocol in ibid., D, XI, 124.
81. Ibid., 30, 125, and n. 4.
82. For the economic agreement drafts between the Spanish economic delegation and the German Foreign Ministry's economic policy department, see ibid., 125, 126. On the debt issue, see Leitz, *Economic Relations,* 132.
83. *KTB/Skl.*, XIII, 17 and 18 September 1940.
84. *KTB/OKW,* I, 25 September 1940.

Chapter 6. October Illusions

1. Hencke to Foreign Ministry, Nr. 43, 25 September 1940, AA, StS, FF, II, 207041; memorandum by Grote, 30 September 1940, idem., 207061; Schellert to Deutsche Waffenstillstandsdelegation für Wirtschaft, 26 September 1940, AA, Büro des Reichsaussenministers, Afrika; *KTB/Skl.,* XIV, 5 October 1940.
2. All nine battalions, leaving Casablanca between 28 September and 6 October 1940, were deployed in West Africa by 19 November 1940. Memorandum by Grote of 9 October 1940, AA, StS, FF, II, 207123–26; memorandum by Grote, idem., 207278–80; *KTB/Skl.,* XIII, 23, 30 September 1940; idem., XIV, 2 October 1940.
3. The aircraft moved between 23 September and 2 October 1940 consisted of two fighter groups, one bomber group, and four seaplane staffs. See memorandum by Grote, 2 October 1940, ibid., 207082–85. The French request for munitions for *Richelieu* was presented on 29 September and approved on 10 October. See memorandum by Grote, 1 October 1940, ibid., 207074–76; memorandum by Grote, 10 October 1940, ibid., 207127–29; *DFCAA,* I, 392–95; idem., II, 70, 117; *KTB/OKW,* I, 11 October 1940. The French also mined the waters surrounding Dakar. See *KTB/Skl.,* XIII, 28 September 1940.
4. DWStK, Der Chef des Stabes, Nr. 8/40 gKdos. Chefs., 4 October 1940, BA/MA, RW 34/9. See also *KTB/Skl.,* XIII, 30 September 1940.
5. *KTB/OKW,* I, 30 September 1940 and 1 October 1940. Warlimont had also requested information on transport possibilities from North to West Africa on 25 September. See idem., 25 September 1940; memorandum by Grote, 2 October 1940, AA, StS, FF, II, 207082–85.
6. *ADAP,* D, XI, 149.
7. *DFCAA,* I, 392–95; memorandum by Grote, 1 October 1940, AA, StS, FF, II, 207074–76; memorandum by Grote, 30 September 1940, idem., 207078–80.

8. The *Strasbourg* group was defined as the battleship *Strasbourg,* three first-class cruisers, two second-class cruisers, five torpedo-boat destroyers and three torpedo boats. Memorandum by Stein, 14 October 1940, AA, StS, FF, II, 207137–40; Senger to German Armistice Commission, GPR 1, 3 October 1940, BA/MA, RW 34/9; "Von Senger Reports," 18 October 1940; *DFCAA,* II, 113.

9. *KTB/Skl.,* XIII, 30 September 1940.

10. *KTB/OKW,* I, 1 October 1940.

11. Ibid.

12. Jacobsen, ed., *Halder Diary,* II, 3 October 1940.

13. Muggeridge, ed., *Ciano Diary,* 4 October 1940. For the protocol, see *ADAP,* D, XI, 149; Muggeridge, ed., *Ciano Papers,* 395–98.

14. The idea that the continental coalition was more an intended compromise of interests is contained in Hillgruber, *Strategie,* 317, which suggests that the prime motivation for the scheme lay in the maritime aims of closing the western Mediterranean and attacking the British supply lines from bases in North Africa, and hints that future war with the United States was secondary.

15. Hitler's statement on this issue says the following: "If a compromise between the French and the Spanish interests should not be possible, however, one should consider very carefully which of the then available possibilities to prefer. An attack on Gibraltar was technically quite feasible. Germany possessed certain specialized troops that had successfully accomplished similar tasks in the West, and they could doubtless also achieve the conquest of the Rock. At any rate the war was won for the Axis Powers unless they should do something very inept." Hitler also stated, in a disparaging tone, that without the possibility of setting up bases on the Northwest African coast, Spanish entry into the war "was of strategic significance only in connection with the conquest of Gibraltar." *ADAP,* D, XI, 149.

16. Hillgruber, *Strategie,* 679; *KTB/OKW,* I, 5 October 1940; Fröhlich, ed., *Goebbels Diary,* IV, 6 October 1940.

17. *ADAP,* D, XI, 158 and n. 1.

18. Memorandum by Stein, 14 October 1940, AA, StS, FF, II, 207137–40.

19. Memorandum by Grote, 19 October 1940, ibid., 207160–64; memorandum by Grote, 23 October 1940, ibid., 207172–73; memorandum by Grote, 31 October 1940, ibid., 207195–200. The French received authorization in Turin for ninety light armored vehicles, thirty-six antitank vehicles, four 15.5-centimeter batteries and two 10.5-centimeter batteries. It should also be remembered that the Italian concessions regarding the armament of the *Strasbourg* group in Toulon came following the Brenner meeting.

20. Memorandum by Grote, zu Pol. IM, 13 735g., 8 October 1940, ibid., 207114; memorandum by Ritter, 14 October 1940, ibid., 207144; memorandum by Stein, 13 October 1940, ibid., 207137–40; *KTB/OKW,* I, 15 October 1940.

21. Muggeridge, ed., *Ciano Diary,* 1 October 1940; idem., *Ciano Papers,* 393–94.

22. Ibid., *Ciano Diary,* 5 October 1940; Tusell and Queipo de Llano, *Franco y Mussolini,* 107–108.

23. *ADAP*, D, XI, 172.

24. German military intelligence had already learned a full week earlier that the Spaniards had bolstered their troop strength in the Canaries to a potential of 40,000 men. See OKH/GenStdH/Abt. Fremde Heere West/IV Lageberichte West, Nr. 419, 3 October 1940 in AA, Handakten, Hasso von Etzdorf (Foreign Ministry Representative with German Army High Command), 1940–41; *KTB/Skl.*, XIV, 4 October 1940. The Italians received the same intelligence about ten days after the Germans, and noted simultaneously that the normal peacetime strength of the Canary Islands was a single division. See memorandum by Stein, 14 October 1940, AA, StS, FF, II, 107137–40.

25. There are no available Spanish sources on the troops in Spanish Morocco due to the secrecy of the *Servicio Historico Militar*. German army intelligence picked up the movement in the first week of October, and Serrano announced the movement to Ribbentrop on 10 October. The seven infantry divisions did not include the 20,000 Califate troops also in Spanish Morocco under Spanish command. See OKH/GenStdH/Abt. Fremde Heere West/IV Lageberichte West, Nr. 419, 3 October 1940, AA, Handakten, Hasso von Etzdorf, 1940–41; memorandum by Stein, 14 October 1940, AA, StS, FF, II, 107137–40; For the most detailed German accounting of Spanish troop strength in Spanish Morocco, see OKH/GenStdH/Op. Abt. IIb, Vortragsnotiz, gKdos.: Sperrung der Meerenge von Gibraltar, 13 November 1940, BA/MA, RH 2/444.

26. *ADAP*, D, XI, 172; Tusell and Queipo de Llano, *Franco y Mussolini*, 108.

27. Lequerica to Beigbeder, no. 1137, 30 September 1940, AMAE, L 2295, Ex 5; Charles-Roux, *Cinq Mois*, 243–48. Pétain was aptly concerned that Hitler was using Franco to push into North Africa. The issue is covered in Ricardo de la Cierva, *Hendaya: Punto Final*, 123–24, but the author of this semi-official Spanish account cites no source material.

28. The importance of Piétri's appointment should not be underestimated, since the previous ambassador, Robert-Renom de la Baume, had been Baudouin's primary contact with the British government via the British ambassador in Madrid, Sir Samuel Hoare. In his memoirs, Hoare assumes that Piétri's replacement of de la Baume was due to Laval's Anglophobia. Hoare apparently made this assumption owing to the fact that Piétri did not actually arrive in Madrid until after Laval had replaced Baudouin as foreign minister on 28 October. See Hoare, *Mission*, 90. Yet Baudouin had made the appointment in early October, and Piétri's experience as the director-general of Finances in Morocco (1917–24) and as a delegate to the technical conference on Tangier (1920), and his scholarly work on Joseph Bonaparte's tenure in Spain can only lead one to believe that Baudouin made the appointment with consideration toward a possible future settlement with the Spaniards over Morocco. A lengthy evaluation of Piétri is in Lequerica to Beigbeder, no. 1774, 7 October 1940, AMAE, L 2295, Ex 5, which describes Piétri as having to understand the experience and intelligence. See also and François Piétri, *Mes anées en Espagne, 1940–1948;* Cierva, *Hendaya*, 124; Matthieu Séguéla, *Pétain-Franco: Les secrets d'une alliance*, 199ff.

29. There is no evidence to support de la Baume's assertion in Charles-Roux, *Cinq Mois,* 247, that Beigbeder's refusal was due to German pressure.

30. There is no evidence to support French and British rumors that Hitler demanded Beigbeder's removal. See *Baudouin Diary,* 16 October 1940; Smyth, *Survival,* 99–100. Beigbeder's fall will be covered in greater detail below.

31. Memorandum by Grote, Pol. IM, 14022g, 17 October 1940, AA, StS, FF, II, 207154; memorandum by Grote, 18 October 1940, idem., 207155–58; memorandum by Grote, Pol. IM, 14069g, 19 October 1940, idem., 207165–66.

32. *ADAP,* D, XI, 149; *KTB/OKW,* I, 26 September 1940, 5 October 1940; Jacobsen, ed., *Halder Diary,* II, 11 and 16 October 1940; Jäckel, *Frankreich,* 110–11.

33. The original plan was to meet Pétain on both occasions, reaching a firm agreement with the French chief of state on the second visit. The reason for the change in plans is unclear. See Jäckel, *Frankreich,* 110–11.

34. *ADAP,* D, XI, 207, 208.

35. This is also the interpretation offered in Jäckel, *Frankreich,* 113. Jäckel does not exclude the further possibility that the relevant clauses also referred to German use of the French fleet.

36. Ibid., 113–14.

37. *ADAP,* D, XI, 212. For analyses, see Jäckel, *Frankreich,* 116–17; Paxton, *Vichy France,* 74–75.

38. The reasons behind Beigbeder's removal have recently been the subject of discussion. It is the argument here that whatever the reasons for Beigbeder's removal, excessive Anglophilia, as is argued in Smyth, *Survival,* 99–101, may not have been one of them. The colonel's tendency to balance the belligerent sides against one another is described in chapter 4 above and in Tusell and Queipo de Llano, *Franco y Mussolini,* 108. It would seem that the reasons for Beigbeder's fall lay more in this characteristic, which still irritated the Axis, than in an outspoken preference for the British side. Moreover, although there were growing complaints from Berlin and Rome about the colonel's attitudes, there is no hard evidence that the Germans had demanded Beigbeder's removal. Cierva, *Hendaya,* 124, even includes a comment from Franco from 1955, which states that Beigbeder was in fact a "complete germanophile" but was involved with a woman said to be a British spy. Payne, *Franco Regime,* 271, adds to the explanation that Beigbeder's work was rather haphazard and that his reputation as a playboy caught up with him when his list of women was said to include an agent from the British secret service, known as "Miss Fox." It was also rumored at the time that Beigbeder had accepted a bribe from Samuel Hoare and that the Germans had become increasingly unwilling to work closely with him. Payne also points out that Franco would naturally want his closest collaborator in the Foreign Ministry at the crucial phase of negotiations with Berlin. Whatever the reason for the change at the Foreign Ministry, the appearance of a greater shift toward the Axis, given Beigbeder's equivocation and Serrano's position in the *Falange* and his previous visits to the Axis capitals, was of course a natural byproduct of the govern-

mental change in Madrid. The international reaction to the appointment of Serrano Suñer as foreign minister is covered in Tusell and Queipo de Llano, *Franco y Mussolini,* 109–10.

39. Lequerica to Serrano Suñer, Nos. 663–665, 22 October 1940, AMAE, L 1190, Ex 97.

40. Present at this famous and oft-described meeting were Hitler, Ribbentrop, Franco, Serrano, and two interpreters: a German (Herr Gross) and a Spaniard (Baron de las Torres). Hitler's usual interpreter and stenographer, Dr. Paul Schmidt did not know Spanish and was not present. There are thus problems with the sources of the Hitler-Franco meeting. The only primary sources of the meeting are the incomplete protocol by Gross in *ADAP,* D, XI, 220, and the protocol of the Ribbentrop-Serrano meeting of the same day in idem., 221, which alludes to the Hitler-Franco discussion. Also helpful is the account in Serrano Suñer, *Memorias,* 289–301, since Serrano was present at both meetings. The detail of Serrano's account of the day at Hendaye suggests strongly that he kept a record of some sort. His account should be read with some caution, although his tendency lies more toward the omission of certain aspects rather than in the insertion of falsehoods. The accounts presented in Paul Schmidt, *Statist auf diplomatischer Bühne, 1923–1945,* and in the memoirs by Ribbentrop's secretary, Erich Kordt, *Wahn und Wirklichkeit,* 265–69, are based on hearsay and sometimes imaginative memory. Neither man was present at the meeting. For the source problems in general, see David Wingeate Pike, "Franco and the Axis Stigma," 376–78.

Regarding the events at Hendaye as a whole, the best secondary account for the Spanish side are in Paul Preston, "Franco and Hitler: The Myth of Hendaye 1940," and Tusell and Queipo de Llano, *Franco y Mussolini,* 112–13. The account in Cierva, *Hendaya,* is of some interest but should be used cautiously, particularly with regard to Franco's motives. The best existing account for the German side is Detwiler, *Gibraltar,* 51–67, but his assumption that Franco was stalling the Germans is not followed here. Smyth, *Survival,* 102, n. 91, argues that Franco was no longer considering entrance into the war on the German side as he was in September. Regarding the myth that Franco sought to rattle Hitler by his late arrival at Hendaye, see Detwiler, *Gibraltar,* 56, n. 17; Pike, "Axis Stigma," 376–78; Serrano Suñer, *Memorias,* 289–90; Preston, *Franco,* 394–95. The times of day provided by Serrano for the various meetings at Hendaye are used here.

41. *ADAP,* D, XI, 220, my emphasis. Serrano Suñer, *Memorias,* 294, confirms that Hitler's preoccupations at Hendaye concerned Gibraltar, the Canary Islands, and Morocco.

42. Hitler did not state explicitly that Spanish demands alone would suffer, but he did say that France would lose Tunisia, Corsica, Nice, and Alsace-Lorraine. The Germans had also made it clear to Serrano in September that they would have an empire in central Africa. This left Spain's demands alone for diminishment. The account in Serrano Suñer, *Memorias,* 294, states that Hitler told Franco that if it were up to Berlin alone, Spain would receive all of

Morocco and Oran, but that Germany could not give what it did not have.

43. On the issue of Hitler's reluctance to go into specifics regarding territorial rewards for Spain, the comment by Hitler to Ribbentrop overheard by Paul Schmidt on the Hendaye train platform before the Hitler-Franco meeting is of some use. According to Schmidt's memory, Hitler instructed the foreign minister that "we cannot now give the Spaniards . . . written promises on the distribution of territory from the French colonial holdings. If they get something in writing on this delicate problem, the French sooner or later will learn something of it due to Latin talkativeness." See Schmidt, *Statist*, 500. Hitler made a similar comment to Mussolini during their Florence meeting of 28 October 1940, covered in detail below.

44. Franco's explanation to Hitler on what the Spaniards could do militarily to minimize the Gaullist threat in North Africa are not covered in the incomplete protocol of the meeting, and they receive little ink in the account in Serrano Suñer, *Memorias*. Yet Franco must have gone into considerable detail. Both Ribbentrop and Hitler would tell the Italians after the Hendaye meeting that the Spaniards grossly overestimated their capabilities in North Africa, and that it had been difficult to convince them that alone they could not handle the Gaullist threat. See *ADAP*, D, XI, 228, 246.

45. For Hitler's comments after the discussion, see also Pike, "Axis Stigma," 376–78; Payne, *Franco Regime*, 273. The German memoir literature cited in note 40 above says that Hitler lost his patience and threatened to leave on one or two occasions. Serrano Suñer, *Memorias*, 298–99, states that Hitler did not make such a threat, although the Führer was occasionly reduced to yawns during Franco's monologue.

46. Muggeridge, ed., *Ciano Papers*, 402. Hitler's statement that his meeting with Franco lasted nine hours is an exaggeration. He must have counted his formal meeting with Franco and the subsequent dinner. Serrano Suñer, *Memorias*, 299, says that the meeting lasted three hours.

47. *ADAP*, D, XI, 221.

48. The original draft of the Hendaye Protocol described in this conference no longer survives. The only existing draft is that received by Ciano from Ribbentrop on 4 November 1940, the fifth article of which Ciano altered with Ribbentrop's approval to guarantee Rome's colonial claims. This draft is printed in full in ibid., pp. 394–95. Even before this draft was presented to Ciano, Serrano had on 24 October agreed with angry reluctance on a version of Article 5 which differed from the original version presented by Ribbentrop on the 23rd but which the Germans still found acceptable. Thus, though the original wording of Article 5 seen by Franco and Serrano on 23 October is unknown, it probably could not have differed substantially from the newer version of the 24th. This version of the 24th reads as follows: "5. Apart from the reunion of Gibraltar with Spain, the Axis Powers state that in principle they are ready to provide, in the course of a new general settlement in Africa, such as is to be carried out in the peace treaties after the defeat of England, that Spain be ceded certain areas in Africa in precisely the same extent to

which France can be compensated by other cessions of territorial possessions in Africa of equal value. The claims to be made on France by Germany shall not be affected thereby." For the text, see ibid., 224 and n. 2. Ribbentrop's argument at Hendaye that Berlin was also making colonial sacrifices to assuage the French is belied by the final sentence. The supposition that the fundamentals of the original German draft of Article 5 remained intact in this new text is borne out by the Spanish bitterness with the Germans over the refusal to accept more sweeping changes in the article and the Spanish attempt to guard their colonial claims in a supplementary economic protocol, described below. It is the account in Serrano Suñer, *Memorias,* that claims Hitler had presented the draft of the protocol to Franco during their meeting. Although Serrano records Franco's indignation, he forgets to mention his own.

49. Serrano Suñer, *Memorias,* 294–300.

50. Jäckel, *Frankreich,* 118.

51. Quoted in Serrano Suñer, *Memorias,* 299.

52. For the draft of the Spanish supplementary protocol, see *ADAP,* D, XI, 222. Ribbentrop did not sign the protocol *specifically* due to the words, "in the French zone of Morocco, which is later to belong to Spain." See AA, StS, Spanien, II, 74442–43.

53. See note 48 above. For Serrano's acceptance of Article 5, see *ADAP,* D, XI, 224 and n. 2. The draft of the article was signed both by Stohrer and Espinosa de los Monteros.

54. It has been argued that the original German draft of the Hendaye Protocol stated that Germany would decide the moment of Spanish entry, whereas the draft amended at the behest of the Spaniards and accepted by the Germans left the timing of Spanish entry to Spain after further consultation with Germany and Italy. Such a change might well have occurred, but there is no contemporary documentary evidence for this assertion, since only the latter version of the relevant provision (Article 4) exists. See Serrano Suñer, *Memorias,* 299–301; Payne, *Franco Regime,* 273–74. The only proof on this issue is the statement, made in an indignant tone by Hitler and recorded by Ciano on 28 October in Florence, that the Spaniards were reserving for themselves the moment of their entry into the war while making heavy demands. The tone suggests that the original draft of the protocol might have left the timing of Spanish entry into the war to Berlin. See Muggeridge, ed., *Ciano Papers,* 401.

55. Stohrer to Ribbentrop, 26 October 1940, *ADAP,* D, XI, 235.

56. Baudouin resigned on 28 October 1940. For the struggle between him and Laval during the week of the Montoire discussions, see *Baudouin Diary,* 23–28 October 1940. For a more skeptical view of Baudouin's resignation, See Paxton, *Vichy France,* 76, n. 54.

57. The protocol is printed in *ADAP,* D, XI, 227. For the best summary, see Jäckel, *Frankreich,* 118–21. The account in Paxton, *Vichy France,* 74–75, deemphasizes the importance of the meeting.

58. See p. 30 above.

59. Four days after the meeting, Jodl told Stülpnagel, doubtless on information from Hitler, that the French at Montoire had been prepared to cooperate with Germany in a far-reaching way. The French did not go into specifics, said Jodl, and a French declaration of war was out of the question. But, he continued, Vichy would likely be prepared not only to defend the empire but *also* if need be to grant Germany bases in Africa. *KTB/OKW*, I, 28 October 1940.

60. Ribbentrop to Mackensen, 25 October 1940, *ADAP*, D, XI, 228.

61. Abetz to Ribbentrop, 26 October 1940, ibid., 234.

62. Ibid, 228; *Muggeridge*, ed., *Ciano Diary*, 24 October 1940.

63. Protocol printed in *ADAP*, D, XI, 246; Muggeridge, ed., *Ciano Papers*, 399–404.

64. Knox, *Mussolini*, 202–30. Hitler's remarks at Florence regarding the Greek campaign were minimal. He offered two divisions for the protection of Crete against a British landing.

65. *ADAP*, D, XI, 199 and n. 10. Mussolini had broached the idea of a separate peace with France at the Brenner as well. See also Muggeridge, ed., *Ciano Diary*, 20, 24 October 1940; Knox, *Mussolini*, 222–23.

66. *ADAP*, D, XI, 246; Muggeridge, ed., *Ciano Papers*, 399–404.

67. *ADAP*, D, XI, 246.

68. Warlimont told his staff the following day that Pétain had made an "outstanding" impression on the Führer. *KTB/OKW*, I, 29 October 1940. Goebbels noted after a discussion with Hitler on 31 October that Pétain had made a "deep impression" on the Führer as an honorable man with a clear mind for the realities of the French situation. Fröhlich, ed., *Goebbels Diary*, IV, 1 November 1940.

69. See also Fröhlich, ed., *Goebbels Diary*, IV, 1 November 1940.

70. The text of the directive is printed in Hubatsch, ed., *Weisungen*, 67–71. The drafting of the directive in the High Command began on 4 November 1940 and by 7 November Keitel approved it as a basis for practical staff work. Keitel's approval would have come earlier, but Warlimont's first draft of the directive was rejected due to its comments on the ultimate fate of Operation *Seelöwe*. See *KTB/OKW*, I, 4–9 November 1940. Hitler arrived back in Berlin on the evening of 30 October. See Hillgruber, *Strategie*, 680.

71. *ADAP*, D, XI, 326.

72. Ibid., 328.

Chapter 7. Winter Collapse I: Iberia

1. See Rich, *Hitler's War Aims*, II, 394 ff.; Salewski, ed., *Seekriegsleitung*, I, 288.

2. Herwig, *Frustration*, 210–15, correctly assesses the seriousness with which Berlin pursued the Atlantic island project in general but paints the German navy, not Hitler, as the prime mover in this scheme. The best military-naval

account of the issue is in DRuZW, III, 190–211, which views the Atlantic island issue primarily within the context of a German Mediterranean strategy.

3. *KTB/OKW*, I, 5 September 1940; DRuZW, III, 192, n. 162.

4. Hitler made this argument to Serrano on 25 September 1940. See *ADAP*, D, XI, 117.

5. Halstead, "Consistent and Total Peril from Every Side: Portugal and its 1940 Protocol with Spain," 15. For text, see Great Britain, Foreign and Commonwealth Office, *British Foreign and State Papers, 1939,* vol. 143, 673–75.

6. For Serrano's meeting with Pereira of 30 June 1940, see memorandum by Teixeira de Sampaio (secretary-general in Portuguese Foreign Ministry), 30 June 1940, Portugal, Ministério dos Negócios Estrangeiros, *Dez anos de política externa (1936–1947) a Naçao Portuguesa e a Segunda Guerra Mundial,* (herafter cited as *DAPE),* vol. VII, 929. For Franco's two-hour discussion with Pereira on 6 July, see Pereira to Salazar, 6 July 1940, idem., 972. See also Halstead, "Peril," 17.

7. Halstead, "Peril," 16. For the text of the protocol draft, see *DAPE,* VII, 929 and annex.

8. Pereira to Salazar, *DAPE,* VII, 943.

9. Stohrer to Foreign Ministry, 3 July 1940, *ADAP,* D, X, 95.

10. Stohrer to Foreign Ministry, Nr. 2340, 12 July 1940, AA, StS, Spanien, II, 74217–18. The following day, Beigbeder showed Stohrer a Spanish counterproposal to Salazar's protocol draft that, although still stronger than the original Portuguese suggestion, still fell far short of what Serrano had described as possible on the preceding day. See Stohrer to Foreign Ministry, Nr. 2353, 13 July 1940, idem., 74219. For Beigbeder's stance on the possible separation of Portugal from Britain, see Pereira to Salazar, 12 July 1940, *DAPE,* VII, 1002.

11. Ribbentrop to Stohrer, Nr. 1058, 16 July 1940, AA, StS, Spanien, II, 74228.

12. Ribbentrop to Huene, 16 July 1940, *ADAP,* D, X, 176.

13. For the text of the 29 July 1940 protocol, see *DAPE,* VII, 1066. For analysis, see Halstead, "Peril," 16–19.

14. Huene to Foreign Ministry, Nr. 706, 18 July 1940, AA, StS, Portugal; Huene to Foreign Ministry, 29 July 1940, *ADAP,* D, X, 255.

15. Stohrer to Foreign Ministry, 22 August 1940, *ADAP,* D, X, 374.

16. Huene to Foreign Ministry, Nr. 1008, 3 September 1940, AA, StS, Portugal, 120984–85. Nicolás Franco and Salazar had the same conversation in mid-December. See Huene to Foreign Ministry, Nr. 1676, 17 December 1940, idem., 121013. In each case Salazar insisted that there was no threat to the Azores either from Great Britain or from the United States.

17. *KTB/OKW*, I, 5 September 1940.

18. *ADAP,* D, XI, 117.

19. LIK (naval liaison officer to OKW, Captain Rolf Junge), Vortragsnotiz, 22 September 1940, BA/MA, RM 6/73.

20. Ibid. Junge based his assessments on information then available to the Naval Command, which stated that in the Azores, the two main islands of São Miguel

and Fayal were presently receiving three and four guns of 15 and 12 centimeters, respectively, while the remaining islands in the Azores, if fortified at all, possessed obsolete and meaningless defense. Madeira was said to be receiving three medium-caliber guns, and the fortifications in the Cape Verdes were said to be obsolete and neglected. See enclosure 5 of ibid. For similar estimates, see Jacobsen, ed., *Halder Diary*, II, 13 November 1940.

21. For Hitler's reference in this regard to Raeder of 6 and 26 September 1940 and 14 October 1940, see Wagner, ed., *Lagevorträge*, 137, 144, 147. For the memorandum by Falkenstein, see LIL (Luftwaffe liaison officer to OKW, Major Sigismund Freiherr von Falkenstein), memorandum of 22 September 1940, enclosure no. 3 of LIK, Vortragsnotiz, 22 September 1940, BA/MA, RM 6/73.

22. Falkenstein was apparently referring to the Junkers 52/3m g5e, whose landing gear could be interchanged between wheels, skis, and pontoons. Yet this aircraft had a full range of no more than 683 miles, so Falkenstein must have counted on a refueling stop at sea.

23. This four-engine craft had a range of 2,206 miles and a payload of 2,755 pounds. Falkenstein said that the westerly area of Horta could not be bombed.

24. The Dornier 18 had a range of 2,174 miles but could carry no more than 220 pounds of bombs. The Blohm and Voss Ha 138 was a three-engine aircraft with a range of 2,669 miles and a bomb payload of 661 pounds. The navy and air force were also working at this time on a design for a colonial seaplane whose function would lie in securing the fleet bases off the Continent that Germany would set up immediately after the war. The aircraft would have an action radius of 8,000 kilometers, fighting capability, and a bomb payload of 4,000 kg. See *KTB/Skl.*, XIV, 20 October 1940.

25. See Raeder's initial on LIK, Vortragsnotiz, 22 September 1940, BA/MA, RM 6/73. For his meeting with Hitler, see Wagner, ed., *Lagevorträge*, 143–46.

26. *KTB/OKW*, I, 25 September 1940.

27. LIK, Vortagsnotiz, 2 October 1940, BA/MA, RM 6/73. This study was also read by Raeder.

28. Wagner, ed., *Lagevorträge*, 147; *KTB/Skl.*, XIV, 15 October 1940. For the Naval Command's view of cooperation with France and the desire to place German forces in Casablanca, see *idem.*, XIII, 25 September 1940.

29. *KTB/OKW*, I, 23 October 1940.

30. Ibid., 28–29 October 1940. According to Jodl's report, Hitler raised the issue after reading a report by Vice Admiral Karl Dönitz, commander of the navy's submarine arm. No such report was found, but Dönitz at most only reinforced Hitler's enthusiasm.

31. *IMT*, XXV, 376-PS, 392–93. For the recipient of the letter, see Jodl's testimony in idem., XV, 397.

32. *KTB/OKW*, I, 11 November 1940.

33. "Betrachtung zur Frage der Besetzung der atlantischer Inseln durch deutsche Wehrmachtteile," BA/MA, RM 6/73. There is some disagreement on the origins of this document. There are three copies, all in draft form. Salewski, *Seekriegsleitung*, I, 288, states that Captain Hansjürgen Reinicke of Fricke's

operations staff wrote the study in late July 1940. Salewski uses an unmarked copy of the document found in BA/MA, RM 7/1003. Gerhard Schreiber, writing in DRuZW, III, 193, n. 165, argues that Fricke himself wrote it in October 1940. Schreiber bases this statement on the assumption that the navy would not compose such a document until ordered to do so. Schreiber uses Raeder's copy located in BA/MA, RM 6/73 cited above, and Raeder's copy was initialed by both Fricke and Reinicke at the bottom on 31 October. The third copy of the study is in BA/MA, RM 7/1002, and this copy is apparently a first draft by Reinicke. He initialed it at the end on 28 October and there are correction marks in the first part of the text, apparently from Fricke. It would seem, then, that Schreiber dates the document correctly. It was apparently penned by Reinicke on Fricke's directions and in accordance with Fricke's views on the Atlantic islands issue, and then corrected by Fricke and presented to Raeder on 31 October. Nonetheless, it is more difficult to agree with Schreiber that this study was the follow-up to the Junge studies of 22 September and 2 October. Junge was far more enthusiastic about the project than was Fricke, and, as stated above, Junge composed a follow-up study of his own. Schreiber also views the Fricke study as more sincere than does this writer.

34. For the views of the Naval Command in June and July 1940 on the desirability of the Atlantic islands, see chapter 1 above. See also *KTB/Skl.*, XI, 16, 27 July 1940; Salewski, ed., *Seekriegsleitung,* III, 115–16.

35. Hitler had in fact already informed Jodl of this latter aim on 1 November. See *KTB/OKW*, I, 1 and 4 November 1940; Jacobsen, ed., *Halder Diary,* II, 4 November 1940. Halder states that Hitler had not yet decided which island groups to occupy and that he ordered the High Command to look into the issue. The account in the High Command diary, which chronicles Jodl's report on the meeting to Warlimont, states that Hitler was interested in the Cape Verde Islands, thus suggesting that Jodl had recommended this specific group to Hitler based on the earlier studies by Junge. Jodl's account to Warlimont said that German forces would "occupy" the Canaries, but Hitler may well have intended something slightly more benign. The Halder account records Hitler's comment that Germany would simply help Spain to defend the Canary Islands, and Jodl's comments to Fricke later the same day, described below, suggest that this was Hitler's intent. How soon Hitler intended to leave the islands after helping the Spaniards was of course another matter. With regard to a possible march into Portugal, Halder and Brauchitsch decided on 4 November that the Fourth Armored Division and the SS Death's Head Division would serve suitably. Portuguese forces in the homeland were said to comprise no more than five very weak divisions. For further considerations of this issue, see idem., 4, 5, 6, and 13 November 1940.

36. For the memorandum of the 4 November 1940 Jodl-Fricke discussion, see Wagner, ed., *Lagevorträge,* 148–51.

37. For the directive, see Hubatsch, ed., *Weisungen,* 67–71. For the drafting, see *KTB/OKW,* I, 4–9 November 1940.

38. Jacobsen, ed., *Halder Diary,* II, 14 and 18 November 1940.

39. *KTB/OKW,* I, 15 November 1940.

40. See for example *KTB/Skl.,* XIV, 16 October 1940; idem., XV, 8 November 1940. Italy's invasion of Greece on 28 October brought immediate Italian defeats on land and led to the British occupation of Crete the next day and the landing of British forces on the Greek mainland on 3 November. On 11 and 12 November, the British attacked the Italian harbor at Tarent and seriously damaged three Italian battleships, a cruiser, and a destroyer.

41. Ibid., XV, 9 November 1940.

42. Wagner, ed., *Lagevorträge,* 151–65; *KTB/OKW,* I, 15 November 1940.

43. The navy's aversion to the Cape Verde project can be measured by balancing Raeder's statement about air support and supply with the earlier contention made by Falkenstein, and read by Raeder, that the supply of the Cape Verdes from Dakar by air would be a relatively simple undertaking with Junkers 52s.

44. *KTB/OKW,* I, 15, 20 November 1940.

45. B. Nr. 1. Skl. I op. 2497/40 gKdos. Chefs, 22 November 1940, BA/MA, RM 7/1002 and enclosure.

46. *ADAP,* D, XI, 352. See also *KTB/OKW,* I, 5 December 1940; Burdick, *Germany's Military Strategy,* 93, 105–106.

47. Jacobsen, ed., *Halder Diary,* II, 18 November 1940.

48. *KTB/OKW,* I, 19 November 1940.

49. Jacobsen, ed., *Halder Diary,* II, 30 November 1940.

50. *KTB/OKW,* I, 5 December 1940.

51. Ibid., 6 December 1940.

52. Printed in Serrano Suñer, *Memorias,* 301–305. Serrano's claim that the letter was written to buy time does not ring true. On 2 November, he told Stohrer that the intent of the letter lay in clarification of the issues discussed at Hendaye. Stohrer to Foreign Ministry, Nr. 3718, 2 November 1940, AA, StS, Spanien, II, 74437.

53. Hitler received Franco's letter of 30 October on 3 November by a special courier from Serrano's secretariat, who waited in Berlin to take back a reply from Hitler. Yet Hitler made no reply. See Stohrer to Foreign Ministry, 1 November 1940, *ADAP,* D, XI, 273; memorandum by Weizsäcker, AA, StS, Spanien, II, 74440.

54. *KTB/OKW,* I, 4 November 1940; Jacobsen, ed., *Halder Diary,* II, 4 November 1940. Detwiler, *Gibraltar,* 68–73, connects Hitler's decision to press forward with the Gibraltar operation to the recent Italian mishaps with the Greek campaign. There may be a connection with regard to the German navy's increased desire for an operation against the Rock, but not with regard to Hitler's thinking, which, with regard to Gibraltar, underwent no fundamental changes due to events in the eastern Mediterranean. As for the general notion that the Gibraltar operation was part of a Mediterranean strategy for Hitler, it is noteworthy that at the same meeting of 4 November, Hitler announced that Germany would abstain from dispatching forces to Libya. He

mentioned the future German attack on Greece, but primarily in the context of the protection of the Rumanian oil fields.

55. Halder and Brauchitsch decided later in the day that the Third Armored Division, which had until that day been earmarked for service in the Italian North African campaign, would be one of the units sent to Morocco. The SS Division Adolf Hitler was also contemplated for service in Morocco. Subsequent planning revealed that the troops would cross the Strait of Gibraltar on German ships then located in Italy. See Jacobsen, ed., *Halder Diary*, II, 7 November 1940.

56. Muggeridge, ed., *Ciano Diary*, 2–4 November 1940; idem., *Ciano Papers*, 405–408. For the amended protocol, see *ADAP*, D, XI, pp. 394–95

57. *Ciano Papers*, 405–408.

58. Ribbentrop to Stohrer, 6 November 1940, *ADAP*, D, XI, 294 and n. 2.

59. Ribbentrop to Stohrer, 11 November 1940, ibid., 312; Stohrer to Ribbentrop, Nr. 3834, 12 November 1940, AA, StS, Spanien, II, 74454. This evidence should be balanced against the claim made by Serrano, *Memorias*, 305–308, that he and Franco accepted the invitation because they hoped to stall the Germans and because they were afraid of the German reaction should they *not* accept. Serrano accepted the invitation immediately before consulting with Franco, even with the easy, available excuse that he too would be occupied on the 18th. Serrano also neglects to mention that he had in fact signed the Hendaye Protocol. See Serrano Suñer, *Memorias*, 305–308.

60. For the protocol of the meeting, see *ADAP*, D, XI, 352.

61. Stohrer to Ribbentrop, 14 November 1940, ibid., 335. See also Stohrer to Ribbentrop, 20 January 1941, ibid., 677.

62. The scheme for the Swiss grain was first communicated to Berlin on 11 November. See Stohrer to Foreign Ministry, Nr. 3818, 11 November 1940, AA, StS, Spanien, 74450. Stohrer advocated it, but Emil Wiehl in the Foreign Ministry's economic policy department noted that the condition for economic aid had always been Spain's entry into the war, and that a decision to the contrary would have to come from Göring or from Hitler himself. See Stohrer to Ribbentrop, 14 November 1940, *ADAP*, D, XI, 335; memorandum by Wiehl, 15 November 1940, idem., 340.

63. *ADAP*, D, XI, 352. My emphasis.

64. Muggeridge, ed., *Ciano Diary*, 18 November 1940. Ciano met with Hitler later in the day. After lambasting Ciano for the Italian fiasco in Greece, Hitler again said that Spain would have to enter the war as soon as possible and that Spanish Morocco would be occupied by several German divisions. This, argued Hitler, would be the best insurance against a defection by French Morocco. *ADAP*, D, XI, 353; Muggeridge, ed., *Ciano Papers*, 408–11.

65. *ADAP*, D, XI, 357. Serrano's account of his Berghof trip omits mention of the colonial argument and focuses on the food issue. Serrano Suñer, *Memorias*, 305–308.

66. *ADAP*, D, XI, 365. Hitler's positive impression from the meeting was confirmed by reports received by the army High Command and navy as well. See Ja-

cobsen, ed., *Halder Diary*, II, 19 November 1940; *KTB/Skl.*, XV, 22 November 1940.

67. Hitler to Mussolini, 20 November 1940, *ADAP*, D, XI, 369. Hitler justified securing French North Africa against defection by noting the necessity to prevent the setup of British-Gaullist air bases, which the Allies could then use against Italy. One can assume, given other evidence, that Hitler emphasized this to appeal to his reader. Mussolini replied to Hitler on 22 November that the time to play the Spanish card had indeed arrived. See idem., 383.

68. Ibid., 452. My emphasis.

69. Burdick, *Germany's Military Strategy*, 70, 90–94, 105–106.

70. OKH/GenStdH, Op. Abt. IIb, Vortragsnotiz gKdos.: Sperrung der Meerenge von Gibraltar, 13 November 1940, BA/MA, RH 2/444, 444 K-2. The British decided in December as well that an operation against Ceuta would fail to preserve their control of the Strait. See Smyth, *Survival*, 146.

71. *KTB/OKW*, I, 25 November 1940. On the decision not to send armored divisions to Egypt, see idem., 4 November 1940.

72. The army had begun working on the problem after Hitler's first mention of it on 4 November. By 20 November Halder learned that the ships for the crossing of the Strait, twenty vessels located in Italy, would be ready for action by 15 December. Jacobsen, ed., *Halder Diary*, II, 4, 7, 8, 13, 16, and 20 November 1940.

73. *Baudouin Diary*, 23 November 1940.

74. Jacobsen, ed., *Halder Diary*, II, 5 December 1940; *KTB/OKW*, I, 5 December 1940; Burdick, *Germany's Military Strategy*, 71–72.

75. *KTB/OKW*, I, 6 and 7 December 1940. The draft of the nineteenth war directive, which was neither signed by Hitler nor implemented, is printed in Hubatsch, ed., *Weisungen*, 74–77.

76. Burdick, *Germany's Military Strategy*, 102–103 and n. 13.

77. For the protocol of this meeting, written by Vigón, see *ADAP*, D, XI, 500. See also *KTB/OKW*, I, 8 December 1940. The myth propagated by Canaris's earlier biographers, that the Abwehr chief vocally advised Franco not to enter the war, is dispelled in Detwiler, *Gibraltar*, 84, n. 23. Indeed, Franco had enough good reasons not to enter the war before Canaris ever arrived in Madrid. Detwiler in "Spain and the Axis," 48, notes, however, that Canaris had indeed told Vigón earlier in the day that Franco *could safely refuse* Hitler. The statement is based on postwar interviews with Captain Wilhelm Leissner, the head of German military intelligence in Spain, who was present at the evening meeting on 7 December. It is also worth mention however, that both Hitler on 18 November at the Berghof and Canaris on 7 December in Madrid revealed to the Spaniards that the German troops marked for the operation would be needed elsewhere in the spring, and thus that there existed but a rather small window of time for the Gibraltar operation. From these statements, Franco could already have assumed that a lack of acquiescence on his part would likely kill the possibility of German operations in Spain.

78. Stohrer to Ribbentrop, 25 November 1940, *ADAP*, D, XI, 398; Stohrer to For-

eign Ministry, 28 November 1940, idem., 414; Stohrer to Ribbentrop, 29 November 1940, idem., 420. The insistence on a reply from Hitler to Franco's letter of 30 October could revert back to Serrano's suggestion at Hendaye that the colonial compensation issue be handled in an exchange of letters rather than the Hendaye Protocol. Apparently Serrano and Franco both believed that a letter from Hitler would have some legal value after the war. On Spain's unreadiness in general, see Jacobsen, ed., *Halder Diary,* II, 25 November, 3 December 1940.

79. On the incorporation, see Halstead, "Aborted Imperialism," 57; Smyth, *Survival,* 135 ff. For the movement of the Spanish artillery, see Richter to Foreign Ministry, Nr. 28, 4 November 1940, AA, StS, Marokko, I, 58184. On the Spanish press, see Stohrer to Foreign Ministry, Nr. 3752, 5 November 1940, idem., 58187. The Spanish proclamation of 23 November 1940, signed by Franco, is printed in Great Britain, *State Papers,* 1940–1942, vol. 144, 539.

80. Stohrer to Foreign Ministry, 5 November 1940, *ADAP,* D, XI, 286.

81. Stohrer to Foreign Ministry, Nr. 3757, AA, StS, Marokko, I, 58188–90.

82. A long list of German citizens in Spanish Morocco in late 1939 is in AA, DB Madrid, Marokko, Allgemein, Bd. 5. Richter made specific references to Abwehr, SD, and Party agents in Spanish Morocco in early 1941. See Richter to Foreign Ministry, J. Nr. 373/41, 5 March 1941, ibid. See Carlos Collado Seidel, "Zufluchtsstätte für Nationalsozialisten? Spancen, die Alliierten und die Behandlung deutscher Agenten 1944–1947," 133–35.

83. See the lengthy reports of 1 November and 17 December 1940 from Dr. Markus Timmler, the Foreign Ministry representative with the Reichsrundfunkgesellschaft in AA, Kulturpolitische Abteilung, Rundfunkpolitische Abteilung, Referat B, Bd. XIV. In the Spanish zone, German broadcasts were said to have a positive reception among the native Moroccans in spite of jamming signals from Rabat. See Richter to Foreign Ministry, J. Nr. 1416/40, 5 November 1940, idem., Bd. XV; Dr. Theodor Auer (German Foreign Ministry representative in Casablanca) to Foreign Ministry, 57/41, 12 March 1941, idem.; Richter to Foreign Ministry, Nr. 31, 8 November 1940, AA, StS, Marokko, I, 51891.

84. Richter to Stohrer, 24 June 1940, AA, DB Madrid, Marokko Allgemein, Bd. 5.

85. Espinosa to Ribbentrop, Nr. 620, 30 November 1940, AA, StS, Marokko, 58203.

86. Richter to Foreign Ministry, 26 December 1940, *ADAP,* D, XI, 273. The issue of the German legation will be treated below. On the entrance of Germans into Tangier, see German Embassy (Madrid), Note Verbale no. 473/40, 2 July 1940, AMAE, L 1267, Ex 101; Beigbeder to Amieva, unnumbered, 12 July 1940, idem.; Amieva to Beigbeder, no. 76 cif., 14 July 1940, idem. See also Woermann to Stohrer, Nr. 1095, 20 July 1940, AA, StS, Marokko, I, 58166; Stohrer to Foreign Ministry, Nr. 2505, 25 July 1940, idem., 58169. On the cooperation of Spanish authorities, a 25 February 1941 Abwehr report stated that for "some time" Spanish military and administrative authori-

ties had been distancing themselves from Germany. This Abwehr officer blamed Spain's disappointment regarding its colonial aspirations and Jewish influence. The report is enclosed in Richter to Foreign Ministry, J. Nr. 373/41, 5 March 1941, AA, DB Madrid, Marokko-Allgemein, Bd. 5. An SS report of the same time states that German propaganda among the Moroccan natives in the Spanish zone was proceeding effectively with little hindrance from the Spanish authorities, so clearly the Spanish efforts against German meddling were somewhat uneven. See C.S.P. u. S.D. VI E 2 Kei/Li. AZ: VI E 502/41g, 21 January 1941, AA, Inland IIg, Nordafrika, bndl. 335. Spanish-German friction over German propaganda in Morocco continued well into the war. See AMAE, L 2199, Ex 12. See also AA, StS, Marokko, I, passim, for 1941 and 1942.

87. On the confiscation, see Richter to Foreign Ministry, 28 June 1940, AA, DB Madrid, Französisch Marokko u. Nordafrika. For the official fate of German property in Morocco, movable and immovable, following the First World War, see Harold W. V. Temperley, *Peace Conference at Paris*, vol. III, 183–84.

88. Carlos Collado Seidel, "Zufluchtsstätte für Nationalsozialisten? Spanien, die Allierten und die Behandlung deutscher Agenten 1944–1947," 131–58.

89. Richter to Foreign Ministry, unnumbered, 28 June 1940, AA, DB Madrid, Französisch Marokko u. Nordafrika. For reports on the *Mendub*'s affiliations, see C.S.P. u. S.D. VI F 12 Ma/vB AZ: 1781/40g, 12 October 1940, AA, Inland IIg, Berichte und Meldungen zur Lage in und über Nordafrika, bndl. 335.

90. Stohrer to Foreign Ministry, no. 3018, 6 September 1940, AA, StS, Marokko, 58177.

91. C.S.P. u. S.D. VI E 22 To/Kg AZ: VE 5889/40, 8 November 1940, AA, Inland IIg, Nordafrika, bndl. 335. This problem was also a heavy concern of Richter's, and he requested that German radio broadcasting to Morocco exercise the utmost reserve in the Tangier affair. See Richter to Foreign Ministry, J. Nr. 1497, 13 November 1940, AA, Kulturpolitische Abteilung, Rundfunkpolitische Abteilung, Referat B, Bd. XV.

92. Weizsäcker to Stohrer, Pol. III 2751/40, 16 November 1940, AA, StS, Marokko, I, 58197–98.

93. Stohrer to Foreign Ministry, Nr. 3874, 14 November 1940, ibid., 58193; Schroeder to Stohrer, Nr. 2073, 22 November 1940, ibid., 58194. The delegation that was to go to Tangier to accept the return of the legation building included Hans Heinrich Dieckhoff, who had been a member of the expelled legation in 1914. See Stohrer to Foreign Ministry, Nr. 4041, 26 November 1940, ibid., 58200.

94. Stohrer to Foreign Ministry, Nr. 4157, 4 December 1940, ibid., 58202; Stohrer to Foreign Ministry, Nr. 4266, 12 December 1940, ibid., 58204/1; Stohrer to Foreign Ministry, Nr. 4343, 18 December 1940, ibid., 58204/2; Weizsäcker to Stohrer, Nr. 86, 14 January 1941, ibid., 58206–207; Stohrer to Foreign Ministry, Nr. 362, 31 January 1941, ibid., 58222; Stohrer to Foreign Ministry, Nr. 721, 26 February 1941, ibid., 58222.

95. Stohrer to Foreign Ministry, Nr. 875, 6 March 1941, ibid., 58228; Richter to
     Foreign Ministry, Nr. 14, 17 March 1941, ibid., 58230–31; Dr. Herbert
     Nöhring (German Consul in Tangier) to Foreign Ministry, Nr. 5, 9 April 1941,
     ibid. The German Consulate in Tangier was raised to a General Consulate in
     May 1942 when Dr. Kurt Rieth became the new German representative. See
     Stohrer to Foreign Ministry, Nr. 2721, 19 May 1942, ibid., 58330. General
     Noguès protested publically the eviction of the *Mendub* in the name of Sul-
     tan. See his "Une Protestation de sa Majesté le Sultan auprès du Gouvernement
     Espagnol," *L'Echo du Maroc* (Rabat), 8 May 1940, no. 7.136. See also
     Nöhring to Foreign Ministry, B. Nr. 23, 10 May 1941, AA, DB Madrid,
     Tanger Zone, Bd. 3; A. Renschhausen (German consul in Larache) to Heber-
     lein, 10 May 1941, ibid.

96. Nöhring to Foreign Ministry, B. Nr. 1, 4 April 1941, AA, DB Madrid, Tanger
     Zone, Bd. 3; Douglas Porch, *The Conquest of Morocco*, 181–212.

97. For Spanish complaints from 1942, see AMAE, L 2199, Ex 12, passim. A
     poignant German complaint is in Stohrer to Serrano Suñer, 13 August 1941,
     idem., L 1912, Ex 10.

98. See Hoare to Jordana, 21 March 1944, AMAE, L 5162, L3. For the issue in
     general, see Collado Seidel, "Zufluchtsstätte [the full title is provided in n. 88
     above]."

99. For the Hitler-Raeder talks on this issue of 6 and 26 September 1940, see
     Wagner ed., *Lagevorträge,* 134–46. In general, see chapters 4 and 5 above.

100. Serrano commented that Spain was installing machine gun nests, four artil-
     lery batteries, fighter aircraft, and "one of the bravest generals of our Army"
     to command the possible defense against Britain or America. Serrano Suñer
     to Ribbentrop, 10 October 1940, *ADAP,* D, XI, 172. The actual extent of
     Spanish reinforcements in the Canaries is unclear due to the secrecy the Span-
     ish military archives for the period. German army intelligence at this time
     stated that between 22 September and 1 October, Spain had strengthened its
     manpower in the Canary Islands to 40,000 men, but many of these might
     have been potential reserves for emergencies only. In mid-October German
     army intelligence placed 27,552 troops in the Canaries (11,322 on Tenerife
     and 9,970 on Gran Canaria) and noted that the Spaniards could raise that
     number to 38,000 with reserves. The Abwehr placed Spanish strength in the
     Canaries at one division totaling 27,000 men. The brave general to whom
     Serrano referred was General García Escamez, hitherto the military governor
     of Barcelona, who became military governor in the Canary Islands in the fall
     of 1940. See OKH/GenStdH/Abt. Fremde Heere West/IV, Lagebericht West
     Nr. 426, 14 November 1940, AA, Handakten Hasso von Etzdorf. See also
     the Abwehr chart from 5 November 1940 in BA/MA, RW 5/620 K.

101. *ADAP,* D, XI, 220; Serrano Suñer, *Memorias,* 294–98.

102. *ADAP,* D, XI, 246.

103. *KTB/OKW,* I, 4 November 1940; Jacobsen, ed., *Halder Diary,* II, 4 Novem-
     ber 1940, Hubatsch, ed., *Weisungen,* 67–72.

104. *ADAP,* D, XI, 352. In their meeting the next day, Ribbentrop noted that "it

was of great importance that the Canary Islands remain firmly in the hands of the Spaniards," and that military experts would still need to consider the issue. Serrano remained silent on the question. See idem., 357.

105. It has been mentioned above that the Germans already had Madrid's approval for secret submarine refueling in the Canary Islands. Raeder and his subordinates now hoped to use the Canaries as a base for pocket battleships, cruisers, and merchant ships. This hope presupposed that the Canaries would receive new outfitting with munitions and oil stocks, along with German support personnel, all *before* the entrance of Spain into the war. See Wagner, ed., *Lagevorträge,* 151–65.

106. Ibid. There were naval reports on artillery in the Canary Islands in early November, but apparently Raeder and the army felt, correctly as shown below, these reports were overly optimistic. See 3 Abt. Skl. FM b B. Nr. 24223 geh., 6 November 1940, BA/MA, RM 6/73; Jacobsen, ed., *Halder Diary,* II, 13 November 1940.

107. *KTB/Skl.,* XV, 16 November 1940; Burdick, *Germany's Military Strategy,* 76–77, 98, and n. 4. Menzell's departure date is unclear. For Voss's itinerary, see Bericht über die Reise Chef AI nach Spanien vom 15. bis 26.11.1940, BA/MA, RM 7/1002. Burdick says that Menzell filed a detailed report on his return from Madrid as well, but this report was not found.

108. B. Nr. 1. Skl. I op. 2510/40 gKdos. Chefs., 22 November 1940, BA/MA, RM 7/1002.

109. B. Nr. 1. Skl. I op. 2539/40 gKdos. Chefs., 30 November 1940, and enclosure, ibid. Burdick, *Germany's Military Strategy,* 78, n. 4, states that the departure point of the weapons was to be Hamburg. Yet in early December the plan apparently changed. The batteries were to come from coastal defenses in France. See Jacobsen, ed., *Halder Diary,* II, 2 December 1940.

110. B. Nr. 1. Skl. I op. 2560/40 gKdos. Chefs., 3 December 1940, BA/MA, RM 7/1002. On 2 December the navy sent Captain Fritz Krauss to Tenerife to determine the most pressing defense needs of the islands and to help on the other end of the arms shipment. He would return to Berlin on 23 December 1940. See Burdick, *Germany's Military Strategy,* 98, n. 4.

111. Bericht über die Reise Chef AI nach Spanien vom 15. bis 26.11.1940, BA/MA, RM 7/1002. On Tenerife, according to Voss's report Spain had four Munaiz 15-centimeter pieces with a range of 13,500 meters and four Vickers 15.25-centimeter pieces with the same range. On Gran Canaria the Spaniards had six of each. These figures were considerably less than those in the navy's earlier reports. See 3. Abt. Skl. FM b B. Nr. 24223 geh., 6 November 1940, BA/MA, RM 6/73.

112. Wagner, ed., *Lagevorträge,* 165–66.

113. Jacobsen, ed., *Halder Diary,* II, 26 November 1940.

114. *KTB/Skl.,* XV, 4 December 1940.

115. B. Nr. 1. Skl. I op. 2567/40 gKdos. Chefs., 4 December 1940 and enclosure, BA/MA, RM 7/1002. The Spaniards wished to send one of the four motor-

ized batteries to Tarifa to protect the coastline there, but Fricke rejected this scheme, noting that four motorized batteries would be the minimum defense requirement for Gran Canaria and Tenerife. Fricke also ordered that a German ship for the transport of the batteries would be kept in readiness for the eventuality that the Spaniards changed their minds.

116. *KTB/OKW,* I, 6 December 1940. Canaris could have received this order on 4 December as well.

117. B. Nr. 1. Skl. I op. 2575/40 gKdos. Chefs., 7 December 1940, BA/MA, RM 7/1002.

118. Gaus to Stohrer, 8 December 1940, *ADAP,* D, XI, 476. For Stohrer's reports before the refusal, see idem., 398, 414, 420, and 444; Stohrer to Ribbentrop, Nr. 4090, 29 November 1940, AA, StS, Spanien, II, 74489. For his explanations, see Stohrer to Ribbentrop, Nr. 4209, 9 December 1940, idem., 74514. See also his telegrams to the Foreign Ministry of 9 and 11 December 1940, printed in *ADAP,* D, XI, 492, 493, 497. Ribbentrop himself thought the Spaniards were simply taking a Machiavellian wait-and-see approach to the war. See Ribbentrop to Mackensen, 12 December 1940, idem., 498.

119. Franco had indeed asked on 28 November 1940 that Berlin send an officer who enjoyed Hitler's special confidence for this very purpose. See Stohrer to Ribbentrop, 29 November 1940, *ADAP,* D, XI, 420; memorandum by Ritter, 7 December 1940, idem., 473; *KTB/OKW,* I, 6 December 1940.

120. *KTB/OKW,* I, 8 December 1940.

121. *KTB/OKW,* I, 8 December 1940; Jacobsen, ed., *Halder Diary,* II, 8 December 1940. Hitler expressed similar concerns about French reliability on the same day to Alfieri. See *ADAP,* D, XI, 477.

122. Hubatsch, ed., *Weisungen,* 79–81. For the preparation of the directive, see *KTB/OKW,* I, 8, 9, and 10 December 1940.

123. *KTB/OKW,* 7 and 9 December 1940. See also chapter 8 below for full explanation.

124. Jacobsen, ed., *Halder Diary,* II, 9 December 1940. Disgusted by Italian failures in the eastern Mediterranean, Hitler now added that Berlin did not need to consider Rome to an overly large extent in this regard either.

125. *KTB/OKW,* I, 10 December 1940; Hubatsch, ed., *Weisungen,* 78.

Chapter 8. Winter Collapse II: France

1. Abetz to Ribbentrop, 1 November 1940, *ADAP,* D, XI, 272; *KTB/OKW,* I, 1 November 1940; memorandum from Hencke, 2 November 1940, AA, StS, FF, II, 207203–205; DWStK Ia Chefgruppe Nr. 438/40g, 1 November 1940, BA/MA, RW 4/747.

2. The memoranda in German translation are enclosed in DWStK Ia Chefgruppe Nr. 438/40g, 1 November 1940, BA/MA, RW 4/747. Shortly after the meeting in Paris, Admiral Michelier in Wiesbaden would inform the Germans that the Huntziger memoranda of 31 October had been hurriedly composed and

that the French reserved the right to make amendments. See memorandum by Grote, 4 November 1940, AA, StS, FF, II, 207219–20. Accordingly, the French delegation presented the German Armistice Commission with revised memoranda on 12 November 1940. See Landesverteidigung L III, Vortragsnotiz, 18 November 1940, BA/MA, RW 4/747; *DFCAA*, II, 392–418. The differences between the early and late sets of memoranda are issues of detail. The two sets will be treated here as a unit.

3. The army in North Africa had yet to disarm to 120,000. The Italians reported in early November that it would reach this figure by the end of the month. See memorandum by Grote, 5 November 1940, AA StS, FF, II, 207222–23. The supplementary memoranda of 12 November said that the extra 20,000 men would be formed into two mobile detachments of 8,200 men each, with the remainder forming four infantry battalions for those regiments that had only two.

4. The mobile detachment, according to the memoranda of 12 November (see n. 2 above), was to include three motorized infantry battalions, three motorized cavalry squadrons, and mobile artillery with 780 Europeans and 2,360 natives. The French specifically requested the release of Generals Emile-Jaques Carles and Maurice-Emile Falvy, who had held commands in Equatorial and West Africa respectively before the war.

5. In the 12 November memoranda, the French also requested a parachute company for French West Africa.

6. Ritter to Abetz, 4 November 1940, *ADAP*, D, XI, 285; memorandum by Ritter, Pol. I, 1275 GRs, 8 November 1940, AA, StS, FF, II, 207231; Muggeridge, ed., *Ciano Papers*, 405–407.

7. *KTB/OKW*, I, 1 November 1940. Expulsions from Alsace began in early December. Jäckel, *Frankreich*, 75–84.

8. The 6 November memorandum by Dr. Ernst Bielfeld, which even included Nigeria and Dakar, was shown to Ribbentrop and likely Hitler as well. See *ADAP*, D, XI, 298.

9. De Gaulle's army under de Larminat attacked Gabon from Cameroon and Pointe Noire in mid-October. In the first week of November, the Free French forces took Njidolle and Lambarene and Vichy troops held only Libreville and Port Gentile. On 9 November, General Doyen reported in Wiesbaden that de Gaulle's troops had begun their assault on Libreville the previous evening, and that due to the weak government forces there (roughly one battalion), the city would probably fall. On the tenth, the Germans learned that de Gaulle's forces had captured the Vichy governor Têtu during the attack on Libreville, and the next day it was learned that of the two Vichy warships at Libreville, one, a sloop, was captured by de Gaulle and one, a submarine, scuttled itself. Libreville would fall on 10 November, and the Germans would learn it on the twelfth, the same day on which Port Gentile surrendered. See memorandum by Grote, 9 November 1940, AA, StS, FF, II, 207232–34; memorandum by Grote, 11 November 1940, idem., 207235–57; *KTB/OKW*, I, 9,

11, and 12 November 1940; de Gaulle, *Mémoires de Guerre*, I, 111–17; Vincent, *Les Forces Françaises*, 17–18.

10. Welck to Foreign Ministry, Nr. 218, 5 November 1940, AA, StS, FF, II, 207221. The only request rejected was the production of war materials in the occupied territory.

11. *KTB/OKW*, I, 1 November 1940.

12. He even pushed for a full overhaul of the armistice regime for easier collaboration. See *KTB/OKW*, I, 1 and 4 November 1940; L III, Vortragsnotiz, 4 November 1940, BA/MA, RW 4/747. The Naval Command gave their agreement to the French memoranda immediately, with the sole addendum that the French make their ciphers known to Germany. See *KTB/OKW*, I, 4, 7 November 1940.

13. *KTB/OKW*, I, 1 November 1940.

14. Welck to Foreign Ministry, Nr. 219, 5 November 1940, AA, StS, FF, II, 207224.

15. *ADAP*, D, XI, 306. Why Ribbentrop indefinitely postponed his own planned meeting with Laval is not clear. Jäckel, *Frankreich*, 134, says he was tied to prescheduled visits.

16. *DFCAA*, I, 321–25. Doyen's note includes an overview of Vichy and Gaullist forces in Africa. See also *KTB/OKW*, I, 7 and 11 November 1940.

17. *KTB/OKW*, I, 9 November 1940; Hencke to Foreign Ministry, 12 November 1940, *ADAP*, D, XI, 321.

18. Hitler also allowed the use of two transport aircraft groups for food and troop transport, to be taken from North Africa. On the French delegation's request, the personnel of the mobile detachment was raised from 3,140 to 5,000 men. See *KTB/OKW*, I, 12 November 1940; Hencke to Foreign Ministry, 14 November 1940, *ADAP*, D, XI, 321 and n. 5; memorandum by Grote, 18 November 1940, AA, StS, FF, II, 207265–66; memorandum by Grote, 20 November 1940, idem. The French delegation attributed the German change of heart to events in Gabon. See *DFCAA*, II, 352–53, 356–57, 448.

19. Hitler's thoughts on strengthening the French in Morocco might have also been reinforced by Bötticher's report at this time that Britain was planning to attack Casablanca. See *KTB/OKW*, I, 29 October 1940. On Stülpnagel's inquiry the next day, Doyen stated that Casablanca was safe from a Gaullist coup and that based on aerial reconnaissance over Freetown and Gibraltar, he expected no British attack there. *DFCAA*, II, 269.

20. "Von Senger Reports," 31 October 1940, 7 and 14 November 1940.

21. Memorandum by Grote, 9 November 1940, AA, StS, FF, II, 207232–34; memorandum by Grote, 16 November 1940, idem., 207259–62; memorandum by Grote, 19 November 1940, idem., 207278–80; memorandum by Grote, 11 November 1940, idem., 207235–37; Hencke to Foreign Ministry, Nr. 234, 14 November 1940, idem., 207255.

22. *KTB/OKW*, I, 4, 7 November 1940.

23. Ibid., 14, 15 November 1940.

24. Badoglio had requested the meeting on 24 October in order to discuss coop-

eration in general. See ibid., 25 October 1940. For the meeting itself, see ibid., 19 November 1940; OKW/WFSt/L IV, Nr. 33 371/40 gKdos. Chefs., 25 November 1940, BA/MA, RW 34/9; "Von Senger Reports," 21 November 1940. Badoglio admitted in the talks with Keitel that the French army in North Africa had still not disarmed to the level of 120,000 men. Badoglio's orders after the meeting to General Pintor, chief of the Italian Armistice Commission, are not clear. According to Hemmen, he might have ordered Pintor only to check with Wiesbaden on nonmilitary decisions. See Hemmen to Foreign Ministry, Nr. 200, 23 November 1940, AA, StS FF, II, 207300–302. Senger had already demanded before the Keitel-Badoglio meeting, on the orders of Wiesbaden, that Turin permit the fuel tankers whose movement had been suspended earlier to move to West Africa. See memorandum by Grote, 19 November 1940, idem., 207278–80.

25. General Enno von Rintelen, military attaché in Rome, reported on 9 December that Mussolini had approved the increase, but only with much hesitation due to his mistrust of General Weygand. The French received official approval on 12 December. See *KTB/OKW*, I, 11 December 1940; memorandum by Kramarz, 11 December 1940, AA, StS, FF, II, 207394–96; memorandum by Stein, 12 December 1940, idem., 207402–405.

26. Memorandum by Grote, AA, StS, FF, II, 207298–92; Hencke to Foreign Ministry, Nr. 252, 22 November 1940, idem., 207293–94; memorandum by Grote, idem., 207319–21.

27. The Germans allowed coded contact as of 13 November 1940, and the Italian commission agreed by the twenty-sixth. See memorandum by Grote, 18 November 1940, ibid., 207265–66; Hencke to Foreign Ministry, no. 241, 18 November 1940, ibid., 207267–68; memorandum by Grote, 26 November 1940, ibid., 207308–10.

28. Memorandum by Grote, 18 November 1940, ibid., 207265–66. As far as one can tell, the French ignored the Italian demand. Its stone structures along the 450-kilometer front remained intact.

29. Schleier to Abetz, 15 November 1940, *ADAP*, D, XI, 343. The number of Spanish troops comes from a French count. See also Lequerica to Serrano Suñer, no. 1301, 8 November 1940, AMAE, L 2295, Ex 5.

30. DWStK, Gruppe Auswärt., Nr. 233, 14 November 1940, AA, StS, FF, II, 207254.

31. See *KTB/OKW*, I, 26, 27, 29 November 1940. Achenbach and Schleier to Abetz, 23 November 1940, *ADAP*, D, XI, 385; memorandum by Woermann, 25 November 1940, idem., 401; memorandum by Ritter, 26 November 1940, idem., 408; Schwarzmann to Schleier, 27 November 1940, idem., 410.

32. Vice Admiral Kurt Assmann, "Die Bemühungen der Skl. um einen Ausgleich mit Frankreich und um die Sicherstellung des französischen Kolonialreiches in Afrika" (hereafter cited as "Bemühungen"), 23–24, BA/MA, RM 8/1209.

33. For the meeting, see the memorandum by Achenbach, 29 November 1940, BA/MA, RW 4/747. See also Abetz to Ribbentrop, 30 November 1940, *ADAP*, D, XI, 428; Abetz to Ribbentrop, 1 December 1940, idem., 434.

34. *ADAP*, D, XI, 434.

35. *KTB/OKW*, I, 2 December 1940, 1–4 December 1940.

36. Ibid., 4 December 1940. Warlimont's impression that Hitler had been pleased with the outcome of the meeting should be seen in light of other evidence.

37. Hitler to Mussolini, 5 December 1940, *ADAP*, D, XI, 452.

38. Ibid., 477.

39. Jacobsen, ed., *Halder Diary*, II, 9 December 1940, pp. 134–35 above.

40. *KTB/OKW*, I, 7 December 1940.

41. Ibid., 6–7 December 1940.

42. Ibid., 7 and 9 December 1940; Jacobsen, ed., *Halder Diary*, II, 9 December 1940.

43. *KTB/OKW*, I, 10 December 1940; Hubatsch, ed., *Weisungen*, 78.

44. *Baudouin Diary*, 30 October, 10 November and 7–11 December 1940. For a further evaluation of the French memoir literature on the Chad issue, see Warner, *Laval*, 257. An excerpt from a French ministerial discussion on the Chad expedition from 7 December is printed in *DFCAA*, V, 445–46, which supports the theory above. Laval pressed for plans for anti-British reprisals, with agreement from Pétain and Huntziger. Laval also argued that the Chad operation would strengthen the French position vis-à-vis Italy.

45. The most complete memorandum is in *KTB/OKW*, I, Dokumenten-Anhang, 984–94. See also *DFCAA*, V, 446–62. For summaries, see Abetz to Ribbentrop, 10 December 1940, *ADAP*, D, XI, 490; memorandum by Warlimont, 12 December 1940, idem., 506.

46. According to Stehlin, there were four bomber groups and two fighter groups in French West Africa. The French wanted to keep one fighter group and two bomber groups in Dakar to fight possible British reprisals there.

47. KTB/OKW, I, Dokumenten-Anhang, 984–94. Huntziger spoke *ad nauseum* on optimum percentages, but he wanted 262 white officers and 920 NCOs, plus 2,000 extra colonial troops and 12 Senegalese officers.

48. Memorandum by Warlimont, 12 December 1940, *ADAP*, D, XI, 506. It is of note that the words "political and" were struck from the record once the memorandum reached the German Foreign Ministry. Warlimont also commented to Jodl that French planning corresponded in objective and timing to the German hopes. *KTB/OKW*, I, 11 November 1940.

49. Memorandum by Warlimont, 12 December 1940, *ADAP*, D, XI, 506; *KTB/OKW*, I, 12 December 1940.

50. Warner, *Laval*, 253–54 and n. 1; Jäckel, *Frankreich*, 140. This was to be Pétain's first journey to the occupied territory. No copy of the invitation has been found in the German records. For references, see *ADAP*, D, XI, 510, n. 2; *DFCAA*, III, 221, n. 1.

51. The events of 13 December are well described in Warner, *Laval*, 254–57, and Paxton, *Vichy France*, 92–93.

52. The most thoughtful consideration is in Paxton, *Vichy France*, 92–101.

53. For a summary of the memoirs, see Warner, *Laval*, 257.

54. See ibid., 257–58; Jäckel, *Frankreich*, 141–42; Paxton, *Vichy France*, 92–101. Pétain's explanation of the event as a domestic affair was first made to

Hitler in a letter of 13 December, and in another letter of 18 December. See *ADAP*, D, XI, 510, 530. The argument in Elmar Krautkrämer, "Die Entmachtung Lavals im Dezember 1940: Ein Außenpolitisches Kalkül Vichys," 79–112, that the dismissal was aimed at American economic aid for French Africa, is another interesting interpretation.

55. See for example *Baudouin Diary*, 16 and 23 June 1940, 6, 12, 18, 19, and 22 July 1940, 3, 7, and 19 August 1940, 9 September 1940.

56. The most prominent instance was the sale of the French-owned Bor copper mines in Yugoslavia and the presentation to the Germans of the two hundred tons of Belgian gold that the French had been keeping in West Africa. See Warner, *Laval*, 246–47.

57. See p. 188 below.

58. *ADAP*, D, XI, 510, 530.

59. Ibid., 510. Pétain had already drafted a letter to the same effect on 9 December but refrained from sending it at the last moment. See Jäckel, *Frankreich*, 142. Darlan would explain to Hitler on Christmas Day that Pétain had refrained from sending the first letter for fear of ruining the military negotiations to take place on 10 December in Paris. See *ADAP*, D, XI, 564. The fact that this original announcement antedates the 10 December talks strengthens the possibility that Laval's dismissal had less to do with the Chad expedition as such than with his failure to gain concessions for the *Metropole*.

60. Hencke to Foreign Ministry, 16 December 1940, *ADAP*, D, XI, 521; memorandum by Stein, 17 December 1940, AA, StS FF, III, 207438–40. Doyen to Stülpnagel, 16 December 1940, *DFCAA*, III, 222.

61. Hencke also told the French not to make any more public announcements about the changes already made. Pétain had already made one on the evening of 14 December. Hencke to Foreign Ministry, Nr. 304, AA, StS, FF, II, 207419; Hencke to Foreign Ministry, 15 December 1940, *ADAP*, D, XI, 517. On Pétain's announcement, see Warner, *Laval*, 256–57.

62. The demands are listed in Abetz to Ribbentrop, 18 December 1940, *ADAP*, D, XI, 530. For the meeting, see Abetz to Ribbentrop, 18 December 1940, idem., 531. On the discussion between Abetz and Darlan on 15 December in Paris, there is a memorandum by Darlan on Abetz's comments in Alain Darlan, *L'Amiral Darlan parle*, 261–62.

63. Quoted by Abetz in *ADAP*, D, XI, 531.

64. Ibid. This original draft offered only to make Laval the minister of agriculture or labor, and even that "after a certain time had elapsed."

65. For the final draft of the Pétain letter of 17 December, see *ADAP*, D, XI, 530. Regarding the "investigation," see ibid.; Abetz to Ribbentrop, 18 December 1940, ibid.

66. *ADAP*, D, XI, 531.

67. Abetz to Ribbentrop, 18 December 1940, ibid., 530; Welck to Foreign Ministry, Nr. 325, 21 December 1940, AA, StS, FF, II, 207446.

68. Quoted in Lequerica to Serrano Suñer, no. 1471, 18 December 1940, AMAE, L 2295, Ex 6.

69. Jacobsen, ed., *Halder Diary,* II, 18 December 1940.

70. Bankwitz, *Weygand,* 340–45, 349–50; Destremau, *Weygand,* 662–63, 677–82.

71. *DFCAA,* II, 455–56, n. 1.

72. *KTB/OKW,* I, 30 November 1940. Weygand, *Mémoires,* III, 461–65, says he opposed the ground plans (apparently of 29 November 1940) for geographic and logistical reasons, and Huntziger agreed with his objections. Yet Weygand's memoir account does not mention the 10 December planning for aerial assault.

73. *KTB/OKW,* I, 8 December 1940.

74. Memorandum by Warlimont, 12 December 1940, *ADAP,* D, XI, 506. Ribbentrop expected Weygand's recall to occur after Huntziger's comment. On 12 December, Abetz asked Ribbentrop if he should raise the issue in case the then-foreseen Ribbentrop-Laval meeting were to receive further delay. Abetz suggested the possibility of having Weygand detained in France or in Germany for a few months under the pretext of consultations with the German military. See Abetz to Ribbentrop, 12 December 1940, Abetz, *Pétain et les Allemands,* 42–43. No reply from Ribbentrop has been found.

75. For Warlimont's comments, see *KTB/OKW,* I, 2 December 1940.

76. Leahy arrived in Vichy on 5 January. In fact, the German assessment of his mission was rather accurate in that Roosevelt viewed Pétain as a pillar of possible resistance to German demands. See Admiral William D. Leahy, *I Was There,* 6 ff.; Julian G. Hurstfield, *America and the French Nation, 1939–1945,* 67–69; William L. Langer, *Our Vichy Gamble,* 118–20. The German assessment of the Murphy mission was also generally accurate. Murphy as the personal representative of Roosevelt was in French Africa from 18 December 1940 through 5 January 1941, and in his travels from Algiers to Dakar to Gau to Morocco he made contact with a number of high French military and civilian officials, including Weygand and Boisson. Weygand told Murphy that he would resist a German attack on French Africa, but it was also clear that the delegate-general had no intention of breaking with the marshal or of joining de Gaulle. The seeds of the March 1941 economic agreement between Murphy and Weygand for American economic aid to North Africa were planted at this time, however. See idem., 128–29, 138; Robert Murphy, *Diplomat among Warriors,* 66–81; Bankwitz, *Weygand,* 340–50. Murphy's movements in Africa are well covered in United States, Department of State, *Foreign Relations of the United States: Diplomatic Papers,* (hereafter cited as *FRUS*), 1940, vol. II, 622–23, 627–28, 632, 635–36.

77. Memorandum by Woermann, 18 December 1940, *ADAP,* D, XI, 529; memorandum by Altenburg, 24 December 1940, idem., 561 and n. 2. According to Murphy's later account, the German representative then in Casablanca, Dr. Theodor Auer, telephoned Murphy immediately after the latter's arrival in that city on 30 December 1940 and pressed him amid frequent cocktails for the reason behind his visit to Africa. See Murphy, *Diplomat,* 78.

78. *KTB/OKW,* I, 20 December 1940.

79. Abetz to Ribbentrop, 21 December 1940, *ADAP,* D, XI, 543.

80. Ribbentrop to Abetz, 21 December 1940, ibid., 546.

81. Pétain's letter is printed in ibid., 566.

82. Paul Stehlin, *Témoignage pour l'histoire,* 304.

83. For the protocol, see *ADAP,* D, XI, 564. There is also a brief memorandum by Admiral Darlan in Darlan, *Darlan Parle,* 263–67. See also Abetz's reports to Ribbentrop of 25 and 26 December 1940, *ADAP,* D, XI, 565, 569.

84. *ADAP,* D, XI, 569.

85. Hitler to Mussolini, 31 December 1940, ibid., 586.

86. *KTB/OKW,* I, 9 January 1941; Jacobsen, ed., *Halder Diary,* II, 16 January 1941.

87. See Jäckel, *Frankreich,* 152; Paxton, *Vichy France,* 101, n. 107, for Keitel's relay of this message on 10 January to General Georg Thomas, chief of the High Command's War Economy and Armaments Office. Thomas had wanted increased collaboration with French industry despite the recent political tensions. Yet it was no longer the German intent, wrote Keitel, to bring about collaboration with France by political discussions, concessions, or guarantees. Of course, added Keitel, the economic assets of the occupied area could still be plundered, while in the unoccupied area, Germany could invoke the preamble to the Armistice Convention as a pretext to take what it needed. See also *Jacobsen, ed., Halder Diary,* II, 16 and 28 January 1941. By 28 January Hitler was talking about keeping Laval in Paris for the eventuality of a colonial defection, total occupation of the *Metropole,* and the need to create an entirely new French government.

88. Rosenman, *Roosevelt Papers,* IX, 604–15; William L. Langer and S. Everett Gleason, *The Undeclared War, 1940–1941,* 213–51.

89. On 9 December 1940, the British under General Archibald Wavell opened their first desert offensive, ruining the Italian position at Sidi el Barrini. By 17 December the Italians had lost Sidi Omar and Sollum, and the British would take Tobruk by 22 January.

90. For the opinions of the War Economy and Armaments Office and the Naval Command, see *KTB/Skl.,* XVI, 16, 20 and 22 December 1940.

91. Ibid., XVII, 4, 7 January 1941.

92. Assmann, "Bemühungen," BA/MA, RM 8/1209, 26–27.

93. Weizsäcker to Ribbentrop, 8 January 1941, AA, StS, FF, III, 209358; *ADAP,* D, XI, 628. In Wiesbaden, Hemmen argued that Germany should not allow economic contact with Vichy to lapse, especially since the issues of the transport of gold from Dakar, the supply of colonial products, foreign border control, and aircraft contracts were still not completed. Ribbentrop approved Hemmen's negotiations, but purely on an economic level. See Hemmen to Ribbentrop, Nr. 22, 16 January 1941, AA, StS, FF, III, 209386–89; memorandum by Wiehl, 22 January 1941, *ADAP,* D, XI, 689.

94. Assmann, "Bemühungen," BA/MA, RM 8/1209, 22–23, 26–27; Hencke to Foreign Ministry, 6 January 1940, *ADAP,* D, XI, 609; Hemmen to Wiehl, 14 January 1941, idem., 654; memorandum by Grote, 8 January 1941, AA,

StS, FF, III, 209359–60; memorandum by Rintelen, 7 January 1941, AA, StS, FF, III, 209382–85; memorandum by Grote, 10 January 1941, idem., 209369–70; memorandum by Grote, 15 January 1941, idem., 209379–81.

95. Stülpnagel was assigned to the command of Seventeenth Army, which at that time had a relatively insignificant task of replacing the Twelfth Army in the *Generalgouvernement*. The first report of the transfer came on 12 February, and the actual change took place two days afterward. See memorandum by Grote, 12 February 1941, AA, StS, FF, III, 209458; memorandum by Grote, 15 February 1941, idem., 209461–62. The account in Heinrich Bücheler, *Carl-Heinrich von Stülpnagel*, 212–13, does not mention the possibility of political reasons for the change of assignment.

96. Memorandum by Grote, Pol. IM, 353 GRs, 14 February 1941, AA, StS, FF, III, 209459–60/II. This policy had really been in effect since Laval's dismissal. In mid-January, Germany had rejected Huntziger's 10 December request for the release of numerous colonial officers, along with a number of smaller petitions. *ADAP*, D, XI, 672.

97. The mission was first requested of the French delegation in Wiesbaden by Hemmen in October 1940. See Doyen to Stülpnagel, 21 March 1941, *DFCAA* IV, 210, n. 1. Exactly when Auer left Paris for Casablanca is unclear, but he reported to Hemmen on 8 December 1940 that he had made contact with Brinon about his trip to Casablanca and that he would probably leave for Casablanca within the week. See Auer to Hemmen, Nr. 1434, 8 December 1940, AA, DB Paris, Auer. The official name of his agency in Casablanca was the *Dienststelle des Auswärtigen Amtes für das Französische Protektorat Marokko* The status of this agency was raised to a General Consulate at the end of 1941, and Auer himself was raised to the rank of consul-general. The timing of the arrivals of Auer's associates, Consuls Klaube and Schellert, are unclear. According to a comment from Stülpnagel from 16 January, Klaube was in Casablanca on 31 October 1941, but no reports from him have been found. Schellert first receives mention in Auer's reports in late February 1941. See Stülpnagel to Doyen, 16 January 1941, *DFCAA*, III, 478–79; Hemmen to Foreign Ministry, Nr. Del. W. 97, 1 March 1941, AA, StS, Marokko, I, 58225. Regarding the true nature of the Auer mission, see idem., Hemmen to Foreign Ministry, Nr. Del. W. 95, 28 February 1941, idem., 58224. For a wild tale of Auer's aid to German agents in French Morocco, see Auer to Foreign Ministry, Pol. 254/41 GRs, 20 August 1941, AA, Abteilung Pol. IM, Abwehr-Afrika Bd. 7.41–8.44.; Auer to Foreign Ministry, Pol.2. Nr. 464141 GRs/Bericht Nr. 65, 17 December 1941 with enclosures, idem.

98. Friedens HWIX to Foreign Ministry, 15 December 1940, AA, StS, FF, II, 207430; Hemmen to Foreign Ministry, Del. Nr. 28, 19 January 1941, idem., 209395; Auer's report enclosed in AA/Pol. II to DB Paris, Pol. II 4209, 2 January 1941, AA, DB Paris, Französische Kolonien, Mandate, Protektorate, Kolonial Ministerium (hereafter cited as franz. Kolonien) bndl. 1312.

99. Auer's report is enclosed in AA/Pol. II to DB Paris, AA/Pol. II 37, 16 January 1941, AA, DB Paris, franz. Kolonien, bndl. 1312.

100. On the Munich discussions of 11 and 12 November 1940, see Neugebauer, *Militärkontrolle,* 122 and n. 7. On the protest from Wiesbaden and the further evolution of the German commission, see memorandum by Grote, Pol. IM, 705g Ang. III, 31 January 1941, AA, StS, FF, III, 209436. For Hitler's role, see memorandum by Grote, idem., 11 January 1941, 209371; *KTB/OKW,* I, 10 January 1941. See also *ADAP,* D, XI, 671, n. 2.

101. Memorandum by Grote, AA, StS, FF, III, 11 January 1941, 209371.

102. The text of the German note Nr. 184/41 signed by Colonel Hünermann, chief of the Armistice Commission's *Gruppe Rüstung,* is in Welck to Foreign Ministry, 25 March 1941, AA, StS, Marokko, I, 58232.

103. Doyen to Stülpnagel, 15 January 1941, *DFCAA,* III, 475–76. On the same day, the head of the French delegation's armament branch, M. Allier, raised similar complaints with Colonel Hünermann himself, again with the same argument that public opinion in Morocco could boil over with the presence of German control commissioners. Here the poignant argument was also raised that there was no war industry in Morocco to speak of and that the Italians already had an oil commission in Casablanca, thus negating the need for such a German commission. See idem., 476–78. Stülpnagel passed word to the German High Command in Berlin that the French were unhappy indeed about the German commission. See *KTB/OKW,* I, 16 January 1941.

104. Abetz to Foreign Ministry, 19 January 1941, *ADAP,* D, XI, 671. Weygand's own protests are mentioned in Weygand, *Mémoires,* III, 409. See also Destremau, *Weygand,* 663–65; Paxton, *Parades,* 221.

105. Hitler would mention Huntziger's petition to Mussolini on 19 January. See *ADAP,* D, XI, 672.

106. Stülpnagel to Doyen, 16 January 1941, *DFCAA,* III, 478–79. See also idem., 448.

107. Hünermann to French Delegation, 16 January 1941, ibid., 479–80.

108. Memorandum by Grote, 22 January 1941, AA, StS, FF, III, 209396–98. In a final appeal to Stülpnagel on 24 January 1941, Doyen expressed his hope that the German officers would act with discretion, that the German commission would remain as small as possible, and that the Italian commission would leave on the arrival of the Germans to give the appearance of a change in inspection responsibilities rather than that of an augmentation. He added the hope that the commission would truly focus on armament and fuel inspection and that it would leave Morocco once it had completed this task. See Doyen to Stülpnagel, 24 January 1941, *DFCAA,* IV, 5–6, n. 1.

109. Auer to German Armistice Commission, Nr. 14, 28 January 1941, AA, StS, Marokko, I, 58210–11. On the makeup and travel of the preliminary group, see Welck to Foreign Ministry, 25 March 1941, idem., 58232. See also the various memoranda by Grote between 11 and 31 January 1941, AA, StS, FF, III, 209371, 209390–91, 209396–89, 209415–57.

110. The charge of the *Rüstungs- und Mineralölkontrollkommission Marokko* is contained in memorandum by Grote, Pol. IM, 705g, 31 January 1941, AA, StS, FF, III, 209433–35. For the Italian agreement, see Hencke to Foreign

Ministry, 2 February 1941, idem., 209437. For armament and fuel stocks issues, the German commission would operate west of the foot of the High Atlas, while the Italian fuel commission would operate to the east. No mention was made on the delineation of responsibility of general military matters between the German armament and fuel commission in Casablanca and the Italian military commissions in Rabat and Fez, but the issue would be resolved soon by the exit of the Italian commissions. See also memorandum by Grote, 31 January 1941, idem., 209428–29; Neugebauer, *Militärkontrolle,* 126. The German liaison officers attached to the Italian fuel commissions in Algeria and Tunisia also had general political and military observatory functions that went above the mere observation of French fuel stocks. The actual order for the setup of these liaison officers and their charges was given on 1 February 1941, and the officers were given one week to prepare to leave for Africa. There were only four officers involved. See idem., 123–24.

111. Auer to German Armistice Commission, Nr. 14, 28 January 1941, AA, StS, Marokko, I, 58210–11.

112. These further comments of 28 January are enclosed in Hemmen to Foreign Ministry, 2 February 1941, AA, StS, FF, III, 209438. Auer's count of Italian officers in Morocco was probably fairly accurate. Weygand wrote later that upon his arrival in Algiers in October 1940, the Italians had in all of North Africa 200 men with 60 officers, and one would assume that due to Italian strategic and colonial interests, most of these officers were in Tunisia and Algeria. In January 1941, he says, there were roughly 570 Italians in all in North Africa, including consular and propaganda agents. See Weygand, *Mémoires,* III, 407.

113. Neugebauer, *Militärkontrolle,* 126–27.

114. On the increase in size of the commission, see memorandum by Grote, 11 January 1941, AA, StS, FF, III, 209371. Hencke to Foreign Ministry, Nr. 36, 2 February 1941, idem., 209437. A commission of this type was considered as early as mid-January, albeit in more inchoate form. Göring pressed firmly for the idea, and General von Waldau of the Luftwaffe Command noted at that time that Wiesbaden was working on the composition of three different commissions for work in Casablanca. See Neugebauer, *Militärkontrolle,* 128–30; *KTB/OKW,* I, 14 January 1941.

115. Memorandum by Grote, Pol. IM, 353 GRs, 14 February 1941, AA, StS FF, III, 209459–60/II.

116. Detwiler, *Gibraltar,* 89; Burdick, *Germany's Military Strategy,* 113–22.

117. Hubatsch, ed., *Weisungen,* 84–88.

118. *KTB/OKW,* I, 5 December 1940; Burdick, *Germany's Military Strategy,* 98–99.

119. Wagner, ed., *Lagevorträge,* 172–74.

120. *ADAP,* D, XI, 538.

121. Wagner, ed., *Lagevorträge,* 172–74. No such *démarche* by Ribbentrop has been found, but as will be seen, the Germans would present a very strong *démarche* to the Spaniards via Stohrer in Madrid.

122. *ADAP,* D, XI, 586.

123. *KTB/OKW,* I, 9 January 1941; Wagner, ed., *Lagevorträge,* 183; Jacobsen, ed., *Halder Diary,* II, 16 January 1940.

124. *KTB/OKW,* I, 10 January 1941.

125. *KTB/Skl.,* XVI, 28, 31 December 1940.

126. *KTB/OKW,* I, 18 January 1941. Halder heard a rumor on this day regarding the resurrection of *Felix,* but this was apparently premature. Jacobsen, ed., *Halder Diary,* II, 18 January 1941.

127. Knox, *Mussolini,* chapter 6.

128. Muggeridge, ed., *Ciano Papers,* 417–19.

129. *ADAP,* D, XI, 672; Muggeridge, ed., *Ciano Papers,* 419–20.

130. *ADAP,* D, XI, 679.

131. *KTB/OKW,* I, 20 January 1941; Hubatsch, ed., *Weisungen,* 96; Jacobsen, ed., *Halder Diary,* II, 20 January 1941.

132. Hubatsch, ed. *Weisungen,* 96–97; *KTB/OKW,* I, 21 January 1941; Jacobsen, ed., *Halder Diary,* II, 23 January 1941.

133. B. Nr. 1. Skl. I op. 73/41 gKdos. Chefs., 23 January 1941, BA/MA, RM 7/1002. See also *KTB/Skl.,* XVII, 22, 23 January 1941.

134. Hitler mentioned this theory to Raeder on 27 December 1940 and to Mussolini on 19 January 1941. See Wagner, ed., *Lagevorträge,* 172–74; *ADAP,* D, XI, 672.

135. Stohrer to Ribbentrop, Nr. 197, 20 January 1941, AA, StS, Spanien, II, 74584–45; Stohrer to Ribbentrop, 20 January 1941, *ADAP,* D, XI, 677.

136. Stohrer to Ribbentrop, Nr. 213, 21 January 1941, AA, StS, Spanien, II, 74592–93; Stohrer to Ribbentrop, Nr. 227, 22 January 1942, idem., 74598.

137. Ribbentrop to Stohrer, 21 January 1941, *ADAP,* D, XI, 682. Stohrer tried to have the words "end of Nationalist Spain" reworded by pointing out that they would only anger Franco. See idem., n. 2; Stohrer to Ribbentrop, Nr. 225, 22 January 1941, AA, StS, Spanien, II, 745987.

138. Stohrer to Ribbentrop, 23 January 1941, *ADAP,* D, XI, 692; Stohrer to Ribbentrop, 23 January 1941, idem., 695. On 25 January, Serrano provided Stohrer with an official answer to Ribbentrop's oral message, which in essence repeated Franco's arguments of 23 January. As will be seen, this Spanish answer came after Ribbentrop had already sent a second oral ultimatum. Germany, said the Spanish note of 25 January, had never understood the economic situation in Spain and had done nothing to contribute toward its alleviation. Spain meant to contribute meaningfully to the war, said the note, but needed time first for economic recovery. The Spanish note also disputed the German statement that Franco owed his entire position to the German and Italian dictators. See Stohrer to Ribbentrop, 25 January 1941, idem., 707; Stohrer to Ribbentrop, Nr. 286, 25 January 1941, AA, StS, Spanien, II, 74610.

139. Ribbentrop to Stohrer, 24 January 1941, *ADAP,* D, XI, 702.

140. Ibid., XII, 21. Franco's discussions with Mussolini are covered below.

141. Ribbentrop had commented in the first oral message that the capture of Gibraltar would open for Spain a route to Africa. He must have raised eye-

brows in Madrid, since Spain had had no trouble getting to Africa before.

142. Ribbentrop to Stohrer, 28 January 1941, *ADAP*, D, XI, 725; Stohrer to Ribbentrop, 29 January 1941, idem., 728.

143. *KTB/OKW*, I, 28 January 1941. For the resurrection of *Felix* in High Command headquarters, see Burdick, *Germany's Military Strategy*, 117–19.

144. *ADAP*, D, XII, 17.

145. Ibid., 22.

146. Franco to Hitler, 26 February 1941, ibid., 95 and n. 7.

147. For the invitation itself, which Ciano wrote on 22 January, see Muggeridge, ed., *Ciano Papers*, 420. For the problem of its delivery and Serrano's reply, see Tusell and Queipo de Llano, *Franco y Mussolini*, 119.

148. Muggeridge, ed., *Ciano Papers*, 422–26; memorandum by Weizsäcker, 14 February 1941, *ADAP*, D, XII, 49; Tusell and Queipo de Llano, *Franco y Mussolini*, 120–22.

149. As Franco mentioned to Mussolini, the Spanish government had on 7 February presented Stohrer with a list of these requirements, which included, among other tremendous estimates, one million tons of grain, 8,000 trucks, 16,000 railroad cars, 400 antiaircraft guns, and three squadrons of aircraft. For Stohrer's description of the list, see Stohrer to Ribbentrop, 7 February 1941, *ADAP*, D, XII, 28. Franco told Mussolini at Bordighera that if Germany fulfilled the list, then Spain would indeed enter the war. Whether Franco expected Berlin to acquiesce is at this point another matter.

150. Abetz to Ribbentrop, 15 February 1941, ibid., 56. No mention of the African issue as discussed at Montpellier was found in the Spanish records. Lequerica's report of a follow-up discussion with Darlan recalls only the admiral's outlook on the war in general. See Lequerica to Serrano Suñer, no. 114, 18 February 1941, AMAE, L 2295, Ex 6.

151. Stohrer to Ribbentrop, 17 January 1941, *ADAP*, D, XII, 62.

152. There were also strong rumors at the time that the British government would support a border rectification in Morocco following the war. See Stohrer to Foreign Ministry, 26 February 1941, ibid., 90; Stohrer to Foreign Ministry, 28 February 1941, ibid., 104. Ambassador Hoare had in fact informed General Muñoz Grandes on 15 October 1940 that Great Britain recognized Spanish claims in Morocco and that London would welcome a Spanish occupation of the entire area. Hoare also said that discussions on Gibraltar would have to come later. See memorandum by Muñoz Grandes to Franco, 15 October 1940, Archivo de la Presidencia del Gobierno, Jefatura del Estado, L 1, Ex 6.2.

153. José María Doussinague (general secretary of Spanish Foreign Ministry) to Conde de Jordana y Souza (foreign minister since 3 September 1942), 17 September 1942, AMAE, L 1913, Ex 6; "Conversación del Señor Doussiague con el Embajador de Francia, día 26 septiembre 1942," idem., L 1686, Ex 4.

154. Ibid., L 1686, Ex 4, passim.

155. See memorandum by Wiehl, 12 February 1941, *ADAP*, D, XII, 46, which echoes this interpretation with the comment that the main parts of the Spanish list of material requests of the previous week, "are so obviously unrealiz-

able that they can only be evaluated as an expression of the effort to avoid entering the war under this pretext."

156. Ibid., 73.

157. Ibid., 110.

158. Ibid., 117.

159. B. Nr. 1. Skl. I op. gKdos. Chefs., 14 February 1941, BA/MA, RM 7/1002.

160. *KTB/Skl.*, XVIII, 17 February 1941.

161. Ibid., 22 February 1941.

Chapter 9. Passing the Torch

1. See his comments to Ciano on 25 October 1941, *ADAP*, D, XIII, 424.

2. Bötticher to Halder, Canaris, and Jeschonnek, 11 March 1941, ibid., XII, 148.

3. Hitler discussion with Matsuoka, 27 March 1941, ibid., 222. Hitler repeated to Mussolini on 2 June that America aircraft production aims were greatly exaggerated. See ibid., 584.

4. Weizsäcker to Ribbentrop, 12 April 1941, ibid., 316; memorandum by Ritter, 9 June 1941, ibid., 608; Wagner, ed., *Lagevorträge*, 190–96, 202–203, 219–20, 263, 264–65, 271.

5. *ADAP*, D, XII, 451, 542. Hitler also toyed in the spring of 1941 with sending Hjalmar Schacht on a propaganda tour of the United States. See Weinberg, *World in the Balance*, 67.

6. Hubatsch, ed., *Weisungen*, 103–105.

7. For the memoranda of the Matsuoka discussions, see *ADAP*, D, XII, 218, 222, 230, 233, 266. For interpretation of the German declaration of war on the United States, see Weinberg, *World in the Balance*, 85–86.

8. Burdick, *Germany's Military Strategy*, 122–24; Jacobsen, ed., *Halder Diary*, II, 317; Operationsabteilung II a, Nr. _/41 gKdos., 10 March 1941, enclosed in Chef der Operationsabteilung to Halder, 11 March 1941, BA/MA, RH 2/439.

9. Darlan would also recreate Weygand's old Ministry of Defense in August 1940 and place himself at its head. See Paxton, *Vichy France*, 109–10.

10. On Darlan's "Grand Design," see ibid., 109–14.

11. Abetz to Ribbentrop, 13 January 1941, *ADAP*, D, XI, 645. See also Ribbentrop to Abetz, 19 January 1941, idem., 673; Abetz to Ribbentrop, 19 January 1941, idem., 674; Abetz to Ribbentrop, 31 January 1941, idem., 736; memorandum by Ritter, 22 January 1941, idem., 690; Jacobsen, ed., *Halder Diary*, II, 28 January 1941.

12. See Ribbentrop to Abetz, 11 February 1941, *ADAP*, D, XII, 44 and n. 1, 2. See also the instructions to the courier of Ribbentrop's note of inquiry in idem., 43.

13. Wagner, ed., *Lagevorträge*, 201–208. On 25 March, Hitler repeated to Ciano his distrust for Vichy, complaining that he could do nothing at this point. "It was a question," he said, "of avoiding as long as possible anything that could

lead to North Africa's being detached from Metropolitan France." See *ADAP,* D, XII, 208.

14. Abetz to Ribbentrop, 4 April 1941, Abetz, *Pétain et les Allemands,* 79–84; Abetz to Ribbentrop, April 1941, idem., 91–96.

15. Memorandum of 25 April, ibid., 96–98.

16. Jäckel, *Frankreich,* 161.

17. Otto Abetz, *Das offene Problem,* 186. This view is shared by Paxton, *Vichy France,* 116–17.

18. On the coup in Iraq and its immediate aftershocks, see Ian Stanley Ord Playfair, *The Mediterranean and the Middle East,* II, 177–97; Geoffrey Warner, *Iraq and Syria 1941,* 67–122; Philipp Schröder, *Irak 1941,* 18–40.

19. Jäckel, *Frankreich,* 161–62; Warner, *Iraq and Syria,* 98–100; Schröder, *Irak,* 64–65.

20. This is the interpretation of Jäckel for Hitler's sudden change of heart. See Jäckel, *Frankreich,* 161–2.

21. Ribbentrop to Keitel, 28 April 1941, *ADAP,* D, XII, 421.

22. Ibid., 422. In May, Serrano Suñer was heard to say that a German march through Spain would meet determined resistance. Stohrer to Foreign Ministry, Nr. 1486, 1 May 1941, AA, StS, Spanien, II, 74808; Stohrer to Foreign Ministry, 4 May 1941, *ADAP,* D, XII, 453.

23. Memorandum by Woermann, 3 May 1941, *ADAP,* D, XII, 442.

24. Abetz to Ribbentrop, Abetz, *Pétain et les Allemands,* 99–100.

25. Abetz to Ribbentrop, 5 May 1941, *ADAP,* D, XII, 459; memorandum by Wiehl, 8 May 1941, idem., 475.

26. Ibid., 490.

27. Ibid., 491.

28. Ibid., 499.

29. Ibid., 511; Muggeridge, ed., *Ciano Diary,* 13, 14 May 1941.

30. Abetz to Ribbentrop, 15 May 1941, *ADAP,* D, XII, 520 and n. 10. Abetz floated the idea of a French attack on Bathurst and Freetown and French naval support in operations against Gibraltar and the Canary Islands, but Ribbentrop shelved these ideas.

31. Jäckel, *Frankreich,* 168–69.

32. Brief memoranda of the meetings of 21 May that covered the Syrian and North African questions are in *DFCAA,* IV, 460.

33. Chef L. Nr. 3/41 gKdos. Chefs., 22 May 1941, BA/MA, RW 4/707.

34. Wagner, ed., *Lagevorträge,* 227–39. On 3 June 1941 at the Brenner, Hitler mentioned to Mussolini that by the end of the year Germany would have a number of such bombers. *ADAP,* D, XII, 584.

35. Abetz to Foreign Ministry, *ADAP,* D, XII, 546.

36. See Warlimont's Nr. 6/41 gKdos. Chefs., 24 May 1941, BA/MA, RW 4/707. According to Benoist-Méchin, Darlan had on 23 May ordered Boisson to list all unreliable French and foreign elements in Dakar. Benoist-Méchin also reported that Darlan intended to have Boisson re-swear in all officers there.

37. *DFCAA,* IV, 461–62.

38. Ibid., 462, 464–69.

39. Ibid., 469–72.

40. The texts of the protocols are printed in *ADAP,* D, XII, 559; *DFCAA,* IV, 472–80.

41. OKM/Skl. B. Nr. 1. Skl. I ga 939/41 gKdos. Chefs., 12 June 1941, BA/MA, RM 7/845; OKM/Skl. Ik 974/41 Op. Chefs., 14 June 1941, idem.; OKM/1. Abt. Skl. Ic 12834/41, 18 June 1941, idem. These measures would still have left one German tanker in Las Palmas.

42. Welck to Foreign Ministry, 10 June 1941, *ADAP,* D, XII, 610.

43. Weygand, *Mémoires,* III, 428–38; Paxton, *Parades,* 233–34; Jäckel, *Frankreich,* 174–75.

44. For these talks between Vogl, Böhme, Abetz and Benoist-Méchin on 10–12 June, see *DFCAA,* IV, 563, 566–71; Abetz to Ribbentrop, 11 June 1941, *ADAP,* D, XII, 616; Jäckel, *Frankreich,* 175–76.

45. Paxton, *Vichy France,* 121–23.

46. Keitel to Ribbentrop, 15 June 1941, *ADAP,* D, XII, 633; memorandum by Ritter, 26 June 1941, idem., XIII, 24; Ribbentrop to Keitel, 27 June 1941, idem., 31; memorandum by Wiehl, Dir. Ha. Pol. Nr. 155, 21 June 1941, AA, StS, FF, III, 209719–20; memorandum by Wiehl, Dir. Ha. Pol. Nr. 158, 24 June 1941, idem. 209741–43.

47. *ADAP,* D, XII, 584.

48. Hubatsch, ed., *Weisungen,* 129–34. This draft, as was customary, was signed by Warlimont and not Hitler. This procedure for the drafting of Hitler's war directives in Warlimont's department was standard, and is no reason to reject the correct hypothesis that the orders contained in the directive indeed came from Hitler himself. See Karl Klee, "Der Entwurf zur Führerweisung Nr. 32 vom 11 Juni 1941: Eine quellenkritische Untersuchung," 127–41.

49. Hitler's brief agreement to lower occupation costs from twenty to ten million marks a day was tempered by the condition that three million marks daily come in gold, securities, and foreign exchange. See Abetz to Ribbentrop, Nr. 569, 30 June 1941, AA, StS, FF, III, 211169.

50. *ADAP,* D, XII, 660.

51. Keitel to Ribbentrop, 2 July 1941, ibid., XIII, 61.

52. Wagner, ed., *Lagevorträge,* 265–71.

53. See Hitler's comments of 21 June and 9 July 1941 in ibid., 263–64.

54. Jacobsen, ed., *Halder Diary,* III, 3 July 1941; Oberquartiermeister I des Generalstab des Heeres Nr. 430/41 gKdos. Chefs., 3 July 1941, BA/MA, RH 2/1520.

55. Wagner, ed., *Lagevorträge,* 230, 263.

56. Skl. B. Nr. 1. Skl. IIIa 17233/41 gKdos., 31 July 1941, BA/MA, RM 6/83. Planning for new expanded wharves for postwar shipbuilding in sites other than Trondheim was also moving forward at this time. See Hauptamt Kriegsschiffbau KVT 1572/41 gKdos., 2 August 1941, idem. See also Weinberg, *World in the Balance,* 89–90.

57. Skl. Qu. A. Sf. 6255/42 gKdos., July 1942, BA/MA, RM 6/83.

58. Wagner, ed., *Lagevorträge,* 263, 264.

59. Quoted in Herwig, *Frustration,* 224.

60. Quoted in ibid., 228.

61. Wagner, ed., *Lagevorträge,* 264–71.

62. Ribbentrop to Ritter, Nr. 645, 13 July 1941, AA, Handakte Ritter, Azoren; Thermann (Buenos Aires) to Foreign Ministry, 27 July 1941, idem.; Huene to Foreign Ministry, Nr. 1630, 28 July 1941, idem.

63. Esebeck to General Gerhard Matzky (Fremde Heere West, Oberquartiermeister IV), 12 May 1941, BA/MA, RH 2/2929.

64. German reports said that the Portuguese were also strengthening their air defenses. See OKH, GenStdH, Abt. Fremde Heere West/IV, Lagebericht(e) West, Nrs. 477 (20 May 1941), 486 (10 June 1941), 504 (3 July 1941), 511 (26 July 1941), 520 (11 September 1941), AA, Handakte Hasso von Etzdorf.

65. On the Sakowski affair, see Deutsche Gesandschaft (Lisbon)/Der Marine-attaché/Mar. Nr. 2009g, 6 November 1942, BA/MA, RW 5/429; Huene to Foreign Ministry, Nr. 8134/42 II, 12 October 1942, idem.; Deutsche Gesandschaft/Der Militärattaché Nr. 41/42 gKdos., 20 July 1942, BA/MA, RH 2/2929; HQu. OKH Nr. 1739/42 gKdos., 1 August 1942, idem. The Germans also had no more than an honorary consul on Madeira.

66. *ADAP,* D, XIII, 523. Serrano did not mention how the Spaniards proposed to launch this attack.

67. Klaus-Jörg Ruhl, *Spanien im zweiten Weltkrieg,* 124 and n. 5.

68. See the German army intelligence report of the following March, Generalstab des Heeres Abt. Fremde Heere West Nr. 632/42 gKdos. Chefs., 1 March 1942, RH 2/1521. This comprehensive report on Western defenses also places 30,000 troops in the Canary Islands. See also Stohrer to Foreign Ministry, 20 January 1942, *ADAP,* E, I, 149.

69. *ADAP,* E, I, 149; Stohrer to Foreign Ministry, 29 September 1942, idem., III, 323; Stohrer to Foreign Ministry, Nr. 3155 GRs, 14 April 1942, AA, DB Madrid, Meldungen über Landungsabsichten der Allierten (Schaffung einer 2. Front) (hereafter cited as "Meldungen"); Stohrer to Foreign Ministry, unnumbered, 6 November 1942, idem.; Grote to DB Madrid, Pol. IM, (Att.) 7680g, 28 October 1942 and enclosures, idem. Colonel Remer, the representative in Tangier of Colonel Günther Krappe, the German military attaché in Madrid, further reported in September 1942 that the Spaniards had concentrated strong forces on the southwestern border of Spanish Morocco. See idem; Remer to Krappe, Nr. 155/42 geh., 28 September 1942, idem.

70. See Stohrer to Foreign Ministry, 3 April 1942, *ADAP,* E, III, 108; Stohrer to Foreign Ministry, 29 September 1942, idem., 323. See also Amt Ausland/Abwehr, Abt. Ausland, Nr. 643/42 gKdos. Ib, 23 April 1942 and enclosures, BA/MA, RW 5/429; Stohrer to Foreign Ministry, Nr. 5632/4, 4 November 1942, AA, DB Madrid, "Meldungen"; Stohrer to Foreign Ministry, Nr. 5664/5, 5 November 1942, idem.; Stohrer to Foreign Ministry, unnumbered, 6 November 1942, idem.

71. See Amt Ausland/Abwehr, Abt. Ausland Nr. 1696/42 geh. Ib, 4 June 1942 and enclosures, BA/MA, RW 5/429. See also Weizsäcker to Stohrer, Nr. 3907/8, 8 October 1942, AA, DB Madrid, "Meldungen."

72. Stohrer to Foreign Ministry, 6 November 1942, AA, DB Madrid, "Meldungen."

73. Auswärtiges Amt Nr. 339 GRs, 21 November 1942, ibid.

74. Hemmen to Foreign Ministry, Nr. Del. W. 97, 1 March, 1941, AA, StS, Marokko, I, 58225.

75. Canaris to Ritter, 14 May 1942, AA, Abt Pol. IM, Abwehr-Afrika, 2.42–1.44. On the problem of balancing German business and espionage interests in Morocco, see the file cited above as well as Abetz to Foreign Ministry, Nr. 2580, 30 August 1941, AA, StS, Marokko, I, 58287; Abetz to Foreign Ministry, 15 May 1941, ADAP, D, XII, 520.

76. In general, see Neugebauer, *Militärkontrolle*, 128–30. See also Hencke to Foreign Ministry, Nr. 36, 2 February 1941, AA, StS, FF, III, 209437; memorandum by Grote, 8 February 1941, idem., 209447–50; memorandum by Grote, 20 February 1941, idem., 209465–66; memorandum by Grote, 7 March 1941, idem., 209487–89; memorandum by Grote, Pol. IM, 1641g, 7 March 1941, idem., 209490–91.

77. DWStK Gruppe Wehrmacht/Ia, Nr. 401/41 geh. II. Ang., 10 October 1941, BA/MA, RW 34/116. For an organizational chart, see Neugebauer, *Militärkontrolle*, 167. *KIA* would also command new liaison delegations with Italian agencies in Algeria and Tunisia.

78. Memorandum by Grote, 20 February 1941, AA, StS, FF, III, 209465–66. Boselli assumed his post in Algiers in August 1940, before Weygand became delegate-general there.

79. Memorandum by Grote, 8 February 1941, ibid., 209447–50; memorandum by Grote, 11 February 1941, ibid., 209453–55; memorandum by Grote, 1 March 1941, ibid., 209477–78; memorandum by Grote, Pol. IM, 1641g, 7 March 1941, ibid., 209490–91; memorandum by Grote, 25 March 1941, ibid., 209520–22; memorandum by Grote, 2 April 1941, ibid., 209535–36; Jacobsen, ed., *Halder Diary*, II, 291. See also Senger, "Waffenstillstand," 19–20; Neugebauer, *Militärkontrolle*, 129–30.

80. These latter German commissions were of course never created. For the final delineation agreement, see memorandum by Grote, Pol. IM, 2824g, 29 April 1941, AA, DB Rom, Frankreich auch franz. Kolonien.

81. Memorandum by Grote, 8 February 1941, AA, StS, FF, III, 209447–50; memorandum by Grote, 25 March 1941, idem., 209520–22; Hencke to Foreign Ministry, Nr. 1067, 1 April 1941, idem., 209529–34; memorandum by Grote, 8 April 1941, idem., 209545–56; Abetz to Foreign Ministry, Nr. 1034, 1 April 1941, StS, Marokko, I, 58237–40. The German Armistice Commission solved the problem by issuing ultimatums to the French delegation and claiming extraterritoriality for commission members.

82. Abetz to Foreign Ministry, Nr. 927, 21 March 1941, AA, StS, FF, III, 209516–

18; *DFCAA,* IV, 287–88; Hemmen to Foreign Ministry, 26 March 1941, AA, StS, Marokko, I, 58234.

83. Huntziger to Darlan, 17 March 1941, *DFCAA,* IV, 287–88.

84. Abetz to Foreign Ministry, Nr. 927, 21 March 1941, AA, StS, FF, III, 209516–18.

85. Doyen to Vogl, 21 March 1941, *DFCAA,* IV, 210–12, n. 1. Stülpnagel's statement of 16 January 1941 is printed in idem., III, 478–79.

86. Memorandum by Grote, 25 March 1941, AA, StS, FF, III, 209529–34.

87. *DFCAA,* VI, 289–91. The German text is included in Hencke to Foreign Ministry, Nr. 1067, 1 April 1941, AA, StS, FF, III, 209529–34.

88. Abetz to Foreign Ministry, Nr. 1034, 1 April 1941, AA, StS Marokko, I, 58237–40. See also the note from Darlan's office to Weygand of 2 April 1941 in *DFCAA,* IV, 291–92.

89. Hencke to Foreign Ministry, Nr. 1067, 1 April 1941, AA, StS, FF, 209529–34. French protests would continue well into the month. For Weygand's call to the government to refuse the German demand, see Weygand to Darlan, 3 April 1941, *DFCAA,* VI, 292; Weygand to General Louis Koeltz, 19 April 1941, idem., 292–93; Paxton, *Parades,* 222–23. For later protests by Noguès, see idem.; Hoisington, *Casablanca,* 201. For Doyen's dramatic protest of 18 April 1941, see *DFCAA,* IV, 317.

90. Klaube to Foreign Ministry, Nr. 50, 4 April 1941, AA, StS, Marokko, I, 58241–43. For similar objections by Auer and Lieutenant Colonel Pietri of the armament and fuel commission, see Neugebauer, *Militärkontrolle,* 135–36 and n. 43.

91. On the French acceptance, see memorandum by Grote, 17 April 1941, AA, StS, FF, III, 209550; memorandum by Grote, 21 April 1940, idem., 209553–54. On the assumption of control, see memorandum by Grote, 23 April 1940, idem., 209555–57; *DFCAA,* IV, 409.

92. A. Ausl./Abw. B. Nr. 12 887/42g IM West S, 26 January 1942, AA, Pol. IM, Abwehr-Afrika, 7.41–8.44; Pol. II to Pol. IM, 834 GRs, 24 June 1942, idem.

93. Auer to DB Paris, Pol. II, Westafrika, Nr. 524/42, 16 April 1942, enclosure 2 of DB Paris to Foreign Ministry, Nr. 4056/42, 30 April 1942, AA, DB Paris, franz. Kolonien, Bd. 3, bndl. 1326.

94. The above figures come from the November 1941 study, "Das franz. Übergangsheer in Marokko," which *KIA* compiled on a working basis and which was to be updated periodically. For the study, see BA/MA, RW 34/138. In September 1942, the German army control commission reckoned with 45,312 men in the regular army units, which was 4 percent under the permitted strength, plus 5,246 men in the various allowed supplementary units. See K.K. Heer Br.B. Nr. 435/42g, 4 October 1942, BA/MA, RW 34/131.

95. Auszug aus Studie der K.I. Afrika vom 28.5 [1942] über franz. Abwehrmöglichkeiten bei engl. amerik. Angriff auf Marokko, BA/MA, RM 7/255.

96. Commandement Superieur de l'Air en Afrique du Nord/Commandement de l'Air au Maroc/Etat-Major no. 15054/4 A., 4 November 1942, BA/MA, RW 34/196. See also the undated German strength charts, Flugzeugbestand der

Luftwaffen Einheiten in Marokko, BA/MA, RW 34/195. See also the un-dated chart, "Nordafrika: Verbände der Fliegertruppe," BA/MA, RW 34/189.

97. The above is a composite summary gathered from the general order to *KIA* contained in DWStK Gruppe Wehrmacht/Ia, Nr. 401/41 geh. II Ang., 10 Octo-ber 1941, BA/MA, RW 34/116, and the monthly army inspection reports contained in RW 34/130 and RW 34/131.

98. On Béthouart, see Paxton, *Parades,* 224, 337–38, 350, 418.

99. See for example K.K.(Tr. Heer) Oberstlt. v. Loßnitzer, Sammel-Kontrollberichte für die Zeit vom 30.5–21.6.41., 22 June 1941, BA/MA, RW 34/130.

100. The Germans began inspecting the Rif in August 1941 regardless of French protests, and without incident. On this affair, see K.K. Heer Kommandeur Sammel-Kontollbericht für die Zeit vom 22.6.41–12.7.41, 13 July 1941, idem.; K.I. Afrika Br.B. Nr. 1542/41geh., 8 August 1941, ibid.; K.K. Heer Kommandeur Br.B. Nr. 610/41, 1 September 1941, idem.

101. Der Vorsitzende der DWStK Gruppe Heer II, Nr. 5500/41, 21 November 1941, BA/MA, RW 34/117.

102. K.K. Heer Kommandeur Br.B. Nr. 610/41, 1 September 1941, BA/MA, RW 34/117; K.I. Afrika Ia, Br.B. Nr. 1765/41 geh. 18 September 1941, BA/MA, RW 34/130.

103. Der Vorsitzende der DWStK Gruppe Heer II, Nr. 5500/41, 21 November 1941, BA/MA, RW 34/117.

104. K.I. Afrika Ia, Az. D. Br.B. Nr. 2039/41 geh., 9 October 1941, BA/MA, RW 34/130.

105. K.I. Afrika Ia, Nr. 1213/42, 13 March 1942, BA/MA, RW 34/195. Wühlisch arrived in Casablanca to relieve Schultheiss on 13 January 1942. The official transfer was made on 22 December 1941. See KIA Ia, Inspektionsbefehl Nr. 1, 5 January 1942, BA/MA, RW 34/125; KIA Abteilung IIa/IIb Az. 13, 12 Janu-ary 1942, ibid.

106. Hemmen to Foreign Ministry, Nr. Del. W. 137, 26 March 1941, AA, StS, Marokko, I, 58223; Auer to Foreign Ministry, Nr. 80, 19 June 1941, idem., 58257–58; Foreign Ministry memorandum, Nr. 295 GRs, 15 July 1941, idem., 58267; Sonnenhol to Foreign Ministry, Nr. 163, 14 July 1942, idem., 58354; Sonnenhol to Foreign Ministry, Nr. 164, 16 July 1942, idem., 58355–56. Darlan had in fact complained to Abetz in Paris in April 1941 about exces-sive German contact with the natives. Abetz to Foreign Ministry, Nr. 1034, 1 April 1941, idem., 58237–40. Paxton, *Parades,* 225, adds that Weygand had actually had two Arab informants executed.

107. Leon Borden Blair, "Amateurs in Diplomacy: The American Vice-Consuls in North Africa, 1941–3," 607–20.

108. Auer to Foreign Ministry, Nr. 138, 26 June 1942, AA, StS, Marokko, I, 58349–50; Abetz to Foreign Ministry, Nr. 24, 2 June 1942, idem., 58335–36. This demand, had Laval honored it, would also have eliminated the American Consulate at Dakar, which had been opened in September 1940. Abetz also demanded French restrictions on American trips to Morocco, as well as mail inspection, and complained about the American goods deliveries. On Auer's

complaints on American activity in Morocco, see Auer to Foreign Ministry, Pers R Nr. 138/42, 4 February 1942, AA, DB Paris, franz. Kolonien, Bd. 3, bndl. 1325.

109. Hoisington, *Casablanca*, 220–21. Auer to Foreign Ministry, Nr. 138, 26 June 1942, AA, StS, Marokko, I, 58349–50.

110. Auer to Foreign Ministry Pol. 225/41, 9 August 1941, enclosed in Foreign Ministry to DB Paris Pol. II 2279, 21 August 1941, AA, DB Paris, franz. Kolonien, Bd. 3, bndl. 1325; Sonnenhol to DB Paris, 18 April 1942, idem., Bd. 3, bndl. 1326.

111. K.I. Afrika Ia, Az. A2. Br.B. Nr. 2384/41 geh., 13 November 1941, BA/MA, RW 34/117.

112. On this issue, see K.K. Heer Kommandeur Br.B. Nr. 595/41, 4 August 1941, BA/MA, RW 34/130; K.K. Heer Kommandeur Br.B. Nr. 610/41, 1 September 1941, idem.; K.I. Afrika Ia, Br.B. Nr. 2072/41g, 10 October 1941, idem.; K.I. Afrika Ia, Br.B. Nr. 2281/41g, 8 November 1941, idem; K.K. Heer Br.B. Nr. 709/41g, 4 November 1941, idem.; K.K. Heer Marokko Br.B. Nr. 755/41g, 1 December 1941, idem.; K.I. Afrika Ia, Nr. 2539/41g, 6 December 1941, idem. See also BA/MA, RW 34/147, passim.

113. K.U.K. I Heer Marokko Br.B. Nr. 91/42, 11 June 1942, BA/MA, RW 34/117. Numerous examples of red herrings can be found in this file.

114. K.I. Afrika Ia, Az. Nr. 2063 geh., 10 August 1942, BA/MA, RW 34/130.

115. On Noguès's comments, see for example Auer to Foreign Ministry, Nr. 80, 19 June 1941, AA, StS, Marokko, I, 58257–58. The report on Béthouart in June 1942 read, "Doubtless a man not resigned to present conditions and believes he will still play a role in the future." See K.K. Heer Marokko Br.B. Nr. 255g, 1 June 1942, BA/MA, RW 34/130. For the positive German impression of the other divisional commanders and troop morale, see K.K. Heer Marokko Br.B. Nr. 110/42, 4 March 1942, idem; DWStK Gruppe Marine B. Nr. 1596/42 gKdos., 31 May 1942, BA/MA, RM 7/255; Auszug aus Studie der K.I. Afrika vom 28.5 über franz. Abwehrmöglichkeiten bei engl. amerik. Angriff auf Marokko, idem.

116. Numerous examples of troop movement, training, and equipment replacement can be found in BA/MA, RW 34/130, RW 34/131, passim.

117. Auszug aus dem Turiner Protokoll, 29 March 1941, BA/MA, RW 34/195.

118. Truppenkontrollkommission der Kontrollinspektion Afrika, unnumbered report to *KIA*, 26 June 1941, BA/MA, RW 34/197; K.K. Lw. Br.B. Nr. 3/41 II, 24 June 1941, idem.; K.K. Lw. _/41, 15 July 1941, idem.; Ausbildungstätigkeit der französischen Luftwaffe in Marokko, BA/MA, RW 34/195.

119. DWStK Gruppe Luftwaffe Abt. I, Nr. 1118/41, 7 July 1941, BA/MA, RW 34/197.

120. DWStK Gruppe Luftwaffe Abt. I, Nr. 1865/41, 13 November 1941, ibid.

121. DWStk Gruppe Luftwaffe II, Nr. 2093/41, 15 December 1941, ibid.; DWStK Gruppe Luftwaffe II, Nr. 1416/41, 26 August 1941, ibid.; Bewaffnung der Flugzeuge bei den Verbände Marokkos, 19 December 1941, ibid.

122. K.K. (Tr. Heer) Oberstlt. v. Loßnitzer, Sammel-Kontrollberichte für die Zeit v. 30.5.–21.6.41, 22 June 1941, ibid., RW 34/130.

123. The German army control commission reported in the spring of 1941 that
     troops spent most of their time on road building detail and noticed in No-
     vember that troop training did not occur above the battalion level. Still, the
     Germans noted improvements in this trend over the course of 1942. In March
     regimental exercises were observed, and in April the French began to plan
     exercises between army and air force units. See K.K. (Tr. Heer) Oberstlt. v.
     Loßnitzer, Sammel-Kontrollberichte für die Zeit v. 30.5.–21.6.41, 22 June
     1941, ibid.; K.I. Afrika Ia, Nr. 2539/41g, 6 December 1941, ibid.; K.K. Heer
     Marokko Br.B. Nr. 170/42g, 2 April 1942, ibid.; K.K. Heer Marokko Br.B.
     Nr. 225/42, 4 May 1942, ibid.; K.I. Afrika Ia, Az. Nr. 1265/42 geh., 7 May
     1942, ibid.

124. On troop movements to the coast in the summer of 1942, see K.K. Heer
     Marokko Br.B. Nr. 225/42g, 4 May 1942, ibid.; K.I. Afrika Ia, Az. Nr. 255/
     42 geh., 1 June 1942, ibid.; K.K. Heer Marokko Br.B. Nr. 340/42g, 4 August
     1942, ibid. On general exercises and German impressions, see K.K. Heer
     Br.B. Nr. 371/42g, 4 September 1942, ibid.

125. K.K. Heer Marokko Br.B. Nr. 311/42, 4 July 1942, ibid.; K.K. Heer Marokko
     Br.B. Nr. 255/42g, 1 June 1942, ibid; K.K. Heer Marokko Br.B. Nr. 311/42,
     4 July 1942, ibid.; K.K. Heer Marokko Br.B. Nr. 340/42g, 4 August 1942,
     ibid.; K.K. Heer Br.B. Nr. 435/42g, 4 October 1942, ibid.

126. K.K. Heer Marokko Br.B. Nr. 5/42 geh., 4 January 1942, ibid; K.I. Afrika Ia,
     Br.B. Nr. 92/42 geh., 9 January 1942, ibid.

127. K.U.K. I Heer Marokko Br.B. Nr. 61/42g, 29 April 1942, BA/MA, RW 34/117;
     K.K. Heer Marokko Br.B. Nr. 170/42g, 2 April 1942, BA/MA, RW 34/130.

128. K.K. Heer Br.B. Nr. 371/42g, 4 September 1942, BA/MA, RW 34/130.

129. On the training, see K.I. Afrika, Verbindungskommando Nordafrika Algier
     Br.B. Nr. 1142/42, 1 June 1942, BA/MA, RW 34/197. On Darlan's comment,
     see DWStK Gruppe Wehrmacht Ia, Nr. 10 gKdos. Chefs., 10 November 1942,
     and enclosure, BA/MA, RW 34/10.

130. K.K. Heer Marokko Br.B. Nr. 110/42, 4 March 1942, BA/MA, RW 34/130;
     K.K. Heer Marokko Br.B. Nr. 371/42, 4 September 1942, BA/MA, RW 34/
     131.

131. Anlage zu K.I. Afrika Abt. Ia, Br.B. Nr. 52/42 gKdos., 20 May 1942, BA/MA,
     RW 34/117.

132. For Wever's report, see DWStK Gruppe Marine B. Nr. 1596/42 gKdos., 31 May
     1942, BA/MA, RM 7/255. Wever's group was in Morocco from 8 May through
     17 May 1942.

133. Auszug aus Studie der K.I. Afrika vom 28.5 über franz. Abwehrmöglichkeiten
     bei engl. amerik. Angriff auf Marokko, BA/MA, RM 7/255.

134. K.I. Afrika Abt. Ia, Az. A2 Nr. 1434/42g, 25 May 1942, enclosed in K.K.
     Heer Marokko Br.B. Nr. 254/42 geh., 28 May 1942, BA/MA, RW 34/117.

135. OKW WFSt/Abt. L (IV/K) Nr. 441485/41 gKdos. Chefs., 5 September 1941,
     BA/MA, RW 34/10.

136. For the German demands, see *ADAP*, D, XIII, 415, 419, 445, 463, 478. Final
     arrangements for Weygand's removal were made at the funeral of General

Huntziger, who died in an airplane crash on 12 November. Weygand was officially retired on 20 November 1941. See also Paxton, *Parades*, 270–71; idem., *Vichy France*, 125.

137. Muggeridge, ed., *Ciano Papers*, 460–65.

138. Abetz's expectations are in *ADAP*, D, XIII, 478. The Germans approved Juin's release from prison camp at Königstein as part of the Paris Protocols negotiations. Hitler had expressed his mistrust of both Juin and Noguès to Mussolini at the Brenner on 6 June 1941. See *ADAP*, D, XII, 584.

139. On the connection between Weygand's removal and the Levante troops, see General von Senger to DB Rom, Nr. 32, 22 November 1941, AA, DB Rom, Frankreich auch franz. Kolonien. On the original strength of 13,000, see ibid.; DWStK Gruppe Marine Nr. 4685 gKdos., 22 November 1941, BA/MA, RM 7/255. On the final numbers of Levantine troops in Morocco as of October 1942, see BA/MA, RW 34/138, passim.; K.K. Heer Br.B. Nr. 435/42g, 4 October 1942, BA/MA, RW 34/131. On the arming of the Levante troops, see DWStK Gruppe Marine Nr. 4685 gKdos., 22 November 1941, BA/MA, RM 7/255; K.K. Heer Marokko Br.B. Nr. 5/42 geh., 4 January 1942, BA/MA, RW 34/130; K.I. Afrika Ia, Br.B. Nr. 92/42 geh., 9 January 1942, ibid.; K.I. Afrika Abt. Ia, Nr. 325/42 geh., 6 February 1942, ibid.; K.K. Heer Marokko Br.B. Nr. 50/42 geh., 4 February 1942, ibid.; K.K. Heer Marokko Br.B. Nr. 340/42, 4 August 1940, ibid.; K.K. Heer Marokko Br.B. Nr. 371/42, 4 September 1942, ibid. See also BA/MA, RW 34/148, 164, 165, 168, 169.

140. Memorandum in *ADAP*, D, XIII, 529; Paxton, *Vichy France*, 127–28.

141. *ADAP*, D, XIII, 531 and n. 1.

142. Muggeridge, ed., *Ciano Diary*, 2 and 7 December 1941; Rintelen to Keitel and Warlimont, 2 December 1941, *ADAP*, D, XI, 532. On the problems of supplying the North African theater, see Schreiber, *Revisionismus*, 319–26.

143. DWStK Gruppe Wehrmacht Ia, Nr. 31/41 gKdos. Chefs., 5 December 1941, BA/MA, RW 34/10. Col. Mancinelli (Italian liaison in Wiesbaden) to German Armistice Commission, Nr. 6981, 5 December 1941, idem.

144. DVD bei IWStK Nr. 219/41 gKdos., 5 December 1941, ibid; DWStK Gruppe Wehrmacht Ia, Nr. 31/41 gKdos. Chefs. II Ang., 5 December 1941, ibid.; Langen to DB Rom, Nr. 36, 5 December 1941, AA, DB Rom, Frankreich auch franz. Kolonien.

145. Chef OKW: OKW/WFSt/L (IV/K) Nr. 442051/41 gKdos. Chefs., 4 December 1941, BA/MA, RW 34/10.

146. Ribbentrop to Mackensen, 7 December 1941, *ADAP*, D, XIII, 552, and n. 6.

147. Mackensen to Ribbentrop, 7 December 1941, ibid., 557 and n. 6. See also Muggeridge, ed., *Ciano Diary*, 2, 7 December 1941.

148. Muggeridge, ed., *Ciano Papers*, 468–69; idem., *Ciano Diary*, 10 December 1941.

149. DWStK Gruppe Wehrmacht Ia, Nr. 2592/41 geh., 10 December 1941, BA/MA, RW 34/10.

150. Weizsäcker to Mackensen, Nr. 3514, 23 December 1941, AA, DB Rom, Frankreich und franz. Kolonien.

151. For Warlimont's memo, see DWStK Gruppe Wehrmacht Ia, Nr. 40/41 gKdos. Chefs. II Ang., 24 December 1941, BA/MA, RW 34/10. See also DWStK Gruppe Wehrmacht Ia, Nr. 40/41 gKdos. Chefs. I Ang., 22 December 1941, idem.

152. See DB Madrid, "Meldungen," passim; AA, StS, Zweite Front, I, II, passim.

153. Ribbentrop Multex Nr. 46, 29 June 1942, *ADAP,* E, III, 46.

154. Jochmann, ed., *Monologe,* 1 August 1942, 321.

155. Wagner, ed., *Lagevorträge,* 325.

156. OKW/WFSt/Abt. L (IK Op) Nr. 44 2173/41 gKdos. Chefs., 14 December 1941, BA/MA, RH 2/1521. An abridged version of this report is printed in Salewski, ed., *Seekriegsleitung,* III, 249–61. Warlimont based his assumptions on pre-December 1941 American planning partly on the American "Victory Program," which was published in American newspapers shortly before the attack on Pearl Harbor, and also on German observations of American activity and policy up until December 1941. On the "Victory Plan," see Langer and Gleason, *Undeclared War,* 735–41; 923–24.

157. Generalstab des Heeres/ Abt. Fremde Heere West Nr. 632/42 gKdos. Chefs., 1 March 1942, BA/MA, RH 2/1521.

158. The copy belonging to Fremde Heere West still survives. On Hitler's order and the order for the return of the study to the author agency, see Generalstab des Heeres Abt. Fremde Heere West III, Nr. 761/42 gKdos. Chefs., 13 June 1942, ibid.; Generalstab des Heeres Abt. Fremde Heere West Nr. 632/42 gKdos. Chefs. II Ang., 24 March 1942, ibid.

159. DWStK Gruppe Marine B. Nr. 1596/42 gKdos., 31 May 1942, BA/MA, RM 7/255; Auszug aus Studie der K.I. Afrika vom 28.5 über franz. Abwehrmöglichkeiten bei engl. amerik. Angriff auf Marokko, idem.; *ADAP,* E, III, 46, n. 2.

160. K.K. Heer Br.B. Nr. 435/42, 4 October 1942, BA/MA, RW 34/131; K.I. Afrika Ia, Br.B Nr. 265/42g, 6 October 1942, idem.

161. Keith Sainsbury, *The North African Landings, 1942,* 81–117; Arthur Layden Funk, *The Politics of Torch,* 65–87.

162. For allied shipping woes, see Samuel Eliot Morison, *History of United States Naval Operations in World War II,* vol. II, 25–30; Harry C. Butcher, *My Three Years with Eisenhower,* 18 and 22 August 1942; Howe, *Northwest Africa,* 43–44; Mark Wayne Clark, *Calculated Risk,* 45–53; Sainsbury, *North African Landings,* 130–32.

163. For the Allied deception campaign, see Butcher, *Eisenhower,* 8, 12, 16, 18, 20, and 21 August 1942.

164. Auer to DB Paris, Pol. II, Westafrika, Nr. 524/42, 16 April 1942, enlosure no. 2 of DB Paris to Foreign Ministry, Nr. 4056/42, 30 April 1942, AA, DB Paris, franz. Kolonien, Bd. 3, bndl. 1326.

165. J. R. M. Butler, ed., *History of the Second World War: Grand Strategy,* vol. III, 166, 354.

166. On Liberia, see Stetson Conn, ed., *United States Army in World War II,* Special Studies, vol. VIII, 619–22. The negotiations and agreements between

Washington and Monrovia are covered in *FRUS, 1941,* III, 532–49; idem., *1942,* IV, 355–430. On Equatorial Africa, and in particular Point Noire, see idem., II, 564–96.

167. For this issue, see *FRUS,* 1942, IV, 419–30.

168. Bielfeld felt Konakry and Abidjan were also possible targets. On the Foreign Ministry's discussion of these issues, see DB Paris to Foreign Ministry, Nr. 9776/42, 5 November 1942, AA, DB Paris, franz. Kolonien, Bd.3, bndl. 1326; C.S.P. u. S.D. VI, B 2 b Nr. 26925/42g, 13 October 1942, AA, Inland IIg, Berichte und Meldungen zur Lage in und über Nordafrika, bndl. 335; Notiz zu D II 1533g, 17 October 1942, idem.; Notiz zu D II 1553g, 20 October 1942, idem.; Vortragsnotiz by Bielfeld, zu D II 1533g, 21 October 1942, idem. Most dramatic from the French side was the evacuation of French women and children from Dakar, announced in October 1942 and begun in November. See Paxton, *Parades,* 330.

169. OKW/WFSt/Op. Nr. 551768/42 gKdos. Chefs., 17 October 1942, BA/MA, RW 34/10. Keitel mentioned that the High Command also thought that a landing in Morocco was a possibility, albeit a slighter one.

170. On the French requests and German permission, see DWStK Gruppe Heer III, Nr. 784/42 geh., 21 September 1942, and enclosures, BA/MA, RW 34/129; Franz. Abordnung bei der DWStK/Unterkommission: Forces Terrestres, Nr. 2982/FT/S, 25 September 1942, idem; DWStK Gruppe Heer III, Nr. 805/42g, 29 September 1942, idem; K.K. Heer Gruppe W.u.G. Br.B. Nr. 77/42 geh., 13 October 1942, idem. Paxton, *Parades,* 325, ties the German concessions to French concessions in the area of neutral cargo ships in French ports. Still, as Paxton himself states, German concerns for West Africa as such determined the timing of the material concessions. On Darlan's comment, see DWStK Gruppe Wehrmacht Ia, Nr. 10 gKdos. Chefs., 10 November 1942 and enclosure, BA/MA, RW 34/10.

171. Butcher, *Eisenhower,* 15 August 1942; Clark, *Calculated Risk,* 44.

Conclusion

1. Howe, *Northwest Africa,* 171–75; Hoisington, *Casablanca,* 225–34.

2. Foreign Ministry (Schirmer) to DB Paris, Nr. 5680, 6 December 1942, AA, DB Paris, Maghrebinische Sendungen für Marokko und übriges Nordafrika.

Bibliography
❧

I. Unpublished archival sources

A. Germany

1. POLITISCHES ARCHIV DES AUSWÄRTIGEN AMTES (BONN)

Büro des Reichsaußenministers
Büro des Staatssekretärs
Büro Unterstaatssekretär
Abteilung Pol. IM
Abteilung Pol. II
Abteilung Pol. III
Abteilung Pol. IV
Abteilung Pol. VII
Abteilung Pol. IX
Abteilung Pol. X
Abteilung Pol. XI
Handelspolitische Abteilung
Abteilung Inland
Kulturpolitische Abteilung
Handakten Botschafter Karl Ritter
Handakten Hasso von Etzdorf
Handakten Unterstaatssekretär Andor Hencke
Nachlaß Hans Georg von Mackensen
Deutsche Botschaft Madrid
Deutsche Botschaft Paris
Deutsche Botschaft Rom (Quirinal)
Deutsche Konsulat Tetuán

2. BUNDESARCHIV/MILITÄRARCHIV
(FREIBURG)

RW 4 OKW/Wehrmachtführungsstab
RW 5 OKW/Amt Ausland Abwehr
RW 34 Deutsche Waffenstillstandskommission
RH 2 OKH/Generalstab des Heeres
RM 6 Oberbefehlshaber der Kriegsmarine
RM 7 Seekriegsleitung
RM 8 Kriegswissenschaftliche Abteilung der Marine
RM 11 Marineattachégruppe
RM 12 Marineattachés
N 236 Nachlaß Karl Dönitz
N 391 Nachlaß Erich Raeder
N 323 Nachlaß Friedrich von Bötticher
N 539 Nachlaß Gerhard Wagner

3. INSTITUT FÜR ZEITGESCHICHTE
(MUNICH)

ED 61 Frido von Senger und Etterlin, "Auszüge aus den Wochenberichten."
Frido von Senger und Etterlin, "Der Waffenstillstand."

4. GERMAN RECORDS ON MICROFILM AT THE NATIONAL ARCHIVES, WASHINGTON, D.C. (ORGANIZED BY NATIONAL ARCHIVES MICROCOPY DESIGNATION)

T-77 Records of the Headquarters of the German Armed Forces High Command
T-78 Records of the Headquarters of the German Army High Command
T-120 Records of the German Foreign Office received by the Department of State
T-321 Records of the Headquarters of the German Air Force High Command
T-608 Records of the Headquarters, German Navy High Command
T-1022 Records of the German Navy, 1850–1945, received from the United States Naval History Division

B. Spain

1. ARCHIVO GENERAL DEL MINISTERIO DE ASUNTOS EXTERIORES (MADRID)

The Foreign Ministry Archives of Spain have yet to receive an organizing principle commensurate with their importance. Organization is based on a card catalog, which in turn is based on key-word indexing. Thus, a systematic research strategy is not as easy as in Germany. Documents relating to Germany from 1940 through 1942 in the Spanish Foreign Ministry are few and far between, especially for the period of Ramón Serrano Suñer's tenure as foreign minister. The situation is somewhat better for the tenures of Juan Beigbeder and Count Jordana. The archive is an invaluable source for politics in France and Spanish-French relations during the war years, as it includes a large set of reports to the foreign minister from the Spanish ambassador to Vichy, José Felix de Lequerica. Lequerica, through frequent conversations with key French officials, kept himself unusually well informed. The archive is thus quite useful for the entire Northwest African issue.

2. ARCHIVO DE LA PRESIDENCIA DEL GOBIERNO (MADRID)

This archive houses a collection of documents that passed the desk of Generalissimo Francisco Franco. For the war years, the collection is very small but contains useful items nonetheless, particularly with regard to Spanish aims in Africa and modernization projects in the Spanish Moroccan protectorate.

C. United States

I. NATIONAL ARCHIVES (COLLEGE PARK, MARYLAND)

The National Archives complex in Maryland holds the index to the German records seized in Morocco, as well as the United States Army interrogation reports of those German officers captured following the U.S. landing there (Record Group 165).

II. Official Documentary Collections

Areilza, José María de and Fernando María Castiella. *Reivindicaciones de España.* 2d ed. Madrid: Instituto de Estudios Politicos, 1941.

Besymenski, Lew. *Sonderakte "Barbarossa": Dokumente, Darstellung, Deutung.* Translated by Erich Einhorn. Stuttgart: Deutsche Verlags-Anstalt, 1968.

France. Délégation française auprès de la commission allemande d'armistice. *La Délégation française auprès de la commission allemande d'armistice: Recueil de documents publié par le gouvernement française.* 5 vols. Paris: Imprimerie Nationale, 1947–59.

———. *Documents secrets du ministère des affaires étrangères d'Allemagne.* Vol. III, *La politique allemande en Espagne, 1936–1943.* Translated by Madeleine Eristiov and Michael Eristiov. Paris: Dupont, 1946.

Germany. Auswärtiges Amt. *Akten zur deutschen auswärtigen Politik, 1918–1945: Aus dem Archiv des deutschen Auswärtigen Amtes (Serie D: 1937–1941).* 13 vols. Baden Baden: Imprimerie Nationale, 1950–64.

Germany. Auswärtiges Amt. *Akten zur deutschen auswärtigen Politik, 1918–1945: Aus dem Archiv des Auswärtigen Amtes (Serie E: 1942–1945).* 8 vols. Göttingen: Vandenhoeck & Ruprecht, 1969–79.

Great Britain. Foreign and Commonwealth Office. Librarians Department. *British Foreign and State Papers*. Vols. 143–44. London: HMSO, 1951–52.

———. Foreign and Commonwealth Office. *Weekly Political Intelligence Summaries*. 16 vols. London: Kraus, 1983.

Hillgruber, Andreas, ed. *Staatsmänner und Diplomaten bei Hitler: Vertrauliche Aufzeichnungen über Unterredungen mit Vertretern des Auslandes*. 2 vols. Frankfurt am Main: Bernard & Graefe, 1967–70.

Hillgruber, Andreas and Jürgen Förster, ed. "Zwei neue Aufzeichnungen über 'Führer'-Besprechungen aus dem Jahre 1942." *Militärgeschichtliche Mitteilungen* 22 (January 1972): 109–26.

Hubatsch, Walther, ed. *Hitlers Weisungen für die Kriegführung, 1933–1945: Dokumente des Oberkommandos der Wehrmacht*. 2d ed. Frankfurt am Main: Bernard & Graefe, 1983.

International Military Tribunal. *Trial of the Major War Criminals before the International Military Tribunal, Nuremberg, 14 November 1945–1 October 1946*. 42 vols. Nuremberg: International Military Tribunal, 1949.

Italy. Ministero degli Affari Esteri. Commissione per la Publicazione dei Documenti Diplomatici Italiani. *I Documenti Diplomatici Italiani, Nona Serie: 1939–1943*. 10 vols. Rome: Instituto Polografico dello Stato, 1954–90.

Krautkrämer, Elmar, ed. "Das Ringen um die Erhaltung der französischen Souveränität in Nordafrika im Zusammenhang mit Torch." *Militärgeschichtliche Mitteilungen* 32 (February 1982): 79–136.

Lohmann, Walter and Hans H. Hildebrand. *Die deutsche Kriegsmarine*. 3 vols. Bad Nauheim: Podzun, 1956.

Portugal. Ministerio dos Negocios Estrangeiros. *Dez anos de política externa, 1937–1947: A naçao portuguesa e a segunda guerra mundial*. 11 vols. Lisbon: Ministerio dos Negocios Estrangeiros, 1964–80.

Rahn, Werner and Gerhard Schreiber, ed. *Kriegstagebuch der Seekriegsleitung 1939–1945: Teil A*. 78 vols. Bonn: Mittler, 1988–.

Rosenman, Samuel I. *The Public Papers and Addresses of Franklin D. Roosevelt*. 13 vols. New York: Harper & Brothers, 1938–1950.

Salewski, Michael, ed. *Die deutsche Seekriegsleitung*. Vol. III, *Denkschriften und Lagebetrachtungen, 1938–1944*. Frankfurt am Main: Bernard & Graefe, 1973.

———, ed. "Von Raeder zu Dönitz: Der Wechsel im Oberbefehl der Kriegsmarine 1943." *Militärgeschichtliche Mitteilungen* 23 (February 73): 101–46.

Schramm, Percy Ernst, ed. *Kriegstagebuch des Oberkommandos der Wehrmacht (Wehrmachtführungsstab)*. 4 vols. Frankfurt am Main: Bernard & Graefe, 1961–65.

Spain. Ministerio de Asuntos Exteriores. *Tangier under the Protective Action of Spain during the World War, June 1940–October 1945*. Madrid: Ministerio de Asuntos Exteriores, 1946.

United States. Department of State. *Documents on German Foreign Policy, 1918–1945, Series D: 1937–1945*. 13 vols. Washington, D.C.: GPO, 1956–64.

———. Department of State. *Foreign Relations of the United States: Diplomatic Papers*. Washington, D.C: GPO, 1861–.

————. Department of State. *The Spanish Government and the Axis: Official German Documents*. Washington, D.C.: GPO, 1946.

Wagner, Gerhard, ed. *Lagevorträge des Oberbefehlshabers der Kriegsmarine vor Hitler, 1939–1945*. Munich: Lehmans, 1972.

III. Newspapers

España
L'Echo du Maroc

IV. Individual Sources: Memoirs, Diaries, Published Papers

Abetz, Otto. *Das offene Problem: Ein Rückblick auf zwei Jahrzehnte deutscher Frankreichpolitik*. Cologne: Greven-Verlag, 1951.

Alfieri, Dino. *Dictators Face to Face*. Translated by David Moore. London: Elek, 1954.

Anfuso, Filippo. *Du palais de Venice au lac du Garde*. Translated by Eugéne Bestaux. Paris: Coleman-Levy, 1949.

Baudouin, Paul. *The Private Diaries (March 1940 to January 1941) of Paul Baudouin*. Translated by Sir Charles Petrie. London: Eyre & Spottiswood, 1948.

Bayod, Angel, ed., *Franco visto por sus ministros*. Barcelona: Planeta, 1981.

Bouthillier, Yves. *Le drame de Vichy*. 2 vols. Paris: Plon, 1950–51.

Butcher, Harry C. *My Three Years with Eisenhower: The Personal Diary of Captain Harry C. Butcher, USNR, Naval Aide to General Eisenhower, 1942 to 1945*. New York: Simon & Schuster, 1946.

Calic, Edouard, ed. *Ohne Maske: Hitler-Breiting Geheimgespräch, 1931*. Frankfurt: Societäts-Druckerei, 1968.

Carboni, Giacomo. *Memorie segrete, 1935–1948*. Florence: Parenti, 1955.

Charles-Roux, François. *Cinq mois tragiques aux affaires étrangères (21 mai–1er novembre 1940)*. Paris: Plon, 1949.

Childs, James Rives. *Diplomatic and Literary Quests*. Richmond, Va.: Whittet & Shepperson, 1963.

Churchill, Winston. *The Second World War*. 6 vols. Boston: Houghton Mifflin, 1948–53.

Clark, Mark W. *Calculated Risk*. New York: Harper, 1950.

Darlan, Alain. *L'Amiral Darlan parle . . . .* Paris: Amiot-Dumont, 1952.

De Gaulle, Charles. *Discourses et Messages*. Vol I, *Pendant la Guerre, Juin 1940–Janvier 1946*. Paris: Plon, 1970.

————. *Lettres, notes et carnets*. Vol. III, *Juin 1940–Juillet 1941*. Paris: Plon, 1981.

————. *Mémoires de guerre*. 3 vols. Paris: Plon, 1954–59.

De la Baume, Robert Renom. "L'Espagne 'non-bélligerante' (1940)." *Revue d'histoire diplomatique* 69 (April–June 1955): 126–29.

Dönitz, Karl. *Memoirs: Ten Years and Twenty Days*. Translated by R. H. Stevens. London: Weidenfeld & Nicholson, 1959.

Doussinague, José María. *España tenía razón, 1939–1945*. 2d ed. Madrid: Espasa Calpe, 1950.

Eden, Anthony (Earl of Avon). *The Eden Memoirs*. Vol. II, *The Reckoning*. London: Times, 1965.

Eisenhower, Dwight D. *The Papers of Dwight David Eisenhower: The War Years*. 5 vols. Edited by Alfred D. Chandler Jr. Baltimore: The Johns Hopkins University Press, 1970.

Franco Salgado-Arrajo, Francisco. *Mis conversaciones privadas con Franco*. Barcelona: Planeta, 1976.

———. *Mi vida junto a Franco*. Barcelona: Planeta, 1977.

Fröhlich, Elke, ed. Die Tagebücher von Joseph Goebbels: *Sämtliche Fragmente. Teil I: Aufzeichnungen 1924–1941*. 4 vols. Munich: Sauer, 1987.

———. *Die Tagebücher von Joseph Goebbles. Teil II: Diktate 1941–1945*. 15 vols. Munich: Sauer, 1993–96.

Hayes, Carlton J. H. *Wartime Mission to Spain, 1942–1945*. New York: Macmillan, 1945.

Hill, Leonidas E., ed. *Die Weizsäcker-Papier, 1933–1950*. Frankfurt am Main: Propyläen, 1974.

Hitler, Adolf. *Mein Kampf*. Translated by Ralph Manheim. 2 vols. Munich: Eher, 1925–27. Reprint, Boston: Houghton Mifflin, 1971.

Hoare, Samuel (Viscount Templewood). *Ambassador on Special Mission*. London: Collins, 1946.

Hull, Cordell. *The Memoirs of Cordell Hull*. 2 vols. New York: Macmillan, 1948.

Jacobsen, Hans-Adolf, ed. *Generaloberst Halder: Kriegstagebuch*. 3 vols. Stuttgart: Kohlhammer, 1962–64.

James, Robert Rhodes, ed. *Winston S. Churchill: His Complete Speeches, 1897–1963*. Vol. VI, *1935–1942*. London: Chelsea House, 1974.

Jochmann, Werner, ed. *Adolf Hitler: Monologe im Führerhauptquartier, 1941–1944*. Bindlach: Knaus, 1988.

Juin, Alphonse. *Mémoires (1941–1958)*. 2 vols. Paris: Fayard, 1959–60.

Keitel, Wilhelm. *In the Service of the Reich*. Edited by Walter Görlitz. Translated by David Irving. New York: Stein & Day, 1979.

Kindelan, Alfredo. *La verdad de mis relaciones con Franco*. Barcelona, Planeta, 1981.

Kordt, Erich. *Nicht aus den Akten: Die Wilhelmstrasse in Frieden und Krieg: Erlebnisse, Begegnungen, und Eindrücke, 1928–1945*. Stuttgart: Union Deutsche Verlagsgesellschaft, 1950.

———. *Wahn und Wirklichkeit: Die Außenpolitik des Dritten Reiches: Versuch einer Darstallung*. Stuttgart: Union Deutsche Verlagsgesellschaft, 1947.

Leahy, William D. *I Was There*. New York: Whittlesey House, 1950.

Lomax, John Garnet. *The Diplomatic Smuggler*. London: Becker, 1965.

MacVane, John. *Journey into War: War and Diplomacy in North Africa*. New York: Appleton, 1943.

Muggeridge, Malcolm, ed. *Ciano's Diary, 1939–1943*. Translated by V. Umberto Coletti-Perrucca. London: Heinemann, 1947.

———, ed. *Ciano's Diplomatic Papers*. Translated by Stuart Hood. London: Odhams Press, 1948.

Murphy, Robert. *Diplomat among Warriors.* Garden City, N.Y.: Doubleday, 1964.

Nicolle, Pierre. *Cinquante mois d'armistice: Vichy, 2 juillet 1940–26 août 1944, journal d'un témoin.* 2 vols. Paris: Bonne, 1947.

Pendar, Kenneth. *Adventure in Diplomacy: Our French Dilemma.* New York: Dodd, Mead, 1966.

Picker, Henry, ed. *Hitlers Tischgespräche im Führerhauptquartier.* 3d ed. Stuttgart: Seewald Verlag, 1976.

Piétri, François. *Mes anées en Espagne, 1940–1948.* Paris: Plon, 1954.

Raeder, Erich. *Mein Leben.* 2 vols. Tübingen-Neckar: Schlichtenmayer, 1956–57.

Rauschning, Hermann. *Gespräche mit Hitler.* Zurich: Europa Verlag, 1976.

Ribbentrop, Anneliese von, ed. *Joachim von Ribbentrop: Zwischen London und Moskau.* Leoni: Druffel, 1953.

Rintelen, Enno von. *Mussolini als Bündesgenosse: Erinnerungen des deutschen Militärattachés in Rom, 1936–1943.* Tübingen: Wunderlich, 1951.

Roatta, Mario. *Otto milioni di baionetti: L'esercito italiano in guerra dal 1940 al 1944.* Milan: Mondadori, 1946.

Saña, Heleno. *El franquismo sin mitos: conversaciones con Serrano Suñer.* Barcelona: Grijalbo, 1982.

Schmidt, Paul. *Statist auf diplomatischer Bühne, 1923–1945: Erlebnisse des Chefdolmetschers im Auswärtigen Amt mit den Staatsmännern Europas.* Bonn: Athenaum, 1950.

Serrano Suñer, Ramón. *Entre Hendaye y Gibraltar: noticia y reflexión, frente a una legenda, sobre nuestra politica en dos guerras.* Madrid: Ediciones y Publicaciones Españolas, 1947.

———. *Entre el silencio y la propaganda, la historia como fue: Memorias.* Barcelona: Planeta, 1977.

Speer, Albert. *Erinnerungen.* 6th ed. Berlin: Propyläen, 1970.

Stehlin, Paul. *Témoignage pour l'histoire.* Paris: Laffont, 1964.

Strasser, Otto. *Mein Kampf: Eine politische Autobiographie.* Frankfurt: Streit-Zeit Bücher, 1969.

Trevor-Roper, Hugh, ed. *Hitler's Table Talk, 1941–1944.* Translated by Norman Cameron and R. H. Stevens. London: Weidenfeld & Nicholson, 1952; reprint, London: Oxford University Press, 1988.

Turner Jr., Henry Ashby, ed. *Hitler—Memoirs of a Confidant.* Translated by Ruth Hein. New Haven, Conn.: Yale University Press, 1985.

Warlimont, Walter. *Inside Hitler's Headquarters, 1939–1945.* Translated by R. H. Barry. New York: Praeger, 1964.

Weinberg, Gerhard L., ed. *Hitlers zweites Buch: Ein Dokument aus dem Jahr 1928.* Stuttgart: Deutsche Verlags-Anstalt, 1961.

Weygand, Maxime. *Mémoires.* Vol. III, *Rappelé au service.* Paris: Flammarion, 1950.

Zincone, Vittorio, ed. *Hitler e Mussolini: letteri e documenti.* Milan: Rizzoli, 1946.

V. Secondary Sources: Books

Abendroth, Hans-Henning. *Hitler in der spanischen Arena: Die deutsch-spanischen Beziehungen im Spannungsfeld der europäischen Interessenpolitik vom Ausbruch des Bürgerkrieges bis zum Ausbruch des Weltkrieges, 1936–1939.* Paderborn: Schöningh, 1973.

Abshagen, Karl Heinz. *Canaris.* Translated by A. H. Brodrick. Stuttgart: Union Deutsche Verlagsgesellschaft, 1949.

Ades, Lucien. *L'adventure algerienne, 1940–1944: Pétain, Giraud, de Gaulle.* Paris: Belfond, 1979.

Amouroux, Henri. *La grande histoire des Français sous l'occupation.* 6 vols. Paris: Laffont, 1976–88.

Andrew, Christopher. *Théophile Delcassé and the Making of the Entente Cordiale: A Reappraisal of French Foreign Policy, 1898–1905.* London: Macmillan, 1968.

Ansel, Walter. *Hitler and the Middle Sea.* Durham, N.C.: Duke University Press, 1972.

———. *Hitler Confronts England.* Durham, N.C.: Duke University Press, 1960.

Arquéz, Enrique. *El Momento de España en Marruecos.* Madrid: Vicesecretaría de Educación Popular, 1942.

Bailey, Thomas A. and Paul B. Ryan. *Hitler vs. Roosevelt: The Undeclared Naval War.* New York: Free Press, 1979.

Bankwitz, Philip C. F. *Maxime Weygand and Civil-Military Relations in Modern France.* Cambridge: Harvard University Press, 1967.

Baum, Walter and Eberhard Weichold. *Der Krieg der "Achsenmächte" im Mittelmeer-Raum: Die "Strategie" der Diktaturen.* Göttingen: Musterschmidt, 1973.

Berghahn, Volker. *Germany and the Approach of War in 1914.* New York: St. Martin's Press, 1973.

———. *Der Tirpitzplan: Genesis und Verfall einer innenpolitischen Krisenstrategie unter Wilhelm II.* Düsseldorf: Droste, 1971.

Berque, Jaques. *French North Africa: The Maghreb Between Two World Wars.* Translated by Jean Stewart. New York: Praeger, 1967.

Berteil, Louis. *L'Armée de Weygand: La chance de la France, 1940–1942.* Paris: Albatross, 1975.

Bidwell, Robin. *Morocco under Colonial Rule: French Administration of Tribal Areas, 1912–1956.* London: Cass, 1973.

Bird, Keith W. *Weimar, the German Naval Officer Corps, and the Rise of National Socialism.* Amsterdam: Gruner, 1977.

Böhme, Hermann. *Der deutsch-französische Waffenstillstand im zweiten Weltkrieg.* Vol. I, *Entstehung und Grundlagen des Waffenstillstandes von 1940.* Stuttgart: Deutsche Verlags-Anstalt, 1966.

Bourgi, Robert. *Le Général de Gaulle et l'Afrique Noire, 1940–1949.* Paris: Librairie Général de Droit et de Jurisprudence, 1980.

Bragadin, Marc Antonio. *The Italian Navy in World War II.* Annapolis, Md.: United States Naval Institute, 1977.

Browning, Christopher. *The Final Solution and the German Foreign Office.* New York: Holmes & Meier, 1978.

Bücheler, Heinrich. *Carl-Heinrich von Stülpnagel: Soldat, Philosoph, Verschwörer: Biographie.* Berlin: Ullstein, 1989.

Buchheit, Gert. *Der deutsche Geheimdienst: Geschichte der militärischen Abwehr.* Munich: List, 1969.

Bullock, Alan. *Hitler: A Study in Tyranny.* Rev. ed., New York: Harper & Brothers, 1960; reprint, New York: Bantam, 1960.

———. *Hitler and Stalin: Parallel Lives.* New York: Knopf, 1992.

Burdick, Charles B. *Germany's Military Strategy and Spain in World War II.* Syracuse, N.Y.: Syracuse University Press, 1968.

———. *Unternehmen Sonnenblume: Der Entschluß zum Afrika-Feldzug.* Neckargemünd: Vowinckel, 1972.

Burns, James MacGregor. *Roosevelt 1940–1945: The Soldier of Freedom.* New York: Harcourt Brace Jovanovich, 1970.

Butler, James Ramsey Montagu et al., ed. *History of the Second World War: Grand Strategy.* 6 vols. London: HMSO, 1956–76.

Castor, Elie and Raymond Tracy. *Félix Éboué: Gouverneur et Philosophe.* Paris: Editions L'Harmattan, 1984.

Cave Brown, Anthony. *The Last Hero: Wild Bill Donovan.* New York: Random House, 1982.

Chambrun, René de. *Pierre Laval: Traitor or Patriot?* Translated by Elly Stein. New York: Scribner's, 1984.

Cierva, Ricardo de la. *Franco.* Barcelona: Planeta, 1986.

———. *Hendaya: Punto Final.* Barcelona: Planeta, 1981.

Compton, James V. *The Swastika and the Eagle: Hitler, the United States, and the Origins of World War II.* Boston: Houghton Mifflin, 1967.

Conn, Stetson, ed. *United States Army in World War II: Special Studies,* Vol. VIII, *The Employment of Negro Troops,* by Ulysses Lee. Washington, D.C.: Office of the Chief of Military History, United States Army, 1954–66.

Coutau-Bégarie, Herve and Claude Huan. *Darlan.* Paris: Fayard, 1989.

———. *Mers el-Kebir (1940): La nupture franco-britannique.* Paris: Economica, 1994.

Coverdale, John F. *Italian Intervention in the Spanish Civil War.* Princeton, N.J.: Princeton University Press, 1975.

Crozier, Brian. *Franco: A Biographical History.* London: Eyre & Spottiswood, 1967.

Dankelmann, Otfried. *Franco zwischen Hitler und die Westmächten.* Berlin (East): VEB Deutscher Verlag der Wissenschaften, 1970.

Deist, Wilhelm, ed. *The German Military in the Age of Total War.* Dover, N.H.: Berg, 1987.

Destremau, Bernard. *Weygand.* Paris: Perrin, 1989.

Detwiler, Donald S. *Hitler, Franco und Gibraltar: Die Frage des spanischen Eintritts in den zweiten Weltkrieg.* Wiesbaden: Steiner, 1962.

Dougherty, James J. *The Politics of Wartime Aid: American Economic Assistance to France and French Northwest Africa, 1940–1946.* Westport, Conn.: Greenwood Press, 1978.

Dülffer, Jost. *Weimar, Hitler, und die Marine: Reichspolitik und Flottenbau, 1920–1939.* Düsseldorf: Droste, 1973.

Feis, Herbert. *The Spanish Story: Franco and the Nations at War.* New York: Knopf, 1948; reprint, New York: Norton, 1966.

Ferro, Marc. *Pétain.* Paris: Fayard, 1987.

Fest, Joachim. *Hitler.* Translated by Richard Winston and Clara Winston. New York: Harcourt Brace Jovanovich, 1974.

Forstmeier, Friedrich and Hans-Erich Volkmann, ed. *Kriegswirtschaft und Rüstung, 1939–1945.* Düsseldorf: Droste, 1979.

Friedländer, Saul. *Prelude to Downfall: Hitler and the United States.* Translated by Aline B. Werth and Alexander Werth. New York: Knopf, 1967.

Frye, Alton. *Nazi Germany and the American Hemisphere, 1933–1941.* New Haven, Conn.: Yale University Press, 1967.

Funk, Arthur Layden. *The Politics of Torch: The Allied Landings and the Algiers Putsch 1942.* Lawrence, Kans.: University Press of Kansas, 1974.

Funke, Manfred, ed. *Hitler, Deutschland, und die Mächte: Materialen zur Außenpolitik des dritten Reiches.* Düsseldorf: Droste, 1976.

García Figueras, Tomás. *Marruecos: la acción de España en el norte de Africa.* Madrid: Ediciones Fe, 1939.

García Lahiguera, Fernando. *Ramón Serrano Suñer: un documento para la historia.* Barcelona: Editorial Argos Vergara, 1983.

Garriga, Ramón. *Las relaciones entre Franco y Hitler.* Buenos Aires: Alvarez, 1965.

Gassert, Philipp. *Amerika im Dritten Reich: Ideologie, Propaganda und Volksmeining 1933–1945.* Stuttgart: Steiner, 1997.

Gemzell, Carl-Axel. *Organization, Conflict, and Innovation: A Study of German Naval Strategic Planning, 1888–1940.* Lund: Berlingske Boktryckeriet, 1973.

———. *Raeder, Hitler, und Skandinavien: Der Kampf für einen maritimen Operationsplan.* Lund: Gleerup, 1965.

Geschke, Gunter. *Die deutsche Frankreichspolitik 1940: Von Compiègne bis Montoire. Das Problem einer deutsch-französischen Annährung nach dem Frankreichfeldzug.* Berlin: Mittler, 1970.

Gómez-Jordana Souza, Francisco (Conde de Jordana). *La tramoya de nuestra actuación en Marruecos.* Madrid: Editoria Nacional, 1976.

Greenfield, Ken Roberts, ed. *United States Army in World War II: The Mediterranean Theater of Operations.* Vol. I, *Northwest Africa: Seizing the Initiative in the West,* by George F. Howe. Washington, D.C.: Office of the Chief of Military History, United States Army, 1957.

Greiner, Helmuth. *Die Oberste Wehrmachtführung, 1939–1943.* Wiesbaden: Limes, 1951.

Greiselis, Waldis. *Das Ringen um die Brückenkopf Tunesien, 1942–1943: Strategie der "Achse" und Innenpolitik im Protektorat.* Frankfurt am Main: Lang, 1976.

Gröner, Erich. *Die Schiffe der deutschen Kriegsmarine und Luftwaffe, 1939–1945 und ihr Verbleib.* 8th ed. Munich: Lehmanns, 1976.

Gruchmann, Lothar. *Nationalsozialistische Großraumordnung: Die Konstruktion einer "deutschen Monroe-Doktrin."* Stuttgart: Deutsche Verlags-Anstalt, 1962.

Gundelach, Karl. *Die deutsche Luftwaffe im Mittelmeer, 1940–1945.* 2 vols. Frankfurt am Main: Bern, 1981.

Guth, Rolf. *Die Marine des deutschen Reiches, 1919–1939.* Frankfurt am Main: Bernard & Graefe, 1972.

Hall, Luella J. *The United States and Morocco, 1776–1956.* Metuchen, N.J.: Scarecrow Press, 1971.

Halstead, John P. *Rebirth of a Nation: The Origins and Rise of Moroccan Nationalism, 1912–1944.* Cambridge: Harvard University Press, 1967,

Harper, Glenn T. *German Economic Policy in Spain during the Spanish Civil War, 1936–1939.* The Hague: Mouton, 1967.

Hass, Gerhart, ed. *Deutschland im zweiten Weltkrieg.* Vol. I, *Vorbereitungen, Entfesselung, und Verlauf des Krieges bis zum 22 Juli 1941.* Berlin (East): Akademie-Verlag, 1974; Cologne: Rugenstein, 1974.

Hearden, Patrick J. *Roosevelt confronts Hitler: America's Entry into World War II.* De Kalb, Ill.: Northern Illinois University Press, 1987.

Heckmann, Wolf. *Rommel's War in Africa.* Translated by Stephen Sago. Garden City, N.Y.: Doubleday, 1981.

Henke, Josef. *England in Hitlers politischen Kalkül, 1935–1939.* Boppard am Rhein: Boldt, 1973.

Herwig, Holger H. *The Politics of Frustration: The United States in German Naval Planning, 1889–1941.* Boston: Little, Brown, 1976.

Herzstein, Robert E. *Roosevelt and Hitler: Prelude to War.* New York: Paragon House, 1989.

Hildebrand, Klaus H. *The Foreign Policy of the Third Reich.* Translated by Anthony Fothergill. Berkeley: University of California Press, 1973.

———. *The Third Reich.* Translated by P. S. Falla. London: Allen & Unwin, 1984.

———. *Vom Reich zum Weltreich: Hitler, NSDAP, und koloniale Frage, 1919–1945.* Munich: Fink, 1969.

Hillgruber, Andreas. *Deutschlands Rolle in der Vorgeschichte der beiden Weltkriege.* 2d ed. Göttingen: Vandenhoeck & Ruprecht, 1979.

———. *Hitlers Strategie: Politik und Kriegführung, 1940–1941.* 2d ed. Frankfurt am Main: Bernard & Graefe, 1982.

———. *Der Zenit des zweiten Weltkrieges: Juli 1941.* Wiesbaden: Steiner, 1977.

———. *Die Zerstörung Europas: Beiträge zur Weltkriegsepoche, 1914 bis 1945.* Frankfurt am Main: Bernard & Graefe, 1988.

———. *Der zweite Weltkrieg, 1939–1945: Kriegsziele und Strategie der grossen Mächte.* Stuttgart: Kohlhammer, 1982.

Hills, George. *Franco: A Man and His Nation.* New York: Macmillan, 1967.

———. *Rock of Contention: A History of Gibraltar.* London: Hale, 1974.

Hilton, Stanley E. *Hitler's Secret War in South America, 1939–1945: German Military Espionage and Allied Counterespionage in Brazil.* Baton Rouge, La.: Louisiana State University Press, 1981.

Hinsley, Francis H. *Hitler's Strategy.* Cambridge: Cambridge University Press, 1951.

Hinsley, F.H., et al. *British Intelligence in the Second World War.* 5 vols. New York: Cambridge University Press, 1979–90.

Hirschfeld, Gerhard, and Lothar Kettnacker, ed. *The "Führer State": Myth and Re-*

ality—Studies on the Structures and Politics of the Third Reich. Stuttgart: Ernst Klett, 1981.

Höhne, Heinz. *Canaris.* Translated by J. Maxwell Brownjohn. Garden City, N.Y.: Doubleday, 1979.

Hoisington, Jr., William A. *The Casablanca Connection: French Colonial Policy, 1936–1943.* Chapel Hill, N.C.: University of North Carolina Press, 1984.

———. *Lyantey and the French Conquest of Morocco.* New York: St. Martin's, 1994.

Howard, Michael. *The Mediterranean Strategy in the Second World War.* New York: Praeger, 1968.

Hurstfield, Julian G. *America and the French Nation, 1939–1945.* Chapel Hill, N.C.: University of North Carolina Press, 1986.

Jäckel, Eberhard. *Frankreich in Hitlers Europa: Die deutsche Frankreichpolitik im zweiten Weltkrieg.* Stuttgart: Deutsche Verlags-Anstalt, 1966.

———. *Hitlers Weltanschauung: A Blueprint for Power.* Translated by Herbert Arnold. Middletown, Conn.: Wesleyan University Press, 1972.

Jackson, Gabriel. *The Spanish Republic and the Civil War, 1931–1939.* Princeton, N.J.: Princeton University Press, 1965.

Jackson, William G. F. *The North African Campaign, 1940–1943.* London: Batsford, 1975.

Jacobsen, Hans-Adolf. *Nationalsozialistische Außenpolitik, 1933–1938.* Frankfurt am Main: Metzner, 1968.

Jonas, Manfred. *The United States and Germany: A Diplomatic History.* Ithaca, N.Y.: Cornell University Press, 1984.

Junker, Detlef. *Franklin D. Roosevelt: Macht und Vision, Präsident in Krisenzeiten.* Göttingen: Musterschmidt, 1979.

———. *Kampf um die Weltmacht: Die USA und das Dritte Reich, 1939–1945.* Düsseldorf: Schwann, 1988.

———. *Der unteilbare Weltmarkt: Das ökonomische Interesse in der Außenpolitik der USA, 1933–1941.* Stuttgart: Klett, 1975.

Kahn, David. *Hitler's Spies: German Military Intelligence in World War II.* New York: Macmillan, 1978.

Kay, Hugh. *Salazar and Modern Portugal.* New York: Hawthorn Books, 1970.

Kent, John. *The Internationalization of Colonialism: Britain, France, and Black Africa, 1939–1956.* Oxford: Clarendon Press, 1992.

Killingray, David, and Richard Rathbone. *Africa and the Second World War.* New York: St. Martin's Press, 1986.

Klee, Karl. *Das Unternehmen "Seelöwe": Die geplante deutsche Landung in England 1940.* Göttingen: Musterschmidt, 1958.

Kleinfeld, Gerald R. and Lewis Tambs. *Hitler's Spanish Legion: The Blue Division in Russia.* Carbondale, Ill.: Southern Illinois University Press, 1979.

Knox, MacGregor. *Mussolini Unleashed, 1939–1941: Politics and Strategy in Fascist Italy's Last War.* Cambridge: Cambridge University Press, 1982.

Krautkrämer, Elmar. *Frankreichs Kriegswende 1942: Die Rückwirkungen der alliierte*

Landung in Nordafrika: Darlan, de Gaulle, Giraud, und die royalistiche Utopie. Bern: Lang, 1989.

Krebs, Gerhard. *Japans Deutschlandpolitik, 1935–1941: Eine Studie zur Vorgeschichte des pazifischen Krieges.* 2 vols. Hamburg: MOAG Mitteilungen, 1984.

Kum'a N'dumbe III, Alexandre. *Hitler voulait l'Afrique: La projet du 3e Reich ser le continent africain.* Paris: Harmatten, 1980.

Kupferman, Fred. *Laval.* Paris: Balland, 1987.

Lacouture, Jean. *De Gaulle.* Vol I, *The Rebel, 1890–1944.* Translated by Patrick O'Brien. New York: Norton, 1990.

Landou, Rom. *Moroccan Drama, 1900–1955.* San Francisco: American Academy of Asian Studies, 1956.

Langer, William L. *Our Vichy Gamble.* New York: Knopf, 1947; reprint, New York: Norton, 1966.

Langer, William L. and S. Everett Gleason. *The Undeclared War, 1940–1941.* New York: Harper & Brothers, 1953.

Leitz, Christian. *Economic Relations between Nazi Germany and Franco's Spain, 1936–1945.* London: Oxford University Press, 1996.

Lengyel, Emil. *Dakar: Outpost of Two Hemispheres.* New York: Random House, 1941.

Mack Smith, Denis. *Mussolini.* London: Weidenfeld & Nicolson, 1982.

———. *Mussolini's Roman Empire.* New York: Viking, 1976.

Marder, Arthur J. *From the Dardenelles to Oran: Studies of the Royal Navy in War and Peace.* London: Oxford University Press, 1974.

———. *Operation "Menace": The Dakar Expedition and the Dudley North Affair.* London: Oxford University Press, 1976.

Martin, Bernd. *Friedensinitiativen und Machtpolitik im zweiten Weltkrieg, 1939–1942.* Düsseldorf: Droste, 1976.

Medlicott, W. N. *The Economic Blockade.* 2 vols. London: HMSO, 1952–59.

Merkes, Manfred. *Die deutsche Politik gegenüber dem spanischer Bürgerkrieg, 1936–1939.* 2d ed. Bonn: Rohrscheid, 1969.

Meskill, Johanna M. *Hitler and Japan: The Hollow Alliance.* New York: Atherton Press, 1966.

Michalka, Wolfgang. *Ribbentrop und die deutsche Weltpolitik, 1933–1940: Außenpolitische Konzeptionen und Entscheidungsprozesse im dritten Reich.* Munich: Fink, 1980.

———, ed. *Der zweite Welthrieg: Analysen, grundzüge, Forschungsbilanz.* Munich: Piper, 1989.

Miller, Michael B. *Shanghai on the Métro: Spies, Intrigue, and the French between the Wars.* Berkeley: University of California Press, 1994.

Milward, Alan S. *The New Order and the French Economy.* Oxford: Clarendon Press, 1970.

Militärgeschichtliches Forschungsamt, gen. eds. Das deutsche Reich und der Zweite Weltkreig. 10 vols.(in progress). Stuttgart: Deutsche Verlags-Anstalt, 1979–.

Morales Lezcano, Victor. *El colonialismo hispanofrancés en Marruecos (1898–1927).* Madrid: Siglo XXI de España Editores, 1976.

————. *España y el norte de Africa: el protectorado en Marruecos (1912–1956).* 2d ed. Madrid: Universidad Nacional de Educación a la Distancia, 1986.

————. *Historia de la no-beligerancia española durante la segunda guerra mundial.* Las Palmas: Plan Cultural, 1980.

Morison, Samuel Eliot. *History of United States Naval Operations in World War II.* Vol. II, *Operations in North African Waters, October 1942–June 1943.* Boston: Little, Brown, 1951.

Mueller, Gene. *The Forgotten Field Marshal: Wilhelm Keitel.* Durham, N.C.: Moore, 1979.

Murray, Williamson. *Strategy for Defeat: The Luftwaffe, 1933–1945.* Maxwell Air Force Base, Ala.: Air University Press, 1983.

Neugebauer, Karl-Völker. *Die deutsche Militärkontrolle im unbesetzten Frankreich und in Französisch-Nordafrika, 1940–1942: Zum Problem der Sicherung der Südwestflanke von Hitlers Kontinentalimperium.* Boppard am Rhein: Boldt, 1980.

Olshausen, Klaus. *Zwischenspiel auf dem Balkan: Die deutsche Politik gegenüber Jugoslawien und Griechenland von März bis Juli 1941.* Stuttgart: Deutsche Verlags-Anstalt, 1973.

Paxton, Robert O. *Parades and Politics at Vichy: The French Officer Corps under Marshal Pétain.* Princeton, N.J.: Princeton University Press, 1966.

————. *Vichy France: Old Guard and New Order, 1940–1944.* New York: Knopf, 1972; reprint, New York: Norton, 1972.

Payne, Stanley G. *Falange: A History of Spanish Fascism.* Palo Alto: Stanford University Press, 1961.

————. *The Franco Regime, 1936–1975.* Madison, Wis.: University of Wisconsin Press, 1987.

————. *Politics and the Military in Modern Spain.* Palo Alto: Stanford University Press, 1967.

Petersen, Jens. *Hitler-Mussolini: Die Entstehung der Achse Berlin-Rom, 1933–1936.* Tübingen: Niemayer, 1973.

Pitt, Barrie. *The Crucible of War: The Western Desert, 1941.* London: Cape, 1980.

Playfair, Ian Stanley Ord et al. *History of the Second World War: The Mediterranean and the Middle East.* 6 vols. London: HMSO, 1954–88.

Pollack, Benny. *The Paradox of Spanish Foreign Policy: Spain's International Relations from Franco to Democracy.* New York: St. Martin's Press, 1987.

Porch, Douglas. *The Conquest of Morocco.* New York: Knopf, 1983.

Preston, Paul. *Franco: A Biography.* New York: Basic Books, 1994.

Proctor, Raymond. *Agony of a Neutral: Spanish German Wartime Relations and the "Blue Division."* Moscow, Idaho: Idaho Research Foundation, 1974.

Puzzo, Dante A. *Spain and the Great Powers, 1936–1941.* New York: Columbia University Press, 1962.

Raeder, Erich. *Der Kreuzerkrieg in den ausländischen Gewässern.* Berlin: Mittler, 1922.

Reile, Oskar. *Geheime Westfront: Die Abwehr, 1935–1945.* Munich: Welser-Mühl, 1962.

Reuth, Ralf Georg. *Entscheidung im Mittelmeer: Die südliche Peripherie Europas in der deutschen Strategie des zweiten Weltkrieges, 1940–1942.* Koblenz: Bernard & Graefe, 1985.

Rich, Norman. *Hitler's War Aims.* 2 vols. New York: Norton, 1973–74.

Roskill, Stephen W. *The War at Sea.* 3 vols. London: HMSO, 1954–61.

Rout, Leslie B. and John F. Bratzel. *The Shadow War: German Espionage and United Stated Counterespionage in Latin America during World War II.* Frederick, Md.: University Publications of America, 1986.

Ruhl, Klaus-Jörg. *Spanien im zweiten Weltkrieg: Franco, die Falange, und das "Dritte Reich."* Hamburg: Hoffman & Campe, 1975.

Sainsbury, Keith. *The North African Landings, 1942: A Strategic Decision.* London: Davis-Poynter, 1976.

Salewski, Michael. *Die deutsche Seekriegsleitung, 1935–1945.* 3 vols. Frankfurt am Main: Bernard & Graefe, 1970–75.

Schmokel, Wolfe W. *Dream of Empire: German Colonialism, 1919–1945.* New Haven, Conn.: Yale University Press, 1964.

Schreiber, Gerhard. *Revisionismus und Weltmachtstreben: Marineführung und deutsch-italienische Beziehungen, 1919 bis 1944.* Stuttgart: Deutsche Verlags-Anstalt, 1978.

Schröder, Bernd Philipp. *Irak, 1941.* Freiburg: Rombach, 1980.

Schröder, Hans-Jürgen. *Deutschland und die Vereinigten Staaten, 1933–1939: Wirtschaft und Politik in der Entwicklung des deutsch-amerikanischen Gegensatzes.* Wiesbaden: Steiner, 1970.

Schumann, Wolfgang, ed. *Konzept für die Neuordnung der Welt: Die Kriegziele des faschisten deutschen Imperialismus im zweiten Weltkrieg.* Berlin (East): Dietz, 1977.

Séguéla, Matthieu. *Pétain-Franco: les secrets d'une alliance.* Paris: Albin Michel, 1992.

Siedentopf, Monika. *Die britische Pläne zur Besetzung der spanischen und portugiesischen Atlantikinseln während des zweiten Weltkrieges.* Münster: Aschendorffsche Verlagbuchhandlung, 1982.

Smyth, Denis. *Diplomacy and the Strategy of Survival: British Policy and Franco's Spain, 1940–1941.* Cambridge: Cambridge University Press, 1986.

Sommer, Theo. *Deutschland und Japan zwischen den Mächten, 1935–1940: Von Antikomminternpakt zu Dreimächtpakt.* Tübingen: Mohr, 1962.

Steele, Richard W. *The First Offensive, 1942: Roosevelt. Marshall, and the Making of American Strategy.* Bloomington: Indiana University Press, 1973.

Stewart, Charles F. *The Economy of Morocco, 1912–1962.* Cambridge: Harvard University Press, 1964.

Stoakes, Geoffrey. *Hitler and the Quest for World Dominion.* Leamington Spa: Berg, 1986.

Stoecker, Hellmuth, ed. *Drang nach Afrika: Die koloniale Expansionspolitik und Herrschaft des deutschen Imperialismus in Afrika von den Anfängen bis zum Ende des zweiten Weltkrieges.* Berlin (East): Akademie-Verlag, 1977.

Stuart, Graham. *The International City of Tangier.* 2nd ed. Palo Alto: Stanford University Press, 1955.

Taylor, Alan J. P. *The Origins of the Second World War.* London: Hamilton, 1961.

Taysen, Adelbert von. *Tobruk 1941: Der Kampf in Nordafrika.* Freiburg: Rombach, 1976.

Temperley, Harold W. V., ed. *History of the Peace Conference at Paris.* 6 vols. Reprint, London: Oxford University Press, 1969.

Thies, Jochen. *Architekt der Weltherrschaft: Die "Endziele" Hitlers.* Düsseldorf: Droste, 1980.

Thomas, Charles S. *The German Navy in the Nazi Era.* Annapolis, Md.: Naval Institute Press, 1990.

Thomas, Hugh. *The Spanish Civil War.* 3rd ed. New York: Harper & Row, 1986.

Tillmann, Heinz. *Deutschlands Araberpolitik im zweiten Weltkrieg.* Berlin (East): Deutscher Verlag der Wissenschaften, 1965.

Truchet, André. *L'armistice de 1940 et l'Afrique du nord.* Paris: Presses Universitaires de France, 1955.

Trythall, John W. D. *El Caudillo: A Political Biography of Franco.* New York: McGraw-Hill, 1970.

Tusell, Xavier and Genoveva García Queipo de Llano. *Franco y Mussolini: La politica española durante la segunda guerra mundial.* Barcelona: Planeta, 1985.

Umbreit, Hans. *Der Militärbefehlshaber in Frankreich, 1940–1944.* Boppard am Rhein: Boldt, 1968.

Van Creveld, Martin. *Hitler's Strategy, 1940–1941: The Balkan Clue.* Cambridge: Cambridge University Press, 1973.

Vincent, Jean-Noël. *Les Forces françaises dans la lutte contre l'Axe en Afrique: Les Forces françaises libres en Afrique, 1940–1943.* Chateau de Vincennes: Ministère de la Défense/État-Major de l'Armée de Terre/Service Historique, 1983.

Vintras, R. E. *The Portuguese Connection: The Secret History of the Azores Base.* London: Bachman & Turner, 1974.

Warner, Geoffrey. *Iraq and Syria, 1941.* London: Davis; Poynter, 1974.

———. *Pierre Laval and the Eclipse of France.* New York: Macmillan, 1968.

Wegener, Wolfgang. *Die Seestrategie des Weltkrieges.* Berlin: Mittler, 1929.

Weinberg, Gerhard L. *The Foreign Policy of Hitler's Germany.* 2 vols. Reprint, Atlantic Highlands, N.J.: Humanities Press, 1994.

———. *Germany and the Soviet Union, 1939–1941.* Leyden: Brill, 1954.

———. *Germany, Hitler, and World War II: Essays on Modern German and World History.* New York: Cambridge University Press, 1995.

———. *A World at Arms: A Global History of World War II.* Cambridge: Cambridge University Press, 1994.

———. *World in the Balance: Behind the Scenes of World War II.* Hanover, N.H.: University Press of New England, 1981.

Weiss, Kenneth G. *The Azores in Diplomacy and Strategy, 1940–1945.* Alexandria, Va.: Center for Naval Analysis, 1980.

Whealey, Robert H. *Hitler and Spain: The Nazi Role in the Spanish Civil War, 1936–1939.* Lexington, Ky.: University Press of Kentucky, 1989.

Wheatley, Ronald. *Operation Sea Lion: German Plans for the Invasion of England, 1939–1942.* Oxford: Clarendon Press, 1958.

Wiskemann, Elizabeth. *The Rome-Berlin Axis: A History of Relations between Hitler and Mussolini*. Rev. ed., London: 1966.

Woodward, Sir Llewellyn. *British Foreign Policy in the Second World War*. 5 vols. London: HMSO, 1970–1976.

Woolman, David S. *Rebels in the Rif: Abd el-Krim and the Rif Rebellion*. Palo Alto: Stanford University Press, 1968.

Zieb, Paul. *Logistik-Probleme der Kriegsmarine*. Neckargemünd: Scharnhorst Buch-kameradschaft, 1961.

VI. Secondary Sources: Articles

Abendroth, Hans Henning. "Spanien: Das Ringen um die Gestaltung des Franco-Staates." In *Innen-und Außenpolitik unter nationalsozialistischer Bedrohung: Determinanten internationaler Beziehungen in historischen Fallstudien*, edited by Erhard Forndran, Frank Golczewski, and Dieter Riesenberger, 110–29. Opladen: Westdeutscher Verlag, 1977.

Ageron, Charles-Robert. "Les populations du Maghreb face à la propagande allemande." *Revue d'histoire de la deuxième guerre mondiale* 29 (April 1979): 1–39.

Al-Quazzaz, Ayad. "The Iraqi-British War of 1941: A Review Article." *International Journal of Middle East Studies* 7 (October 1976): 591–96.

Baptiste, F. A. "Le régime de Vichy à la Martinique (juin 1940 à juin 1943)." *Revue d'histoire de la deuxième guerre mondiale* 28 (July 1978): 1–24.

Bernecker, Walther L. "Neutralität wider Willen: Spaniens verhinderter Kriegseintritt." In *Kriegsausbruch 1939: Beteiligte, Betroffene, Neutrale*. Edited by Helmut Altrichter and Josef Becker, 153–77. Munich: Beck, 1989.

Blair, Leon Borden. "Amateurs in Diplomacy: The American Vice Consuls in North Africa, 1941–1943." *The Historian* 35 (August 1973): 607–20.

———. "The Impact of Franco-American Military Agreements on Moroccan Nationalism, 1940–1956." *Rocky Mountain Social Science Journal* 9 (January 1972): 61–68.

Blinkhorn, Martin. "Spain, the Spanish Problem, and the Imperial Myth." *Journal of Contemporary History* 15 (January 1980): 5–25.

Böhme, Hermann. "Deutschland und Frankreich im zweiten Weltkrieg 1940–1941: Die Geschichte des Waffenstillstandes." *Aus Politik und Zeitgeschichte* 31 (1966): 3–30; 33 (1966): 3–32.

Bouche, Denise. "La retour de l'Afrique occidentale française dans la lutte contre l'ennemi aux côtes des allies." *Revue d'histoire de la deuxième guerre mondiale* 29 April (1979): 40–68.

Broszat, Martin. "Soziale Motivation und Führerbindung des Nationalsozialismus." *Vierteljahrshefte für Zeitgeschichte* 18 (October 1970): 392–409.

Burdick, Charles B. "Moro: The Resupply of German Submarines in Spain, 1939–1942." *Central European History* 3 (September 1970): 256–84.

Clarence-Smith, Gervase. "The Impact of the Spanish Civil War and the Second World War on Portuguese and Spanish Africa." *Journal of African History* 26 (1985): 309–26.

Collado Seidel, Carlos. "Zufluchtsstätte für Nationalsozialisten? Spanien, die Allierten und die Behandlung deutscher Agenten 1944–1947." *Vierteljahrshefte für Zeitgeschichte* 43 (January 1995): 131–58.

Colvin, Ian. "The Hendaye Tapestry: Hitler and Spain." *The National and English Review* 135 (1950): 21–27.

Cortada, James W. "Spain and the Second World War: The Laurel Incident." *Journal of Contemporary History* 5 (September 1970): 65–75.

Crowder, Michael. "World War II and Africa: Introduction." *Journal of African History* 26 (1985): 287–88.

Dankelmann, Otfried. "Zur spanischen 'Nichtkriegführung' im zweiten Weltkrieg." *Zeitschrift für Militärgeschichte* 9 (1970): 683–92.

Derrick, Jonathan. "Free French and Africans in Douala, 1940–1941." *Journal of the Historical Society of Nigeria* 10 (June 1980): 53–70.

Detwiler, Donald S. "Spain and the Axis during World War II." *The Review of Politics* 33 (July 1971): 36–56.

Dumet, Raymond. "Africa's Strategic Minerals during the Second World War." *Journal of African History* 26 (1985): 381–408.

Echenberg, Myron. "'Morts pour la France': The African Soldier in France during the Second World War." *Journal of African History* 26 (1985): 373–80.

Fleming, Shannon. "Spanish Morocco and the *Alzamiento Nacional,* 1936–1939: The Military, Economic, and Political Mobilization of a Protectorate." *Journal of Contemporary History* 18 (January 1983): 27–42.

Fleming, Shannon C. and Ann K. Fleming. "Primo de Rivera and Spain's Moroccan Problem, 1923–1927." *Journal of Contemporary History* 12 (January 1977): 85–99.

Fox, J. D. "Adolf Hitler: The Continuing Debate." *International Affairs* 55 (April 1979): 252–64.

Goda, Norman J.W. "Hitler's Demand for Casablanca in 1940: Incident or Policy?" *International History Review* 26 (August 1994): 441–60.

———. "The Riddle of the Rock: A Reassessment of German Motives for the Capture of Gibraltar in the Second World War." *Journal of Contemporary History* 28 (April 1993): 297–314.

Groehler, Olaf. "Kolonialforderungen als Teil der faschistischen Kriegzielplannung." *Zeitschrift für Militärgeschichte* 4 (1965): 547–62.

———. "Die Rolle Nordafrikas in der Kriegführung des deutschen Imperialismus während des zweiten Weltkrieges." *Militärwesen* 7 (1963): 412–28.

Gruchmann, Lothar. "Die 'verpaßten strategischen Chancen' der Achsenmächte im Mittelmeerraum, 1940–1941." *Vierteljahrshefte für Zeitgeschichte* 18 (October 1970): 456–75.

Hadeler, Wilhelm. "Die Flugzeugträger in der deutschen Marine von 1934 bis 1945." *Marine Rundschau* 53 (October 1956): 162–69.

Halstead, Charles R. "Un 'Africain' méconnu: le colonel Juan Beigbeder." *Revue d'histoire de la deuxième guerre mondiale* 21 (July 1971): 31–60.

———. "Consistent and Total Peril from Every Side: Portugal and its 1940 Protocol with Spain." *Iberian Studies* 3 (Spring 1974): 15–29.

———. "Historians in Politics: Carlton J. H. Hayes as American Ambassador to

Spain 1942–1945." *Journal of Contemporary History* (July 1975): 383–405.

———. "A 'Somewhat Machiavellian' Face: Colonel Juan Beigbeder as High Commissioner in Spanish Morocco, 1937–1939." *The Historian* 37 (November 1974): 46–66.

———. "Spanish Foreign Policy, 1936–1978." In *Spain in the Twentieth Century World: Essays on Spanish Diplomacy, 1878–1978,* edited by James W. Cortada, 41–94. Westport, Conn.: Greenwood Press, 1980.

Halstead, Charles R. and Carolyn J. Halstead. "Aborted Imperialism: Spain's Occupation of Tangier 1940–1945." *Iberian Studies* 7 (Autumn 1978): 53–71.

Hartmann, Peter Claus. "Frankreich im Jahr 1941: Seine militärische, politische, und wirtschaftliche Situation." In *Das Jahr 1941 in der europäischen Politik,* edited by Karl Bosl, 39–55. Munich: Oldenburg, 1972.

Hauner, Milan. "Did Hitler Want a World Dominion?" *Journal of Contemporary History* 13 (January 1978): 15–32.

Headrick, Rita. "African Soldiers in World War II." *Armed Forces and Society* 4 (1978): 501–26.

Herde, Peter. "Japan, Deutschland und die Vereinigten Staaten im Jahre 1941." In *Kriegswende Dezember 1941: Referate und Diskussionsbeiträge des internationalen historischen Symposiums in Stuttgart vom 17. bis 19. September 1981,* edited by Jürgen Röhwer et al., 36–54. Koblenz: Bernard & Graefe, 1984.

Herwig, Holger H. "Prelude to *Weltblizkrieg:* Germany's Naval Policy towards the United States of America, 1939–1941." *Journal of Modern History* 43 (December 1971): 649–68.

Hildebrand, Klaus. "Hitler's War Aims." *Journal of Modern History* 48 (September 1976): 522–30.

Hillgruber, Andreas. "England's Place in Hitler's Plans for World Dominion." *Journal of Contemporary History* 13 (January 1978): 5–22.

———. "Der Faktor Amerika in Hitlers Strategie, 1939–1941." *Aus Politik und Zeitgeschichte* 19 (1966): 3–21.

———. "Politik und Strategie Hitlers im Mittelmeerraum." In *Deutsche Großmacht- und Weltpolitik im 19. und 20. Jahrhundert,* 276–95. Düsseldorf: Droste, 1977.

———. "Tendenzen, Ergebnisse und Perspektiven der gegenwärtigen Hitler-Forschung. *Historische Zeitschrift* 226 (1978): 600–21.

Homze, Edward. "The Luftwaffe's Failure to Develop a Heavy Bomber before World War II." *Aerospace Historian* 24 (1977): 20–26.

Jäckel, Eberhard. "Die deutsche Kriegserklärung an die Vereinigten Staaten von 1941." In *Im Dienst Deutschlands und des Rechtes: Festschrift für Wilhelm G. Grewe zum 70. Geburtstag am 16. Oktober 1981,* edited by Friedrich J. Kroneck and Thomas Oppermann, 117–37. Baden-Baden: Nomos-Verlagsgesellschaft, 1981.

Joffé, E. G. H. "The Moroccan Nationalist Movement: Istiglal, the Sultan and the Country." *Journal of African History* 26 (1985): 289–307.

Junker, Detlef. "The Continuity of Ambivalence: German Views of America, 1933–1945." In *Transatlantic Images and Perceptions: Germany and America since*

1776, edited by David E. Barclay and Elisabeth Glaser-Schmidt. Cambridge: Cambridge University Press, 1997.

———. "Hitler's Perception of FDR and the USA." In *FDR and his Contemporaries: Foreign Perceptions of an American President,* edited by Cornelis A. van Minnen and John F. Sears, 145–56. New York: St. Martin's, 1992.

Kirkland, Faris R. "The French Air Force in 1940: Was It Defeated by the Luftwaffe or by Politics?" *Air University Review* 36 (1985): 101–108.

Klee, Karl. "Der Entwurf zur Führerweisung Nr. 32 vom 11. Juni 1941: Eine quellenkritische Untersuchung." *Wehrwissenschaftliche Rundschau* 6 (1956): 127–41.

Knipping, Franz. "Die deutsche Frankreichpolitik 1940–1942." In *Der zweite Weltkrieg: Analysen, Grungzüge, Forschungsbilanz,* edited by Wolfgang Michalka, 697–709. Munich: Piper, 1989.

Knox, MacGregor. "Fascist Italy Assesses Its Enemies 1935–1940." In *Knowing One's Enemies: Intelligence Assessment before the Two World Wars,* edited by Ernest R. May, 347–72. Princeton, N.J.: Princeton University Press, 1984.

Krautkrämer, Elmar. "Admiral Darlan, de Gaulle und das royalistische Komplott in Algier 1942: Politische Implicationen der Kriegswende in Französische Nordafrika." *Vierteljahrshefte für Zeitgeschichte* 32 (December 1984): 529–81.

———. "Die Entmachtung Lavals im Dezember 1940: Ein außenpolitisches Kalkül Vichys." *Vierteljahshefte für Zeitgeschichte* 27 (March 1979): 79–112.

———. "General Giraud und Admiral Darlan in der Vorgeschichte der alliierte Landung in Nordafrika." *Vierteljahrshefte für Zeitgeschichte* 30 (April 1982): 206–55.

Kroll, Frank-Lothar, "Geschichte und Politik im Weltbild Hitlers." *Vierteljahrshefte für Zeitgeschichte* 44 (July 1996): 327–54.

Link, Werner. "Das nationalsozialistische Deutschland und die USA, 1933–1941." *Neue Politische Literatur* 18 (1973): 225–33.

Marchat, Henri. "Les origens diplomatiques du 'Maroc espagnol' (1880–1912)." *Revue de l'occident musulman et de la Méditerranée* 7 (1970): 101–70.

———. "La France et l'Espagne au Maroc pendant la période du protectorat (1912–1956)." *Revue de l'occident musulman et de la Méditerranée* 10 (1971): 81–109.

Martin, Bernd. "Amerikas Durchbruch zur politischen Weltmacht: Die interventionistische Globalstrategie der Regierung Roosevelt, 1933–1941." *Militärgeschichtliche Mitteilungen* 30 (1981): 57–98.

———. "Das deutsch-japanische Bündnis im zweiten Weltkrieg." In *Der zweite Weltkrieg: Analysen, Grungzüge, Forschungsbilanz,* edited by Wolfgang Michalka, 120–137. Munich: Piper, 1989.

Mason, Tim. "Intention and Explanation: A Current Controversy about the Interpretation of National Socialism." In *The "Führer State": Myth and Reality— Studies on the Structure and Politics of the Third Reich,* edited by Gerhard Hirschfeld and Lothar Kettnacker. 24–41. Stuttgart: Ernst Klett, 1981.

Melka, Robert L. "Darlan between Britain and Germany, 1940–1941." *Journal of Contemporary History* 8 (April 1973): 57–80.

Meyer-Sach, Michael. "Politische Gedanken und Bemühungen der deutschen Seekriegsleitung gegenüber Frankreich in der Zeit vom Waffenstillstand bis zur allierten Landung in Nordafrika, 1940–1942." In *Geschichte der französische Marine*, edited by Wilhelm Treue. 127–91. Herford: Mittler, 1982.

Michaelis, Meier. "World Power Status or World Dominion? A Survey of the Literature on Hitler's Plan of World Domination (1937–1970)." *The Historical Journal* 15 (1972): 331–60.

Moltmann, Gunter. "Weltherrschaftsideen Hitlers." In *Europa und Übersee, Festschrift für Egmont Zechlin*, edited by Otto Brunner and Dietrich Gerhard. Hamburg: Hans Bredow Institut, 1961.

Mommsen, Hans. "Nationalsozialismus." In *Sowjetsystem und demokratische Gesellschaft: Eine vergleichende Enzyklopädie*, Vol. VI, edited by C. D. Kernig. Freiburg: Herder, 1971.

Morales Lezcano, Victor. "Las causas de la no beligerancia española, reconsideradas." *Revista de Estudios Internacionales* 5 (July–September 1984): 609–31.

———. "La cuestión del reajuste de fronteras interzonales en el protectorado hispano-frances en Marruecos." *Revista de Estudios Internacionales* 6 (April–June 1985): 357–77.

Moritz, Erhard. "Plannungen für die Kriegführung des deutschen Heeres in Afrika und Vorderasien." *Militärgeschichte* 16 (1977): 323–33.

Müller, Klaus-Jürgen. "Französisch-Nordafrika und der deutsch-französische Waffenstillstand von 1940." *Wehrwissenschaftliche Rundschau* 7 (December 1957): 687–700.

Overy, R. J. "From 'Uralbomber' to 'Amerikabomber': The Luftwaffe and Strategic Bombing." *Journal of Strategic Studies* 1 (September 1978): 154–78.

———. "The German Pre-War Aircraft Production Plans November 1936–April 1939." *English Historical Review* (October 1975): 778–97.

Philibert, J. "Les forces françaises d'Afrique du nord, septembre 1939–juin 1940." *Revue historique de l'Armée* 9 (December 1953): 105–10.

Pike, David Wingate. "Aspects nouveaux du rôle de l'Espagne dans la seconde guerre mondiale." *Revue d'histoire moderne et contemporaine* 19 (1972): 510–18.

———. "Franco and the Axis Stigma." *Journal of Contemporary History* 17 (January 1982): 369–407.

Potts, E. D. and A. Potts. "The Deployment of Black American Servicemen Abroad during World War II." *Australian Journal of Politics and History* 35 (1989): 92–96.

Preston, Paul. "Franco and Hitler: The Myth of Hendaye 1940." *Contemporary European History* 1 (March 1992): 1–16.

Preston, Paul. "General Franco Reassessed: Inertia and Risk, World War and Cold War, 1939–1953." *Journal of the Association for Contemporary Iberian Studies* 1 (Spring 1988).

Proctor, Raymond L. "The Spanish Army and the Nationalists' Moroccan Allies." *Bulletin of the Society for Spanish and Portuguese Historical Studies* 9 (October 1984): 18–19.

Rahn, Werner. "Der Atlantik in der strategischen Perspektive Hitlers und Roosevelts 1941. In *Der zweite Weltkrieg: Analysen, Grungzüge, Forschungsbilanz*, edited by Wolfgang Michalka, 667–82. Munich: Piper, 1989.

Reed, Rowena. "Central Mediterranean Sea Control and the North African Campaigns 1940–1942." *Naval War College Review* 37 (1984): 82–96.

Robineau, L. "La conduite de la guerra aérienne contre l'Allemagne de septembre 1939 à juin 1940." *Revue Historique des Armées* (1989): 102–12.

Rohwer, Jürgen. "Der Nachschubverkehr zwischen Italien und Libyen vom Juni 1940 bis Januar 1943." *Marine Rundschau* 56 (1959): 105–107.

Romer, Jeffrey A. "The German High Seas Fleet: A Reappraisal." *United States Naval Institute Proceedings* 104 (1978): 56–61.

Salewski, Michael. "Das Kriegstagebuch der deutschen Seekriegsleitung im zweiten Weltkrieg." *Marine Rundschau* 64 (June 1967): 137–45.

Schreiber, Gerhard. "Italien im Machtpolitischen Kalkül der deutschen Marineführung 1919 bis 1945." *Quellen und Forschungen aus italienischen Archiven und Bibilotheken* 62 (1982): 222–69.

———. "The Mediterranean in Hitler's Strategy in 1940: 'Programme' and Military Planning." In *The German Military in the Age of Total War*, edited by Wilhelm Deist, 240–81. Dover, N.H.: Berg, 1987.

———. "Die Rolle Frankreichs im strategischen und operativen Denken der deutschen Marine." In *Deutschland und Frankreich, 1936–1939: 15. Deutsch-Französisches Historikerkolloquim des Deutschen Historischen Instituts Paris (Bonn, 26.–29. September, 1989)*, edited by Klaus Hildebrand and Karl Ferdinand Werner, 167–213. Munich: Artemis, 1981.

Smith, Peter D. "Close Encounters of Another Kind in 1940: Casablanca and Dakar." *Mariner's Mirror* 65 (May 1979): 169–75.

Smyth, Denis. "The Dispatch of the Spanish Blue Division to the Russian Front: Reasons and Repercussions." *European History Quarterly* 24 (October 1994): 537–53.

———. "Franco and the Second World War." *History Today* 35 (November 1985): 10–15.

———. "Screening 'Torch': Allied Counter-Intelligence and the Spanish Threat to the Secrecy of the Allied Invasion of French North Africa in November 1942." *Intelligence and National Security* 4 (1989): 335–56.

Smyth, Rosaleen. "Britain's African Colonies and British Propaganda during the Second World War." *Journal of Imperial and Commonwealth History* 14 (October 1985): 65–82.

Spencer, Clair. "The Spanish Protectorate and the Occupation of Tangier in 1940." In *North Africa: Nation, State, and Region*, edited by George Joffe, 91–110. New York: Routledge, 1993.

Stegemann, Bernd. "Der Entschluß zum Unternehmen Barbarossa: Strategie oder Ideologie?" *Geschichte in Wissenschaft und Unterricht* 33 (April 1982): 205–11.

Stone, Glyn A. "The Official British Attitude to the Anglo-Portuguese Alliance, 1910–1945." *Journal of Contemporary History* 10 (October 1975): 729–46.

Syring, Enrico. "Hitlers Kriegserklärung an Amerika vom 11. Dezember 1941." In *Der zweite Weltkrieg: Analysen, Grungzüge, Forschungsbilanz,* edited by Wolfgang Michalka, 683–96. Munich: Piper, 1989.

Szaluta, Jaques. "Marshal Pétain's Ambassadorship to Spain: Conspiratorial or Providential Rise to Power?" *French Historical Studies* 8 (Fall 1974): 511–33.

Thackrah, J. R. "The Gibraltar Question and Its Effect on Anglo-Spanish Relations 1936–1945." *Iberian Studies* 5 (Spring 1976): 9–17.

Thomas, Martin. "The Anglo-French Divorce over West Africa and the Limitations of Strategic Planning, June–December 1940," *Diplomacy & Statecraft* 6 (March 1995): 252–78.

———. "Plans and Problems of the *Armée de l'Air* in the Defence of French North Africa before the Fall of France," *French History* 7 (December 1993): 472–95.

Trevor-Roper, Hugh. "Hitlers Kriegziele." *Vierteljahrshefte für Zeitgeschichte* 8 (April 1960): 121–33.

———. "Hitler und Franco: Warum nahm Spanien nicht am Krieg teil?" *Der Monat* 5 (1952–53): 625–34.

———. "The Mind of Adolf Hitler." Introduction to *Hitler's Table Talk, 1941–1944,* translated by Norman Cameron and R. H. Stevens; edited by Hugh Trevor-Roper. London: Weidenfeld & Nicholson, 1952; reprint, London: Oxford University Press, 1988.

Truchet, André. "L'armistice de juin 1940 et l'Afrique du nord." *Revue d'histoire de la deuxième guerre mondiale* 1 (June 1951): 27–50.

Viñas, Angel. "Autarquía y Política Exterior en el Primer Franquismo, 1939–1959." *Reviste de Estudios Internacionales* 1 (January 1980): 61–92.

Weinberg, Gerhard L. "Die deutsche Politik gegenüber den Vereinigten Staaten im Jahre 1941." In *Kriegswende Dezember 1941: Referate und Diskussionsbeiträge des internationalen historischen Symposiums in Stuttgart vom 17. bis 19. September 1981,* edited by Jürgen Röhwer et al., 73–80. Koblenz: Bernard & Graefe, 1984.

———. "German Colonial Plans and Policies, 1938–1942." In *Geschichte und Gegenwartsbewußtsein: Historische Betrachtungen und Untersuchungen, Festschrift für Hans Rothfels,* edited by Waldemar Besson and Friedrich Freiherr Hiller von Gaertringen, 462–91. Göttingen: Vandenhoeck & Ruprecht, 1963.

———. "Germany's Declaration of War on the United States: A New Look." In *Germany and America: Essays on Problems of International Relations and Immigration,* edited by Hans L. Trefousse, 54–70. Brooklyn: Brooklyn College Press, 1980.

———. "Hitler and England, 1933–1945: Pretense and Reality." *German Studies Review* 8 (May 1985): 299–309.

———. "Hitler's Image of the United States." *The American Historical Review* 69 (July 1964): 1006–1021.

Index

Abd-el-Aziz, 131

Abd-el-Krim, 54, 55

Abetz, Otto, 31, 73, 82–83; and American representation in French Morocco, 266n 108; and collaboration with Darlan's government, 168–69, 171, 181, 184, 261n 30; and Laval's dismissal, 136, 147–50; and Montoire meeting, 101, 108, 137, 138, 141–42, 143, 144

Abteilung Landesverteidigung (German High Command Planning Staff). *See* Warlimont, General Walter

Abwehr. See Canaris, Admiral Wilhelm; German Intelligence agencies

Alfieri, Dino, 25, 29, 61, 143

Algeria: Allied landing in, 1; French governmental flight to, 10; Italian interest in base (Oran), 10, 21–22, 28–29. *See also* Mers-el-Kebir; Oran

Ali-al-Gailani, Rashid, 168

Alsace-Lorraine: deportations from, 138, 141

Anglo-German Naval Agreement, xx

Anti-Comintern Pact, 53

Ark Royal, 21, 79

Armistice (German-French cease-fire terms, Italian-French cease-fire terms): French concerns, 9–10, 12; German-French negotiations and terms, 4–5, 8–10, 12–15; German intentions, 6; German rescinding of, 201–202; Germany and Italian terms, 4–6, 12, 14; Hitler and preamble to, 13, 23, 28; Italian-French negotiations and terms, 5; Italian intentions, 6; Spanish mediation of cease-fire, 59

Arquéz, Enrique, 220

Asensio, General Carlos, 56, 57, 73; and German propaganda in Morocco, 129; and Spanish invasion of France Morocco, 58, 221n 45

Attila, Operation, 135, 143, 149, 157

Auchinleck, General Claude, 187

Auer, Dr. Theodor: assessment of French colonial loyalty to Pétain, 152–55, 179, 182, 192; assignment to Casablanca, 152, 255n 97; objections to American representatives in Morocco, 183; objection to German inspectors in Africa, 181; problems with French authorities in Morocco, 183–84, 266n 106; and Robert Murphy, 253n 77

Axis (Rome-Berlin and Friendship Treaty), 105, 110

Azores: German concerns over American or British capture of, 74, 119; German consular representation in, 178; German strategic interest in, 8, 90;

Azore (*Continued*)German studies on capture of, 115–22, 237*n* 20, 238*n* 22; Hitler and German capture of, 68, 70, 110–11, 113, 115, 119–21, 172; Spain and, 178. *See also Dwarsläufer,* Operation; Portugal (and Portuguese Islands)

Badoglio, Marshal Pietro: and control of French forces in Africa, 45, 83; and Italian base in Algeria, 21; and Italian control of French forces in North Africa, 140, 249*n* 24; and Italian-French Armistice, 11, 37; and Mixed German-Italian Control Commission 47, 48; and possible attacks on Tunisia and Corsica, 217*n* 66
Balbo, Marshal Italo, 10
Barbarossa, Operation, 156, 161, 168, 175–76, 177
Barham, 79
Battre, Major, 154
Baudouin, Paul: and Gaullist attack on Dakar, 78, 81, 84; and German demand for Casablanca, 30; and Italian base in Algeria, 22; and relations with Spain over Morocco, 72–73, 100–101, 231*n* 28; resignation from French government 107, 235*n* 56
Baum, Robert de la, 100–101
Beigbeder y Atienza, Colonel Juan: and de Gaulle, 85, 225*n* 12, 228*n* 68; designs on French Morocco, 55, 56, 58, 225*n* 12; fall from government, 101, 103, 231*n* 30, 232*n* 38; as High Commissioner of Spanish Morocco, 55–56; negotiations with French over Moroccan border, 59, 61, 100–101, 231*n* 29; and occupation of Tangier, 57–58, 130, 220*nn* 32, 33, 221*n* 40; and Portugal, 114, 237*n* 10; and press in Morocco, 220*n* 32; and Serrano Suñer, 71; and Spanish entry into the war, 60, 222*n* 58, 228*n* 68
Beni Zerual, 55, 59, 72. *See also*

Beigbeder y Atienza, Colonel Juan; Noguès, Resident-General Charles; Border Agreement of 1925 (French-Spanish)
Benoist-Méchin, Jacques, 172
Bergeret, General Jean, 141
Béthouart, General Maurice-Emile, 182–83, 185; German evaluation of, 267*n* 115
Beynet, General Paul, 183
Bielfeld, Dr. Ernst, 192
Bismarck, xx
Böhme, Colonel Hermann, 13, 39, 140, 174
Boisson, Governor-General Pierre, 34, 38, 79, 84, 174, 181, 192
Border Agreement of 1925 (French-Spanish), 55, 59, 73, 101, 103, 163
Bordighera meeting (Italian-Spanish, 12 February 1941), 162
Bötticher, General Friedrich von, xx, 66, 87, 166
Bouthillier, Yves, 137
Brauchitsch, Field Marshal Walther von, 82–83, 119, 121, 127, 156
Brenner Meeting (German-Italian, 4 October 1940), 91, 97–100, 109, 196
Brinon, Fernand de, 147, 149, 180
Bullock, Sir Alan, xv
Bürklin, Captain Wilhelm, 218*n* 91

Cameroons: German recovery of 25, 145, 222*n* 59; Spanish claim on territory in, 222*n* 59
Canaris, Admiral Wilhelm, 38; and intelligence in Morocco, 179; meeting with Franco, 128, 134, 135, 242*n* 77
Canary Islands: and capture of Gibraltar, 110–11; concern over British/American seizure, 69, 90, 96, 113; Franco and German demands, 76; German demands for, 74, 75, 77–78, 86, 99, 199, 225*n* 13; German efforts to fortify, 132–34, 159, 163, 197, 225*n* 104, 246*n* 110; German Navy and

permanent base in xxiv, 7–8; German submarine refueling in, xxiv, 6, 24; Hitler and permanent base in, 27–28, 53, 62, 65, 70; studies on occupation of, 113, 115–22. *See also* Spain

Cape Verde Islands: German Navy and permanent base in, 8; Hitler and occupation of, 68, 70, 90, 110–11, 113, 115–22. *See also* Portugal (and Portuguese Islands)

Carceller, Demetrio, 124

Carles, General Emile-Jacques, 248*n* 4

Carls, Admiral Rolf: on bases and future enemies, 6–7; and relationship with Raeder, 205*n* 18

Casablanca: German demand for bases in, 16–32; German General Consulate in, 152, 179, 255*n* 97; German reconnaissance missions to, 50–51, 84. *See also* Morocco, French Protectorate

Catapult, Operation, 18

Cavallero, General Ugo, 188

Chamberlain, Houston Stewart, xvi

Charles-Roux, François, 72

Churchill, Prime Minister Winston, 18, 23, 78–79

Ciano, Count Galeazzo: and Armistice with France, 12; and Brenner meeting, 97; and collaboration with France, 22; and Florence meeting, 108; and Gaullist attack on Dakar, 81; and German peace appeal (19 July 1940), 23–24; and Hendaye Protocol, 123; and Italian use of Bizerte/meeting with Darlan, 188–89; and Italian war aims, 5–6, 14; and meetings with Hitler, 20, 62, 90–91; and separate peace with France, 25; and Spain, 56, 94, 100, 158–59; and Three Power Pact, 77

Crusader, Operation, 187

Cudahy, John: interview with Hitler and Ribbentrop, 166

Dakar: American consulate in, 66, 266*n* 108; British attacks on (8 July 1940), 19, 24; British-Gaullist attack on 49–50, 51, 71, 78–80; French, Belgian, Polish gold located in, 41, 79, 214*n* 46, 254*n* 93; French evacuation of women and children from, 270*n* 168; French willingness to allow German use, 172–73, 261*n* 36; German allowance of French reinforcements in, 193; German concern of British attack on, 31; German desire for base in (West Africa), 7–8, 46, 69, 70, 84, 95, 108, 117, 138–39, 141, 168–69, 171, 173–75, 176, 235*n* 59; German desire for representation in, 42, 44–46, 49, 84, 181–82, 215*n* 53, 228*n* 78; German expectation of attack in 1942, 192–93, 270*n* 168; German reconnaissance missions to, 46; as jump-off point for Cape Verdes occupation, 117–18, 121; Lufthansa service to, 20. *See also Menace,* Operation

Darlan, Admiral Jean-François: and armed convoys/bombing Gibraltar, 35–36, 42; ascendancy in French government, 167–68, 260*n* 9; and defense of Dakar in 1942, 193; and French fleet, 18–19; and German presence in Africa, 181; and German use of Syria, Tunisia, Dakar, 172, 188, 261*n* 36; and Italian base in Algeria, 21; and Laval dismissal, 147, 149–50; meeting with Hitler (25 December 1940), 156; and reconquest of French Equatorial Africa, 141–43; and surrender to Allies, 201; trip to Berchtesgaden, 170–72. *See also* Paris Protocols

de Gaulle, General Charles: coup in Equatorial Africa, 14, 21, 33, 37–40, 42, 199; failed landing at Dakar, 49–50; and French resistance, 8, 10, 33, 34, 35; German intelligence assessments

de Gaulle (*Continued*) of, 34, 211*n* 2;
Hitler and, 8, 10, 40, 46, 51, 104,
109, 126, 158–59; and New
Hebrides, 214*n* 40; and Vichy authorities, 38. *See also* Gabon; *Menace,* Operation

Delcassé, Théophile, 55

Destroyer-Base Deal, 46; German concerns, 66, 196, 199

*Dienststelle des Auswärtigen Amtes für
das Französische Protektorat
Marokko,* 255*n* 97. *See also* Auer, Dr.
Theodor; Casablanca

Dienststelle Ribbentrop, 68

Dönitz, Vice-Admiral Karl, 158

Dörnberg, Baron Alexander von, 73, 74

Doyen, General Paul, 80–82; and German presence in Morocco, 154, 180–
81, 256*nn* 103, 108; and reconquest
of French Equatorial Africa, 138,
147. *See also* Vichy Government

Dülffer, Jost, xvi

Dunkerque, 21

Duplat, Admiral Emile-André-Henri, 18,
82

Dwarsläufer, Operation, 118–19, 121

Éboué, Félix, 38–39

Erdmann, Lieutenant Colonel, 50–51, 84

Erdmann Commission, 50–51, 84. *See
also* Noguès, Resident-General
Charles

Esebeck, Colonel Freiherr von, 177–78

España, 220*n* 32

Espinosa de los Monteros, General
Eugenio: complaints to Ribbentrop,
129; and Hendaye meeting, 106;
Hitler and, 157, 169; and Serrano
Suñer's Berlin trip, 73, 74

Estéva, Admiral Jean, 174

Falange Española (*FET y de las JONS*),
54, 71

Falkenstein, Major Sigismund Freiherr
von, 113, 116, 118, 120

Falvy, General Maurice-Emile, 142, 144,
248*n* 4

Felix, Operation, 111; cancellation of,
135, 143, 144, 155–56; military
preparations, 126–28; relationship to
Barbarossa, 156; revival of, 156–64,
175–76; timing of, 121, 124–25,
160–61. *See also War Directive Number 18; War Directive Number 19*
(first, for Operation *Felix*)

Felix-Heinrich, Operation, 167, 197

Fernando Po: German demand for, 75,
87; German strategic interest in, 65

Flandin, Pierre-Étienne, 147

Florence Meeting (German-Italian, 28
October 1940), 108–10

France: Armed Forces in Africa, 18, 19,
21, 36–37, 44–49, 79, 80–83, 95,
137–38, 140–45, 172–74, 182, 185–
89, 212*n* 22, 217*n* 70, 227*n* 55, 229*nn*
2, 3, 248*nn* 3, 4, 249*n* 18, 251*nn* 46,
47, 265*n* 94, 267*n* 123; armistice
terms with Germany, 3–6, 8–10, 12;
armistice terms with Italy, 11–12;
colonial trade with Germany, 36, 42,
212*n* 17, 215*n* 52; disarmament in
Metropole, 38, 214*n* 31, 217*n* 70;
Hitler's generalities concerning, 3–4;
occupation costs, 9, 36, 176, 212*n*
17, 262*n* 49. *See also* Vichy Government

François-Poncet, André, 101

Franco Salgado-Arraujo, Francisco, 54

Franco y Bahamonde, Generalissimo
Francisco, 10, 25; and de Gaulle 85,
100, 104–106, 234*n* 44; early career
in Morocco, 54–55; and German
bases on Spanish soil, 76; letter to
Hitler of 30 October 1940, 123, 240*n*
52; and long-term alliance with Germany, 86, 92, 100; meeting with
Hitler, 103–105; and Mussolini, 53,
56, 162, 240*n* 52, 259*n* 149; neutrality and German victory, 53–54, 56,
58; political ideas and practices, 54;

refusals to enter the war, 128, 155, 160–63, 242n 77, 259nn 149; territorial claims as expressed to Hitler, 54, 104–106, 123, 162

Franco y Bahamonde, Nicolás, 115

Frick, Wilhelm, 73

Fricke, Rear Admiral Kurt: collaboration with France in Africa, 174; and defense of the Canaries, 133–34, 159, 246n 115; fleet and base issues, 6–7, 118, 176. *See also Dwarsläufer,* Operation

Gabon, 39, 79; fall of, 138–39, 248n 9; Hitler and fall of, 247n 18

García Figueras, Tomás, 56, 59, 130

German *Afrika Korps,* 169, 189

German-American Bund, xix

German Armament and Fuel Inspection Commission (French Morocco) *(Rüstungs- und Mineralölkontollkommission Marokko),* 153–55, 179, 256n 110

German Armistice Commission, 9–11, 13, 18–19, 20, 22, 30–31, 35, 39, 43, 84, 95–96, 99, 138, 145, 152, 184, 185, 187, 193; and Mixed German-Italian Control Commission, 44, 46–47, 49–50, 84, 99–100, 152; and passage of French merchant ships through Gibraltar Strait, 212n 19; and spheres of inspection responsibility in French Empire, 14, 37–38, 40–41, 43–46, 140, 153, 155, 179–80, 197, 216n 60, 256n 110. *See also* Roatta Agreements; Stülpnagel, General Carl-Heinrich von; Vogl, General Oskar

German Foreign Ministry: assessment of United States in 1942, 193; Azores, 178; France and French Empire, 42–43, 81–82, 83, 84, 138, 149; Italy, 42–44; Spain, 61, 64, 134, 178–79. *See also* Ribbentrop, Joachim von; Weizsäcker, State Secretary Ernst von

German High Command (*OKW*): attack on Gibraltar, 64, 96; cooperation with Japan, 166–67; and de Gaulle/Vichy government, 34, 41, 81, 83, 138, 139, 145, 152, 174; and Italy, 41, 42–46; and Portugal/Portuguese Islands, 65–66, 68, 119; War Economy and Armaments Office, 153, 254n 87. *See also Felix,* Operation; Warlimont, General Walter; *War Directive Number 18*

German Intelligence agencies: and Anglo-American capabilities/intentions in, 1941–42, 190–92; and de Gaulle, 34, 211n 2; and French evasion of armistice terms, 214n 33; and French Morocco, 154, 179, 185; and Portuguese armed forces, 178; and Spanish armed forces, 64, 111, 230n 24, 245n 100, 263nn 68, 69. *See also* Canaris, Admiral Wilhelm

German Luftwaffe, 24; and Hitler's demand for Casablanca, 209n 38; and Me 264, xxi–xxii, 26–27; and Spanish/Portuguese island occupation, 69, 90, 116, 118, 120. *See also Felix,* Operation

German Navy/Naval Command: and "Anglo-Saxon Powers" (Great Britain, United States), 7, 26, 40, 62, 66–67, 68, 89, 151–52, 166, 210n 58; and attack on the USSR, 68; and fleet/wharf construction, xx–xxi, 26–27, 62, 176; fortification of Canary islands, 132–34, 159, 163, 197, 225n 104, 246n 110; and France, French empire, collaboration and use of French ports, 7, 19–20, 35–36, 39–40, 42, 44, 69, 83, 89, 96, 151, 172, 174, 176, 197; and German empire in Central Africa, xxv, 6; and Mediterranean Strategy (Gibraltar, Suez), 68–69, 89, 92–93, 95, 96, 121, 151, 158, 198; and need for permanent bases, xxiv, 6–8, 27–28, 46, 66–67,

German Navy/Naval Command (*Continued*) 198; and occupation of Portuguese islands, 118–20, 240*n* 43; and Operation *Seelöwe,* 68; for surface unit refueling, 245*n* 105; use of Spanish ports for submarine refueling, 6, 24; and Versailles restrictions, xxi. *See also Dwarsläufer,* Operation; Trondheim; *War Directive Number 18*

Gibraltar, 7, 18, 36, 40, 52; French attacks on, 19, 21, 31, 35, 81, 227*n* 41; German plans for attack on, 64, 110–11; German strategic interest in, 33, 38, 46, 52–53, 60–70, 74, 75, 95, 96, 98, 109, 151, 155–56; Spanish claim on, 57, 58, 60, 65. *See also Felix,* Operation

Gloire: British capture of, 79–80, 226*nn* 34, 37

Goebbels, Joseph xxiii, 20, 24

Göring, Hermann xxiv, 64–65, 119; and *Me 264,* xxi; meeting with Juin, 189; and meeting with Laval, 138–39; meeting with Pétain and Darlan, 188

Great Britain: alliance with Portugal, 114; attack on Mers-el-Kebir, 18; attacks on Dakar, 19, 24, blockade of Metropole and influence on French empire, 35; and French Navy, 17; and Italian Mediterranean transport, 187; landing in Crete, attack on Tarent, 239*n* 40; offensives in North Africa, 151, 187, 254*n* 89; and Spanish claim to French Morocco, 259*n* 152; and Spanish claim to Gibraltar, 259*n* 152; and Takoradi route, 192. *See also Menace,* Operation

Greece: German aid to Italy in, 158–59; Italian attack on, 108

Guzzoni, General Alfredo, 158

Halder, *Generaloberst Franz,* 63, 64, 119, 126, 127, 167

H-Class battleships, xx, 26–27

Hemmen, Hans-Richard, 41–42, 49, 137, 152

Hencke, Andor, 207*n* 49, 215*n* 60, 252*n* 61

Hendaye meetings (German-Spanish, 23 October 1940), 103–106, 232*n* 40; German assumptions from, 106, 108, 110, 112, 117, 122–23; Spanish reactions to, 106, 123, 129

Hendaye protocol, 105–106, 108, 123; Italy and, 123, 234*n* 48; Spanish dissatisfaction with, 124–25, 161–62; Spanish signature, 124; text of, 234*n* 48, 235*n* 54

Hermes, 19

Heye, Helmuth, xxiv

Hillgruber, Andreas, xv

Hitler, Adolf: and anti-semitism, xvi; early influences, xvi; early statements on global hegemony xiv, xvii, 195; and German inspection commissions in Africa, 44, 46, 216*n* 63; and Great Britain, British Empire, xxv, 5, 8, 15, 23–27, 52, 60–61, 63–64, 87–88, 97–98, 102–103, 104, 107, 109, 112, 120, 166–67, 198; and interservice cooperation, xxii; and Latin America, xviii; and Japan, xviii, 67–68, 75, 77, 157, 166–67, 190; and Mediterranean Strategy, 69, 92, 240*n* 54, 158, 195; and *Me 264, "Amerika Bomber,"* 120, 172; and Portugal, Portuguese Islands, 65–66, 68, 87–88, 110–11, 113–14, 115, 117, 119, 120–22, 172, 175, 196–97, 239*n* 35; and social Darwinism, xvi; and Soviet Union, xvi, 63, 157, *See also Barbarossa,* Operation

——and France: armistice terms with, 5, 8–10, 12, 13; collaboration with Vichy government, xvii, 90–91, 94, 97–112, 119, 125, 138, 139–40, 142–43, 151, 168, 170–71, 172, 175–76, 200, 235*n* 59, 249*n* 18, 260*n* 13; concerns with French em-

pire, 35, 38, 40, 42, 46–47, 51, 69, 74, 75, 87–89; and de Gaulle, 8, 10, 40, 46, 51, 104, 109, 126, 158–59; demand for Casablanca, 16, 21–23, 31, 60, 62, 69–70, 88, 107, 195; and Laval, Laval dismissal, 101–103, 106–108, 110, 146–51, 168, 196, 254n 87, 260n 13; and Pétain, 101–103, 106–108, 109–10, 146, 150, 158; reaction to British attack on Dakar, 81–83; reaction to British attack on Mers-el-Kebir, 18–19, 62; and reduction of French occupation costs, 176, 262n 49; and Weygand, 48, 126, 134–35, 143, 147–51, 154, 156–57, 158–59, 168, 187–88, 196, 260n 13
———and Italy: and Italian armistice terms with France, 5–6, 12; and Italian attack on Greece, 108–109, 241n 64; and Italian authority in French Africa, 38, 40, 43, 46–48, 140, 153, 216n 63; and Italian use of Bizerte, 189; and Italian war aims, 5–6, 98, 110, 112, 233n 42, 247n 124; Mediterranean as Italian theater, 5, 12, 38
———and Spain: and Franco's refusal to enter war, 134–35, 143, 156–57, 159–60, 161–62, 163, 168–69, 175, 196; general ideas and Spanish civil war, 52; at Hendaye meeting, 234n 45; and "Latin talkativeness," 233n 43; and Spain's economic needs, 64–65, 124, 241n 64; Spanish belligerence, 10, 61–65, 97, 110–11, 123–25, 143, 195, 230n 15, 241n 66; and territorial arrangements with, 28, 58, 65, 74, 75, 77, 78, 86–91, 92, 98–99, 103–106, 109–10, 112, 123–25, 225n 13, 232n 40. See also Felix, Operation
———and United States: general views, xvii–xx; inheritance of British empire, 5, 23, 97; thoughts on war and competition for bases with, 8, 25–27, 46, 66–67, 74–75, 78, 87–88, 90, 97,

104, 109, 111–12, 120, 157, 166–67, 170–71, 176, 177, 190, 191, 195–98, 260n 5
Hoare, Sir Samuel, 78, 85, 231n 28, 232n 38, 259n 152
Hoßbach Conference, xx
Hoyningen-Huene, Baron Oswald von, 115, 177–78
Hünermann, Colonel, 153–54
Huntziger, General Charles-Léon: on Armistice terms with Germany, 9–11, 206n 25; death of, 268n 136; and German presence in Morocco, 154; and German threat to French Empire, 28, 30, 31, 78, 212n 19; and German use of Dakar, 173; Hitler and, 101, 154, 158; and Italy's entrance into the war, 10; memoranda on French military needs in Africa, 137–38, 141–42, 144–45; reconquest of Equatorial Africa, 142–44; and relaxation of disarmament clauses, 18, 19, 28, 37, 40–42, 48–49, 82; and removal of Weygand, 149

Iceland: American occupation and German reaction, 176, 177; German interest in, 7
Iraq: revolt in, German reaction, 168–69
Italian Armistice Commission, 11, 13, 21, 22, 82–83, 96, 99, 140–42, 155, 188, 227n 38; and French merchant shipping, 35, 140, 211n 11, 249n 24; and Italian control of French armed forces in Africa, 37–38, 40, 44, 48, 83, 96, 99, 140–41, 185, 227n 55, 230n 19; representatives and inspectors in French Africa, 37, 155, 180, 257n 112; spheres of supervisory responsibility in French empire, 14, 37–40, 50, 100, 140–41, 154–55, 179–80, 249n 24, 256n 110
Italy: armistice terms with France, 5, 10–15, 21; attack on Greece, 108, 239n 40; demand for base in Algeria, 21–

Italy (*Continued*) 22, 28–29; and German involvement in Africa, 28–29, 47–48, 100; planning for attacks on Corsica and Tunisia, 217*n* 66; war aims, 5–6, 29, 77, 98–99, 110, 123; war with British in Mediterranean, 108, 151, 187, 239*n* 40, 254*n* 89; war with France, 5, 11, 89, 96. *See also* Turin Protocol

Japan: German cooperation with, 166–67; Pacific offensives of, 1941–42, 190; Three Power Pact with Germany and Italy, 67–68, 70, 77
Jean Bart, 24, 182
Jodl, *Generaloberst* Alfred, xxii; and Armistice terms with France, 4, 9–10; and arrangements with Spain, 65, 68, 93, 96, 134, 157–58, 159; and French empire, 41, 81, 82, 83, 96; and Italian authority in French Africa, 43–44; and Portuguese islands, 117, 119, 120, 121, 122; and war against Great Britain, 61
Jordana y Souza, Count Francisco Gómez, 56, 178
Juin, General Alphonse, 187; and defenses in North Africa, 189, 191; Hitler's mistrust of, 187, 268*n* 138; release from prison camp, 268*n* 138
Junge, Captain Rolf, 115, 116, 118

Keitel, Field Marshall Wilhelm, xxii, 120, 143; and armistice with France, 9–10, 41, 64; and collaboration with France, 139, 140, 145, 151–52, 172, 176, 187, 188, 193, 254*n* 87; and Erdmann Commission, 50; and Italian authority in French Africa, 64, 140, 155; and Japan, 166; and Spain, 134
Klaube, German Consul, 49, 181, 255*n* 97
Konakry: German interest in, 215*n* 52
Kontrollinspektion Afrika (*KIA:*) French

objections to, 180–81; inspection duties, 182; planning for and setup of, 155, 179–80, 257*n* 114; relations with French authorities, 182–85, 264*n* 81; replacement of Italian inspection agencies, 179–80; success of mission, 184–85
Krappe, Colonel Günther, 263*n* 69
Krauss, Captain Fritz, 246*n* 110
Kurusu, Saburo, 90

La Laurencie, General Benoit, 147
Larminat, Colonel Edgard de, 39, 248*n* 9
Laval, Pierre, 30, 31, 82–83; becomes foreign minister, 107–108; collaboration with Germany, 101–103, 107–108, 135, 137, 141, 143, 144, 252*n* 56; dismissal and arrest, 146–51
Leahy, Admiral William, 149, 151, 253*n* 76
Leissner, Captain Wilhelm, 242*n* 77
Lend-Lease Plan, 151
Lequerica, José Felix de, 59, 72, 73, 101, 103, 148; and appointment of François Piétri, 231*n* 28
Liberia: American presence in and German expulsion from, 192

Matsuoka, Yosuke, 68, 166–67
Mediterranean Strategy: historiography on, 52–53. *See also* German Navy/Naval Command
Menace, Operation 78–80; French and German responses, 80–85, 86–87, 95–96, 117, 196, 199; Italian reaction to, 81–82, 96; Spanish reaction to, 85, 228*n* 70
Menzell, Captain Hermann, 133, 134
Mers-el-Kebir: and Axis suspension of disarmament terms, 18–19, 28; British attack on, 18, 21, 24, 37, 199
Michelier, Admiral Fritz, 18
Mieth, General Friedrich, 40–41, 44
Mixed German-Italian Control Commis-

sion, 44, 46–47, 49–50, 84, 99–100, 152, 216*n* 64

Molotov, V. M., 111–12

Moltmann, Günter, xv

Monroe Doctrine, 87; "German version of," 88, 112

Montoire Meetings (German-French 22, 24 October 1940), 101–103, 106–108, 109

Montpellier meeting (French-Spanish, 13 February 1941), 162–63

Morocco, French Protectorate: French defense of, 73, 93–94, 100–101; German desire for bases in, 16, 21–32, 46, 53, 62, 65, 69, 70, 74, 75, 84, 87, 89, 95, 99, 102, 108, 109, 117, 125, 138, 168, 171, 175, 235*n* 59; German reconnaissance missions to, 46, 50–51, 64, 84; German representation in, 30, 42, 44–46, 49–50; German strategic interest in, 6, 27–28, 58, 61–62, 73; German subversion and propaganda in, 29, 30, 56, 129–30, 202, 243*n* 83; Italian supervisory responsibilities in, 14, 153; Spanish subversion, claims, possible attack on, 28, 55–56, 58–59, 61, 73, 75, 76, 88, 90–91, 98, 100, 104–106, 110, 123, 163, 178; use for island occupation and defense, 117–18. *See also* German Armament and Fuel Commission (French Morocco); *Kontrollinspektion Afrika (KIA)*

Morocco, Spanish Protectorate: German General Consulate in Tetuán and German propaganda in, 30, 129; German strategic interest in, xxiv, 38, 99, 109, 123, 126, 127–28, 159, 199, 240*n* 55, 241*n* 64; during Spanish civil war, 55; Spanish-German friction in, 129–31, 243*n* 86

Munich Meeting (German-Italian, 18 June 1940), 5–6, 25, 60

Muñoz Grandes, General Agostín, 133, 259*n* 152

Murphy, Robert, 149, 183, 253*n* 76

Murphy-Weygand Agreement (February 1941), 183–84, 253*n* 76

Mussolini, Benito: and armistice terms with France, 10–12, 45; and assessment of United States, 224*n* 87; and attack on Greece, 108; and collaboration with France, 22, 28, 96, 99, 109–10, 140, 188; and French disarmament in Africa, 37, 45, 140, 217*n* 66, 250*n* 25; and German aims in Africa, 28–29, 47–48, 100; and separate peace with France, 109–10; and Spain, 25, 53, 77, 109–10, 158–59, 241*n* 67; and Three Power Pact with Japan, 77; and use of Bizerte, 188; war aims, 5–6, 28, 97–100, 109–10; and Weygand, 250*n* 25. *See also* Italy; Ciano, Count Galeazzo

Nazism, Nazi Party, xv, xvi

Noguès, Resident-General Charles, 34, 37; and American presence in Morocco, 183–84; and collaboration with Germany, 141, 152; and concessions to Spain in Morocco, 57, 59, 72, 163; and defense of Morocco, 50, 59, 95, 185; and de Gaulle, 38, 50; German evaluation of, 50, 95, 152–55, 183–84, 268*n* 138; and German presence in Morocco, 50–51, 84, 154–55, 180–82, 183; harassment of German informants, 183, 266*n* 106; protests against eviction of Mendub in Tangier, 244*n* 95; and surrender to Americans, 201–202

Oran: Italian-German interest in air base, 21–22, 29; Italian proposal for air base in, 21–22, 29; Oran District and Spanish claim, 60, 65, 77, 98, 110, 123; surrender to Allies, 201

Paris Protocols, 173–75, 196

Patton, George S. Jr., 201

Pereira, Dr. Pedro Teotónio, 114

Pétain, Marshal Henri Philippe: and Allied landing in Morocco and Algeria, xii–xiv; and collaboration with Germany, 101, 106–108, 143–45, 146, 188, 251n 50; and de Gaulle, 78, 107; French defeat and armistice terms, 4, 10; and German Casablanca demand (letter to Hitler 17 July 1940), 30–31, 33, 53, 62, 107; and German presence in Africa, 231n 27; and Italian base in Algeria, 21–22; prestige and authority in French empire, 34, 48, 78, 81, 95, 106–108, 180; and relationship with Laval, Laval dismissal, 144, 146–51, 252n 59; and relations with Spain, 73, 162–63

Piétri, Lieutenant Colonel, 154

Piétri, François, 101, 231n 28

Pintor, General Pietro, 15

Platon, Admiral Charles, 78, 173, 189

Portugal (and Portuguese Islands), 8, 47, 53, 111; alliance with Great Britain, 114–15; and Azores, 178; German interest toward and historiography, 113; neutrality in war, 114; proposed alliance with Spain, 114–15. See also Salazar, Dr. Antonio de Olveira; *War Directive Number 18*

Primauguet, 79

Primo de Rivera, José Antonio, 54

Primo de Rivera, Miguel, 55

Raeder, Grand Admiral Erich: and Allied capabilities in 1941–42, 190; and collaboration with France, 19–20, 83, 89–90, 151, 168, 172, 176; and fortification of the Canaries, 132, 133, 172; and Mediterranean strategy, 69, 89–90, 116; and Portuguese island occupation, 116, 117, 119–21, 172; and proposed naval bases, xxiv, 6–8, 62; and views on fleet configuration, xxi, 204n 38; and war with England, 62; and war with Soviet Union, 63;

and Weygand, 151. *See also* German Navy/Naval Command

Reichenau, Field Marshal Walter von, 126

Reichstadt, Duke of, 146, 147

Resolution, 79

Ribbentrop, Joachim von: and approaches to Spain, 6, 58, 64–65; and armistice with France, 5–6, 12; and collaboration with France, 81, 102, 138, 143, 148–50, 168, 169–70, 189; and German interest in Morocco, 5–6, 12, 14, 58; and Great Britain, British Empire, 74, 190; and Italian claims in Africa, 5–6, 12, 48, 123; and Latin America, 25; and Portugal, 114–15; and Serrano Suñer at Berchtesgaden, 124–25; and Serrano Suñer in Berlin, 73–78, 86, 91, 196; and Serrano Suñer at Hendaye, 105–106, 110; and Spanish refusal to enter war, 134, 157, 158, 159–61, 163, 247n 118, 258n 141; and Tangier, 130; and United States, 73, 77, 86–87, 90, 123–24, 190

Rich, Norman, xxii

Richelieu, 19, 79, 80, 95

Richter, Herbert Georg, 56, 58, 59, 129–30

Richthofen, Field Marshal Wolfram Freiherr von, 62

Rif region (French Morocco): German military inspection in, 183, 266n 100

Rintelen, General Enno von, 47

Ripert, Georges, 146

Ritter, Karl, 140

Roatta, General Mario, 5, 11, 14

Roatta Agreements, 14, 15, 38, 43, 140, 153, 207n 49, 215n 60; revision of, 179–80

Rommel, General Erwin, 187–88. *See also* German *Afrika Korps*

Roosevelt, Franklin Delano: and American landing in North Africa, xii–xiv; German evaluations of, 25, 65–66,

74, 77, 151, 170; and Pétain, 253n 76; and Washington Conference, 192

Salazar, Dr. Antonio de Olveira, 114–15, 177–78; and threat to Azores, 237n 16

Santos Costa, Captain Fernando dos, 178

Schacht, Hjalmar, 260n 5

Schellert, Consul-General, 50, 84

Schellert Commission, 84, 226n 37

Schmidt, Dr. Paul, 232n 40

Schniewind, Rear Admiral Otto, 121, 133

Schultheiss, General, 155, 183

Seelisch, Major, 184

Seelöwe, Operation, 24, 61, 62–63, 69. *See also* German Navy/Naval Command; Hitler, Adolf

Senger und Etterlin, Colonel Frido von, 140, 207n 43

Serrano Suñer, Ramón, 55; at Hendaye, 105–106; and Montpellier meeting, 163; position in Spanish government, 71, 103, 232n 38; and proposed alliance with Portugal, 114; and Spain's refusal to enter the war, 258n 138; and Tangier, 129, 130–31; trip to Berchtesgaden, 124–25, 128, 241n 59, 242n 78; trip to Berlin, 70–78, 85–89, 91–93, 94, 100, 199. *See also* Hendaye meetings (German-Spanish, 23 October 1940)

Sonnenblume, Operation, 159

Soviet Union: German attack on 63, 69, 90. *See also Barbarossa,* Operation

Spain, 8; and Allied landing in French Morocco, 178; army, 54–55, 71, 127; and Canary Islands, 74–76, 86, 100, 103, 132–34, 178, 230n 24, 245n 100, 263n 68; civil war in, 28, 53, 54, 55, 91, 92; economic needs, economic concessions to Germany, 64–65, 88, 91, 92, 100, 106, 122, 124,

160–61; and France, 55, 59, 61, 72–73, 101, 162–63, 231n 28; French disarmament in North Africa and de Gaulle, 61, 77, 85, 162, 223n 61; and German demand for Casablanca, 73, 225n 12; and German-French cease fire, 59; German submarine refueling in, xxiv, 6; neutrality and non-belligerency, 6, 53–54, 56–57; occupation of Tangier 6, 57–58; and Portugal, 88, 114; press, 57, 85; scholarly literature on issue of belligerence, 54; and Spanish Morocco, 100, 178, 231n 25, 263n 69; territorial claims and offers to enter the war, 6, 28, 49, 53–55, 56–57, 58–60, 61, 72, 75, 76, 70–78, 85, 88, 92, 100, 104–106, 123, 124, 125, 128, 162, 222n 53. *See also Felix,* Operation; Morocco, French Protectorate; Tangier

Spanish Guinea: German interest in, 87; Spanish claim on, 60, 75, 88, 222n 59

Speidel, Lieutenant Colonel Hans, 143

Stahmer, Heinrich, 68

Stehlin, Major Paul, 142, 145, 147, 150

Stohrer, Eberhard von, 56, 57, 60, 61, 64–65, 71–72, 88, 106, 114, 124, 129, 130, 160–61, 163

Strasbourg Group, 80–82, 89, 90, 96, 227n 38, 229n 8

Stülpnagel, General Carl-Heinrich von, 14, 18, 19, 23, 48, 78, 81, 84; French Africa and Italian authority in, 14, 15, 31, 36, 37–38, 39, 41, 45, 49–50, 81–82, 95, 154, 215n 60; removal as Armistice Commission Chairman, 152, 254n 95. *See also* German Armistice Commission

Stülpnagel, General Otto von, 137

Suez Canal, 52, 63. *See also* German Navy/Naval Command

Syria: German-French collaboration in, 168–69, 171, 173

Tangier: German Legation building/General Consulate/German agents in, 130–31, 244n 93; German stance on Spanish control of, 65, 130; *Mendub* and eviction, 57, 130–31; Noguès's protests concerning eviction of Mendub, 244n 95; Spanish claim for and occupation of, 6, 55, 57–58, 100; Spanish legal incorporation of, 58, 128–29, 244n 91; value as a base (with Ceuta), 127

Teleki, Count Pál, 125

Têtu, General Marcel-Louis: capture of, 248n 9; dispatch to Libreville, 39

Thies, Jochen, xvi

Thomas, General Georg, 254n 87

Thomsen, Hans, 66

Three Power Pact, 90–91, 97, 105, 110

Tirpitz: contracting and construction of, xx

Torch, Operation: Allied preparation for, 192–93; execution of, xiii, 201; German reaction to, 201–202

Trondheim: proposed German naval base at, 7, 27, 176, 196, 262n 56

Tunisia: German interest in use of (Bizerte), 169, 171, 174, 187–89; Italian interest in use of (Bizerte), 11, 188–89. *See also* Italy: armistice terms with France; Italy: war aims

Turin Protocol, 185

United States: and Great Britain, 46, 151; landing in North Africa, xxi, 92–93, 201; and Liberia, 192; representatives in French Africa, 66, 149, 183, 253n 76, 266n 108; and Takoradi route, 192. *See also* Bötticher, General Friedrich von; German Navy/Naval Command; Hitler, Adolf; Roosevelt, Franklin Delano

Vichy Government: collaboration with Germany, 4, 28–29, 101–103, 106–108, 135, 137, 141, 143, 144, 146,

167–68, 170–74, 188, 252nn 56, 59, 261n 36; and de Gaulle, hostilities with Great Britain, re-conquest of Equatorial Africa, 34, 35–37, 39, 42, 78–83, 99, 106–108, 137–38, 141–45, 171–72; and German Casablanca demand, 29–31, 196; and German commissioners/agents in Morocco, 50–51, 84, 154–55, 180–81, 183, 256nn 3, 8; and German use of Dakar, 171–72; insistence on imperial guarantee, 41, 80, 82, 144–45, 173, 212n 19; and Laval dismissal, 144, 146–51, 252n 59; and Moroccan borders, 55, 72, 100–101, 162–63, 200; and sale of trucks to Germany, 169, 171; and Spanish occupation/incorporation of Tangier, 57, 101; trade with and authority in Empire, 17, 20–21, 29–30, 34–36, 39, 41–42, 48–49, 78, 137; views on French resurgence, 4. *See also* Morocco, French Protectorate; Noguès, Resident-General Charles

Victor Emmanuel III, 55

Vogl, General Oskar, 152, 174, 181. *See also* German Armistice Commission

Vigón, General Juan, 6, 58, 62, 133

Voss, Captain Hans-Erich, 132–33

Wagner, Rear Admiral Gerhard, 174

Wagner, Richard, xvi

War Directive Number 18, 110–11, 113, 119, 139. *See also Felix,* Operation

War Directive Number 19 (first, for Operation *Felix*), 128, 155

War Directive Number 19 (second, for *Attila*), 135, 155. *See also Attila,* Operation

War Directive Number 17, 64

War Directive Number 16, See Seelöwe, Operation

War Directive Number 32, 175–76, 262n 48

War Directive Number 21, 156. *See also Barbarossa,* Operation

Warlimont, General Walter, 64, 68, 110–11, 115, 158–59; and Allied capabilities in 1941–42, 190, 270n 156; and collaboration with France, 83, 95–96, 135, 138, 140, 141–42, 145, 158–59, 171–72, 249n 12, 251n 48; and Gibraltar, Portuguese islands, 64, 68, 110–11, 115, 158–59

Wavell, General Archibald, 254n 89

Weinberg, Gerhard L., xvi

Weizenbauer, Leo, 178

Weizsäcker, State Secretary Ernst von, 29, 43–44, 47–48, 61, 81–82, 151–52; and German-Italian interests in French Africa, 43–44, 47–48, 81–82, 215n 60; and Mixed German-Italian Control Commission, 44, 216n 64; and policy toward France, 151–52; and Spanish entry into the war, 61, 222n 59

Wever, Commander Paul 18, 19, 186

Weygand, General Maxime 10, 12, 34; and Armistice, 10, 12, 17; and British attack on Mers-el-Kebir, 18, 21; as delegate general of French government in Africa, 48, 84, 148–50, 174, 180, 252n 72, 253nn 74, 76; removal of, 187, 268n 136

Wiehl, Emil, 241n 62, 259n 155

Wühlisch, General Heinz-Helmut von, 183, 184, 186. See also Kontrollinspektion Afrika (KIA)

Yagüe, General Juan, 56

Yuste, Colonel Antonio, 128

Zamboni, Guelfo, 2

Zechlin, Walter, 222n 59